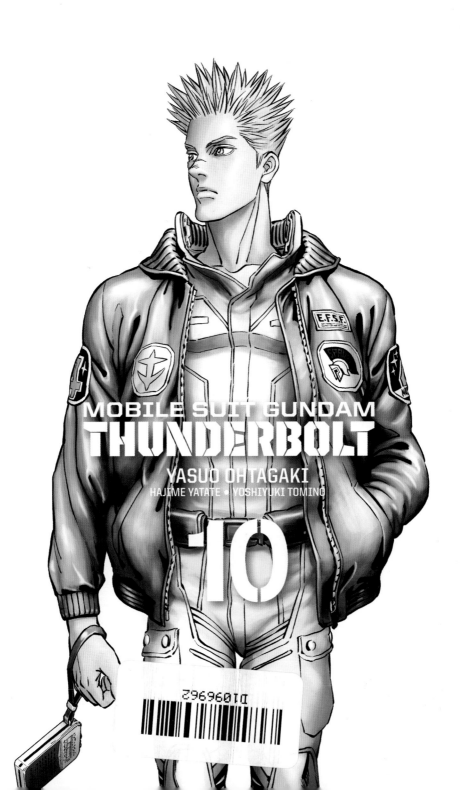

MOBILE SUIT GUNDAM
THUNDERBOLT

YASUO OHTAGAKI
HAJIME YATATE • YOSHIYUKI TOMINO

10

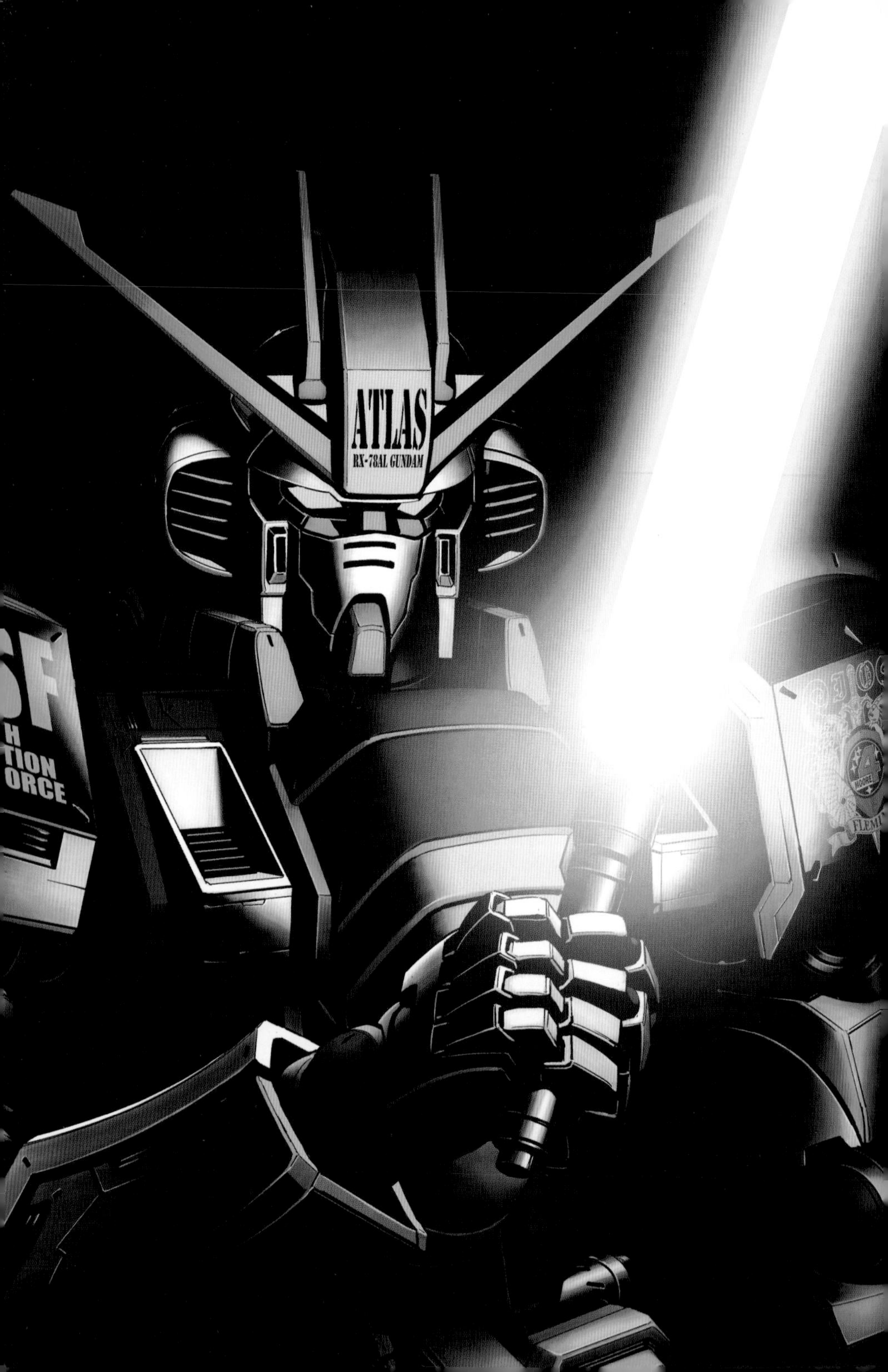
ATLAS
RX-78AL GUNDAM
MOORE

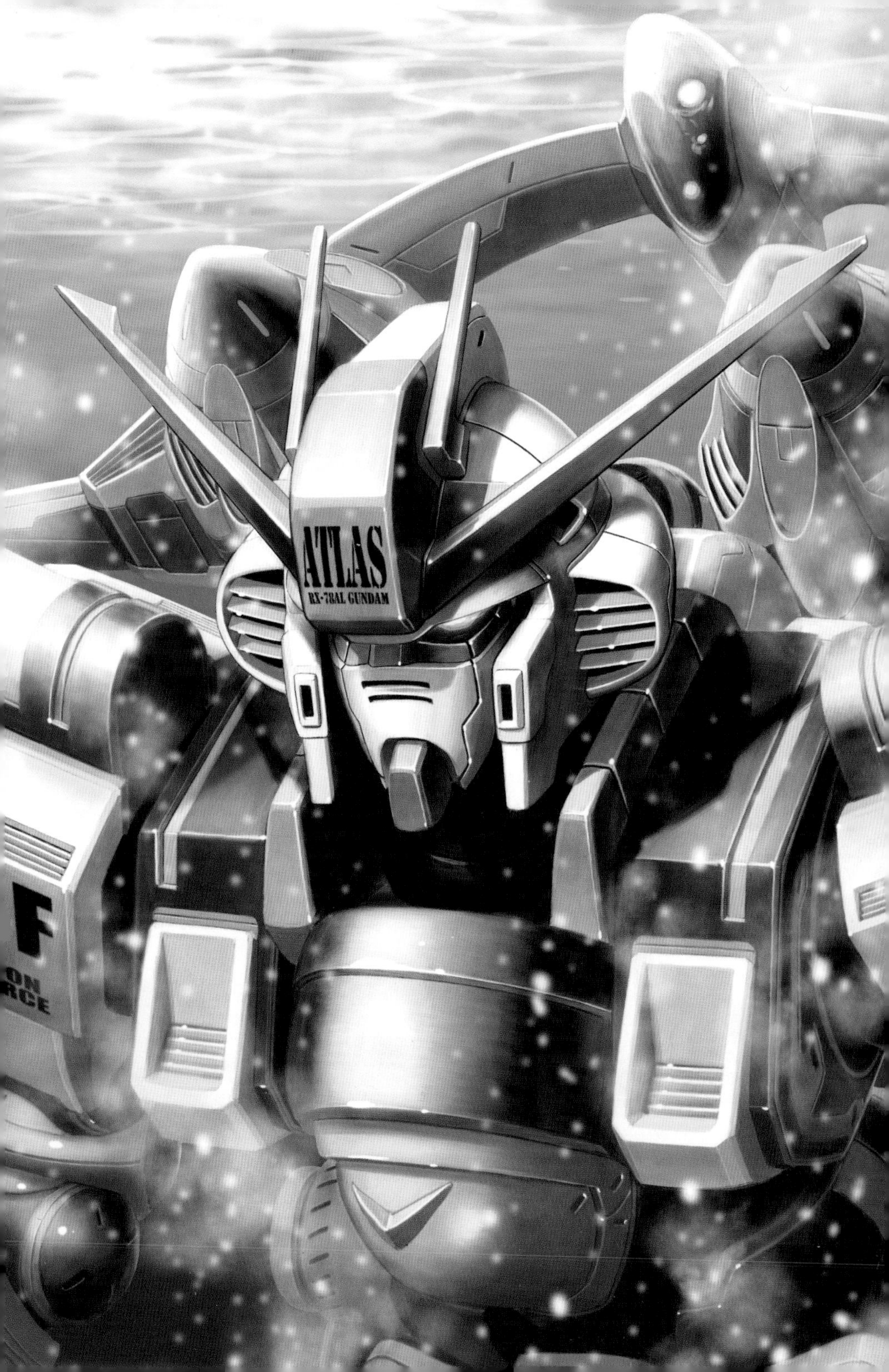
ATLAS
RX-78AL GUNDAM

MOBILE SUIT GUNDAM
THUNDERBOLT
10

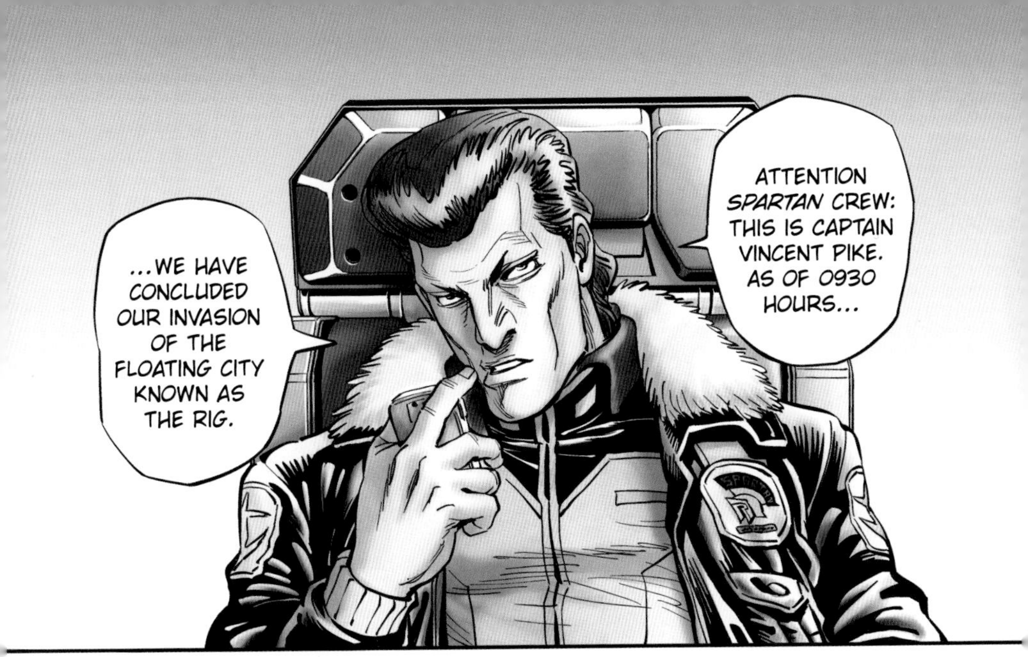
ATTENTION *SPARTAN* CREW: THIS IS CAPTAIN VINCENT PIKE. AS OF 0930 HOURS...
...WE HAVE CONCLUDED OUR INVASION OF THE FLOATING CITY KNOWN AS THE RIG.

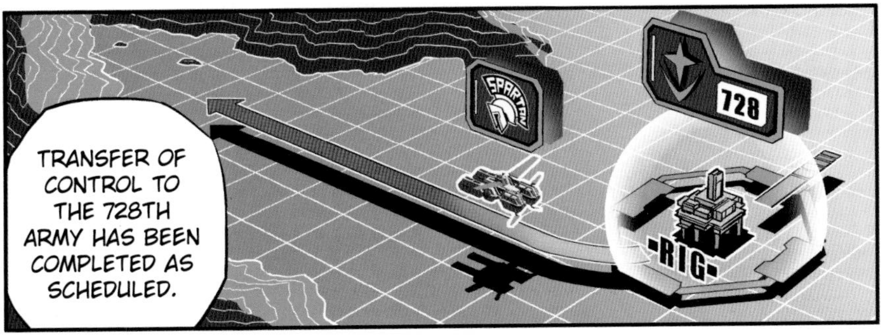
728
SPARTAN
RIG
TRANSFER OF CONTROL TO THE 728TH ARMY HAS BEEN COMPLETED AS SCHEDULED.

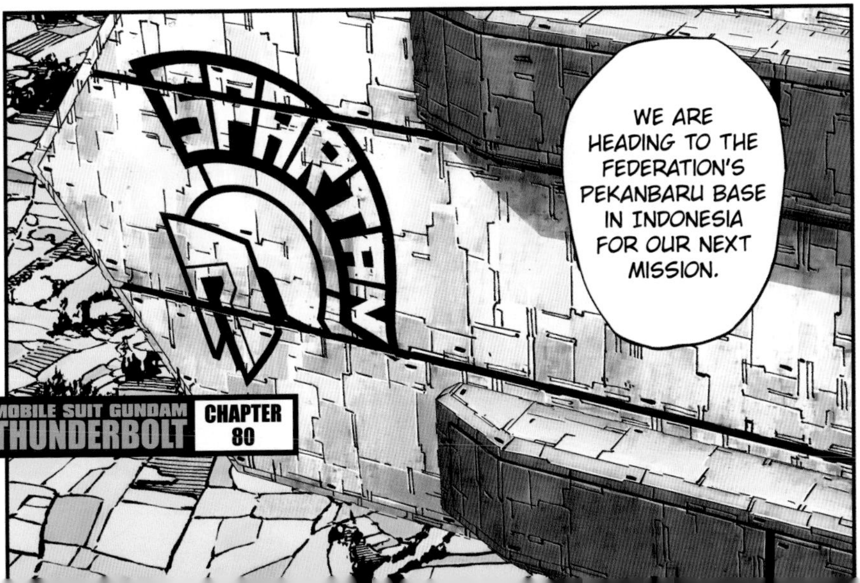
WE ARE HEADING TO THE FEDERATION'S PEKANBARU BASE IN INDONESIA FOR OUR NEXT MISSION.
MOBILE SUIT GUNDAM THUNDERBOLT
CHAPTER 80

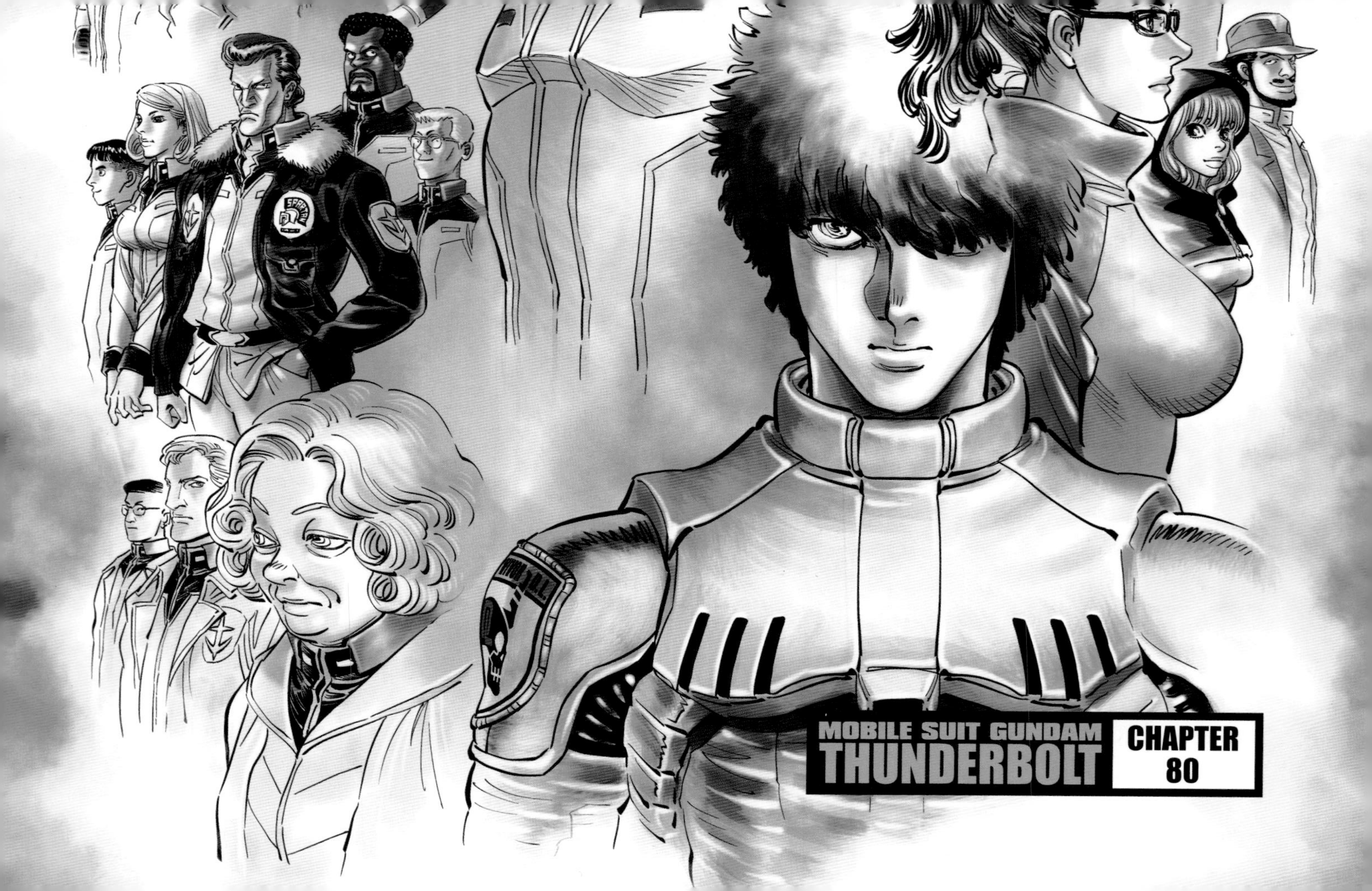
MOBILE SUIT GUNDAM
THUNDERBOLT
CHAPTER
80

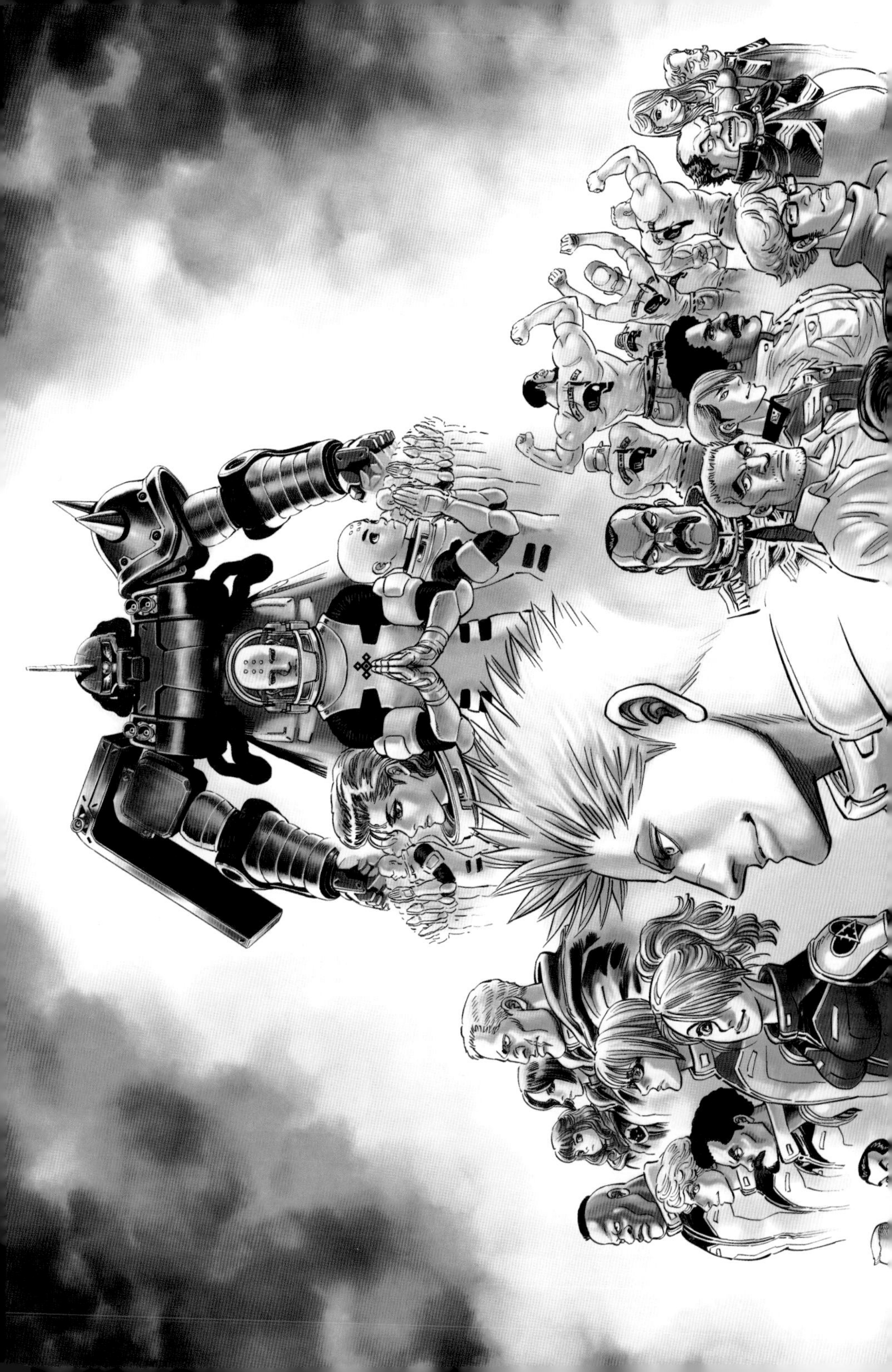

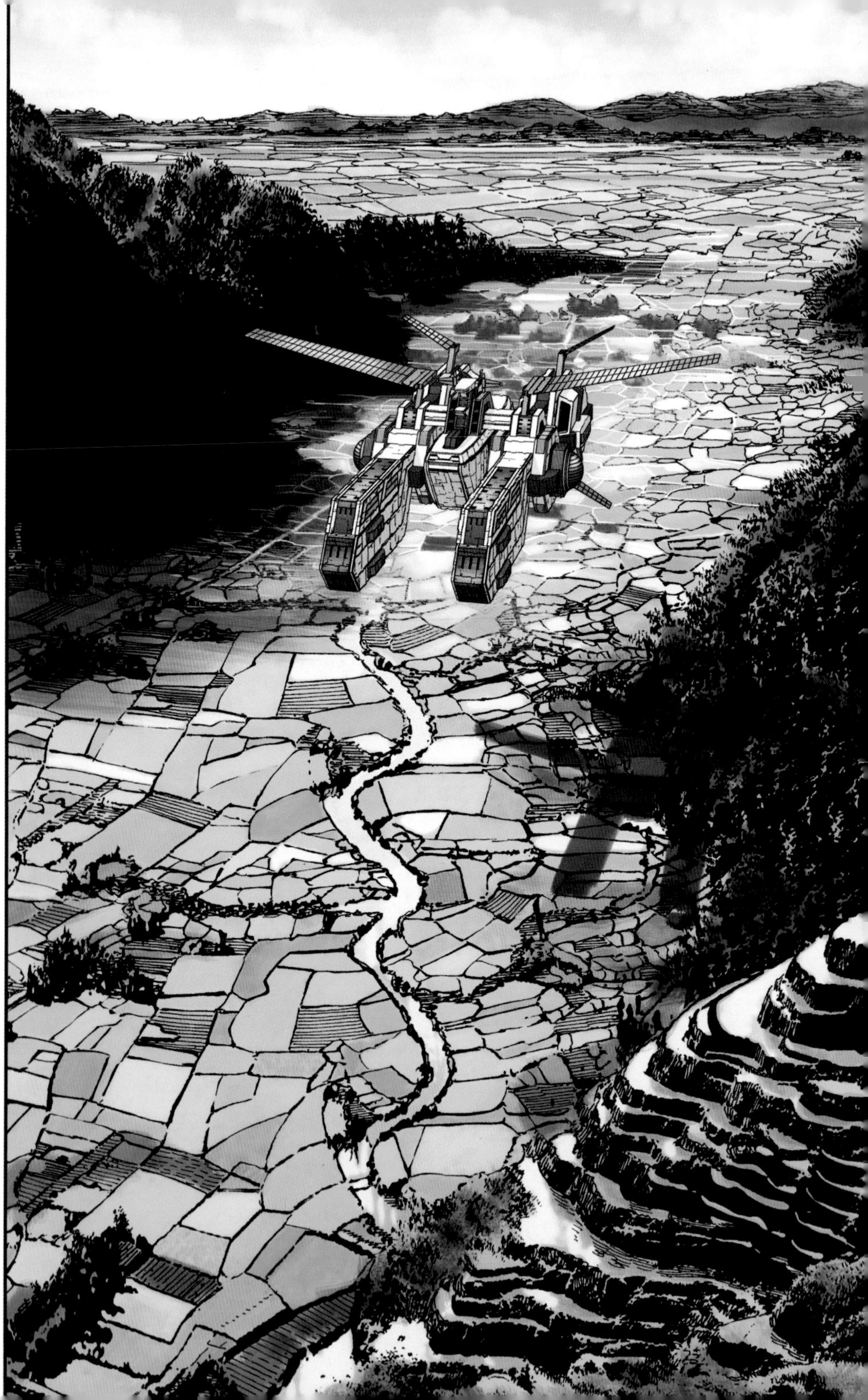

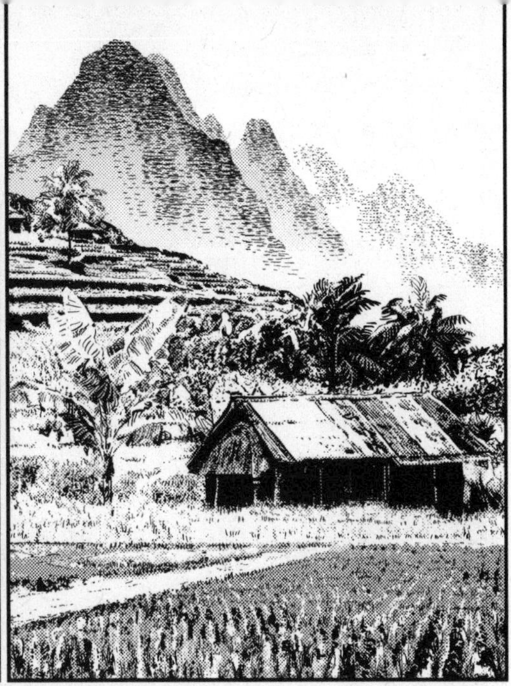
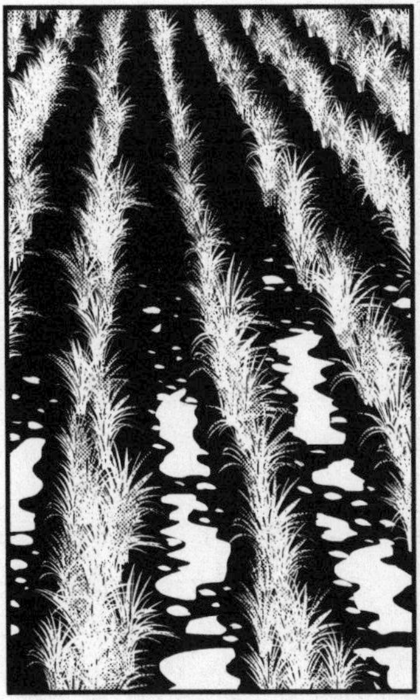
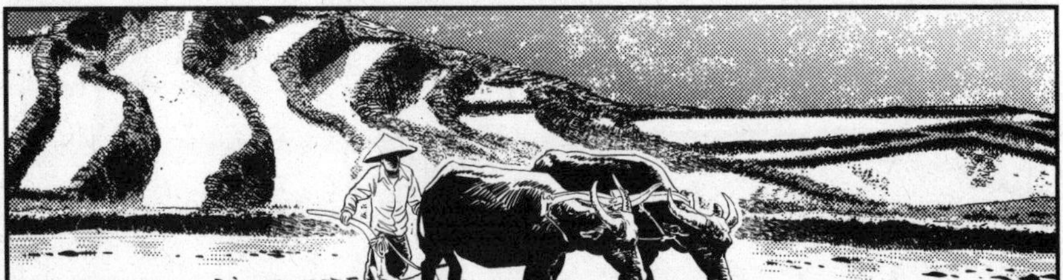
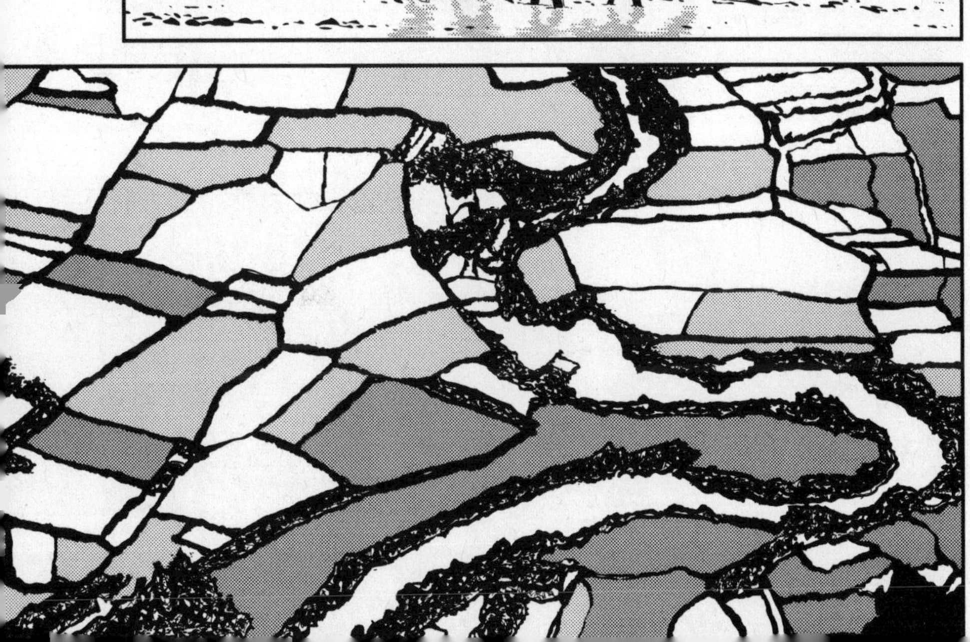

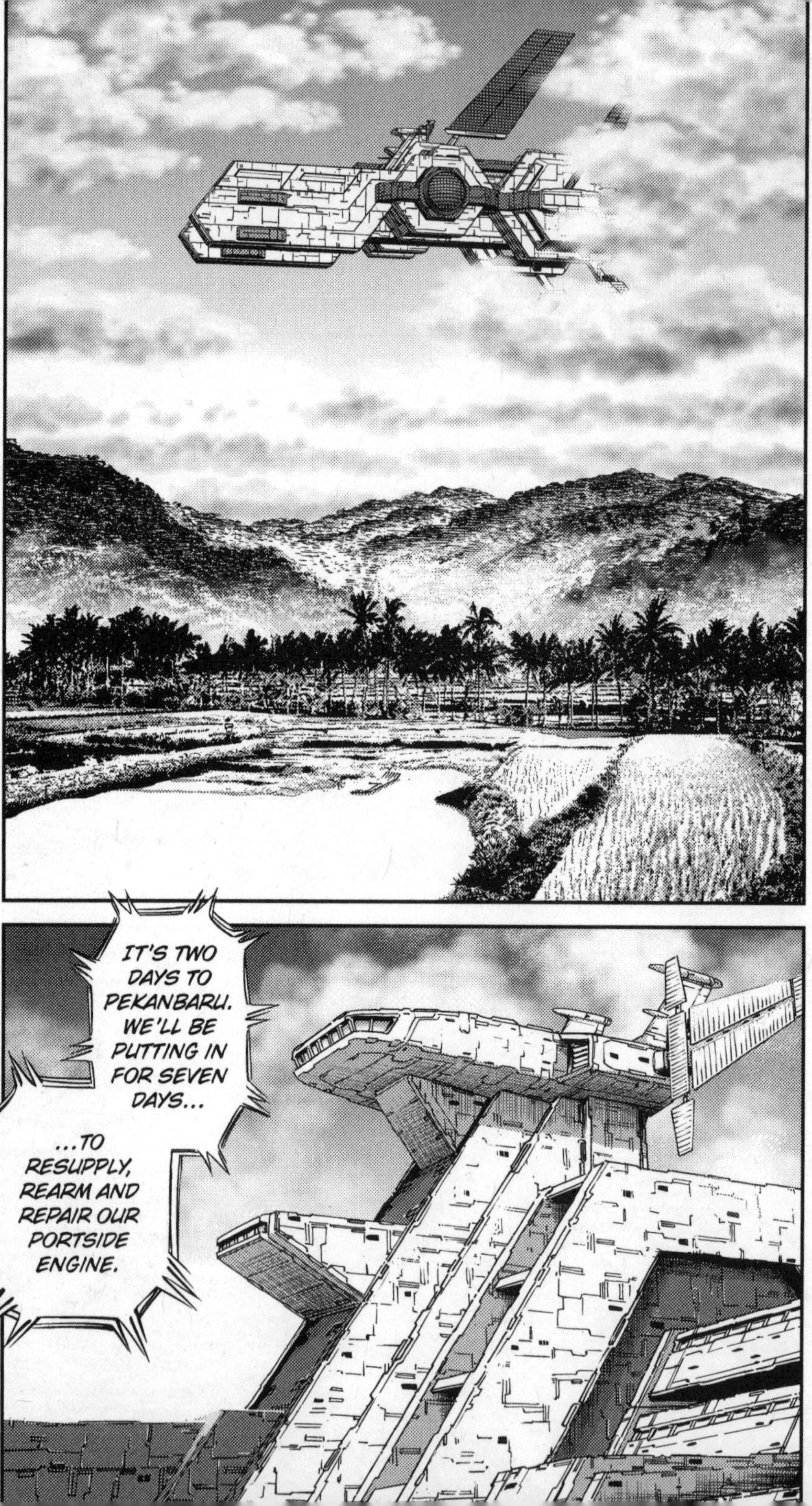
IT'S TWO DAYS TO PEKANBARU. WE'LL BE PUTTING IN FOR SEVEN DAYS...
...TO RESUPPLY, REARM AND REPAIR OUR PORTSIDE ENGINE.

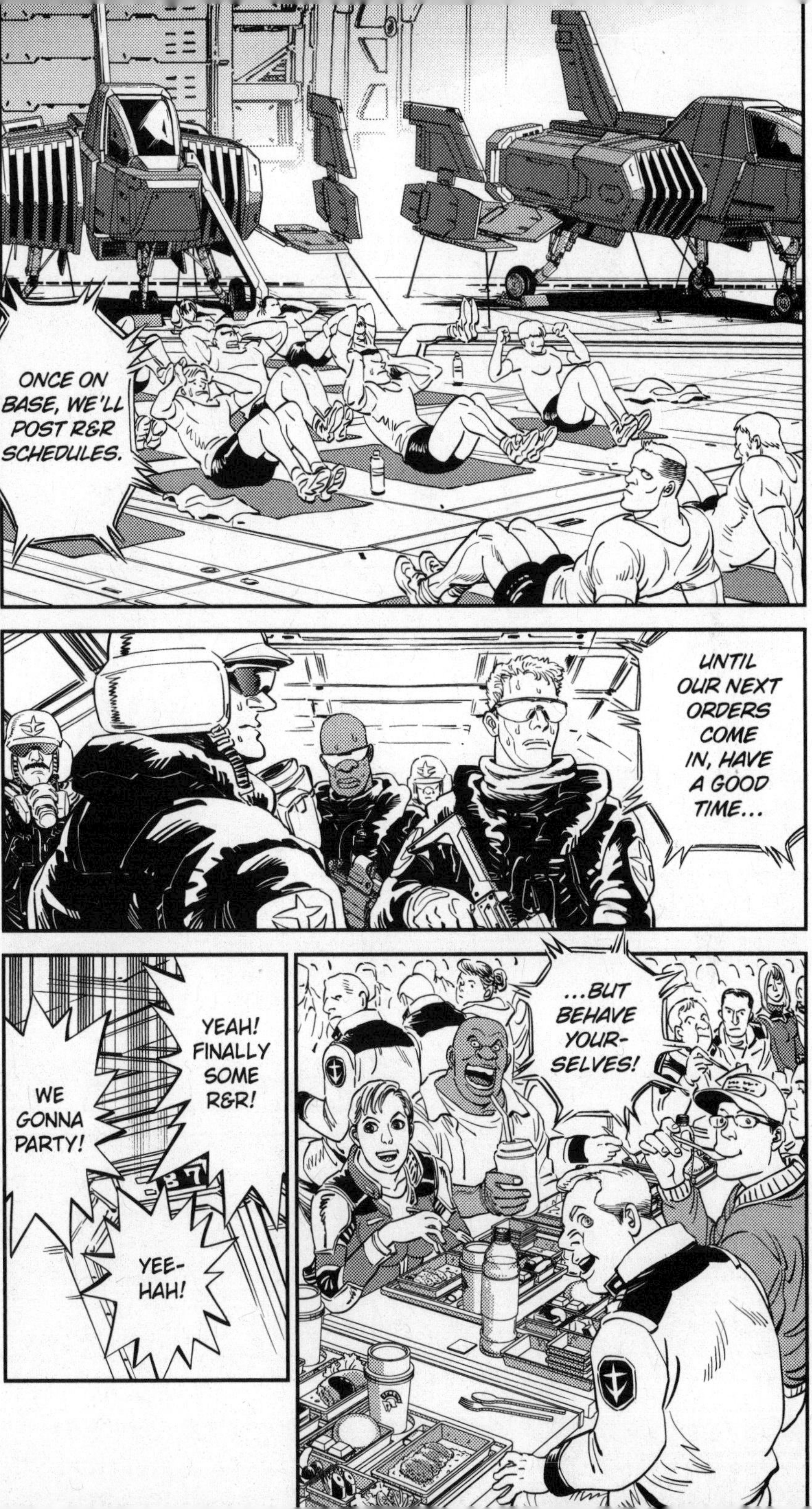
ONCE ON BASE, WE'LL POST R&R SCHEDULES.
UNTIL OUR NEXT ORDERS COME IN, HAVE A GOOD TIME...
...BUT BEHAVE YOUR-SELVES!
YEAH! FINALLY SOME R&R!
WE GONNA PARTY!
YEE-HAH!

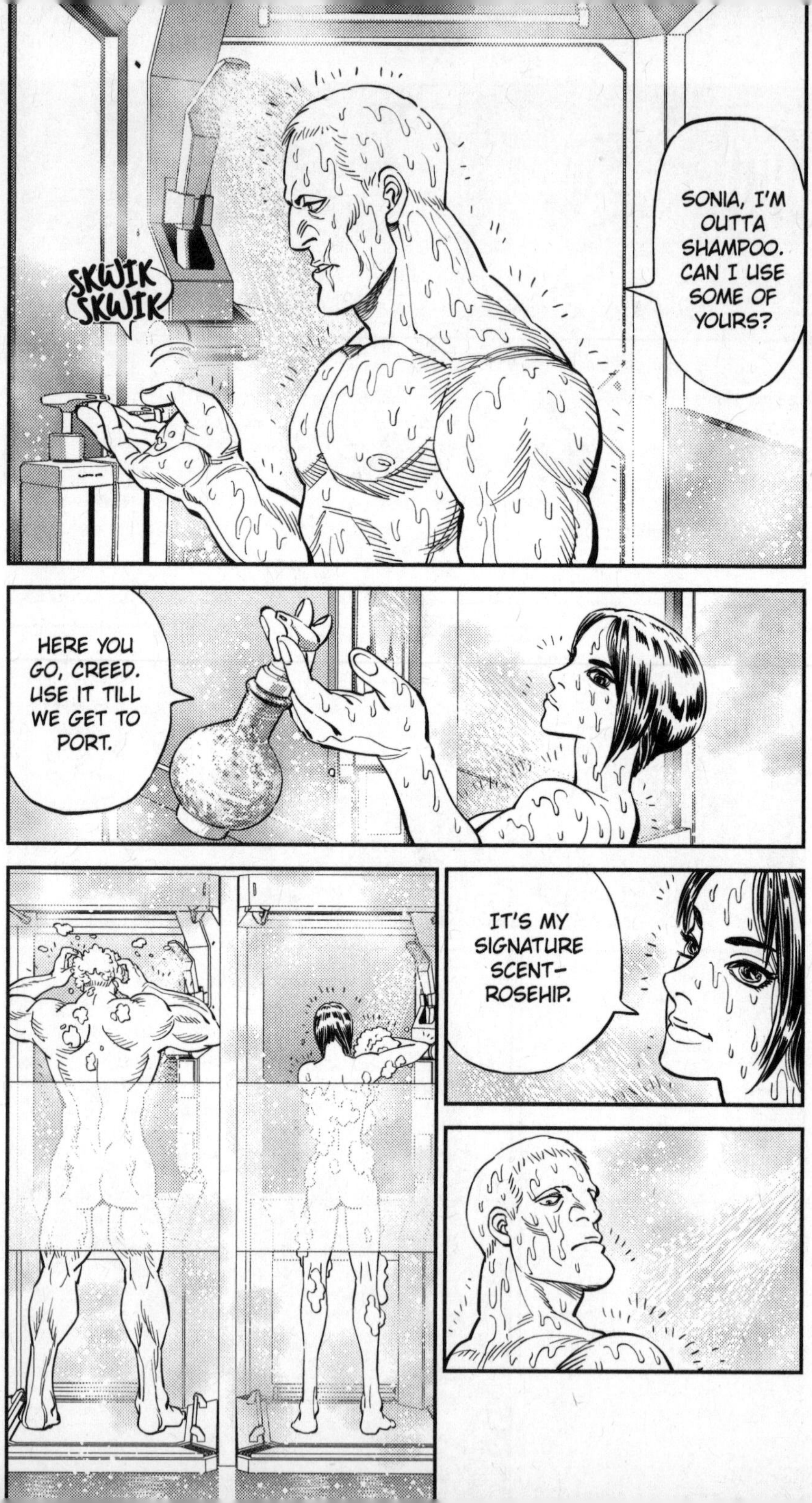
SONIA, I'M OUTTA SHAMPOO. CAN I USE SOME OF YOURS?
SKWIK SKWIK
HERE YOU GO, CREED. USE IT TILL WE GET TO PORT.
IT'S MY SIGNATURE SCENT-ROSEHIP.

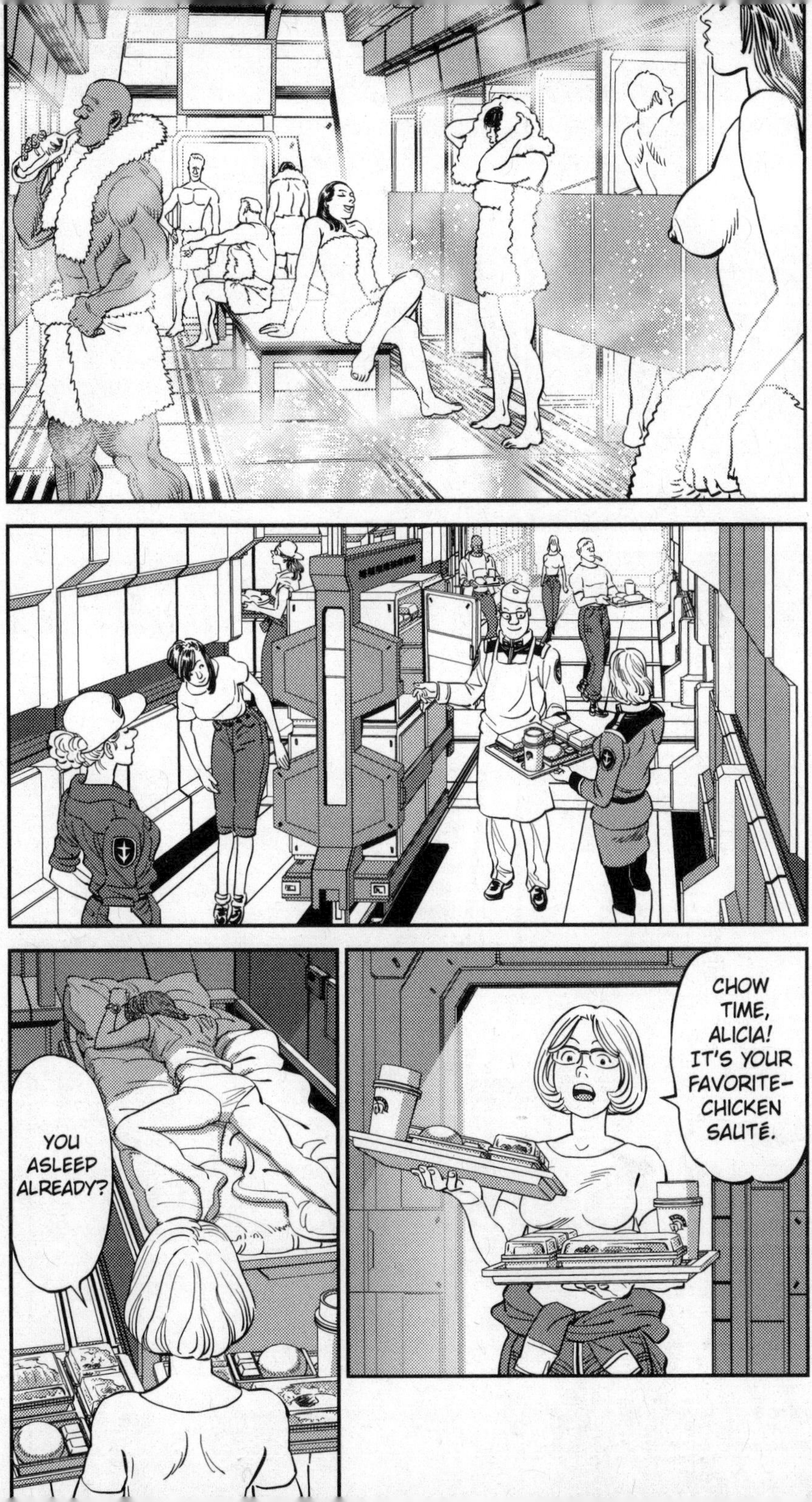
CHOW TIME, ALICIA! IT'S YOUR FAVORITE-CHICKEN SAUTÉ.
YOU ASLEEP ALREADY?

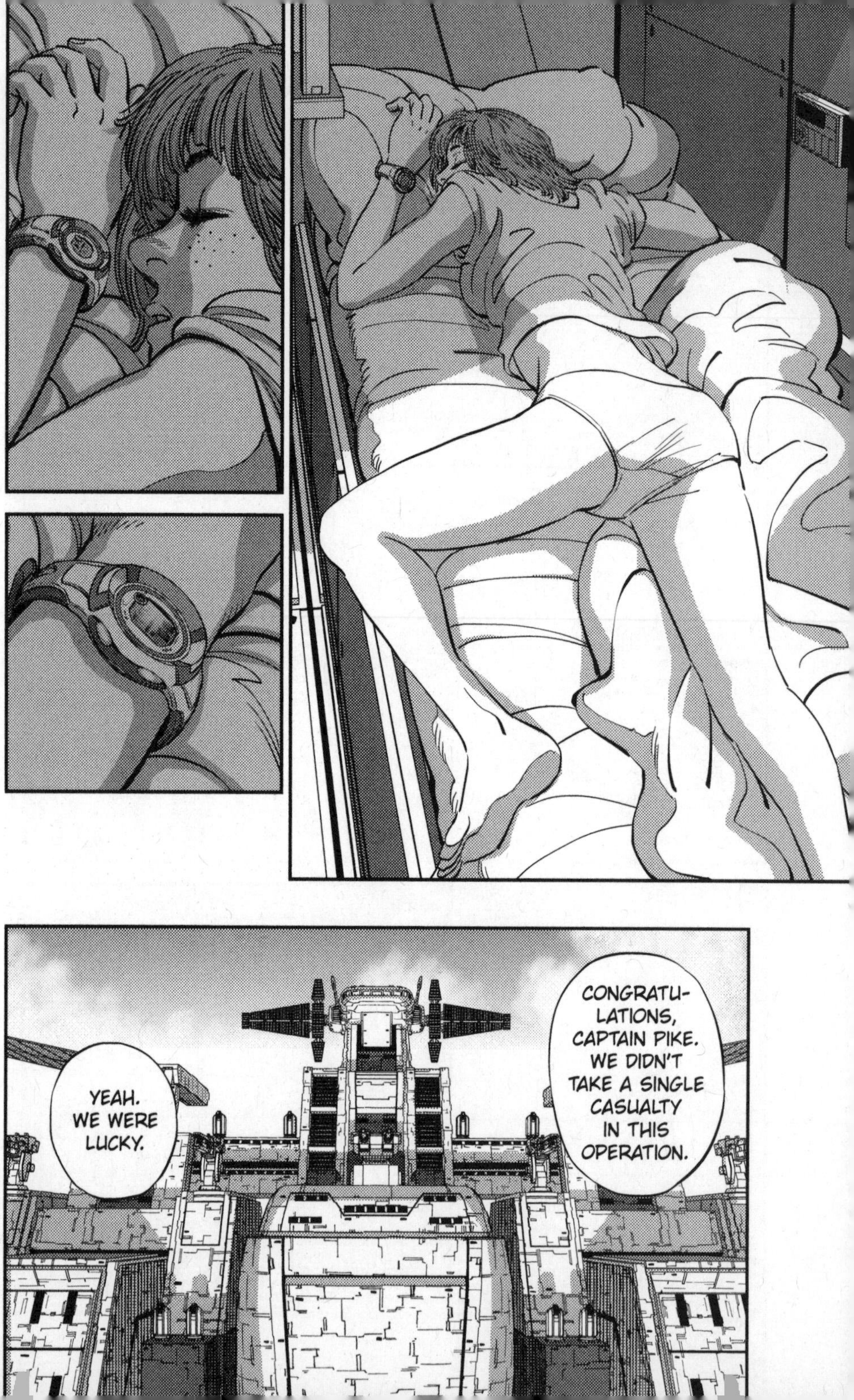
CONGRATU-LATIONS, CAPTAIN PIKE. WE DIDN'T TAKE A SINGLE CASUALTY IN THIS OPERATION.
YEAH. WE WERE LUCKY.

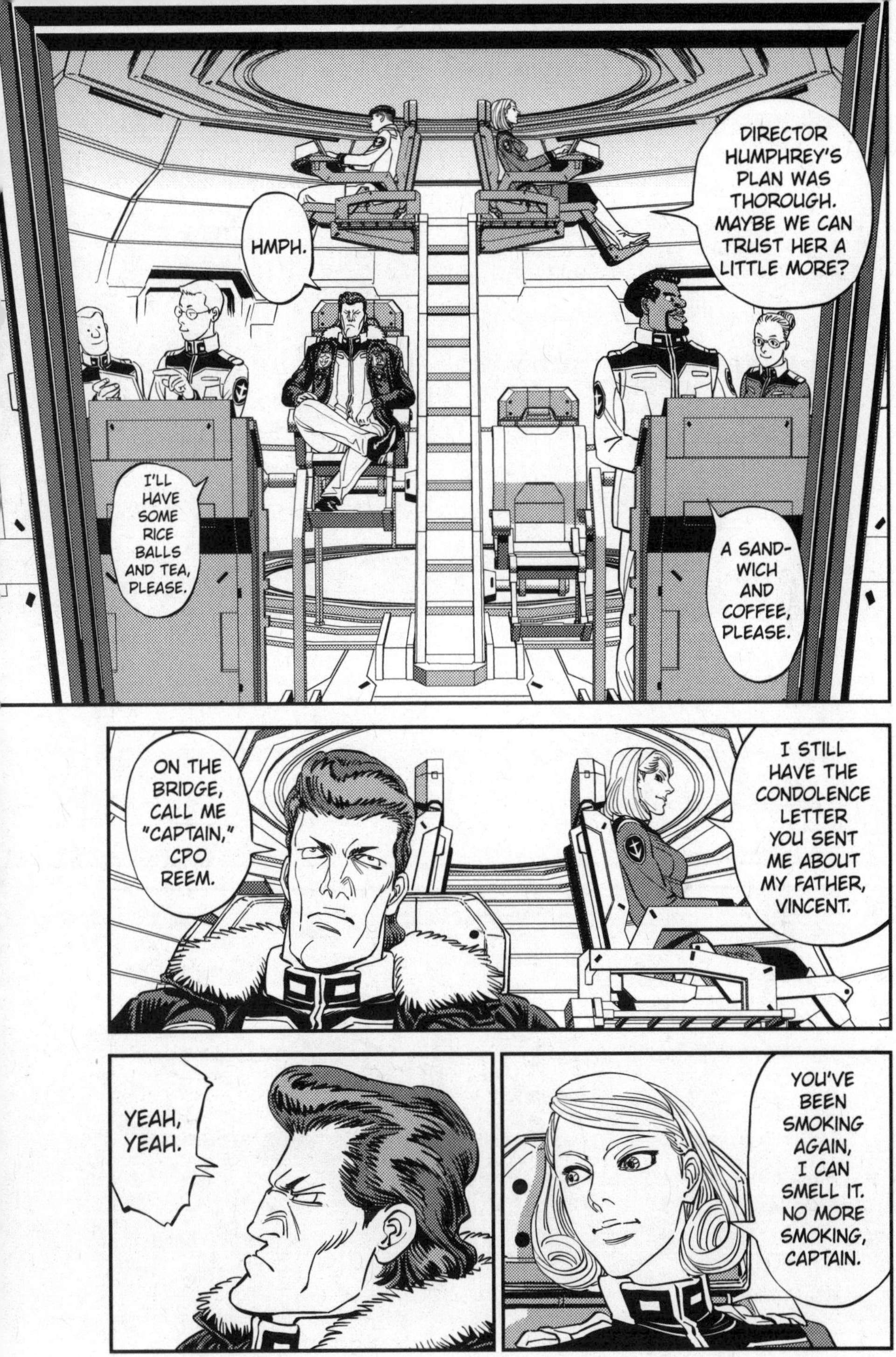
DIRECTOR HUMPHREY'S PLAN WAS THOROUGH. MAYBE WE CAN TRUST HER A LITTLE MORE?
HMPH.
A SAND-WICH AND COFFEE, PLEASE.
I'LL HAVE SOME RICE BALLS AND TEA, PLEASE.
I STILL HAVE THE CONDOLENCE LETTER YOU SENT ME ABOUT MY FATHER, VINCENT.
ON THE BRIDGE, CALL ME "CAPTAIN," CPO REEM.
YOU'VE BEEN SMOKING AGAIN, I CAN SMELL IT. NO MORE SMOKING, CAPTAIN.
YEAH, YEAH.

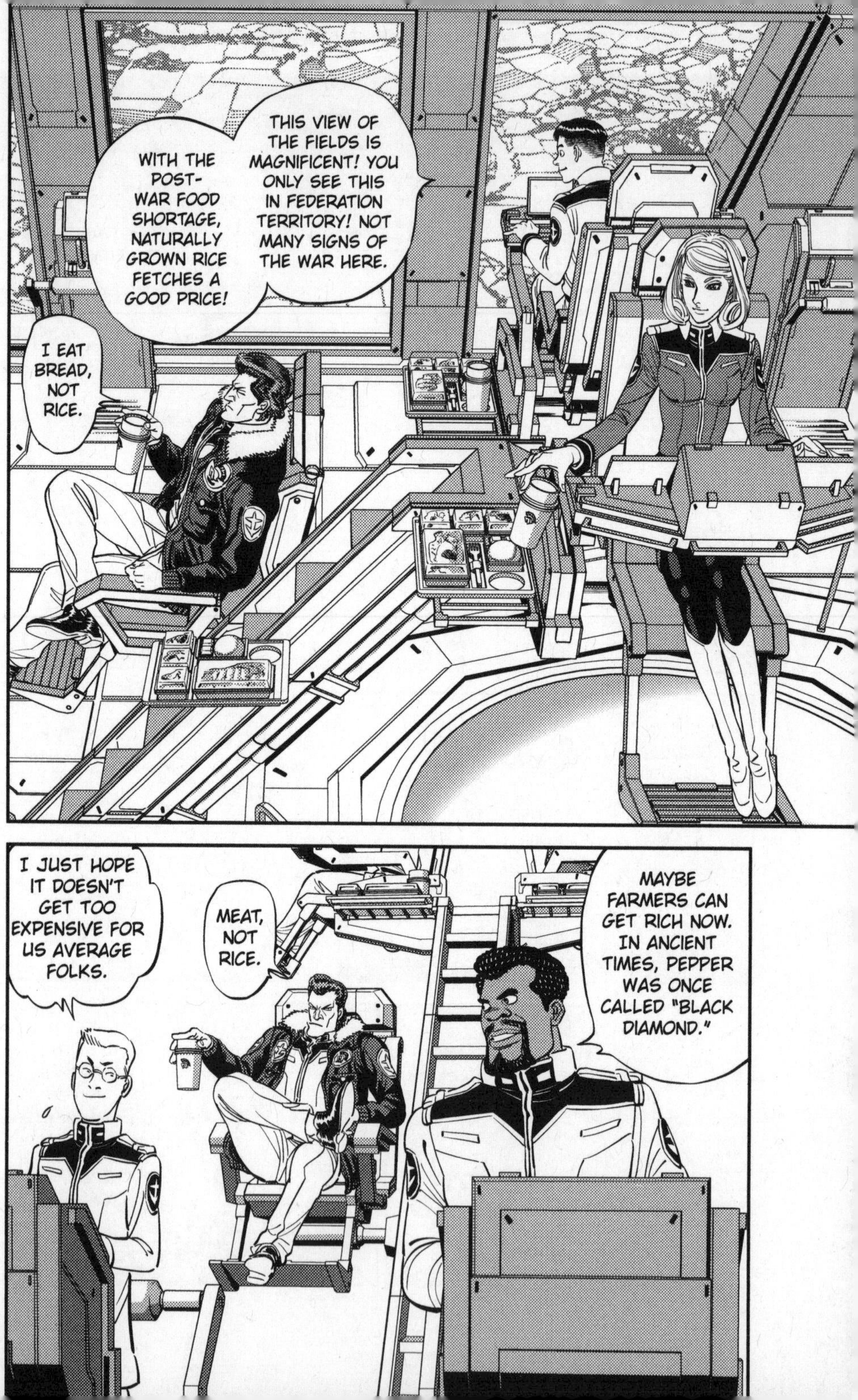
THIS VIEW OF THE FIELDS IS MAGNIFICENT! YOU ONLY SEE THIS IN FEDERATION TERRITORY! NOT MANY SIGNS OF THE WAR HERE.
WITH THE POST-WAR FOOD SHORTAGE, NATURALLY GROWN RICE FETCHES A GOOD PRICE!
I EAT BREAD, NOT RICE.
MAYBE FARMERS CAN GET RICH NOW. IN ANCIENT TIMES, PEPPER WAS ONCE CALLED "BLACK DIAMOND."
MEAT, NOT RICE.
I JUST HOPE IT DOESN'T GET TOO EXPENSIVE FOR US AVERAGE FOLKS.

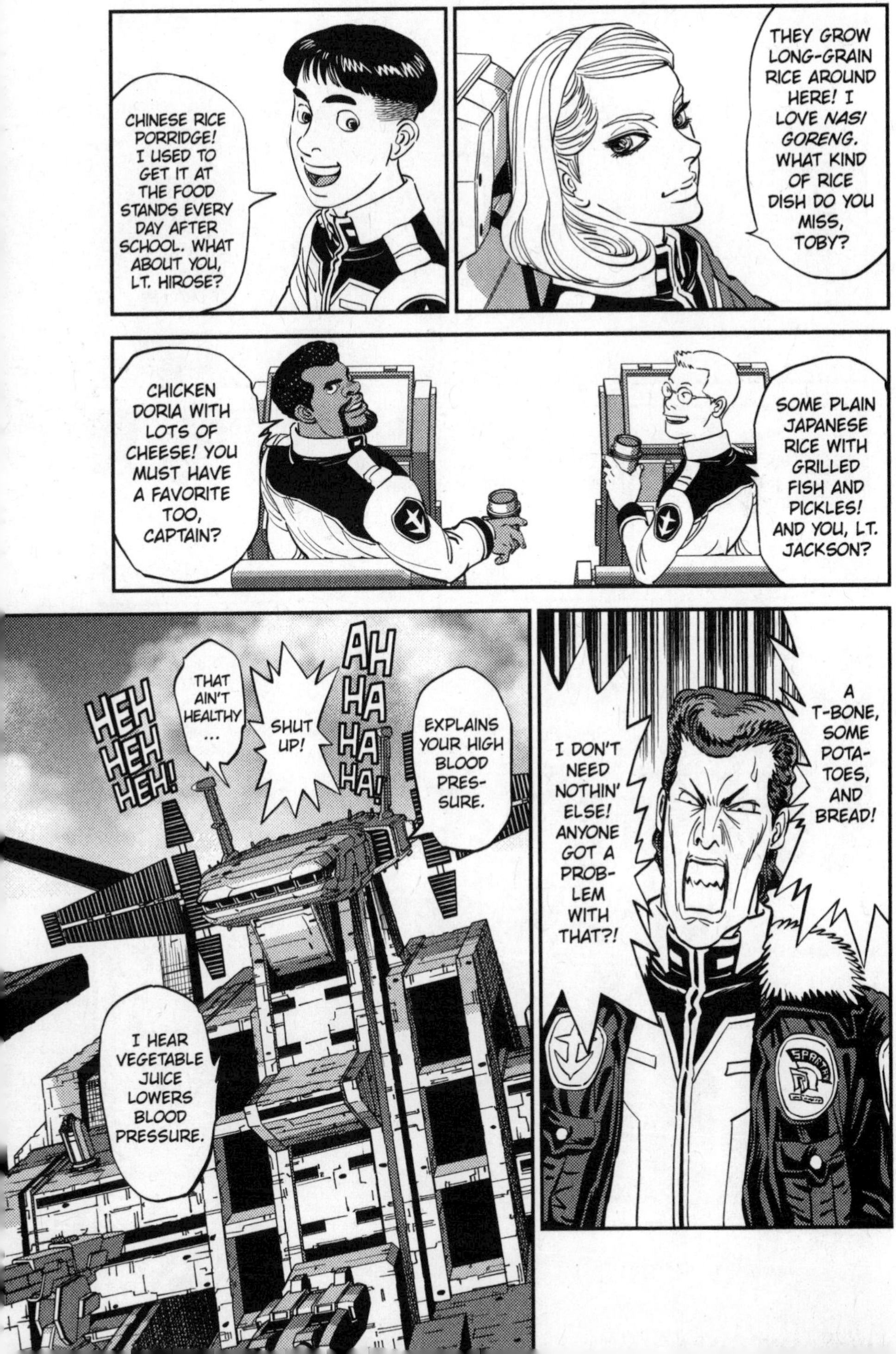
THEY GROW LONG-GRAIN RICE AROUND HERE! I LOVE NASI GORENG. WHAT KIND OF RICE DISH DO YOU MISS, TOBY?
CHINESE RICE PORRIDGE! I USED TO GET IT AT THE FOOD STANDS EVERY DAY AFTER SCHOOL. WHAT ABOUT YOU, LT. HIROSE?
SOME PLAIN JAPANESE RICE WITH GRILLED FISH AND PICKLES! AND YOU, LT. JACKSON?
CHICKEN DORIA WITH LOTS OF CHEESE! YOU MUST HAVE A FAVORITE TOO, CAPTAIN?
A T-BONE, SOME POTATOES, AND BREAD!
I DON'T NEED NOTHIN' ELSE! ANYONE GOT A PROBLEM WITH THAT?!
AH HA HA HA!
EXPLAINS YOUR HIGH BLOOD PRESSURE.
SHUT UP!
THAT AIN'T HEALTHY...
HEH HEH HEH!
I HEAR VEGETABLE JUICE LOWERS BLOOD PRESSURE.

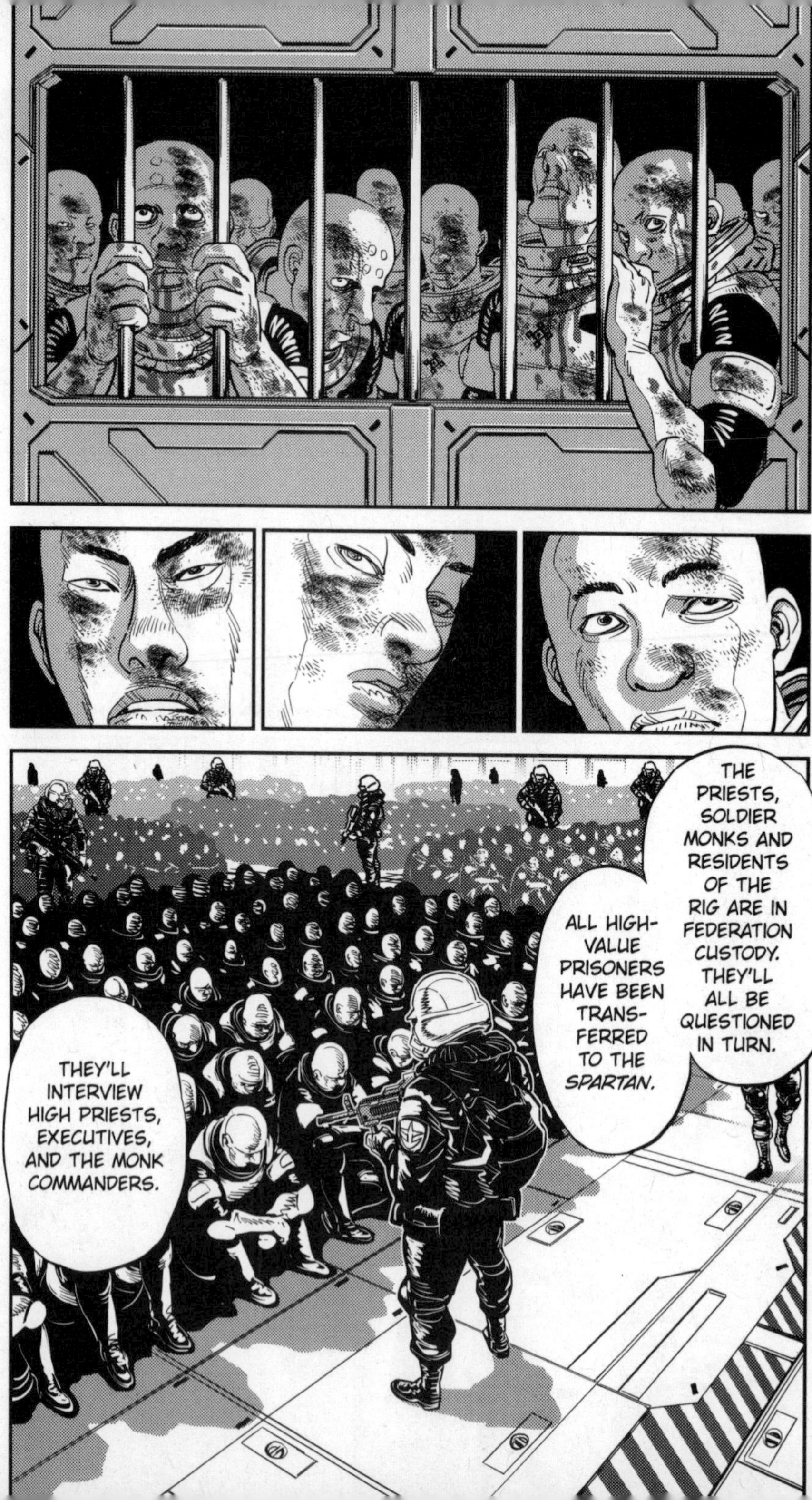
THE PRIESTS, SOLDIER MONKS AND RESIDENTS OF THE RIG ARE IN FEDERATION CUSTODY. THEY'LL ALL BE QUESTIONED IN TURN.
ALL HIGH-VALUE PRISONERS HAVE BEEN TRANS-FERRED TO THE *SPARTAN*.
THEY'LL INTERVIEW HIGH PRIESTS, EXECUTIVES, AND THE MONK COMMANDERS.

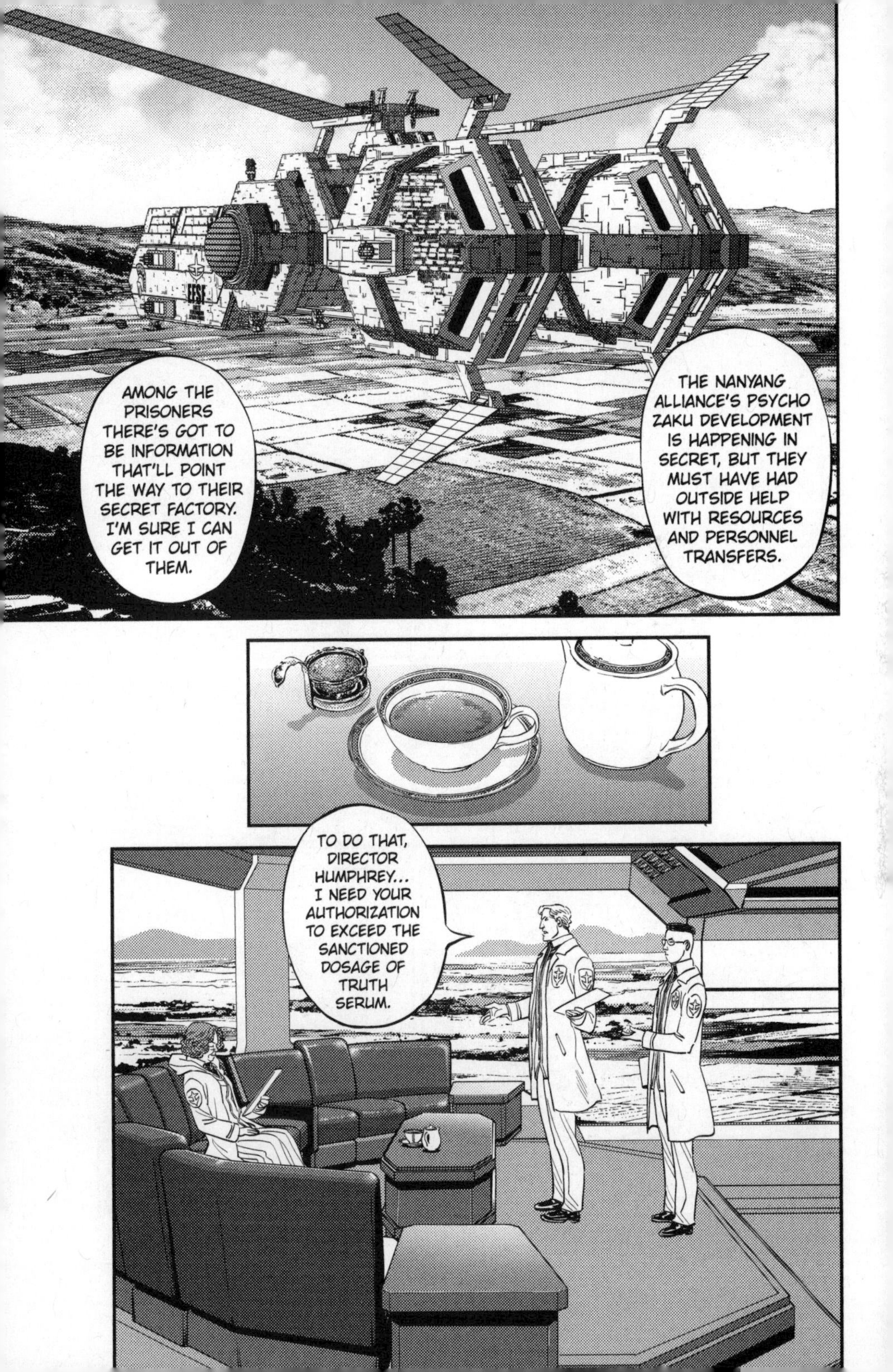
THE NANYANG ALLIANCE'S PSYCHO ZAKU DEVELOPMENT IS HAPPENING IN SECRET, BUT THEY MUST HAVE HAD OUTSIDE HELP WITH RESOURCES AND PERSONNEL TRANSFERS.
AMONG THE PRISONERS THERE'S GOT TO BE INFORMATION THAT'LL POINT THE WAY TO THEIR SECRET FACTORY. I'M SURE I CAN GET IT OUT OF THEM.
TO DO THAT, DIRECTOR HUMPHREY... I NEED YOUR AUTHORIZATION TO EXCEED THE SANCTIONED DOSAGE OF TRUTH SERUM.

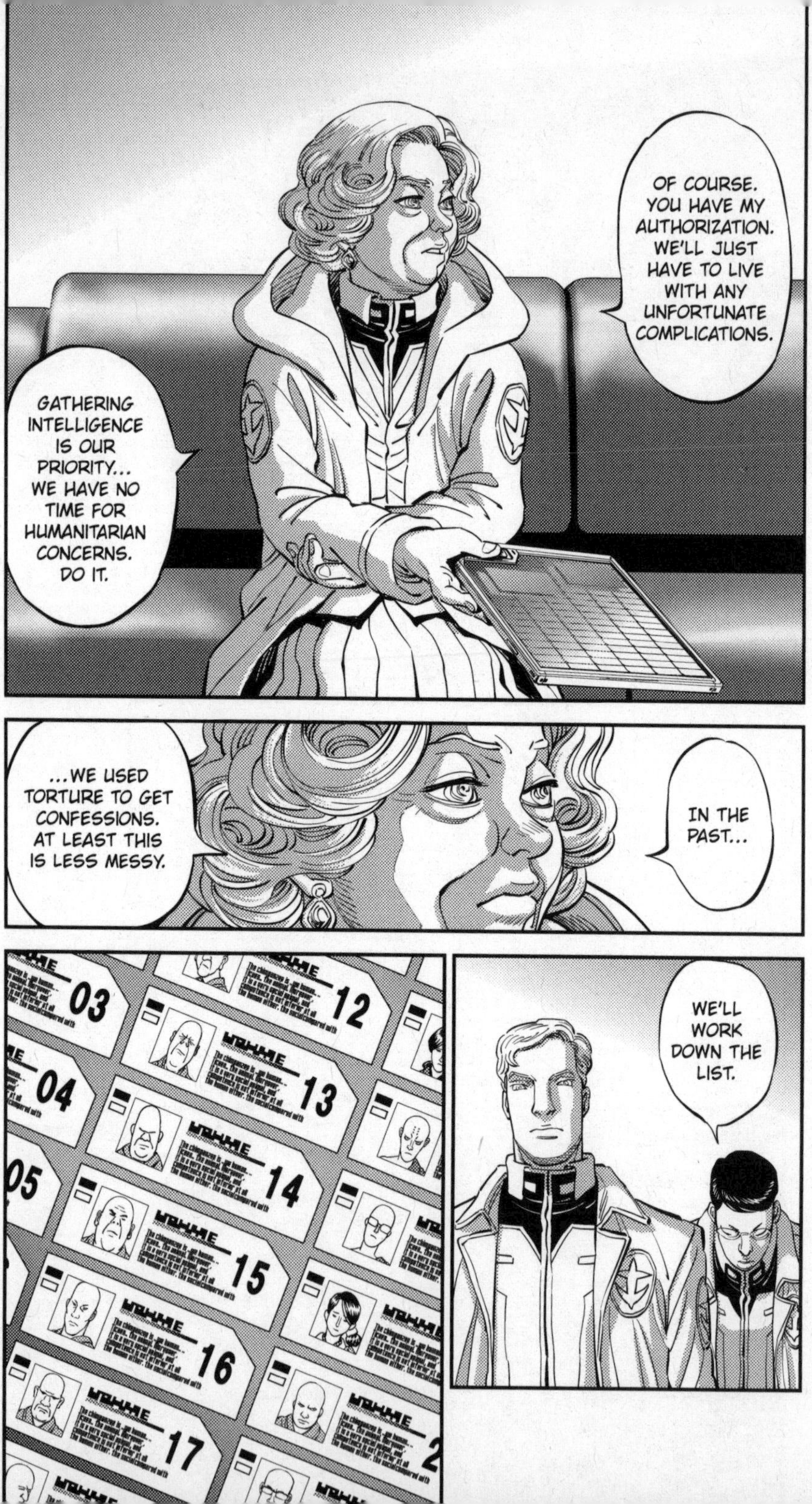
OF COURSE. YOU HAVE MY AUTHORIZATION. WE'LL JUST HAVE TO LIVE WITH ANY UNFORTUNATE COMPLICATIONS.
GATHERING INTELLIGENCE IS OUR PRIORITY... WE HAVE NO TIME FOR HUMANITARIAN CONCERNS. DO IT.
IN THE PAST...
...WE USED TORTURE TO GET CONFESSIONS. AT LEAST THIS IS LESS MESSY.
WE'LL WORK DOWN THE LIST.

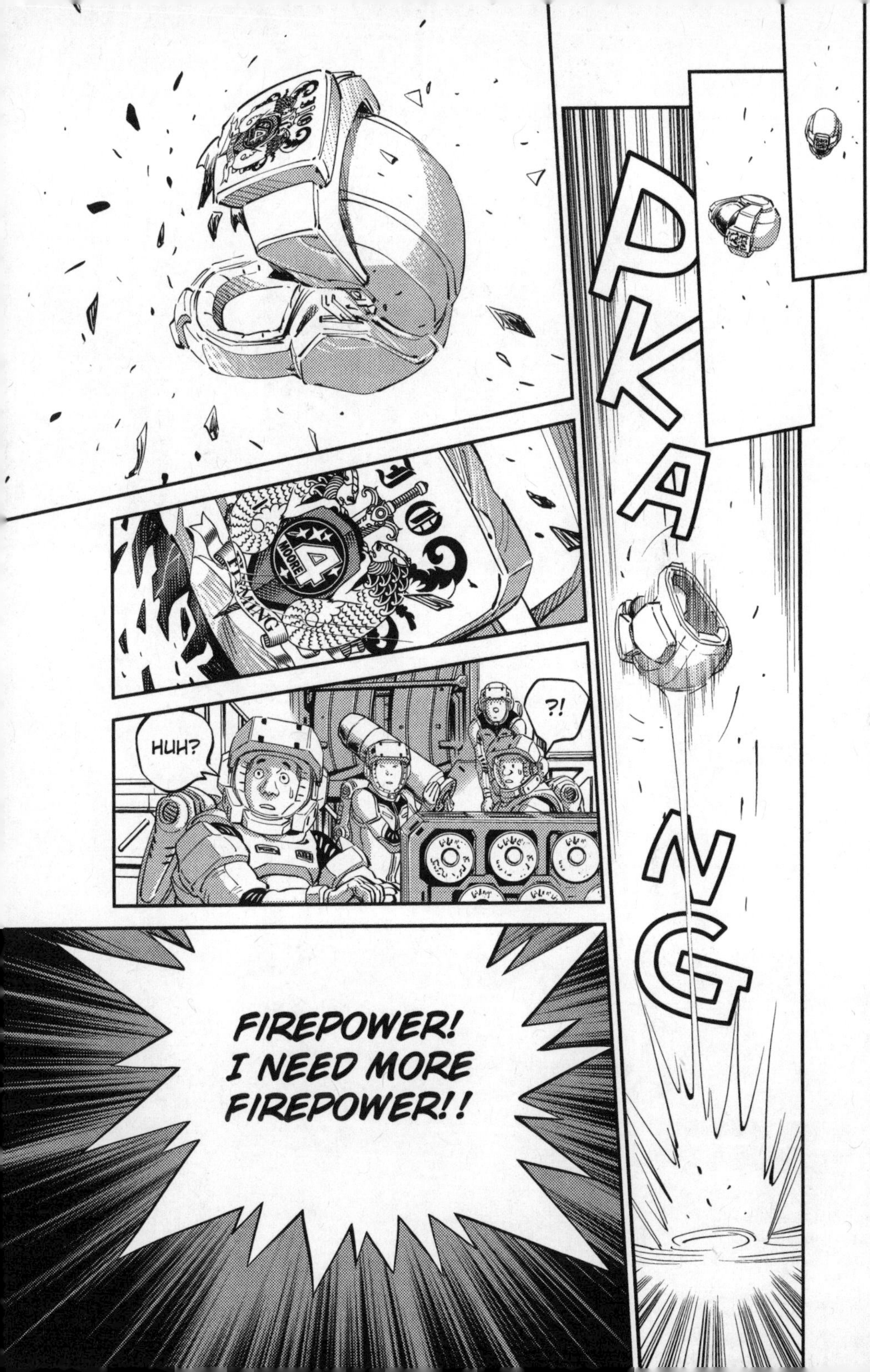
PKANG
MOORE
?!
HUH?
FIREPOWER! I NEED MORE FIREPOWER!!

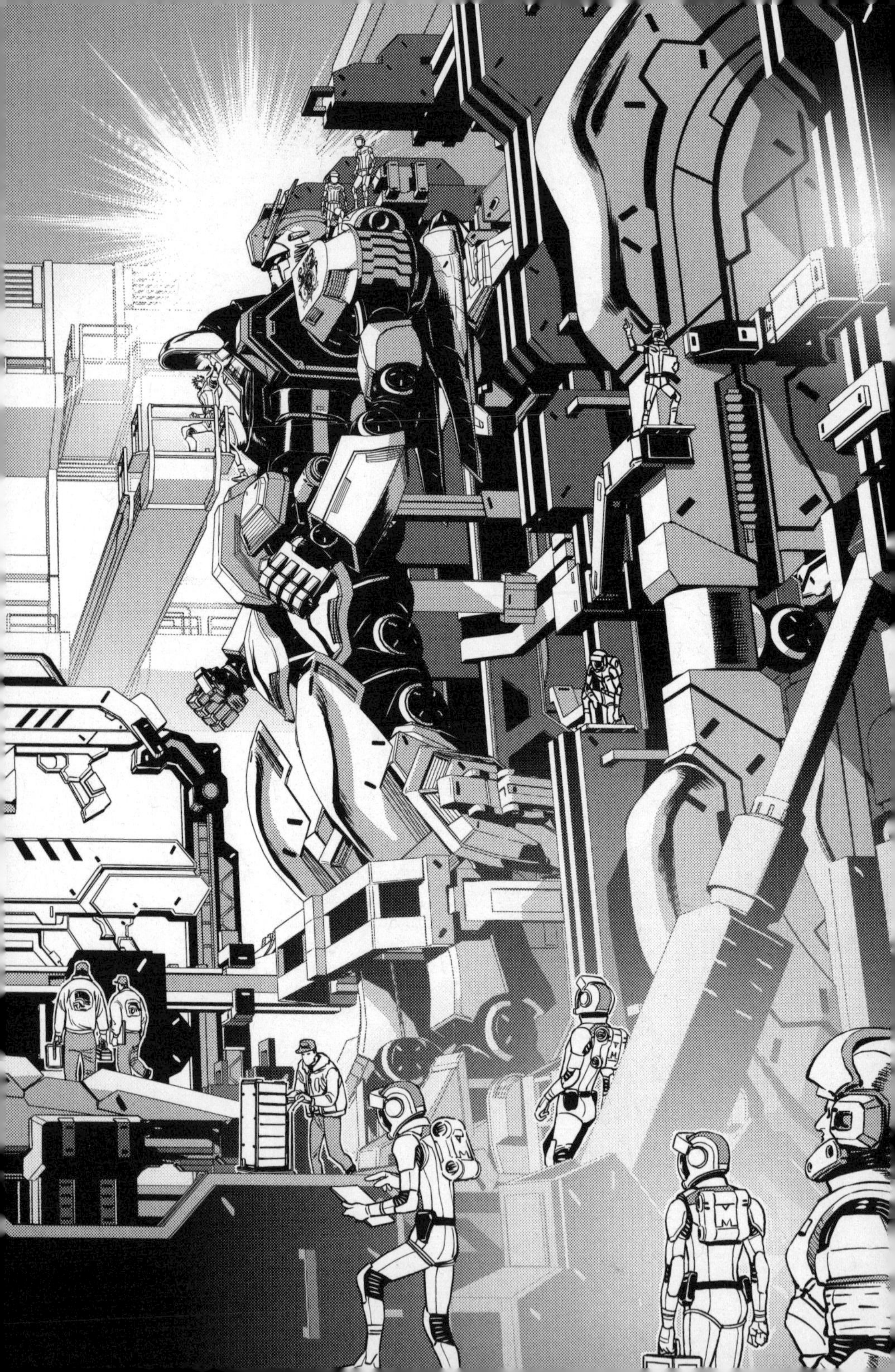

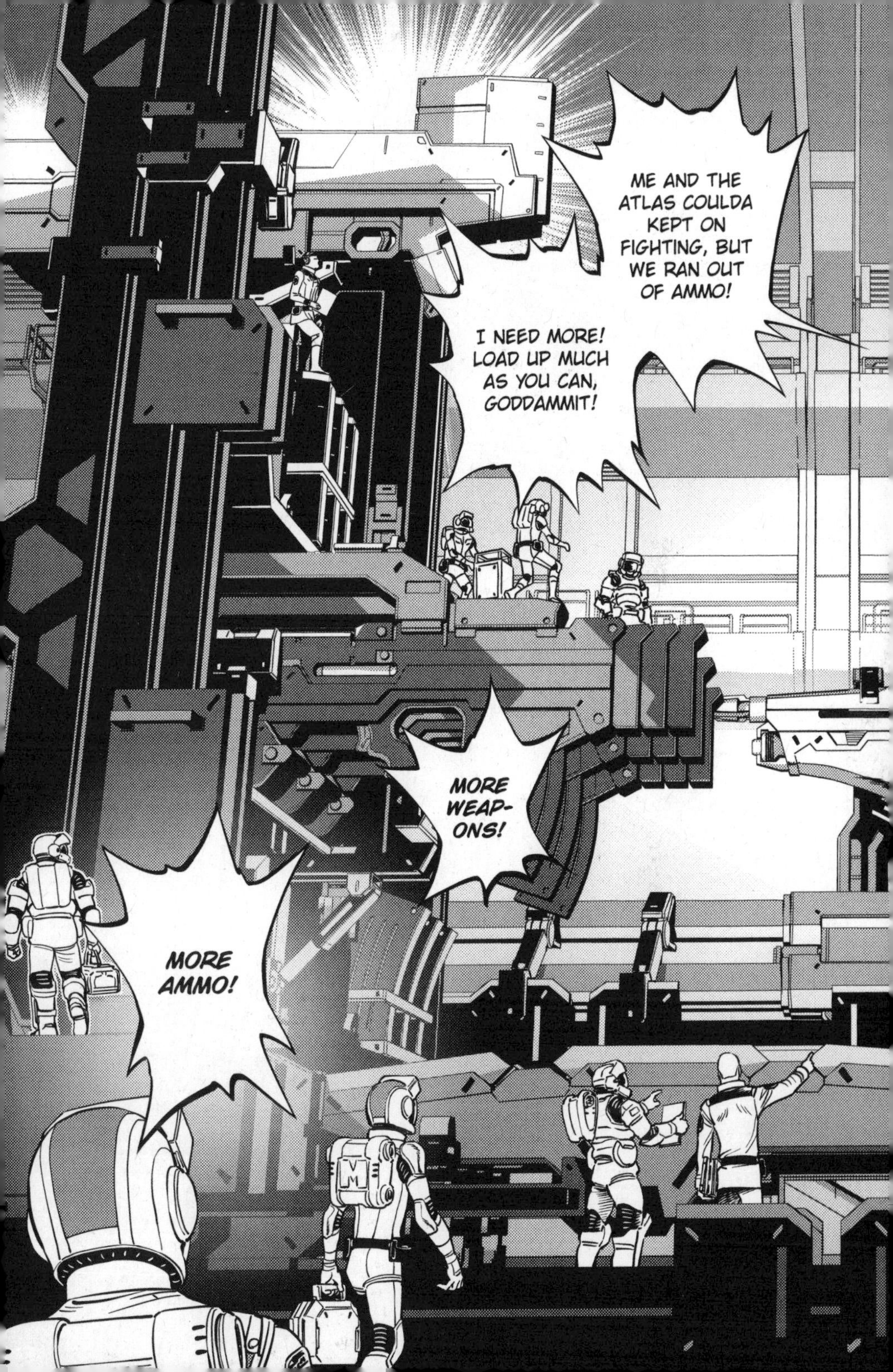
ME AND THE ATLAS COULDA KEPT ON FIGHTING, BUT WE RAN OUT OF AMMO!
I NEED MORE! LOAD UP MUCH AS YOU CAN, GODDAMMIT!
MORE WEAP-ONS!
MORE AMMO!

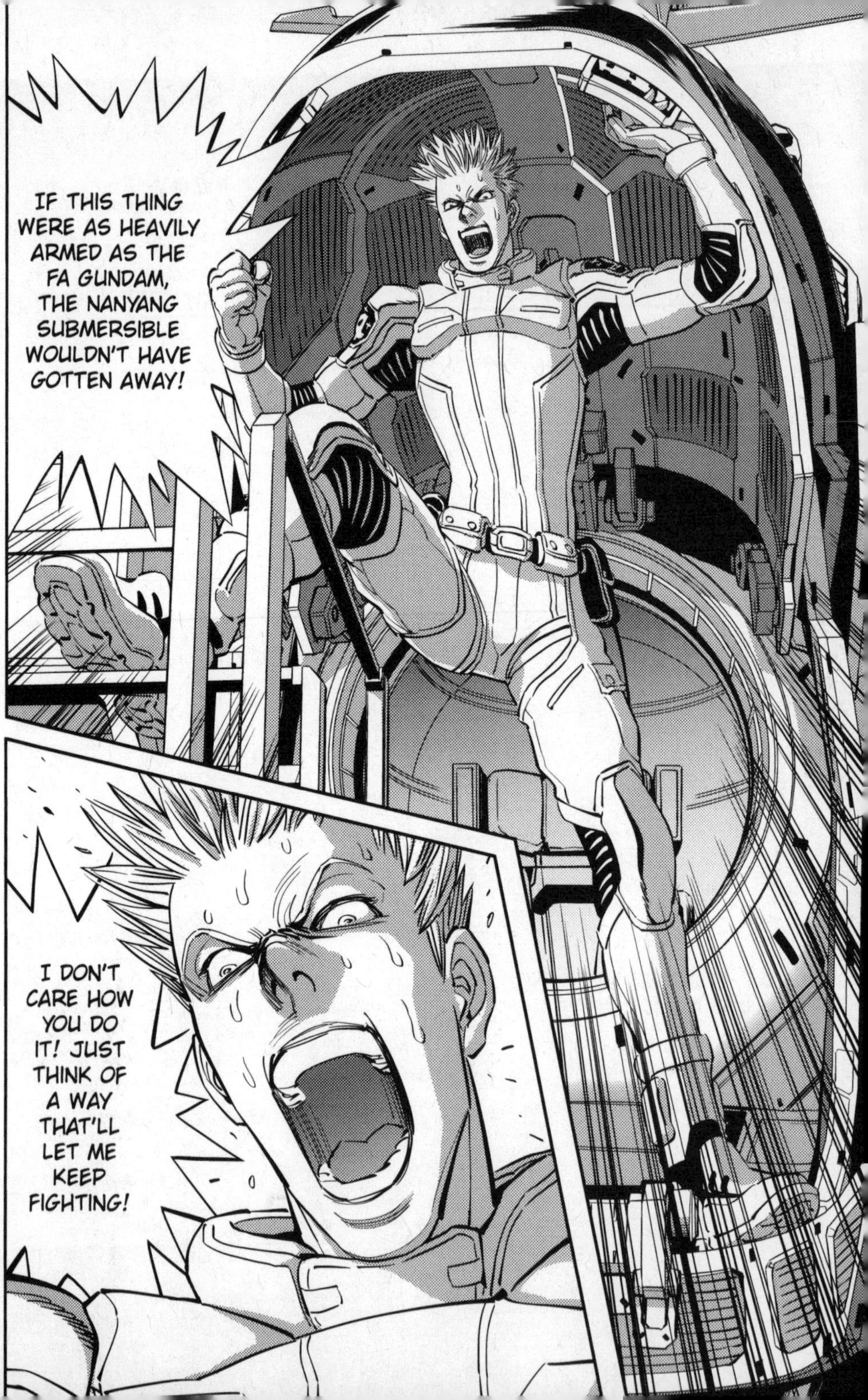
IF THIS THING WERE AS HEAVILY ARMED AS THE FA GUNDAM, THE NANYANG SUBMERSIBLE WOULDN'T HAVE GOTTEN AWAY!
I DON'T CARE HOW YOU DO IT! JUST THINK OF A WAY THAT'LL LET ME KEEP FIGHTING!

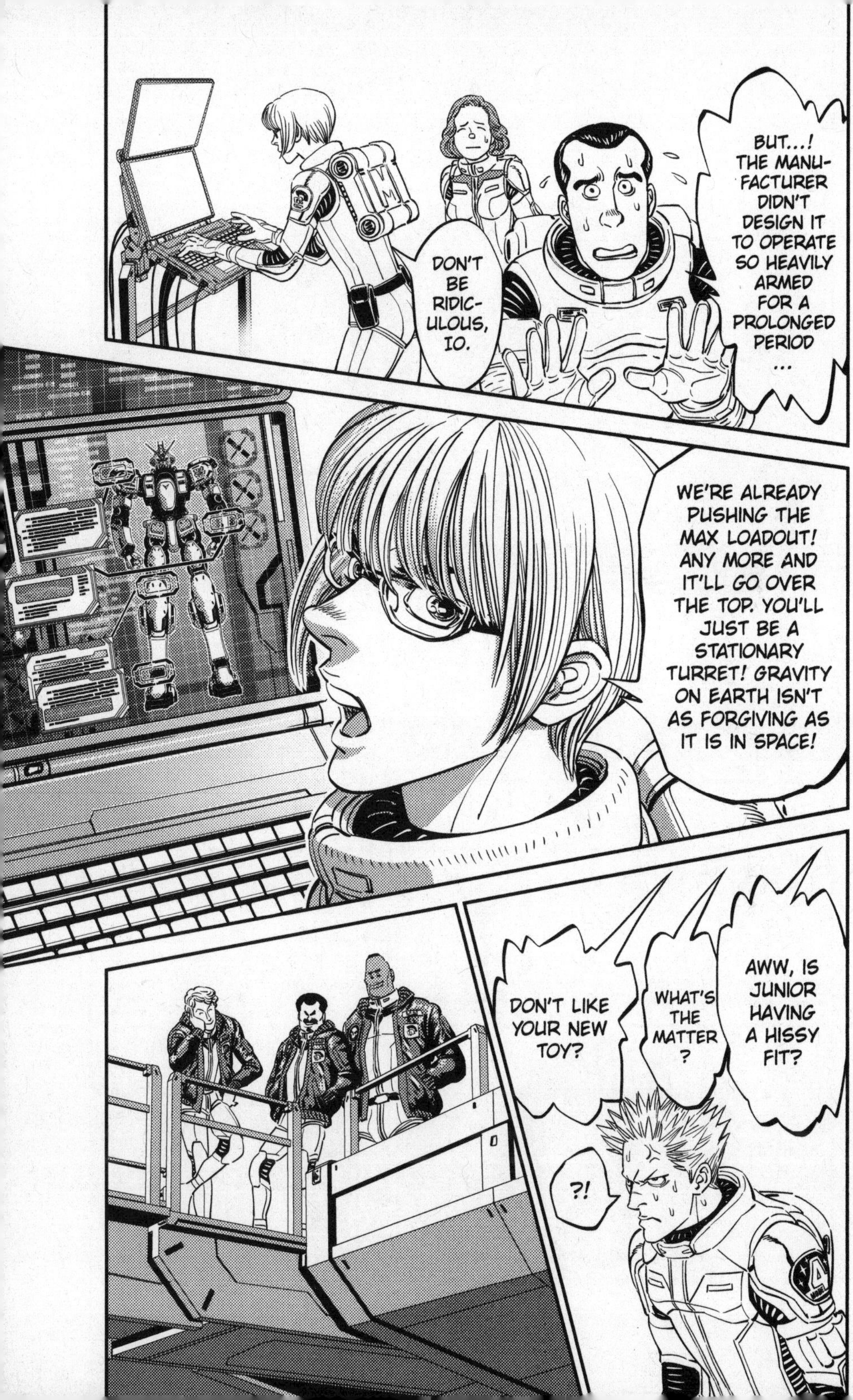
BUT...! THE MANU-FACTURER DIDN'T DESIGN IT TO OPERATE SO HEAVILY ARMED FOR A PROLONGED PERIOD ...
DON'T BE RIDIC-ULOUS, IO.
WE'RE ALREADY PUSHING THE MAX LOADOUT! ANY MORE AND IT'LL GO OVER THE TOP. YOU'LL JUST BE A STATIONARY TURRET! GRAVITY ON EARTH ISN'T AS FORGIVING AS IT IS IN SPACE!
AWW, IS JUNIOR HAVING A HISSY FIT?
WHAT'S THE MATTER ?
DON'T LIKE YOUR NEW TOY?
?!

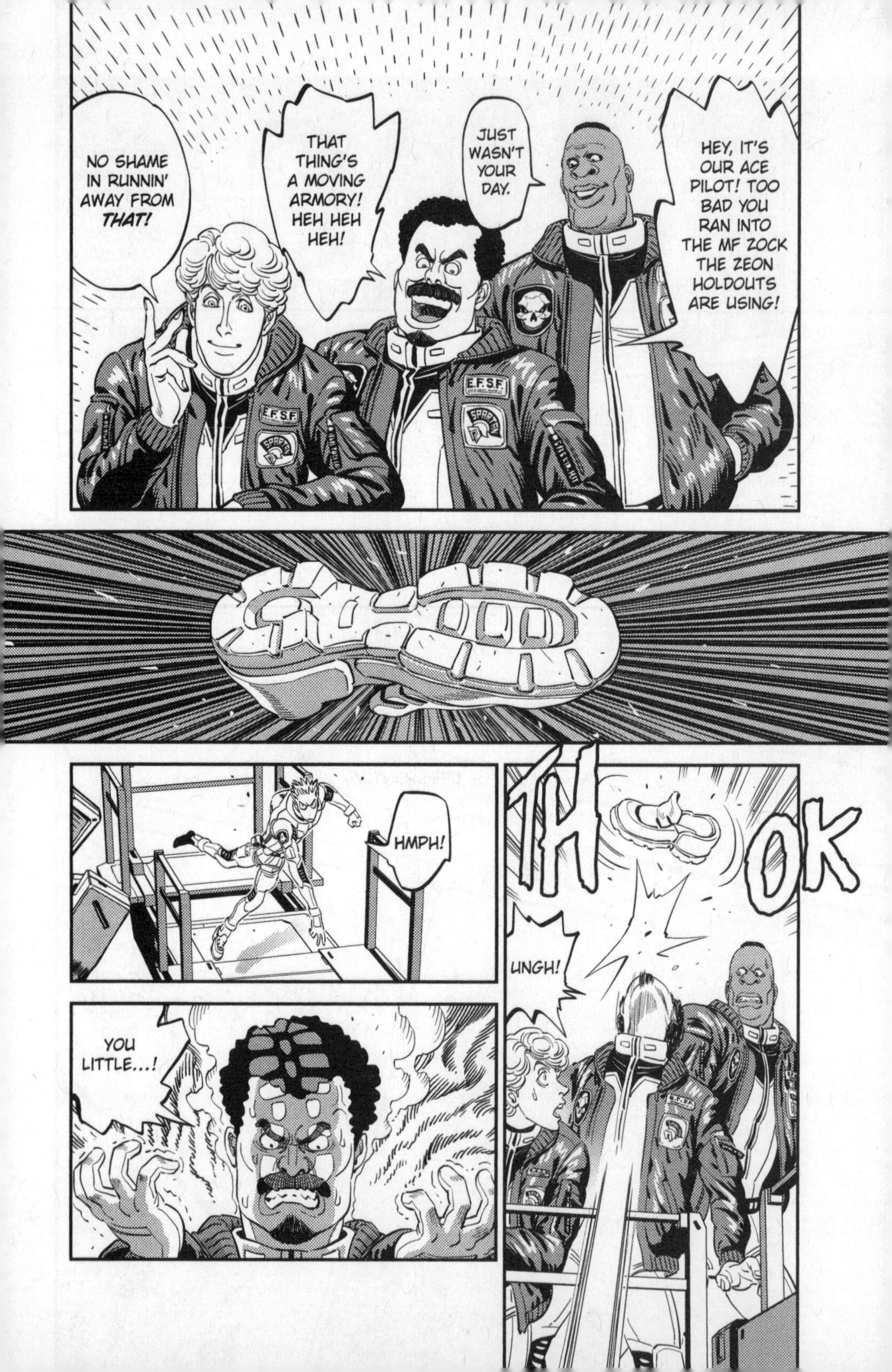
HEY, IT'S OUR ACE PILOT! TOO BAD YOU RAN INTO THE MF ZOCK THE ZEON HOLDOUTS ARE USING!
JUST WASN'T YOUR DAY.
THAT THING'S A MOVING ARMORY! HEH HEH HEH!
NO SHAME IN RUNNIN' AWAY FROM *THAT!*
TH OK
UNGH!
HMPH!
YOU LITTLE...!

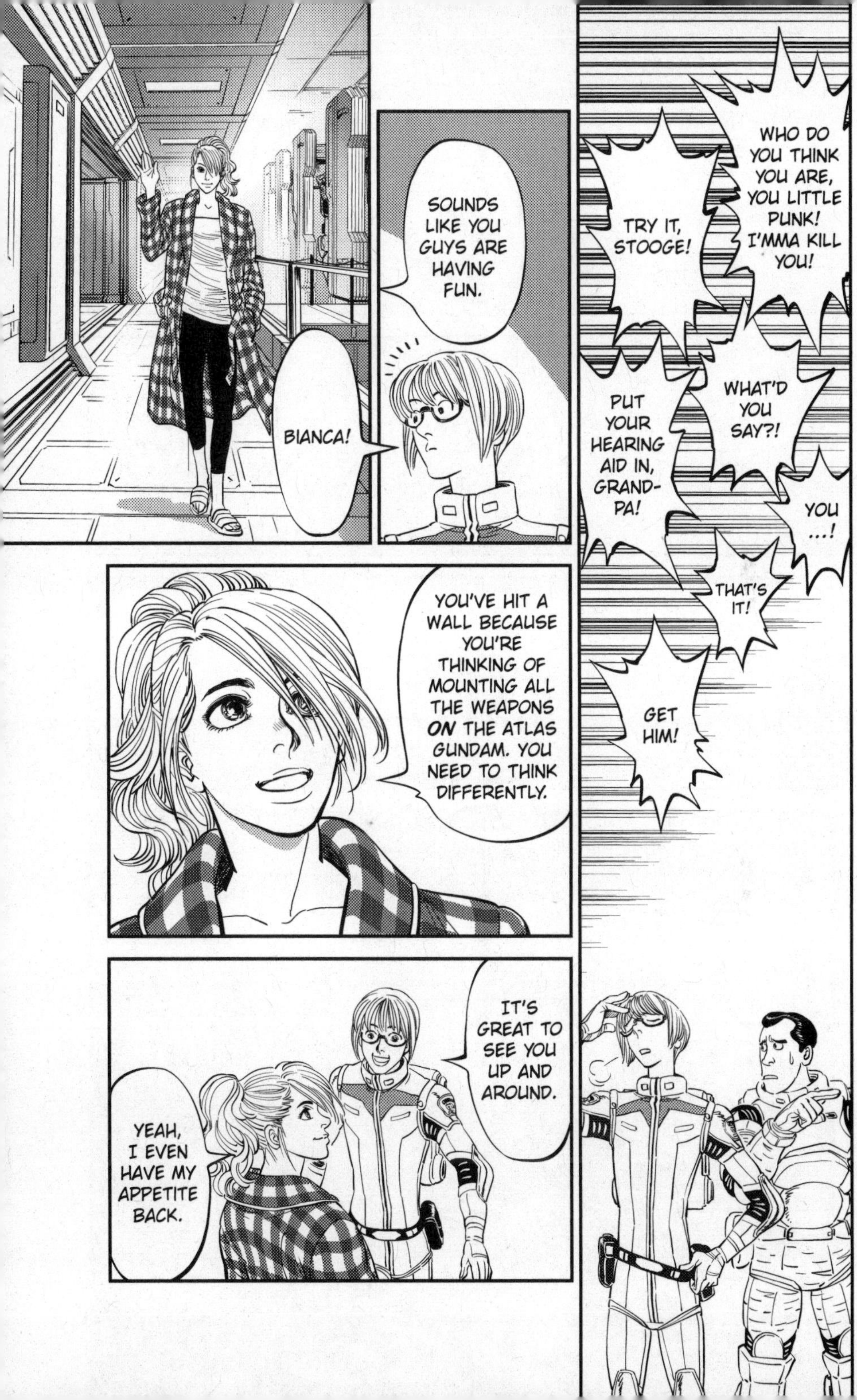
WHO DO YOU THINK YOU ARE, YOU LITTLE PUNK! I'MMA KILL YOU!
TRY IT, STOOGE!
WHAT'D YOU SAY?!
PUT YOUR HEARING AID IN, GRAND-PA!
YOU ...!
THAT'S IT!
GET HIM!
SOUNDS LIKE YOU GUYS ARE HAVING FUN.
BIANCA!
YOU'VE HIT A WALL BECAUSE YOU'RE THINKING OF MOUNTING ALL THE WEAPONS ***ON*** THE ATLAS GUNDAM. YOU NEED TO THINK DIFFERENTLY.
IT'S GREAT TO SEE YOU UP AND AROUND.
YEAH, I EVEN HAVE MY APPETITE BACK.

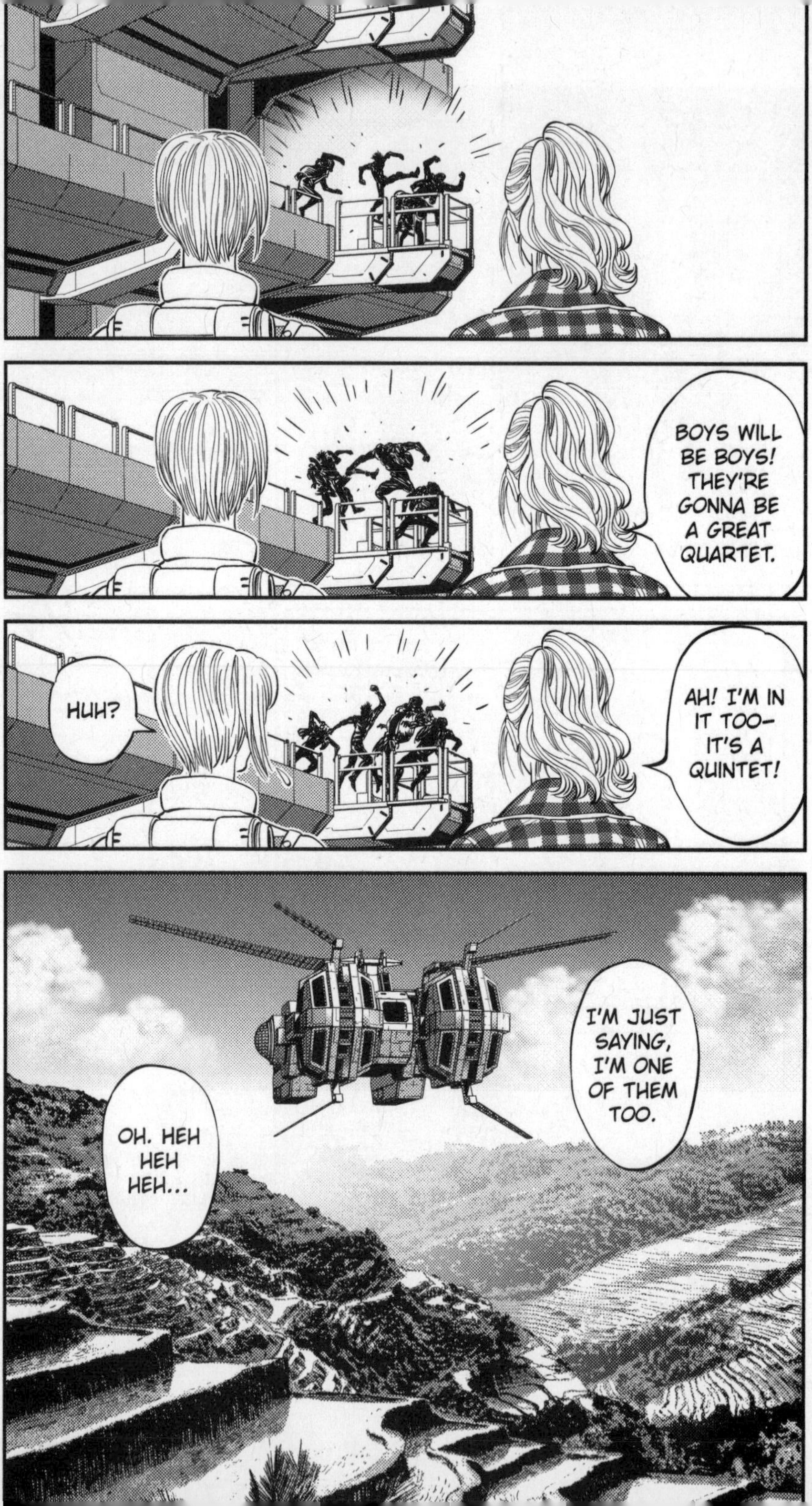

BOYS WILL BE BOYS! THEY'RE GONNA BE A GREAT QUARTET.
AH! I'M IN IT TOO— IT'S A QUINTET!
HUH?
I'M JUST SAYING, I'M ONE OF THEM TOO.
OH. HEH HEH HEH...

MOBILE SUIT GUNDAM THUNDERBOLT

CHAPTER 81

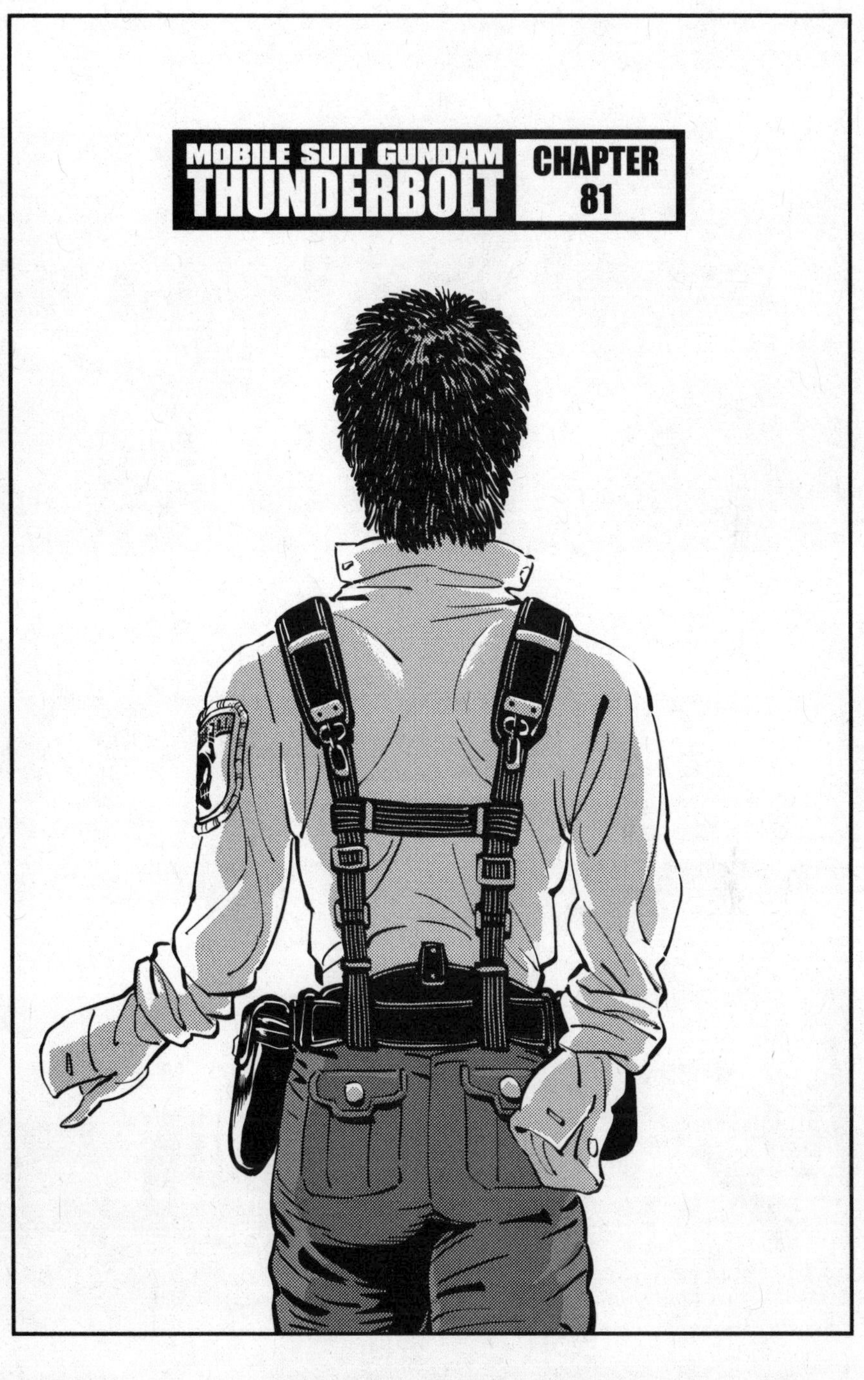

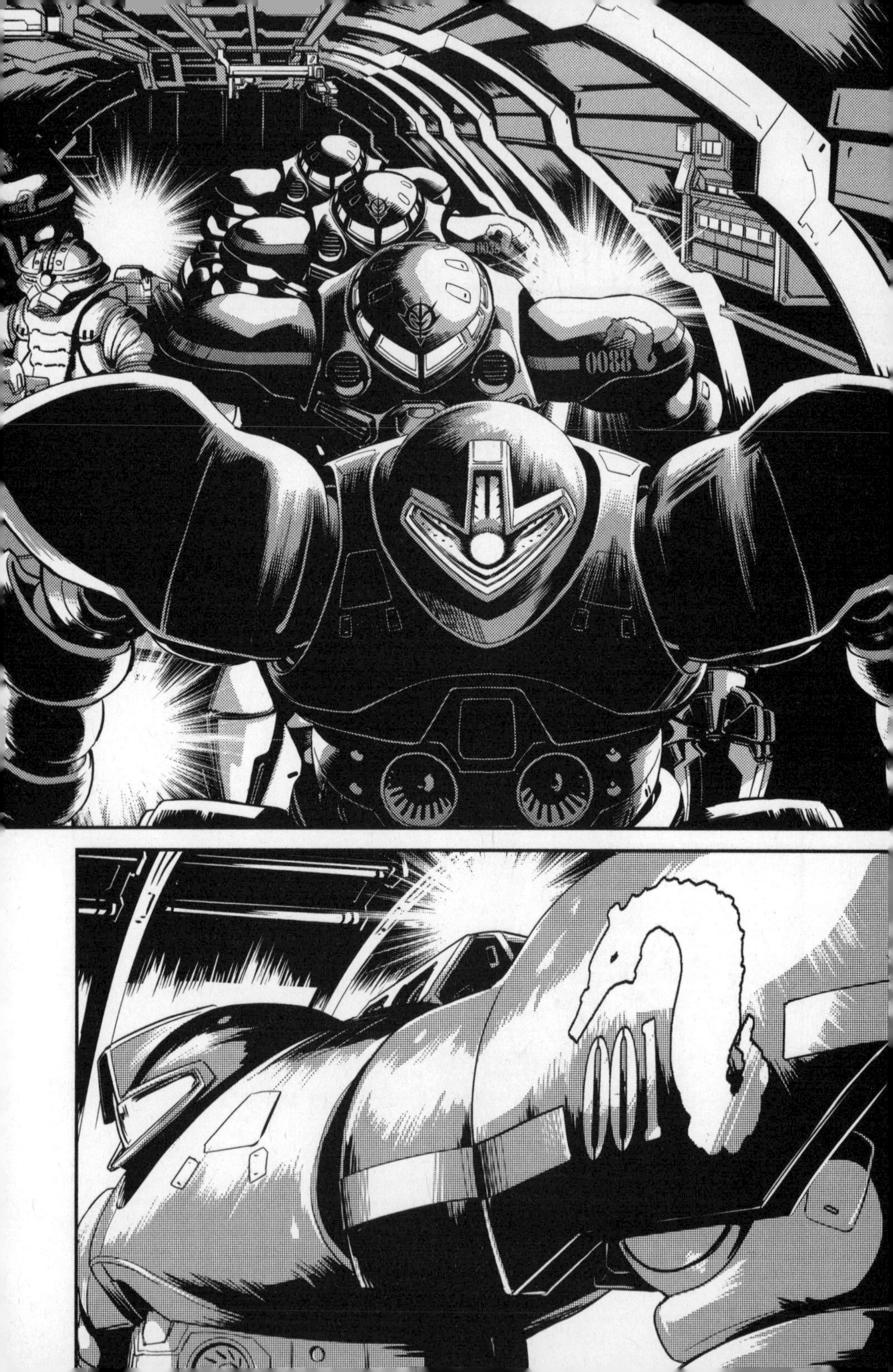
0088

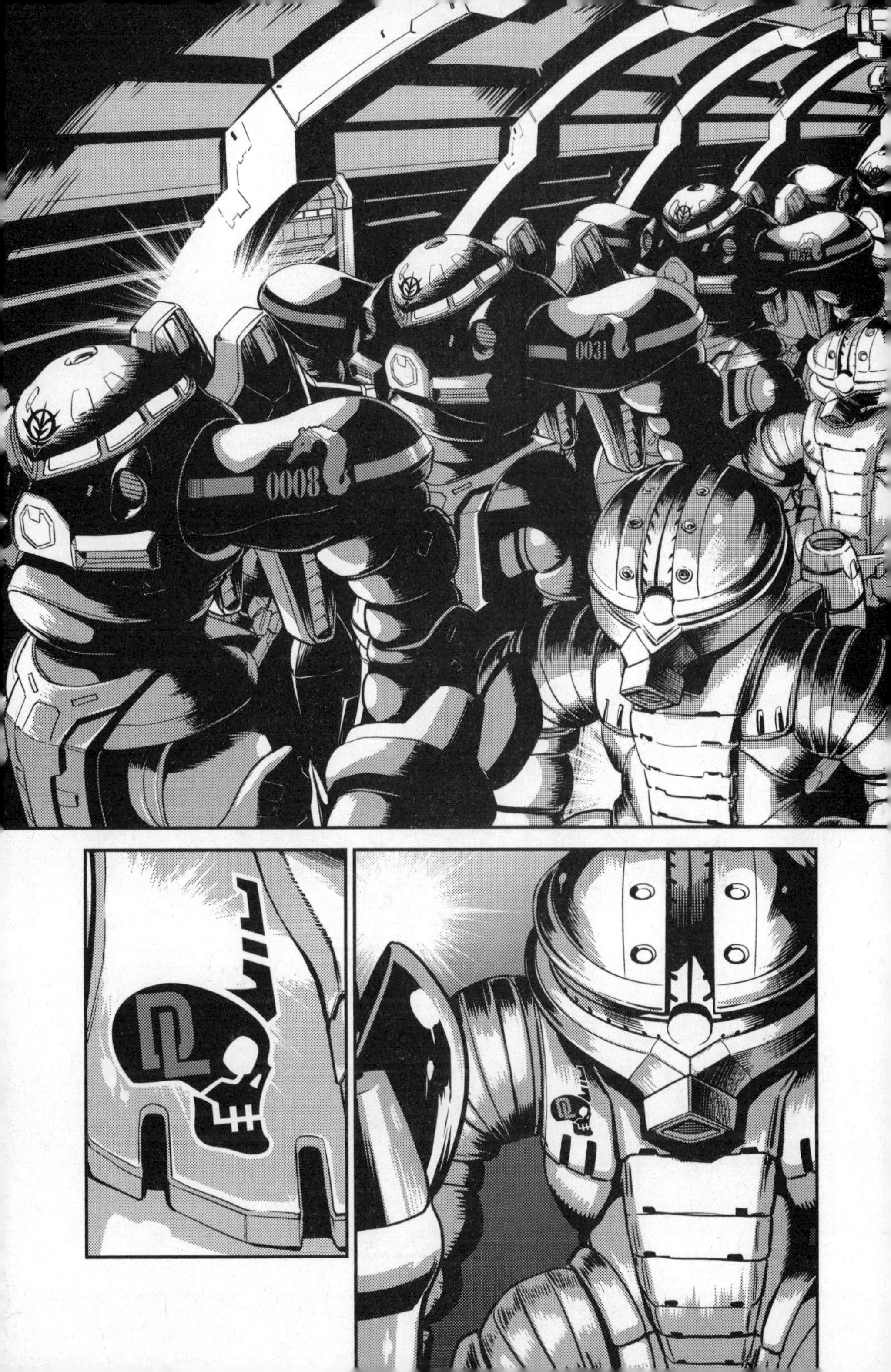
0031
0008

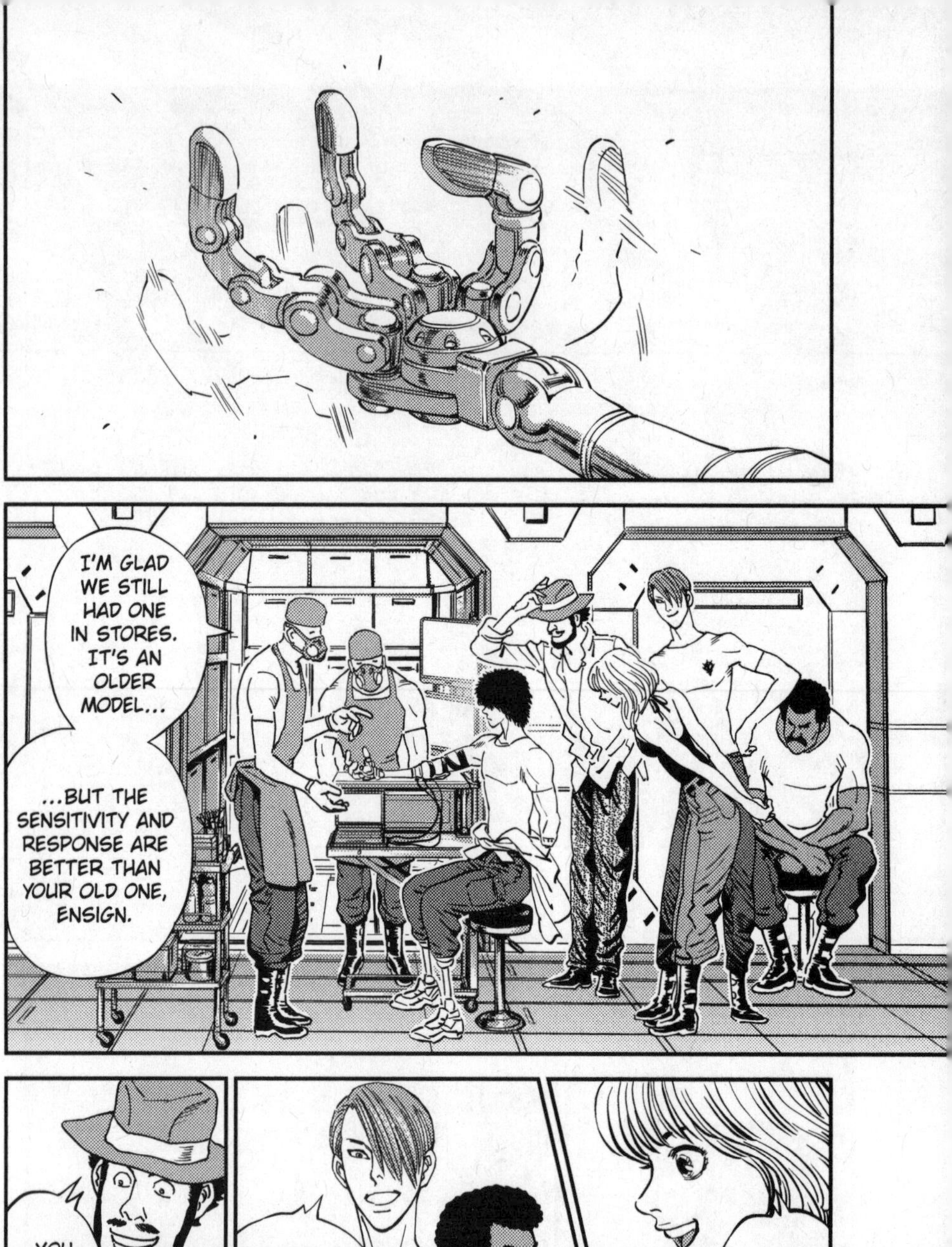
I'M GLAD WE STILL HAD ONE IN STORES. IT'S AN OLDER MODEL...
...BUT THE SENSITIVITY AND RESPONSE ARE BETTER THAN YOUR OLD ONE, ENSIGN.
LOOKS GOOD, DARYL. IT'S COOL!
I'LL HELP WITH THE REHAB TO GET YOU USED TO IT.
YOU GOTTA GET AD-JUSTED QUICK!

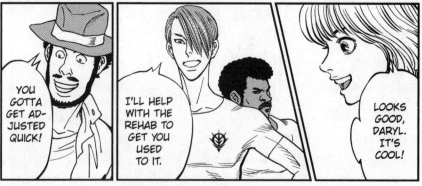

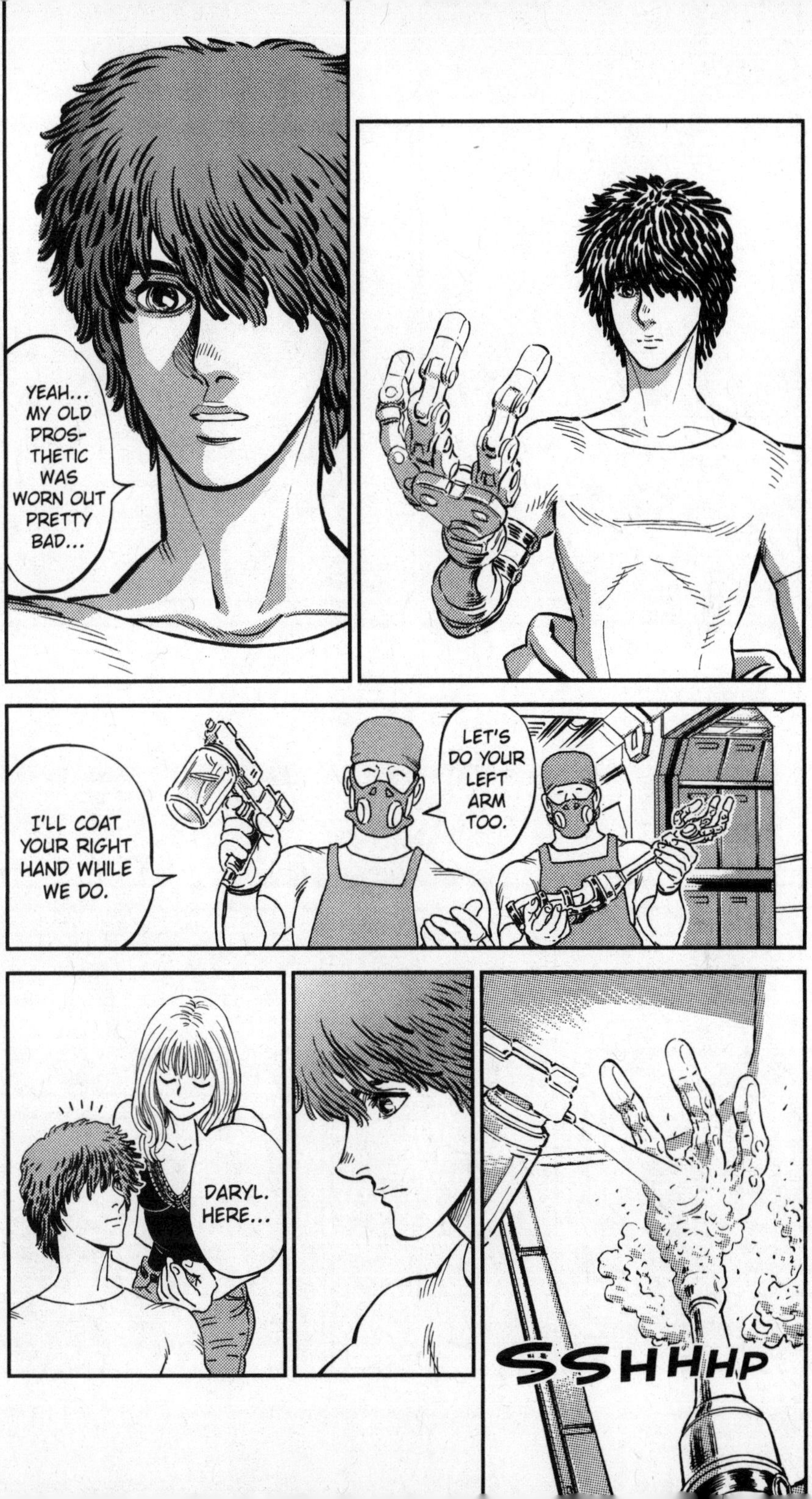
YEAH... MY OLD PROSTHETIC WAS WORN OUT PRETTY BAD...
LET'S DO YOUR LEFT ARM TOO.
I'LL COAT YOUR RIGHT HAND WHILE WE DO.
SSHHHP
DARYL. HERE...

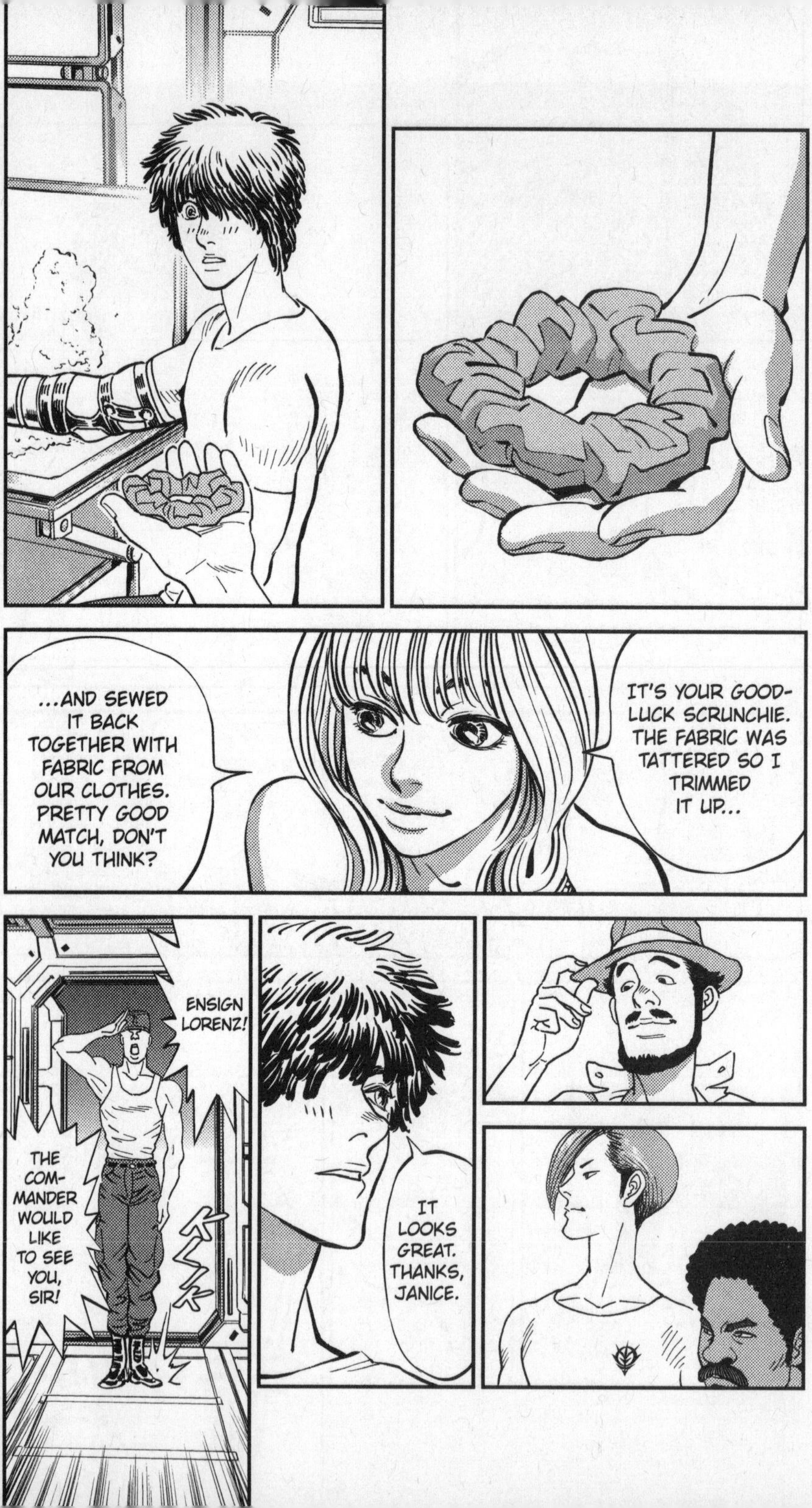
IT'S YOUR GOOD-LUCK SCRUNCHIE. THE FABRIC WAS TATTERED SO I TRIMMED IT UP...
...AND SEWED IT BACK TOGETHER WITH FABRIC FROM OUR CLOTHES. PRETTY GOOD MATCH, DON'T YOU THINK?
IT LOOKS GREAT. THANKS, JANICE.
ENSIGN LORENZ!
THE COMMANDER WOULD LIKE TO SEE YOU, SIR!

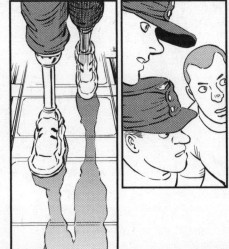

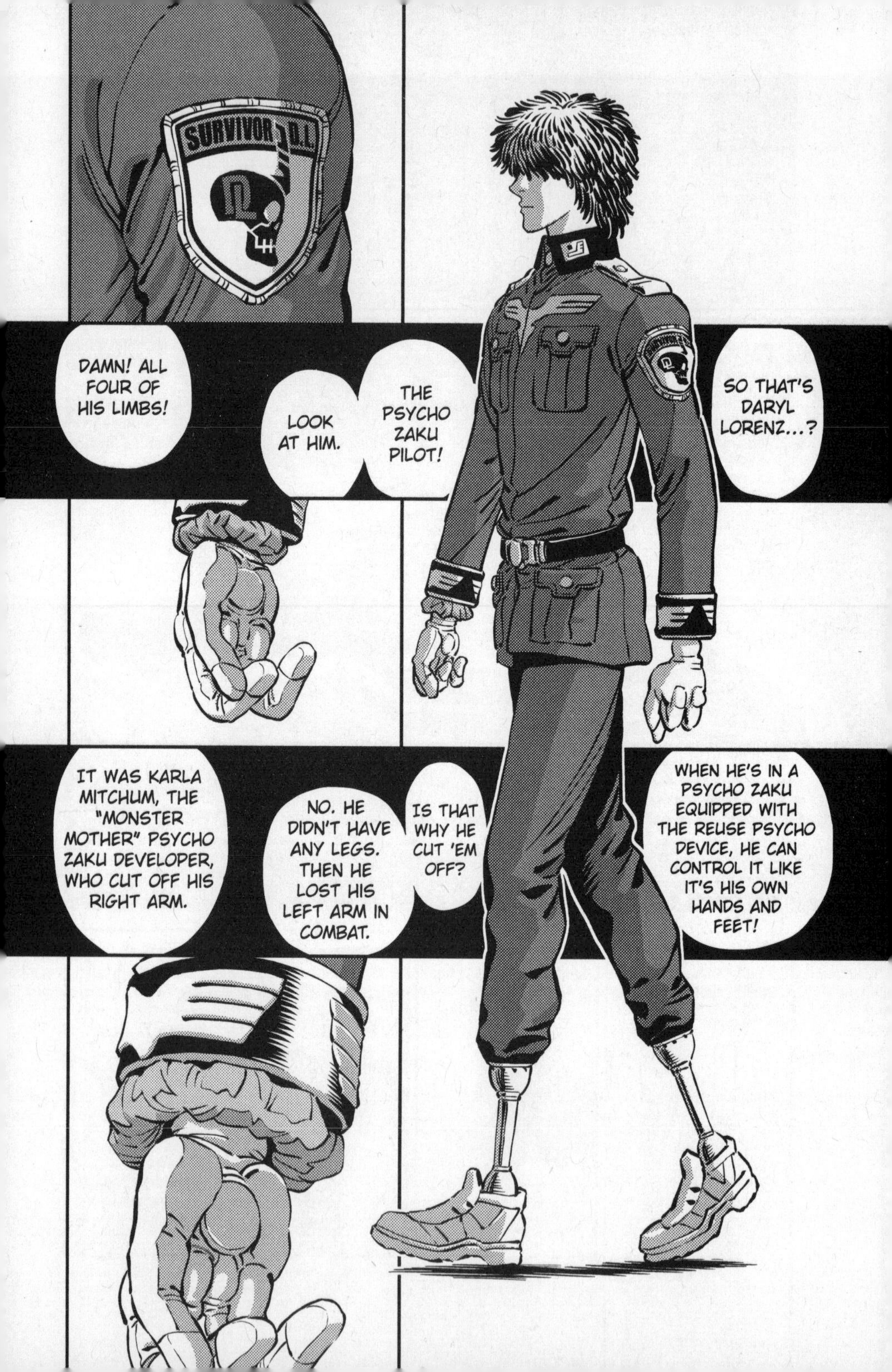
SURVIVOR D.L.
SO THAT'S DARYL LORENZ...?
THE PSYCHO ZAKU PILOT!
LOOK AT HIM.
DAMN! ALL FOUR OF HIS LIMBS!
WHEN HE'S IN A PSYCHO ZAKU EQUIPPED WITH THE REUSE PSYCHO DEVICE, HE CAN CONTROL IT LIKE IT'S HIS OWN HANDS AND FEET!
IS THAT WHY HE CUT 'EM OFF?
NO. HE DIDN'T HAVE ANY LEGS. THEN HE LOST HIS LEFT ARM IN COMBAT.
IT WAS KARLA MITCHUM, THE "MONSTER MOTHER" PSYCHO ZAKU DEVELOPER, WHO CUT OFF HIS RIGHT ARM.

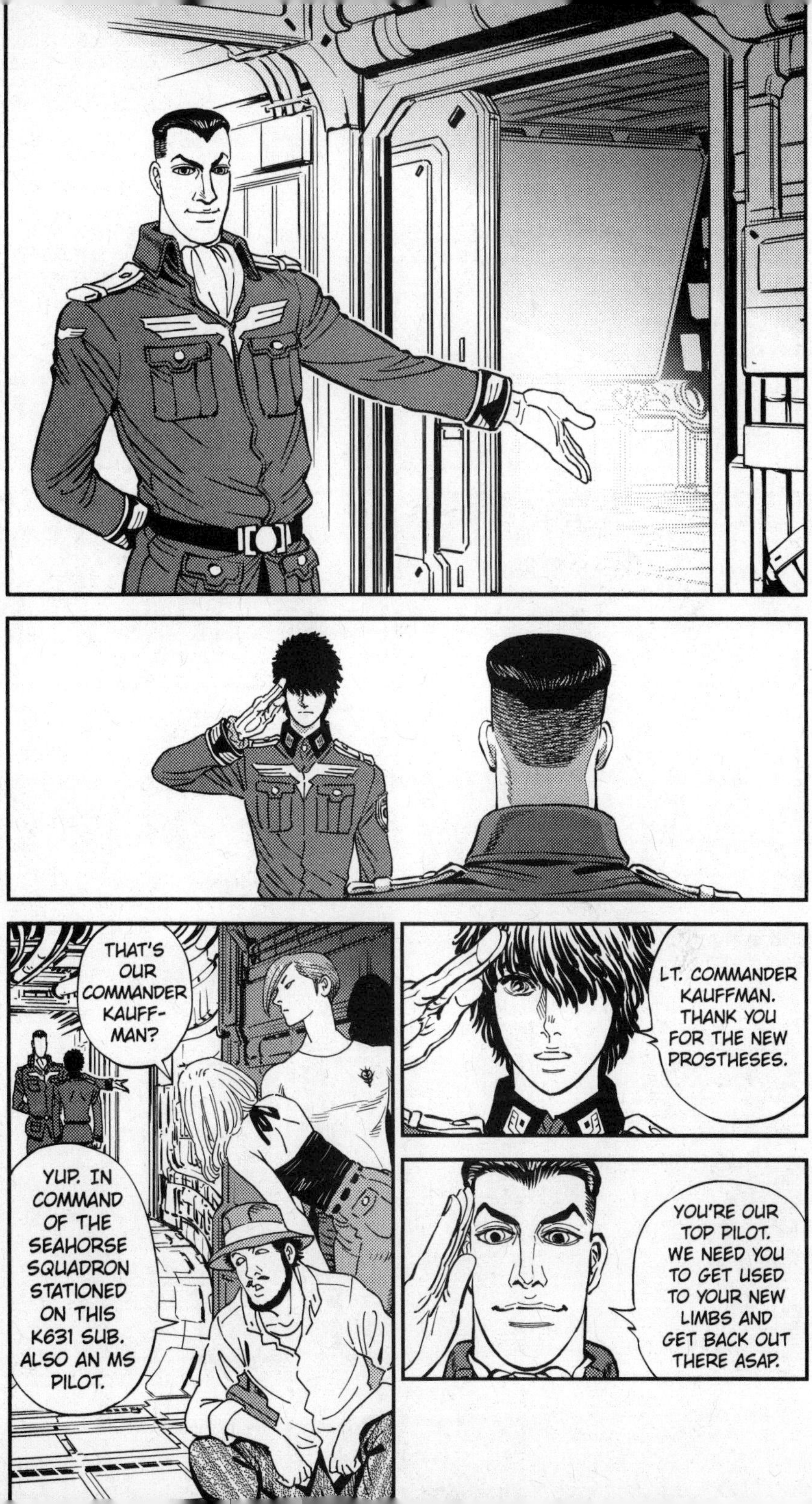
LT. COMMANDER KAUFFMAN. THANK YOU FOR THE NEW PROSTHESES.
YOU'RE OUR TOP PILOT. WE NEED YOU TO GET USED TO YOUR NEW LIMBS AND GET BACK OUT THERE ASAP.
THAT'S OUR COMMANDER KAUFF-MAN?
YUP. IN COMMAND OF THE SEAHORSE SQUADRON STATIONED ON THIS K631 SUB. ALSO AN MS PILOT.

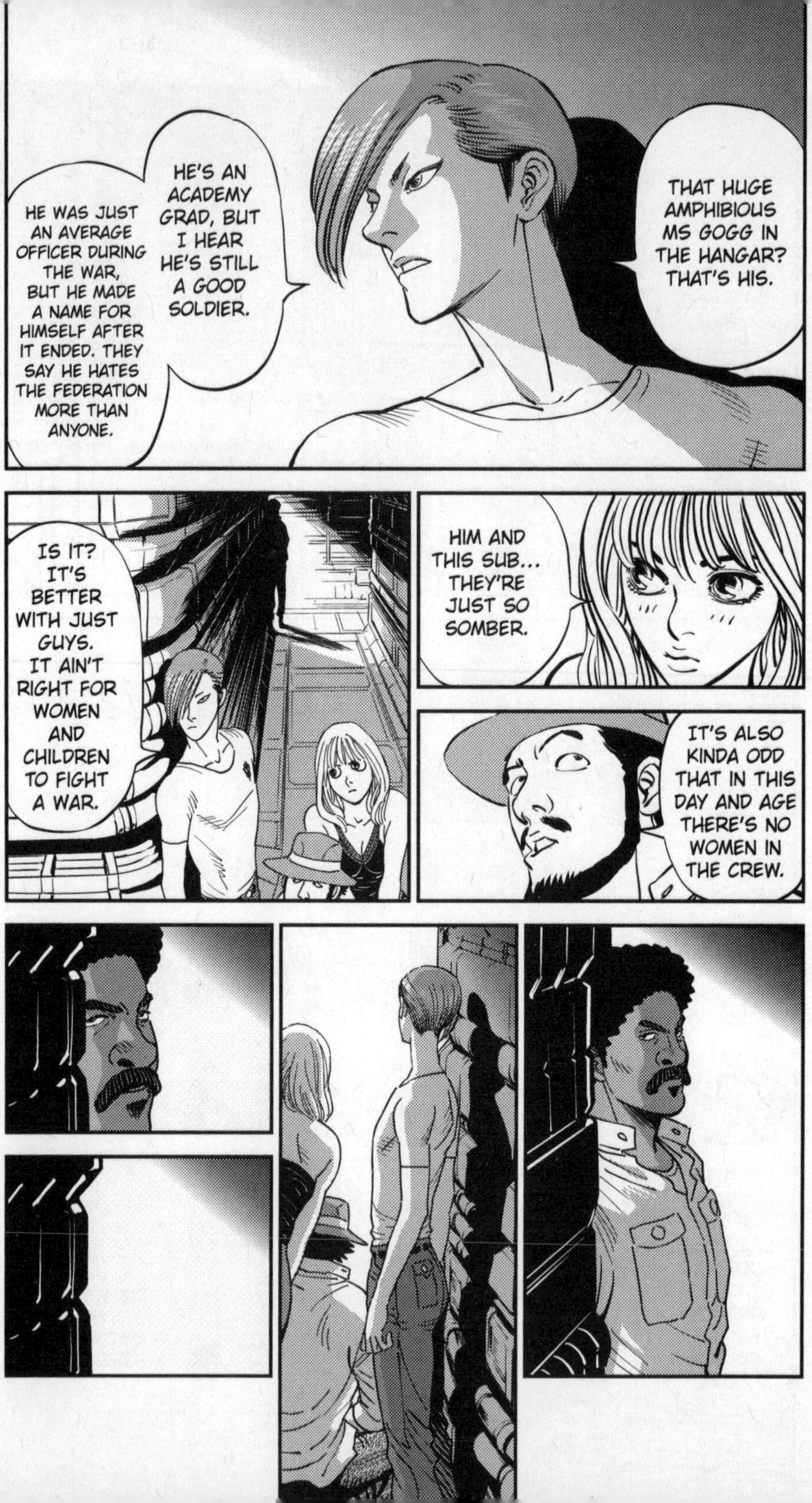
THAT HUGE AMPHIBIOUS MS GOGG IN THE HANGAR? THAT'S HIS.
HE'S AN ACADEMY GRAD, BUT I HEAR HE'S STILL A GOOD SOLDIER.
HE WAS JUST AN AVERAGE OFFICER DURING THE WAR, BUT HE MADE A NAME FOR HIMSELF AFTER IT ENDED. THEY SAY HE HATES THE FEDERATION MORE THAN ANYONE.
HIM AND THIS SUB... THEY'RE JUST SO SOMBER.
IT'S ALSO KINDA ODD THAT IN THIS DAY AND AGE THERE'S NO WOMEN IN THE CREW.
IS IT? IT'S BETTER WITH JUST GUYS. IT AIN'T RIGHT FOR WOMEN AND CHILDREN TO FIGHT A WAR.

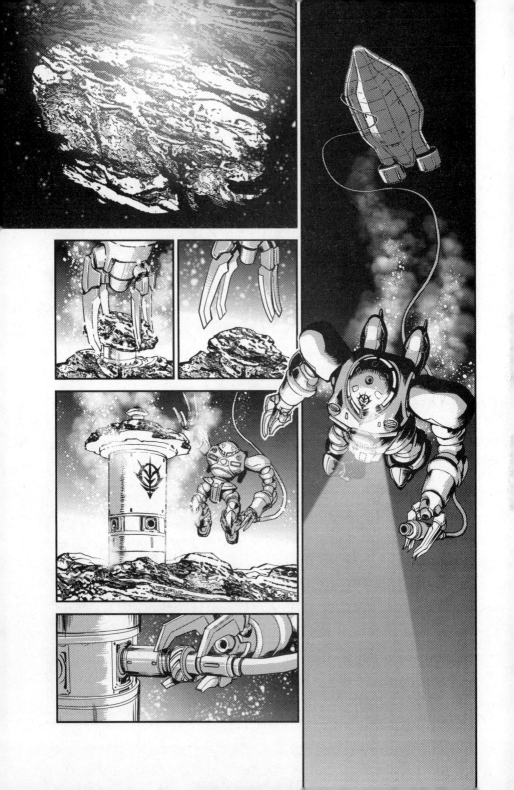

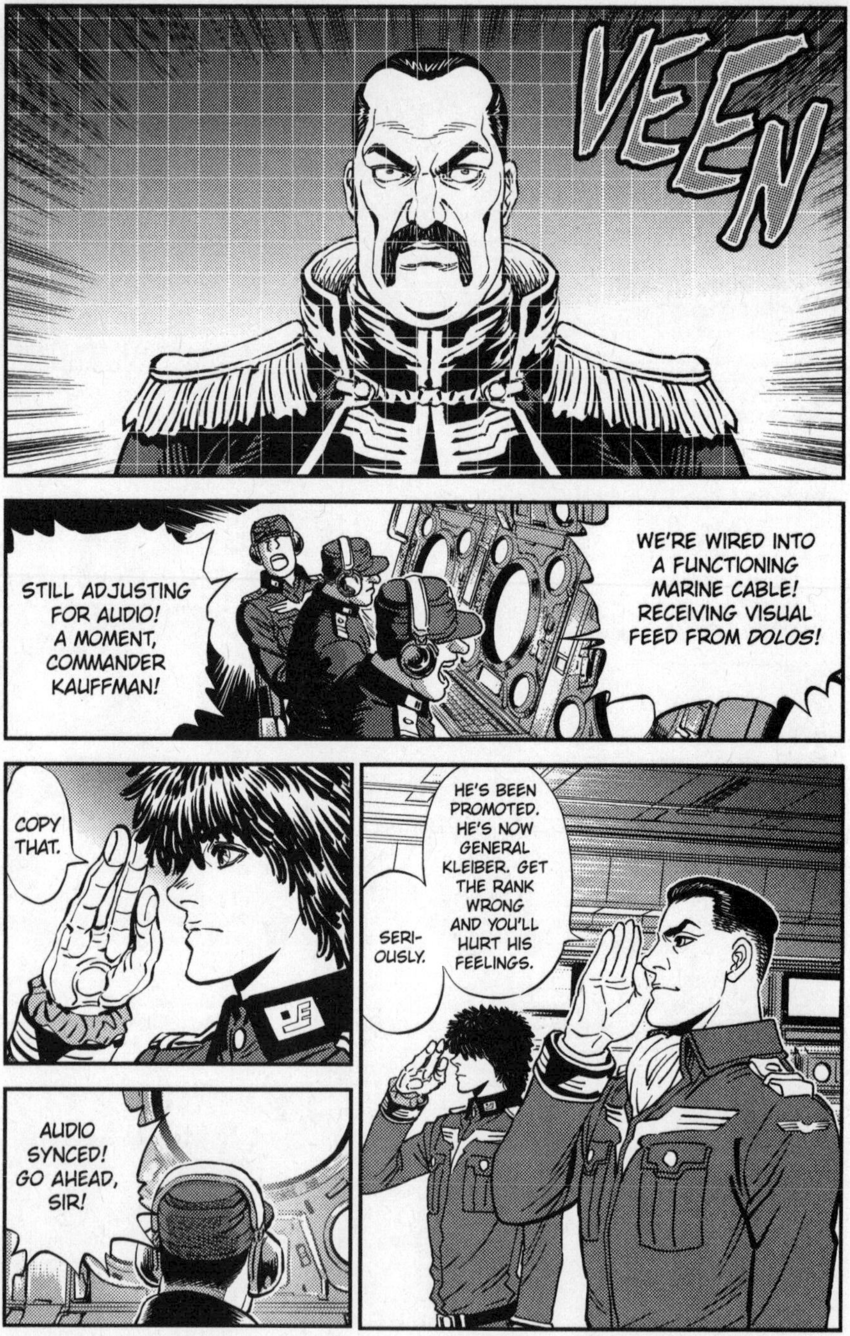
VEEN
WE'RE WIRED INTO A FUNCTIONING MARINE CABLE! RECEIVING VISUAL FEED FROM *DOLOS*!
STILL ADJUSTING FOR AUDIO! A MOMENT, COMMANDER KAUFFMAN!
COPY THAT.
HE'S BEEN PROMOTED. HE'S NOW GENERAL KLEIBER. GET THE RANK WRONG AND YOU'LL HURT HIS FEELINGS.
SERI-OUSLY.
AUDIO SYNCED! GO AHEAD, SIR!

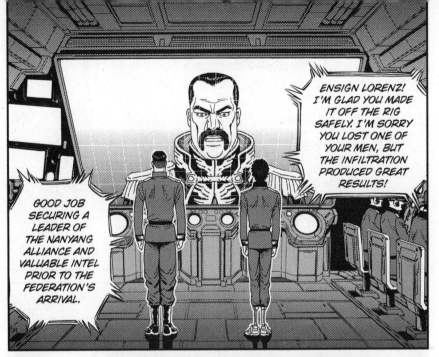

ENSIGN LORENZ! I'M GLAD YOU MADE IT OFF THE RIG SAFELY. I'M SORRY YOU LOST ONE OF YOUR MEN, BUT THE INFILTRATION PRODUCED GREAT RESULTS!

GOOD JOB SECURING A LEADER OF THE NANYANG ALLIANCE AND VALUABLE INTEL PRIOR TO THE FEDERATION'S ARRIVAL.

THANK YOU, GENERAL KLEIBER.

HOW FAR IS THE NANYANG ALLIANCE FROM RESTORING THE PSYCHO ZAKU? WHERE IS THEIR SECRET FACILITY LOCATED? I HAVE A HUNDRED QUESTIONS!

TRANSPORT THIS CLAUDIA PEER TO THE DOLOS! WE'LL INTERROGATE HER THOROUGHLY!

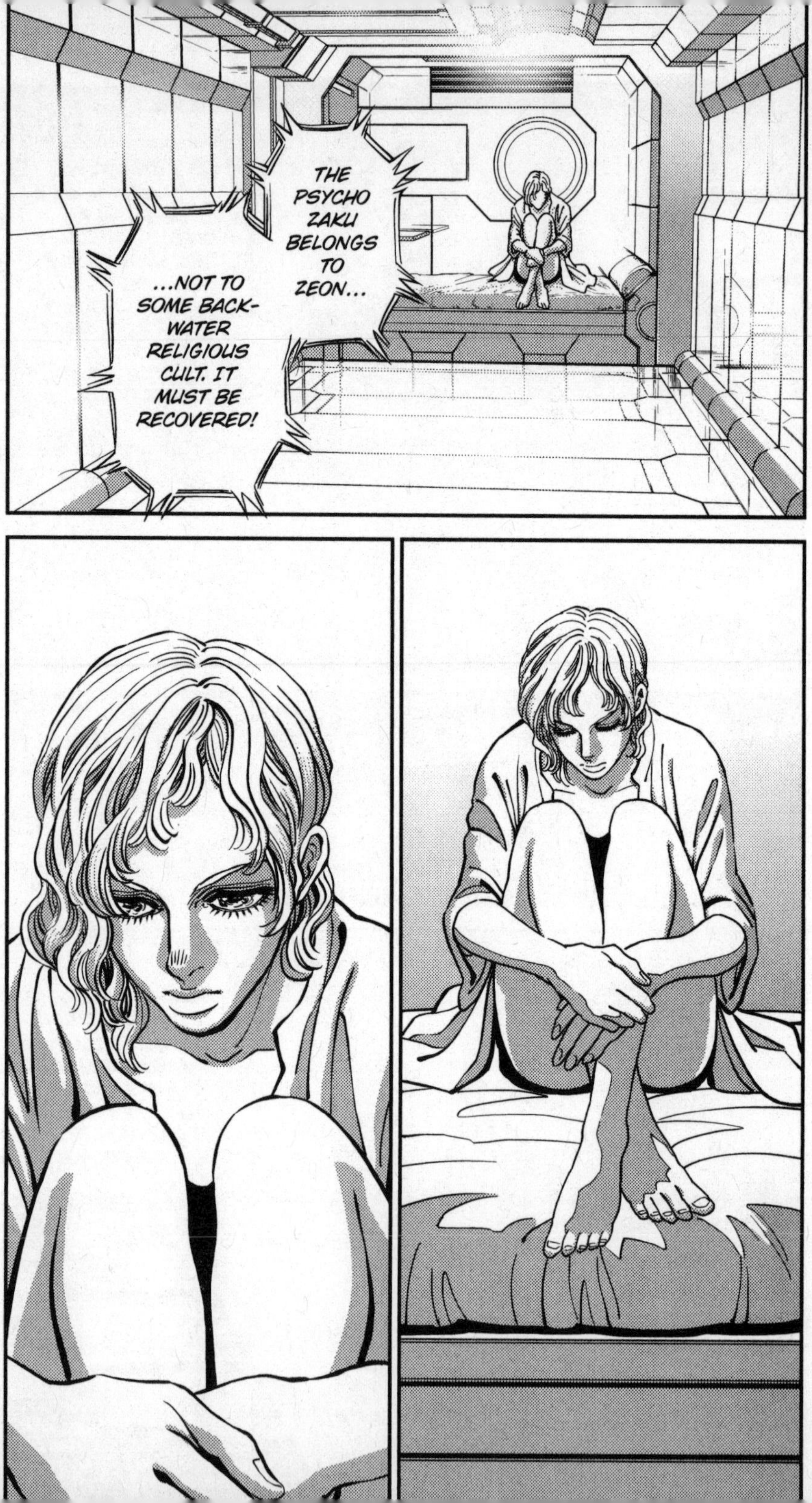
THE PSYCHO ZAKU BELONGS TO ZEON...
...NOT TO SOME BACK-WATER RELIGIOUS CULT. IT MUST BE RECOVERED!

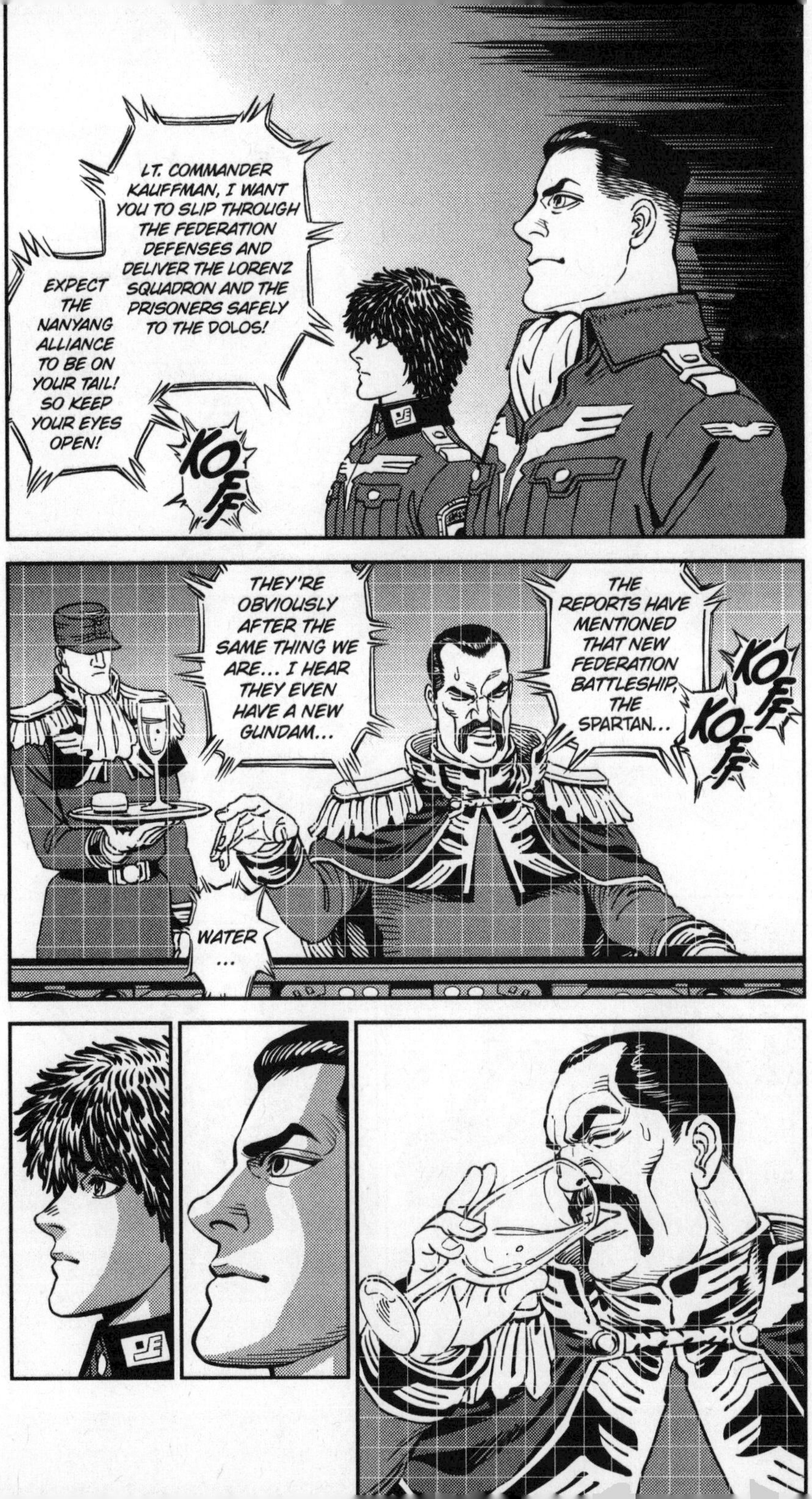
LT. COMMANDER KAUFFMAN, I WANT YOU TO SLIP THROUGH THE FEDERATION DEFENSES AND DELIVER THE LORENZ SQUADRON AND THE PRISONERS SAFELY TO THE DOLOS!
EXPECT THE NANYANG ALLIANCE TO BE ON YOUR TAIL! SO KEEP YOUR EYES OPEN!
KOFF
KOFF KOFF
THE REPORTS HAVE MENTIONED THAT NEW FEDERATION BATTLESHIP, THE SPARTAN...
THEY'RE OBVIOUSLY AFTER THE SAME THING WE ARE... I HEAR THEY EVEN HAVE A NEW GUNDAM...
WATER ...

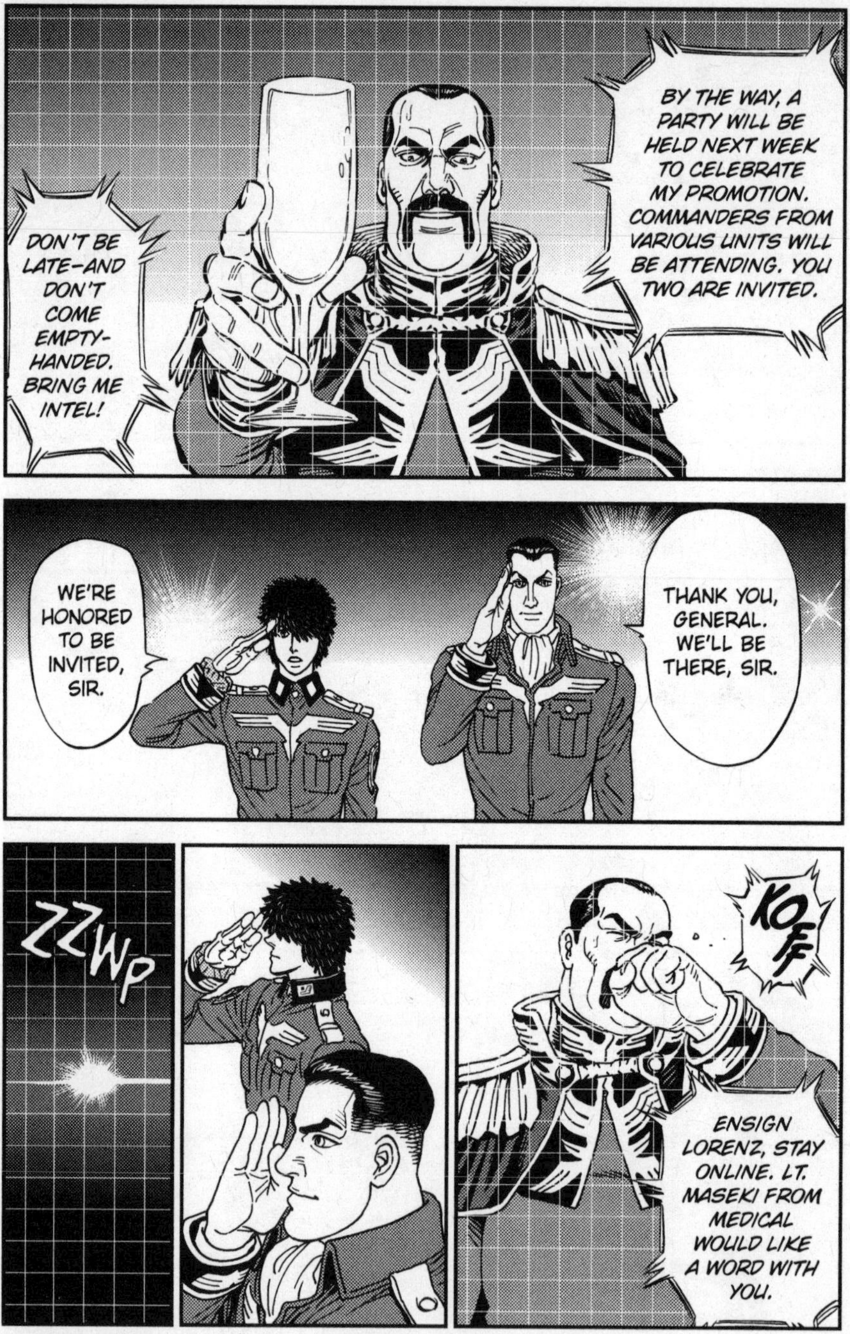
BY THE WAY, A PARTY WILL BE HELD NEXT WEEK TO CELEBRATE MY PROMOTION. COMMANDERS FROM VARIOUS UNITS WILL BE ATTENDING. YOU TWO ARE INVITED.
DON'T BE LATE–AND DON'T COME EMPTY-HANDED. BRING ME INTEL!
THANK YOU, GENERAL. WE'LL BE THERE, SIR.
WE'RE HONORED TO BE INVITED, SIR.
KOFF
ENSIGN LORENZ, STAY ONLINE. LT. MASEKI FROM MEDICAL WOULD LIKE A WORD WITH YOU.
ZZWP

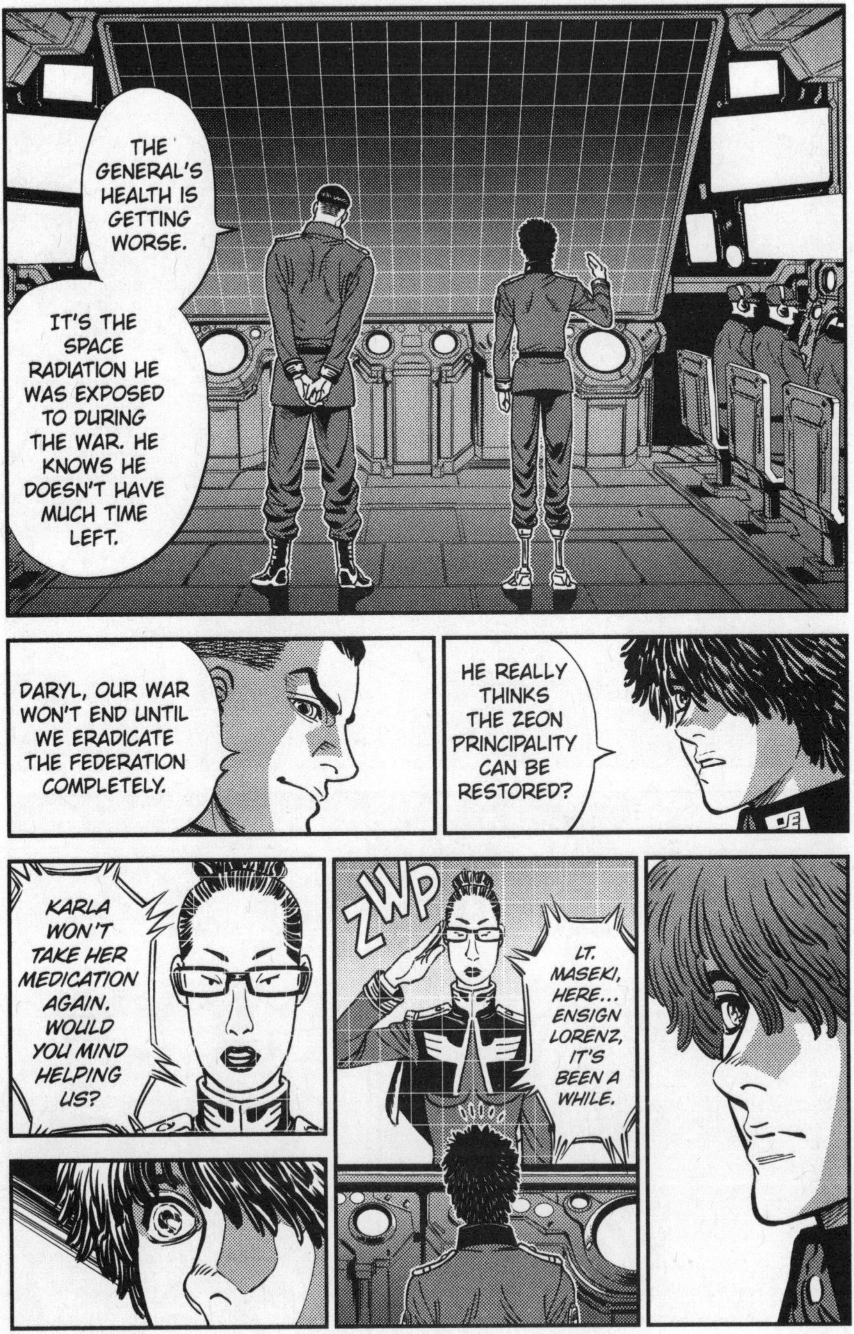
THE GENERAL'S HEALTH IS GETTING WORSE.
IT'S THE SPACE RADIATION HE WAS EXPOSED TO DURING THE WAR. HE KNOWS HE DOESN'T HAVE MUCH TIME LEFT.
HE REALLY THINKS THE ZEON PRINCIPALITY CAN BE RESTORED?
DARYL, OUR WAR WON'T END UNTIL WE ERADICATE THE FEDERATION COMPLETELY.
LT. MASEKI, HERE... ENSIGN LORENZ, IT'S BEEN A WHILE.
ZWP
KARLA WON'T TAKE HER MEDICATION AGAIN. WOULD YOU MIND HELPING US?

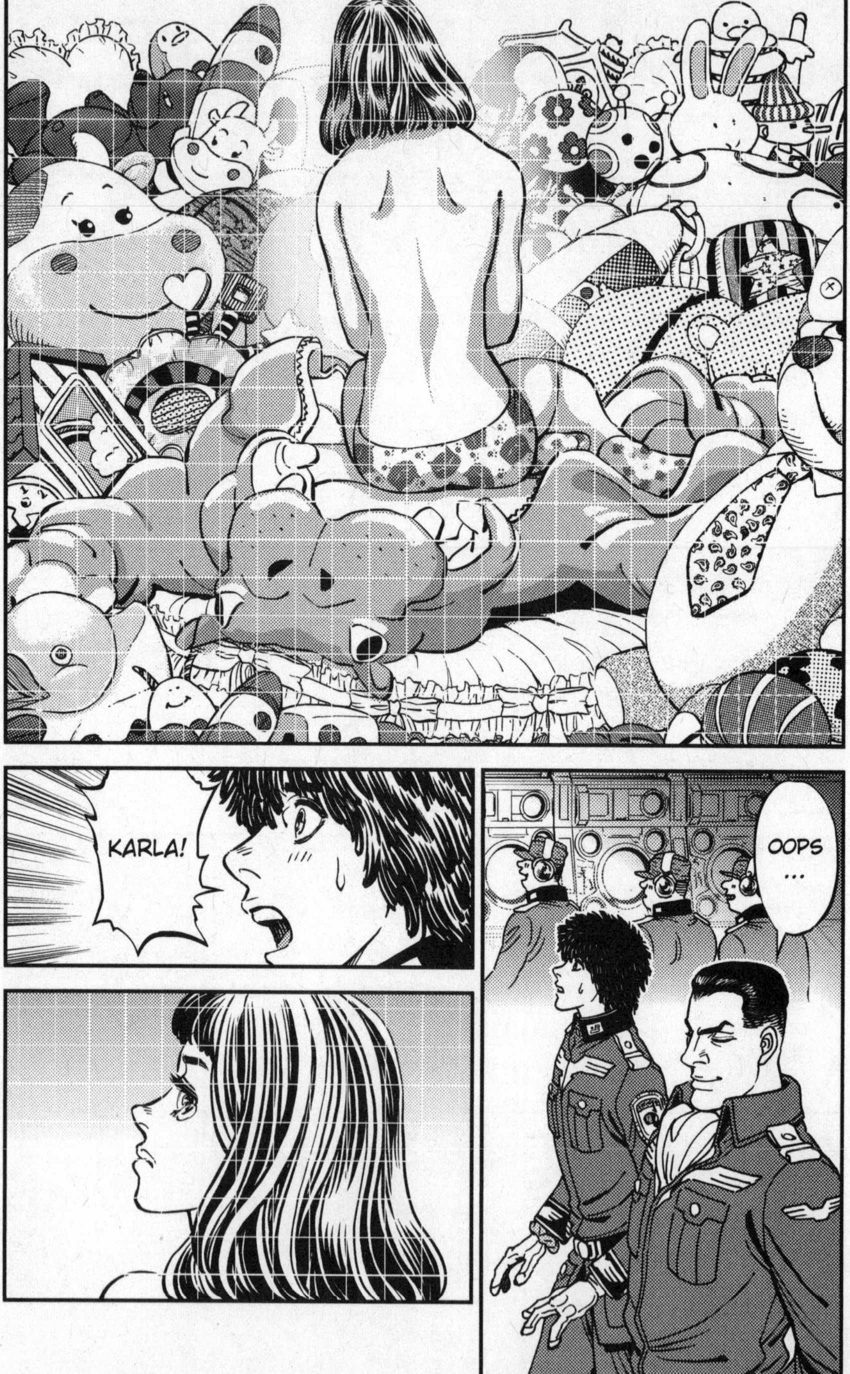
OOPS ...
KARLA!

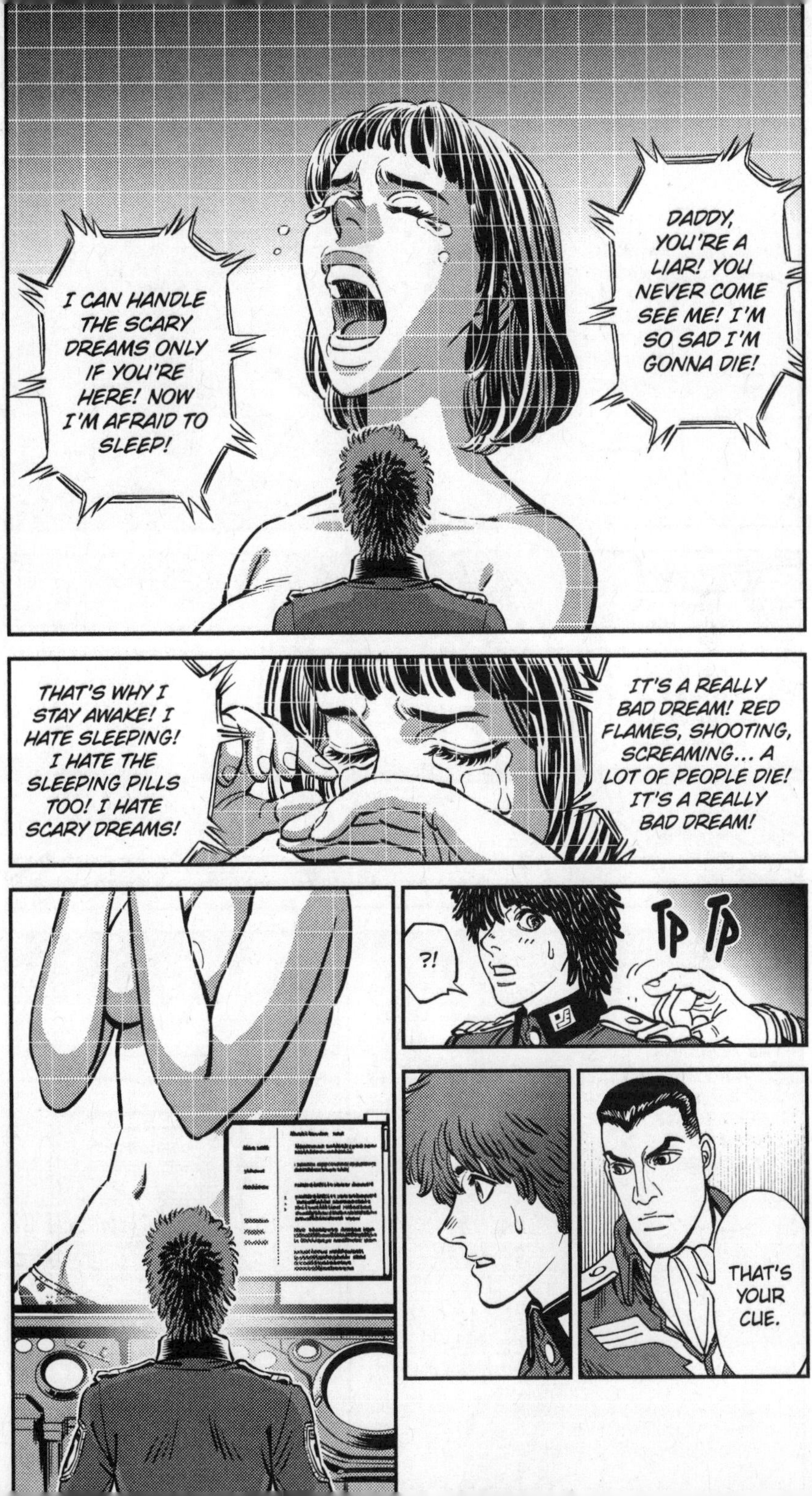

DADDY, YOU'RE A LIAR! YOU NEVER COME SEE ME! I'M SO SAD I'M GONNA DIE!
I CAN HANDLE THE SCARY DREAMS ONLY IF YOU'RE HERE! NOW I'M AFRAID TO SLEEP!
IT'S A REALLY BAD DREAM! RED FLAMES, SHOOTING, SCREAMING... A LOT OF PEOPLE DIE! IT'S A REALLY BAD DREAM!
THAT'S WHY I STAY AWAKE! I HATE SLEEPING! I HATE THE SLEEPING PILLS TOO! I HATE SCARY DREAMS!
TP TP
?!
THAT'S YOUR CUE.

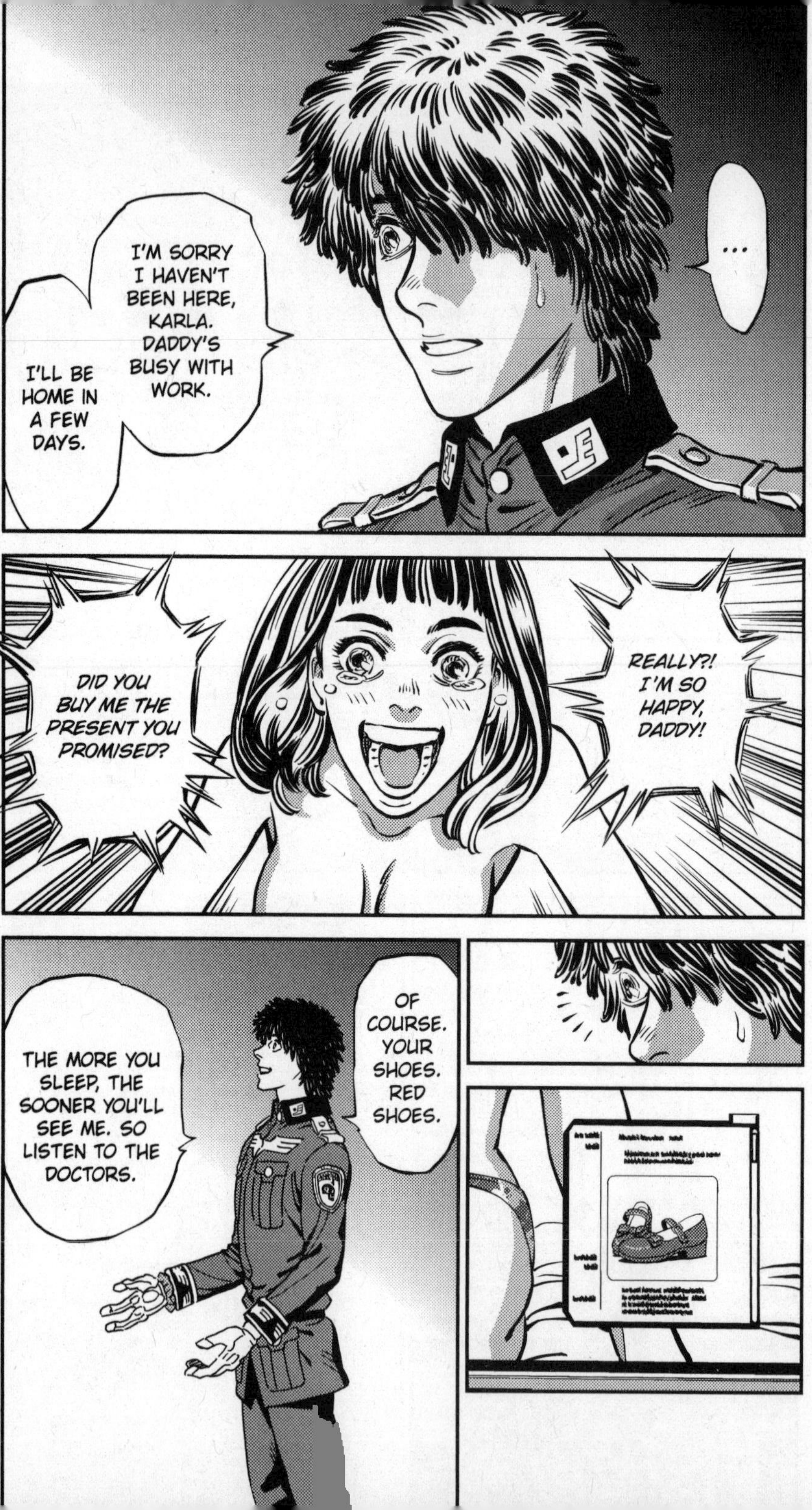
...
I'M SORRY I HAVEN'T BEEN HERE, KARLA. DADDY'S BUSY WITH WORK.
I'LL BE HOME IN A FEW DAYS.
REALLY?! I'M SO HAPPY, DADDY!
DID YOU BUY ME THE PRESENT YOU PROMISED?
OF COURSE. YOUR SHOES. RED SHOES.
THE MORE YOU SLEEP, THE SOONER YOU'LL SEE ME. SO LISTEN TO THE DOCTORS.

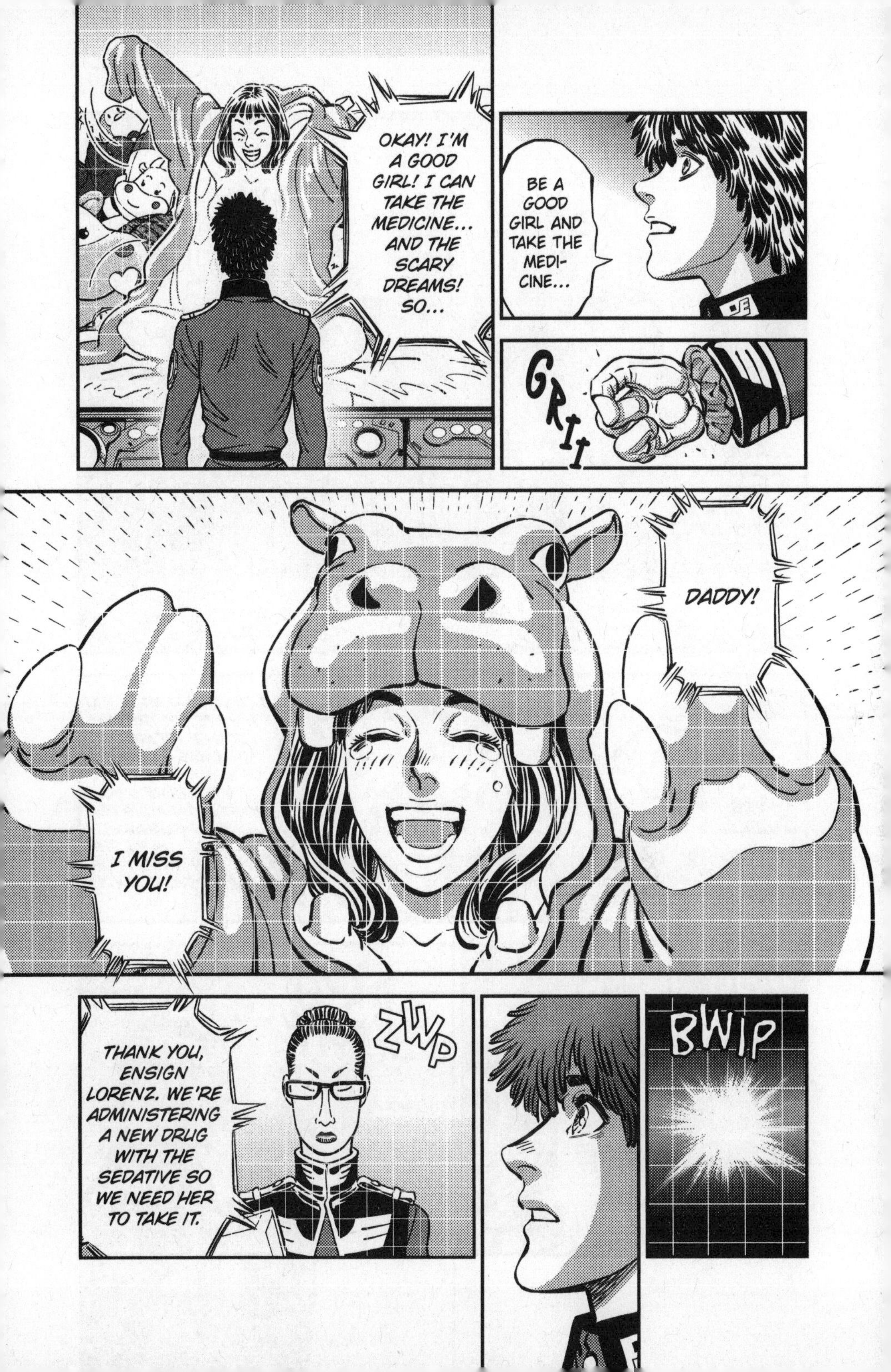
BE A GOOD GIRL AND TAKE THE MEDI-CINE...
GRIII
OKAY! I'M A GOOD GIRL! I CAN TAKE THE MEDICINE... AND THE SCARY DREAMS! SO...
DADDY!
I MISS YOU!
BWIP
ZWP
THANK YOU, ENSIGN LORENZ. WE'RE ADMINISTERING A NEW DRUG WITH THE SEDATIVE SO WE NEED HER TO TAKE IT.

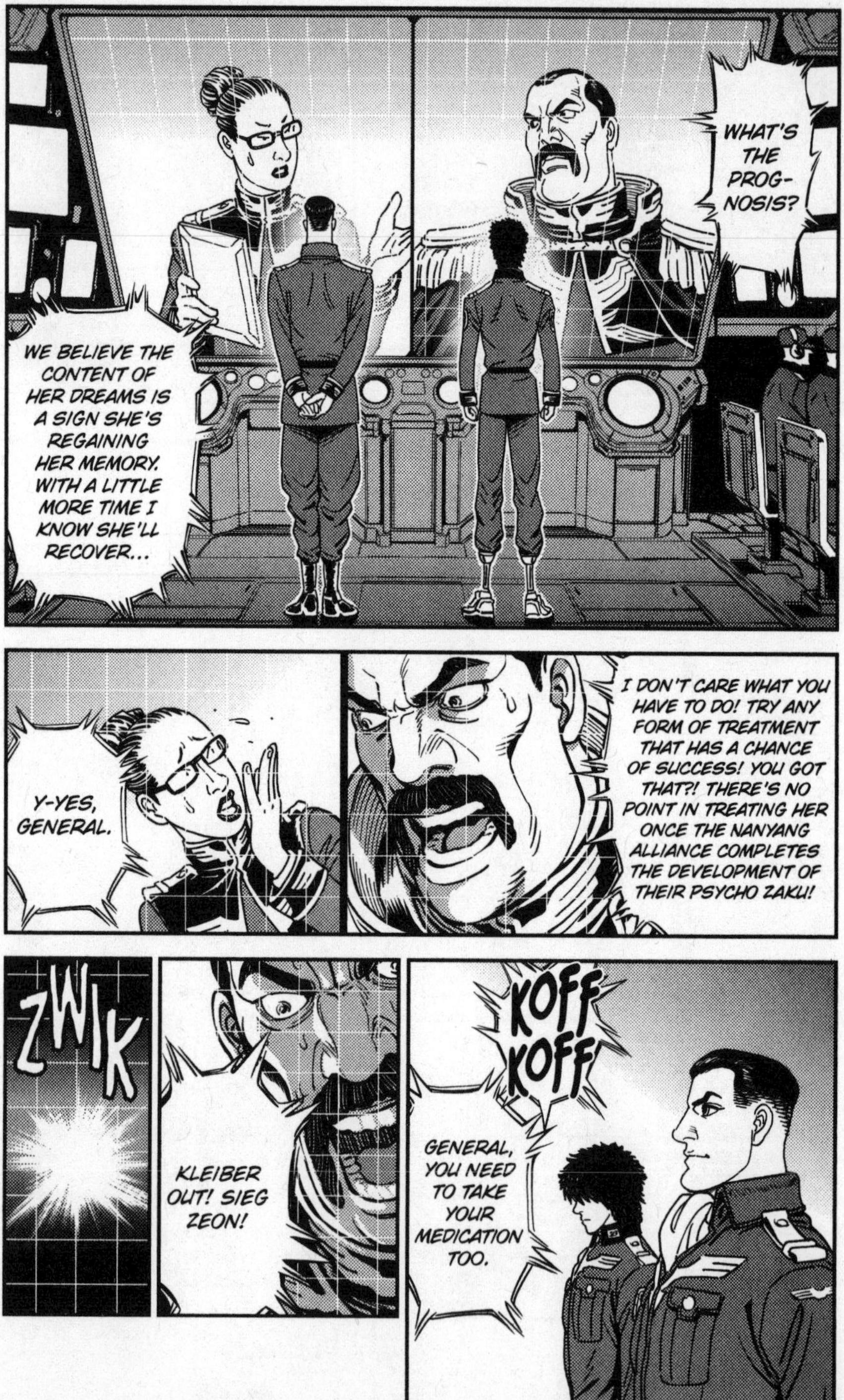
WHAT'S THE PROG-NOSIS?
WE BELIEVE THE CONTENT OF HER DREAMS IS A SIGN SHE'S REGAINING HER MEMORY. WITH A LITTLE MORE TIME I KNOW SHE'LL RECOVER...
I DON'T CARE WHAT YOU HAVE TO DO! TRY ANY FORM OF TREATMENT THAT HAS A CHANCE OF SUCCESS! YOU GOT THAT?! THERE'S NO POINT IN TREATING HER ONCE THE NANYANG ALLIANCE COMPLETES THE DEVELOPMENT OF THEIR PSYCHO ZAKU!
Y-YES, GENERAL.
KOFF KOFF
GENERAL, YOU NEED TO TAKE YOUR MEDICATION TOO.
KLEIBER OUT! SIEG ZEON!
ZWIK

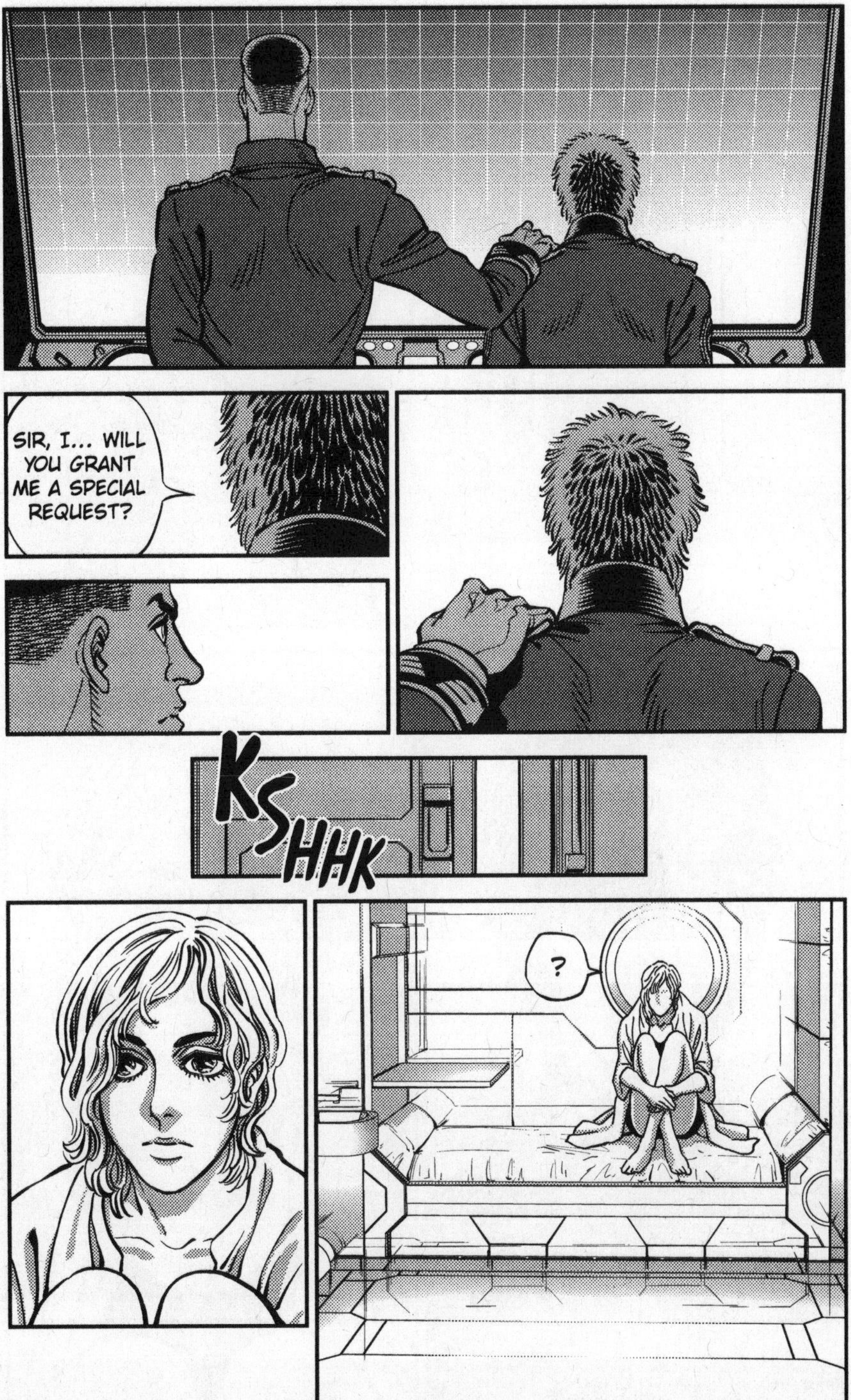
SIR, I... WILL YOU GRANT ME A SPECIAL REQUEST?
KSHHK
?

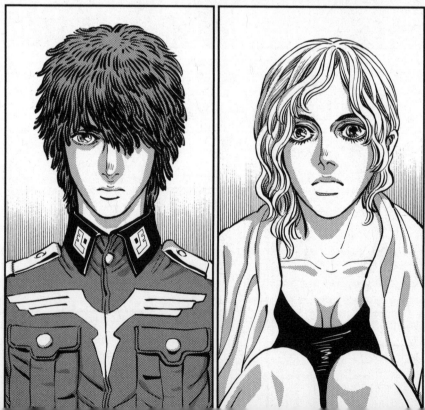

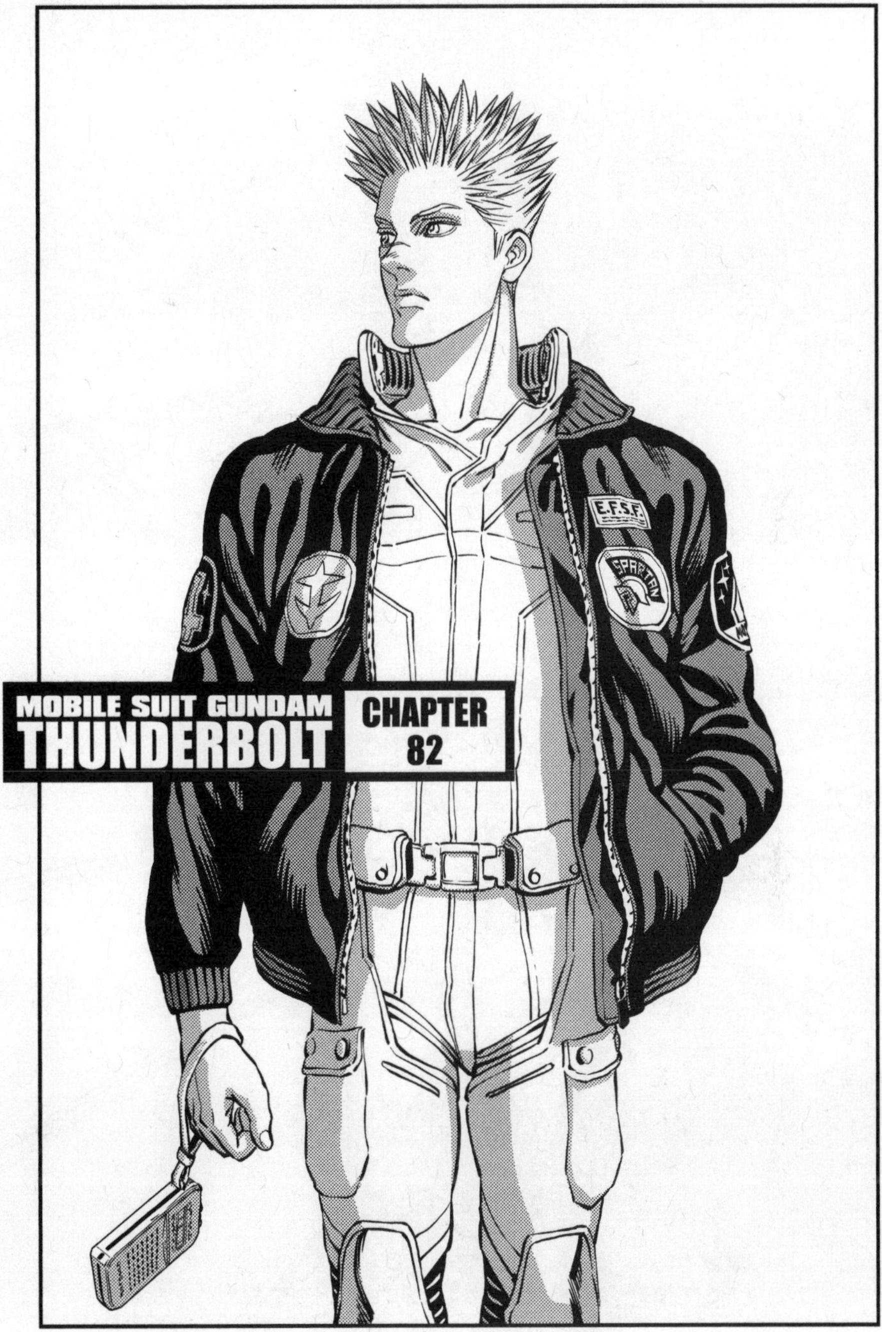
MOBILE SUIT GUNDAM
THUNDERBOLT
CHAPTER
82
E.F.S.F.
SPARTAN

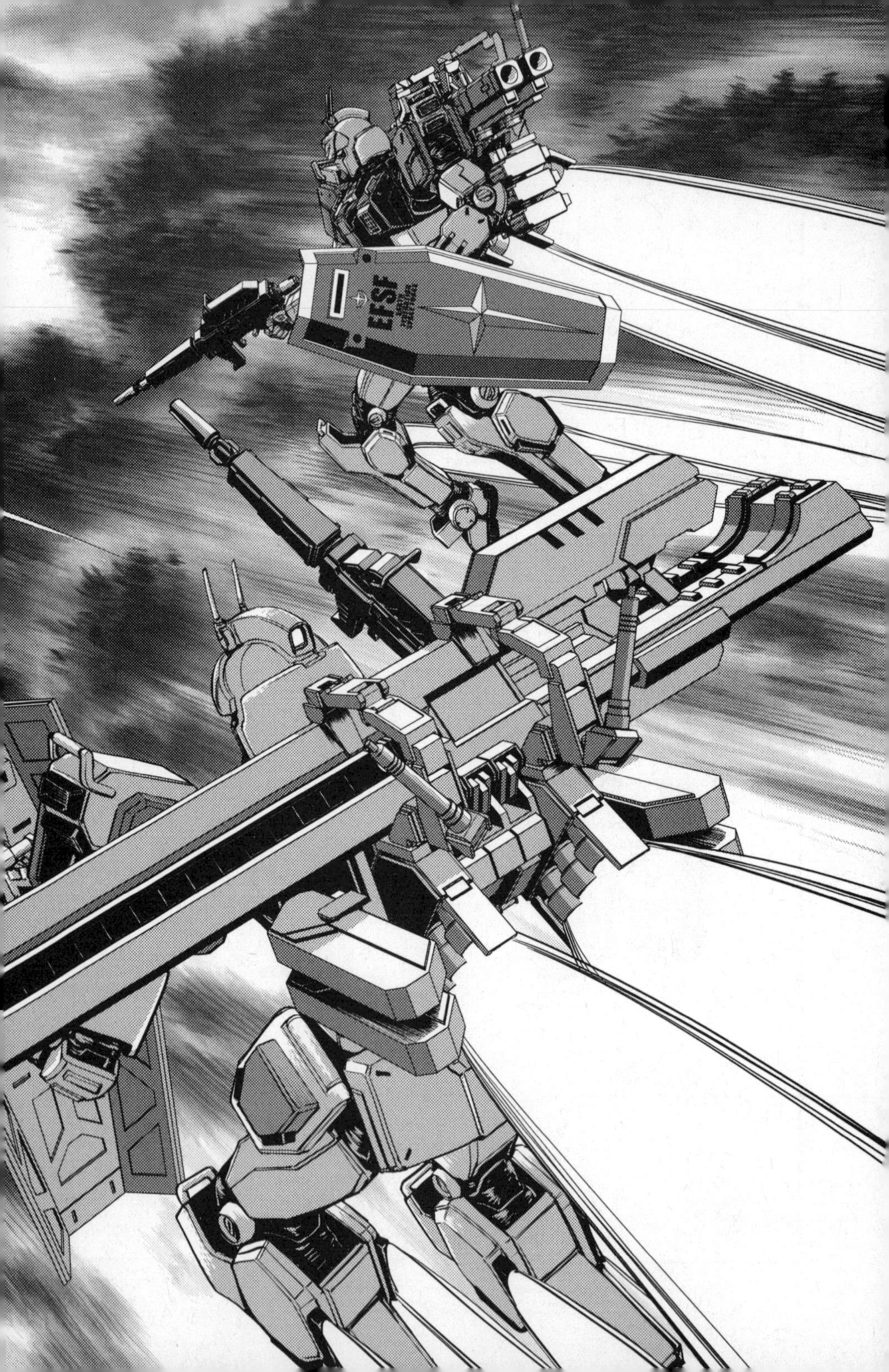
EFSF

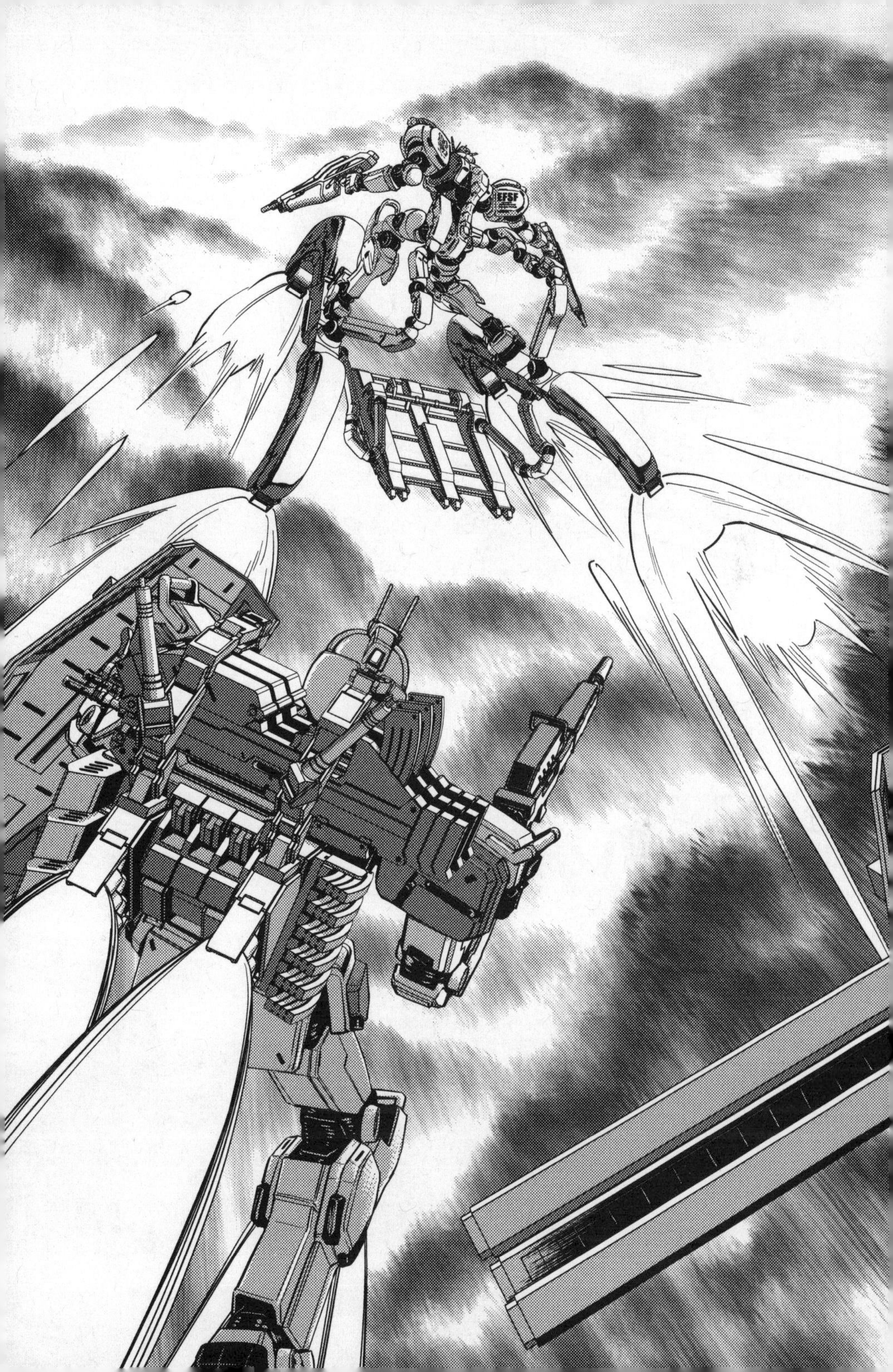
EFSF

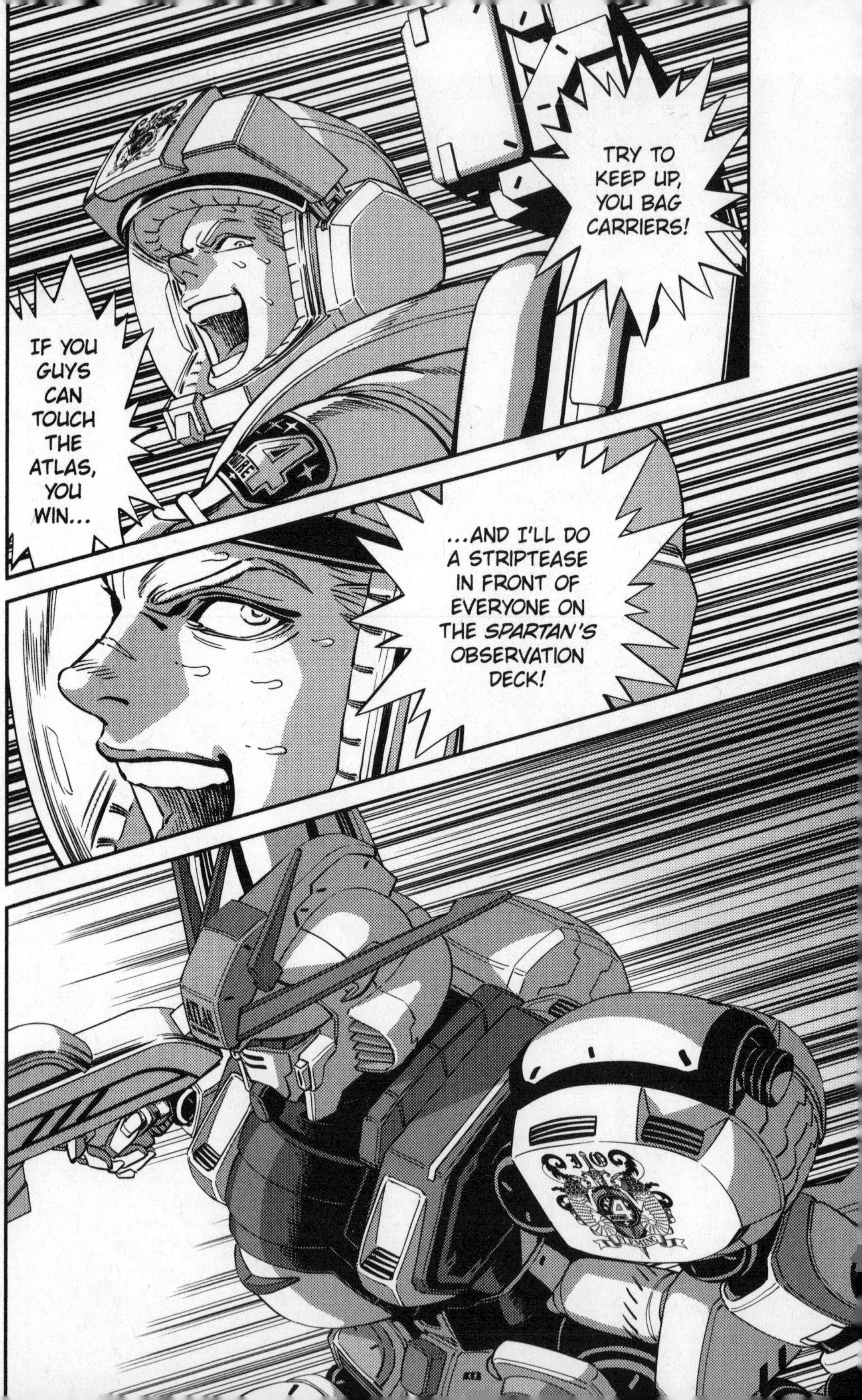
TRY TO KEEP UP, YOU BAG CARRIERS!
IF YOU GUYS CAN TOUCH THE ATLAS, YOU WIN...
...AND I'LL DO A STRIPTEASE IN FRONT OF EVERYONE ON THE *SPARTAN'S* OBSERVATION DECK!

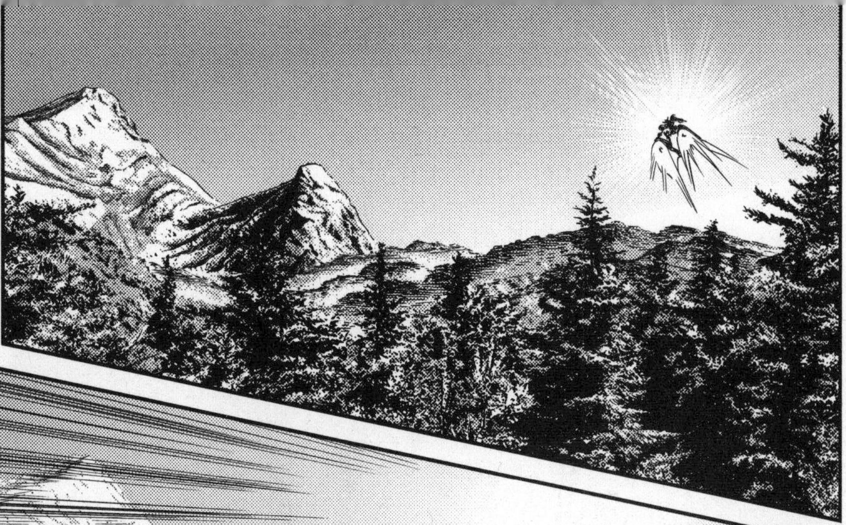
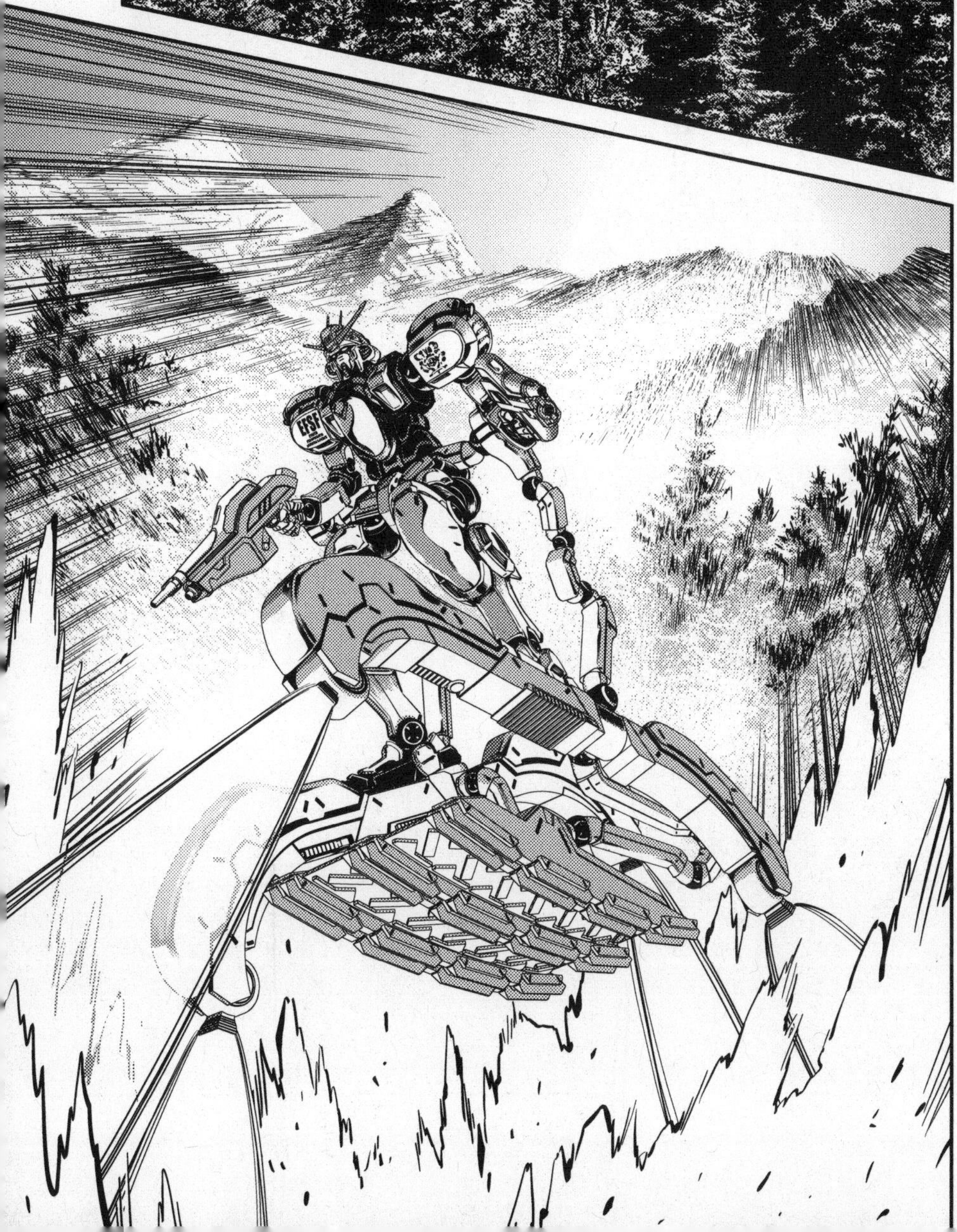
EFSF

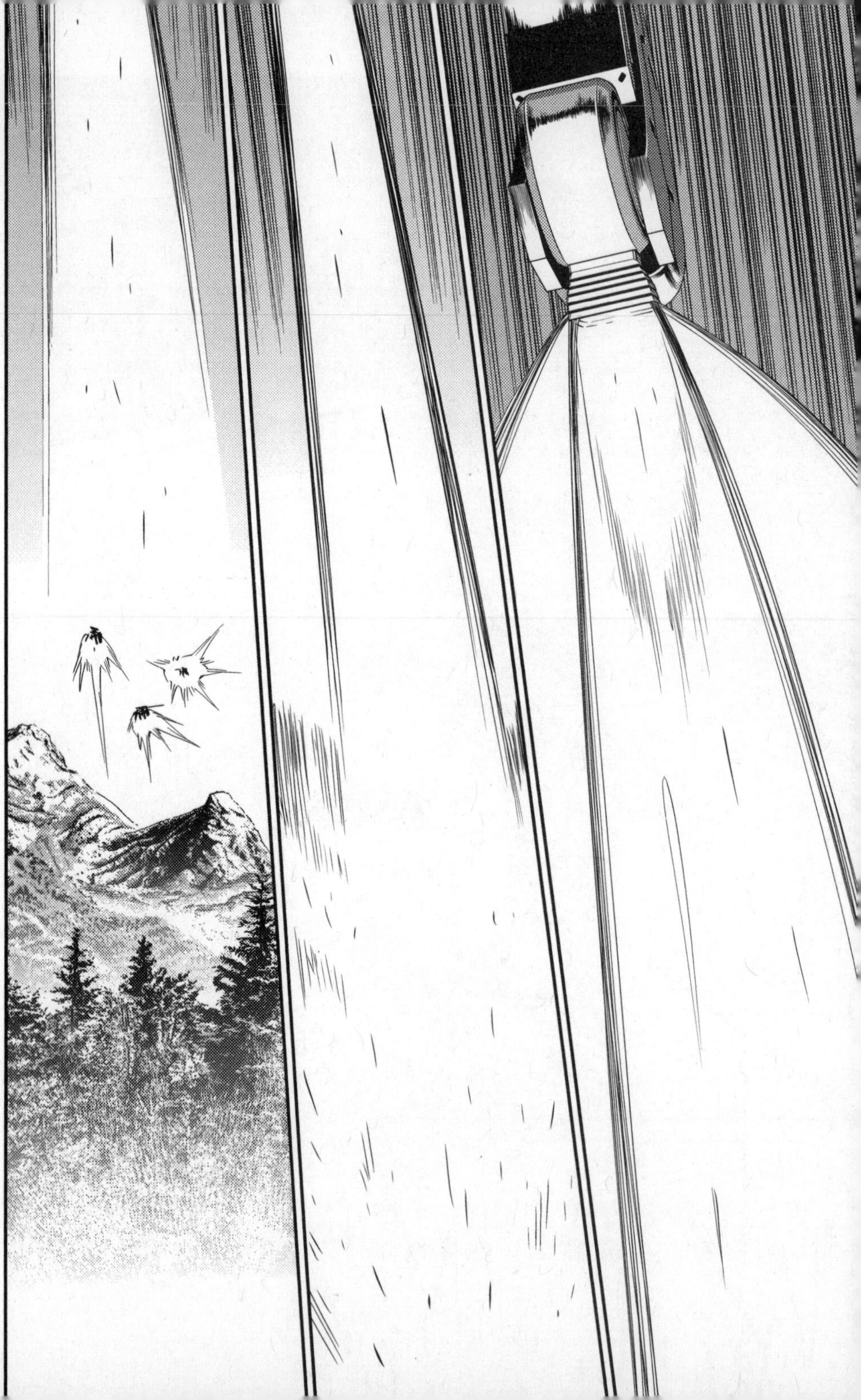

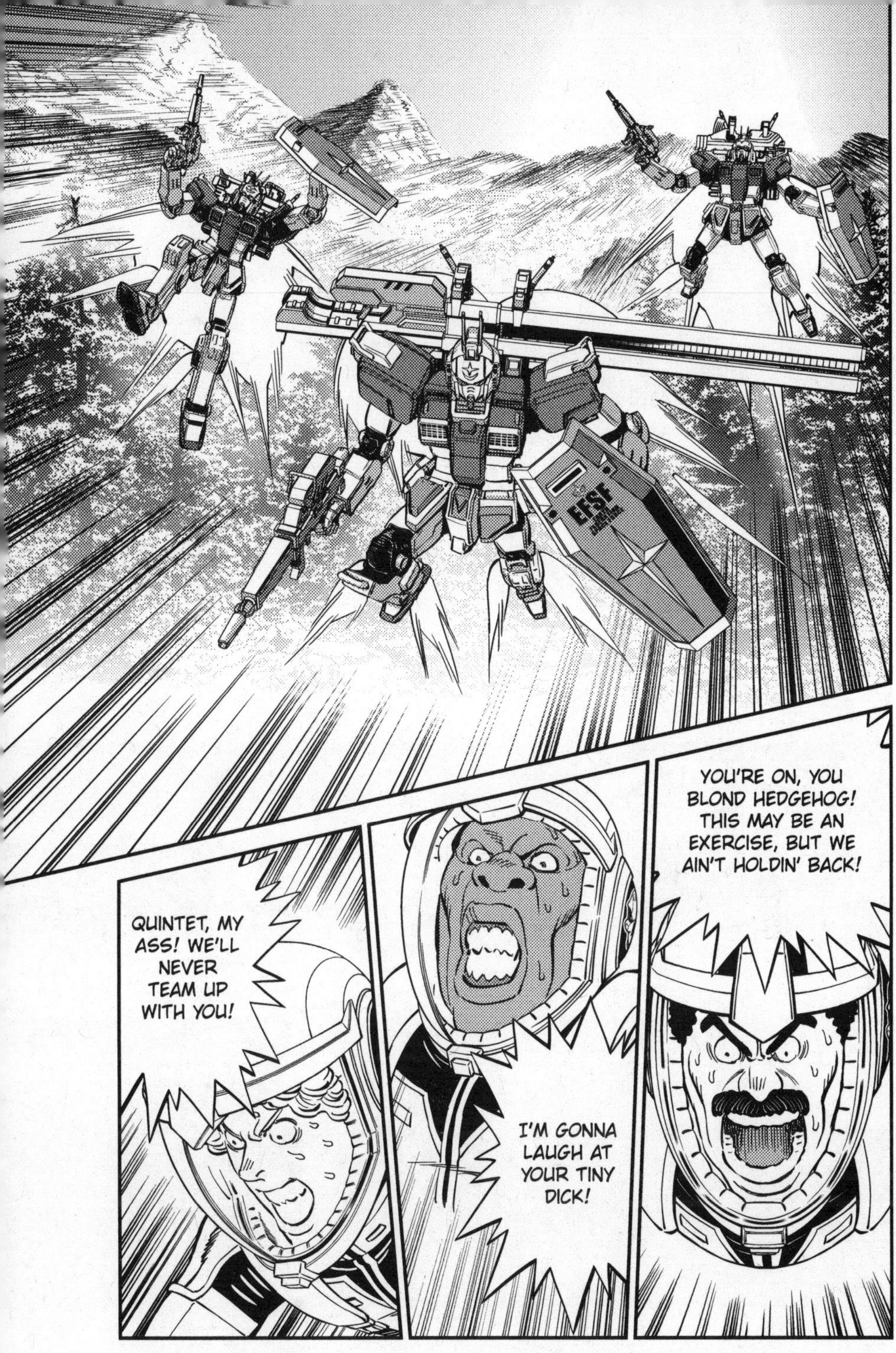
EFSF
YOU'RE ON, YOU BLOND HEDGEHOG! THIS MAY BE AN EXERCISE, BUT WE AIN'T HOLDIN' BACK!
I'M GONNA LAUGH AT YOUR TINY DICK!
QUINTET, MY ASS! WE'LL NEVER TEAM UP WITH YOU!

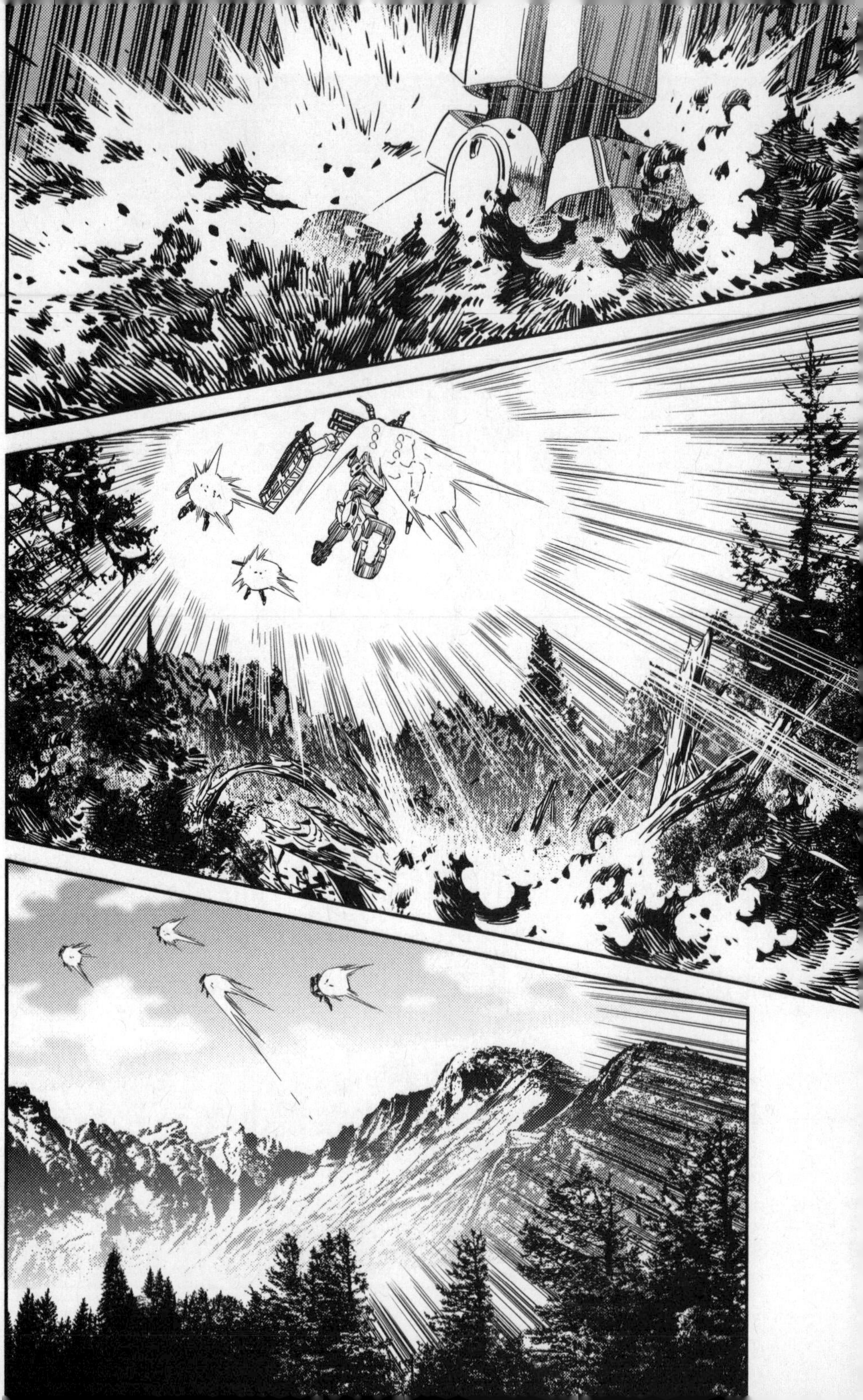

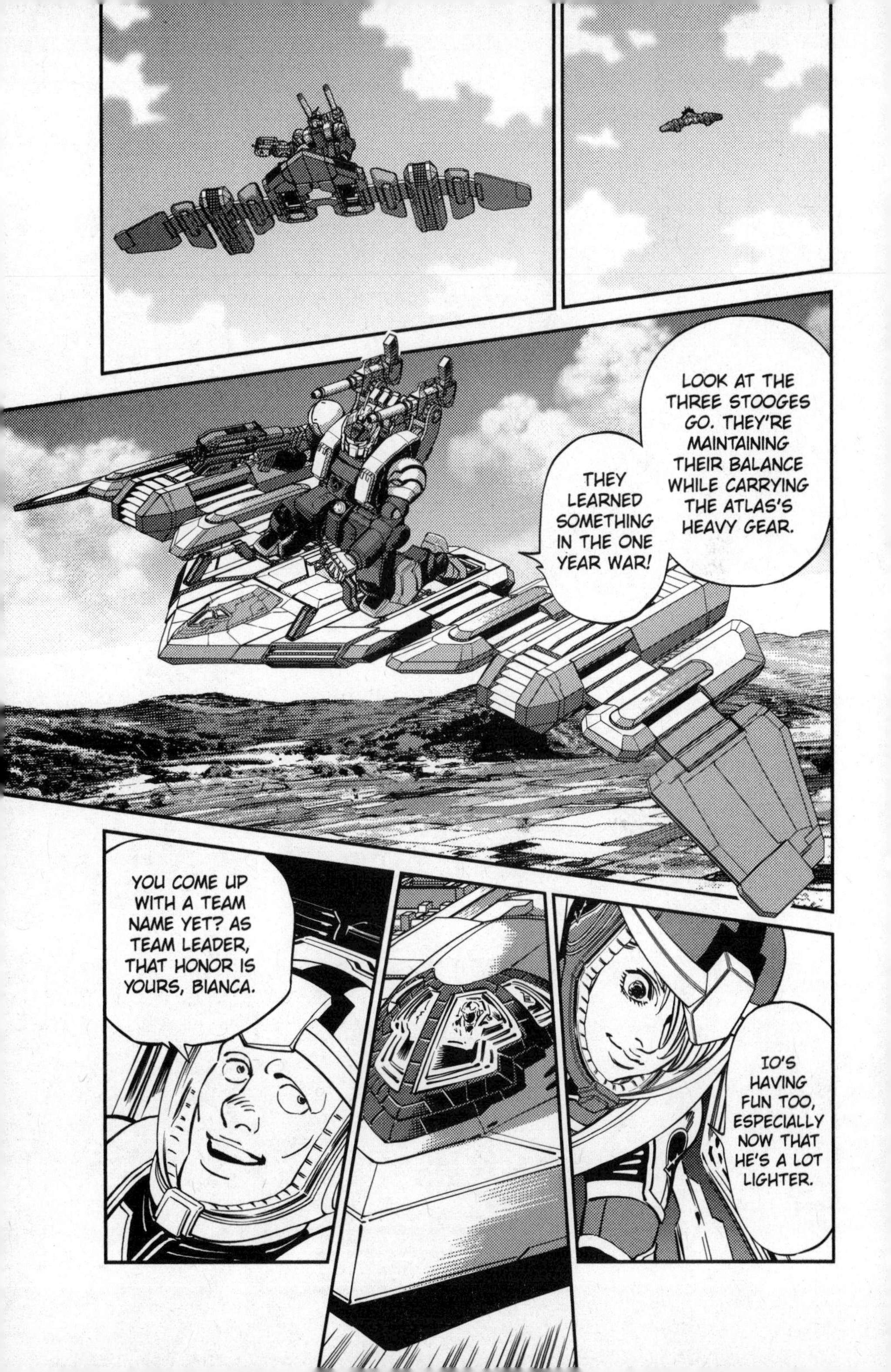
LOOK AT THE THREE STOOGES GO. THEY'RE MAINTAINING THEIR BALANCE WHILE CARRYING THE ATLAS'S HEAVY GEAR.
THEY LEARNED SOMETHING IN THE ONE YEAR WAR!
IO'S HAVING FUN TOO, ESPECIALLY NOW THAT HE'S A LOT LIGHTER.
YOU COME UP WITH A TEAM NAME YET? AS TEAM LEADER, THAT HONOR IS YOURS, BIANCA.

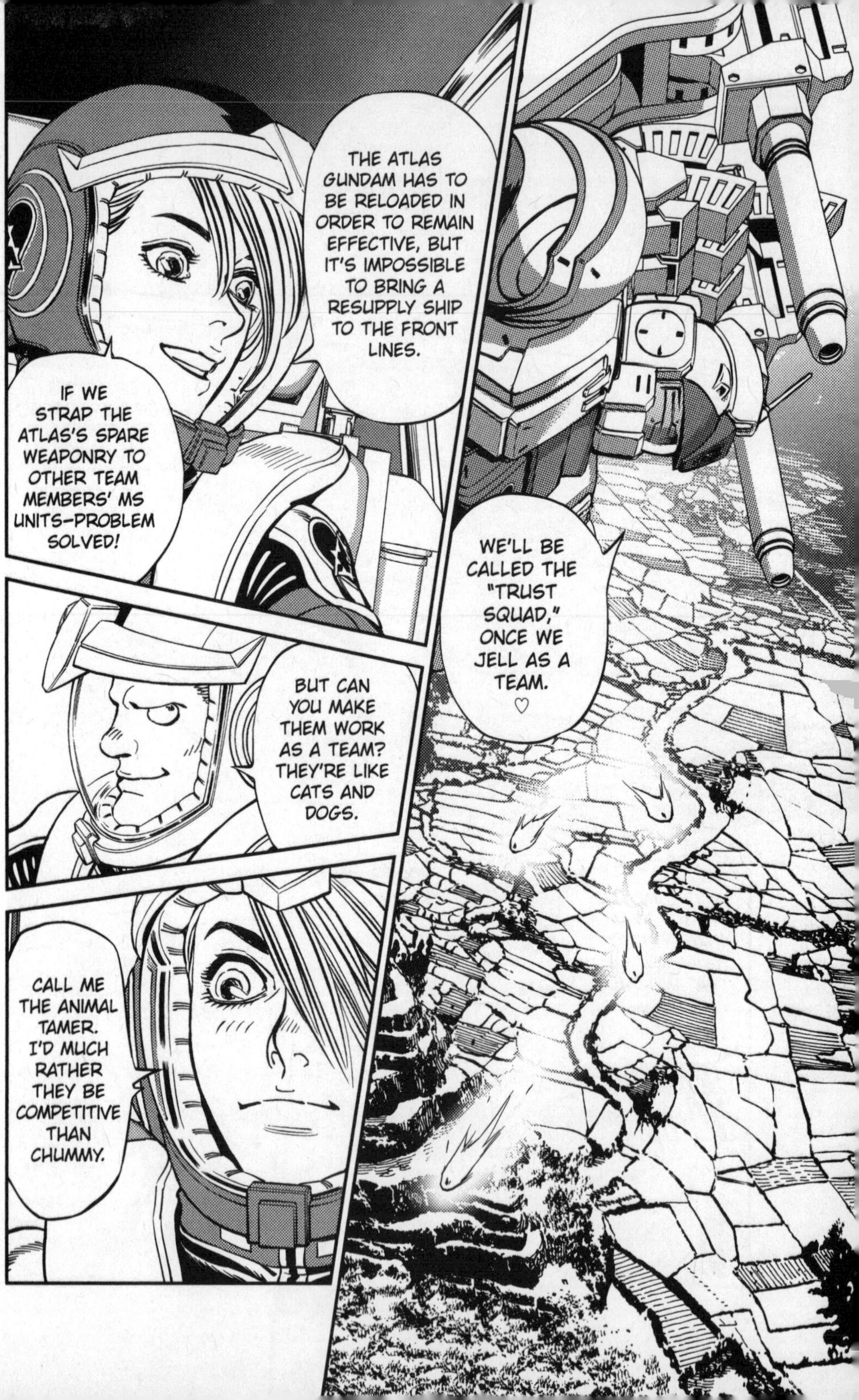
THE ATLAS GUNDAM HAS TO BE RELOADED IN ORDER TO REMAIN EFFECTIVE, BUT IT'S IMPOSSIBLE TO BRING A RESUPPLY SHIP TO THE FRONT LINES.
IF WE STRAP THE ATLAS'S SPARE WEAPONRY TO OTHER TEAM MEMBERS' MS UNITS–PROBLEM SOLVED!
BUT CAN YOU MAKE THEM WORK AS A TEAM? THEY'RE LIKE CATS AND DOGS.
WE'LL BE CALLED THE "TRUST SQUAD," ONCE WE JELL AS A TEAM. ♡
CALL ME THE ANIMAL TAMER. I'D MUCH RATHER THEY BE COMPETITIVE THAN CHUMMY.

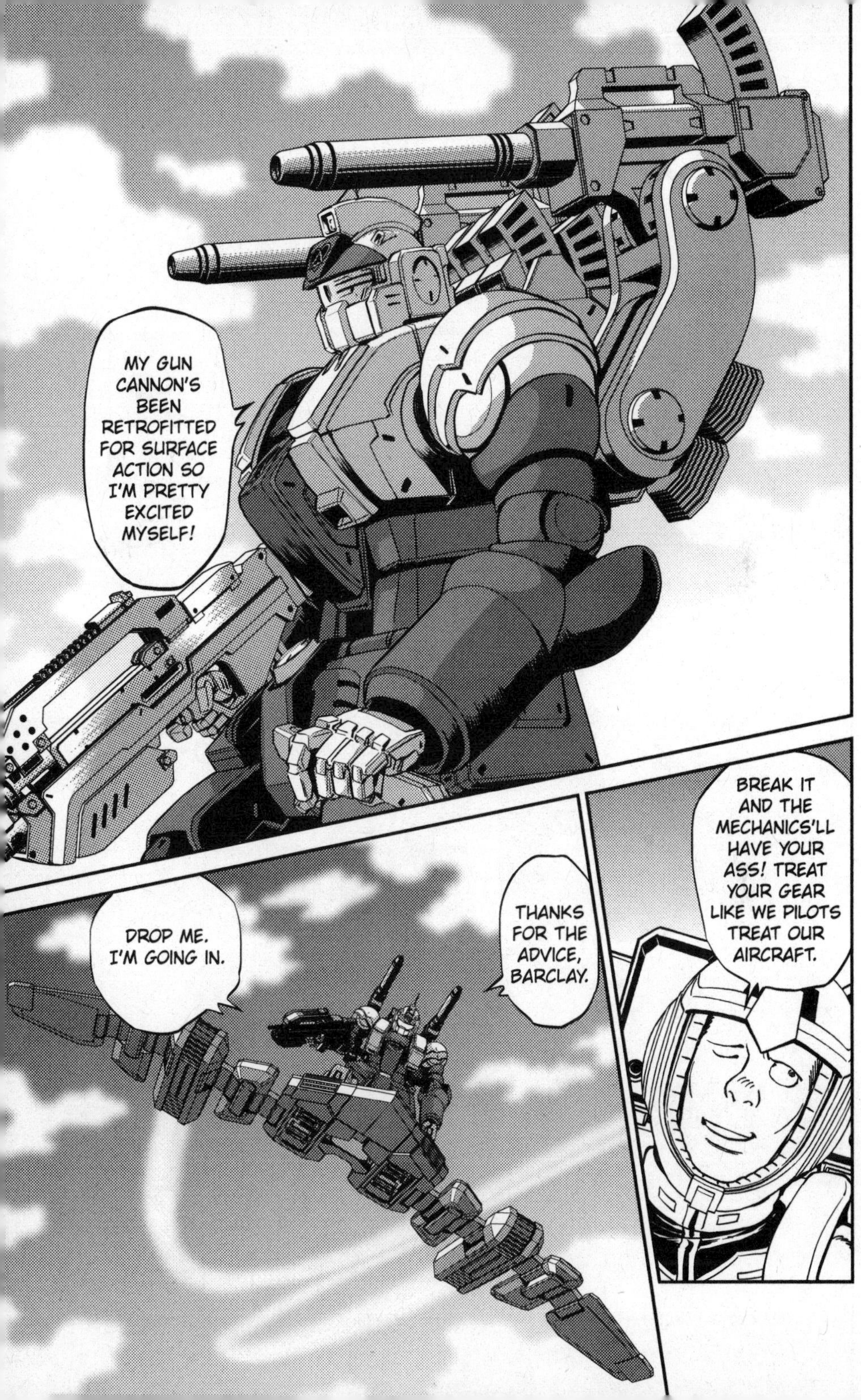
MY GUN CANNON'S BEEN RETROFITTED FOR SURFACE ACTION SO I'M PRETTY EXCITED MYSELF!
BREAK IT AND THE MECHANICS'LL HAVE YOUR ASS! TREAT YOUR GEAR LIKE WE PILOTS TREAT OUR AIRCRAFT.
THANKS FOR THE ADVICE, BARCLAY.
DROP ME. I'M GOING IN.

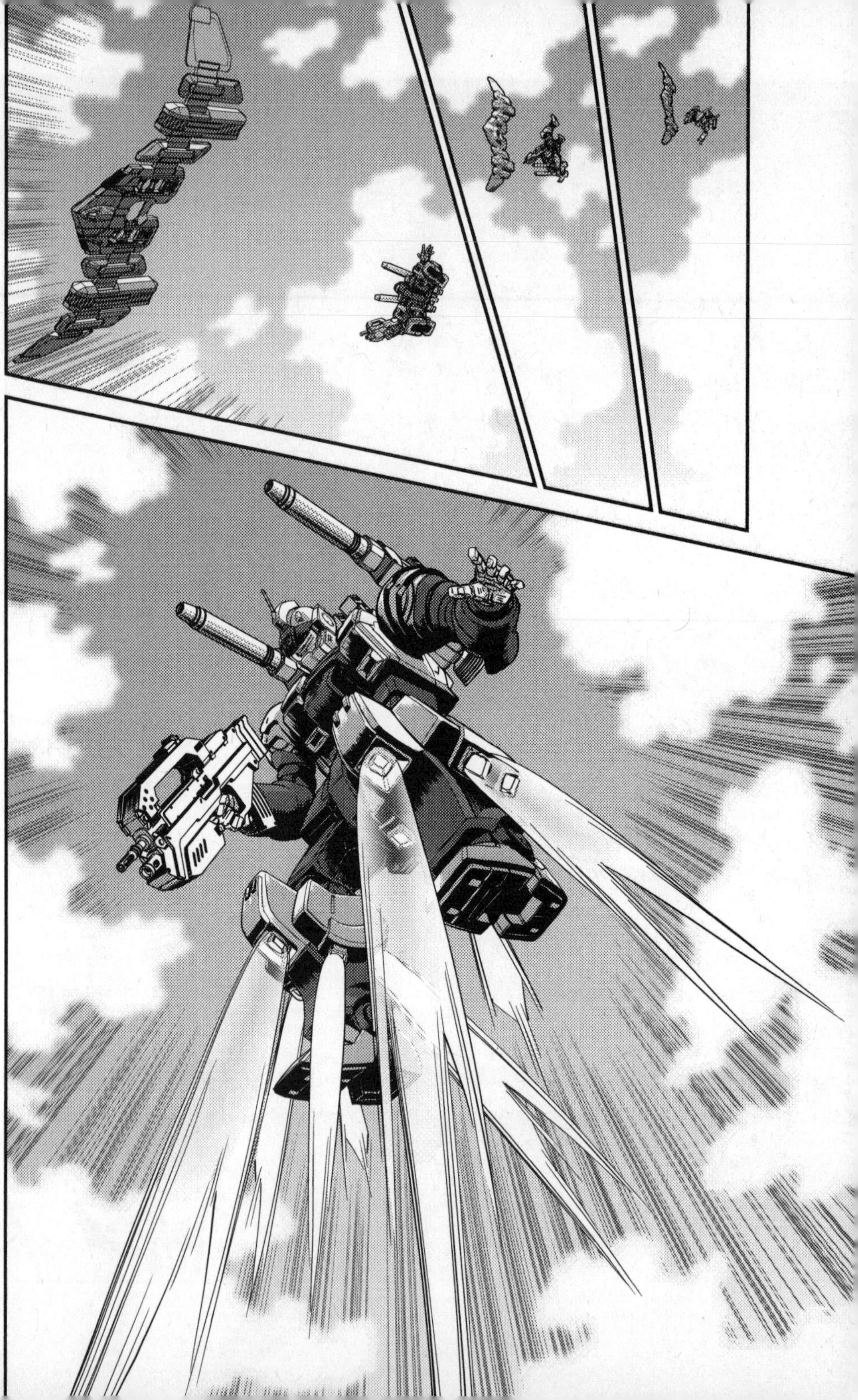

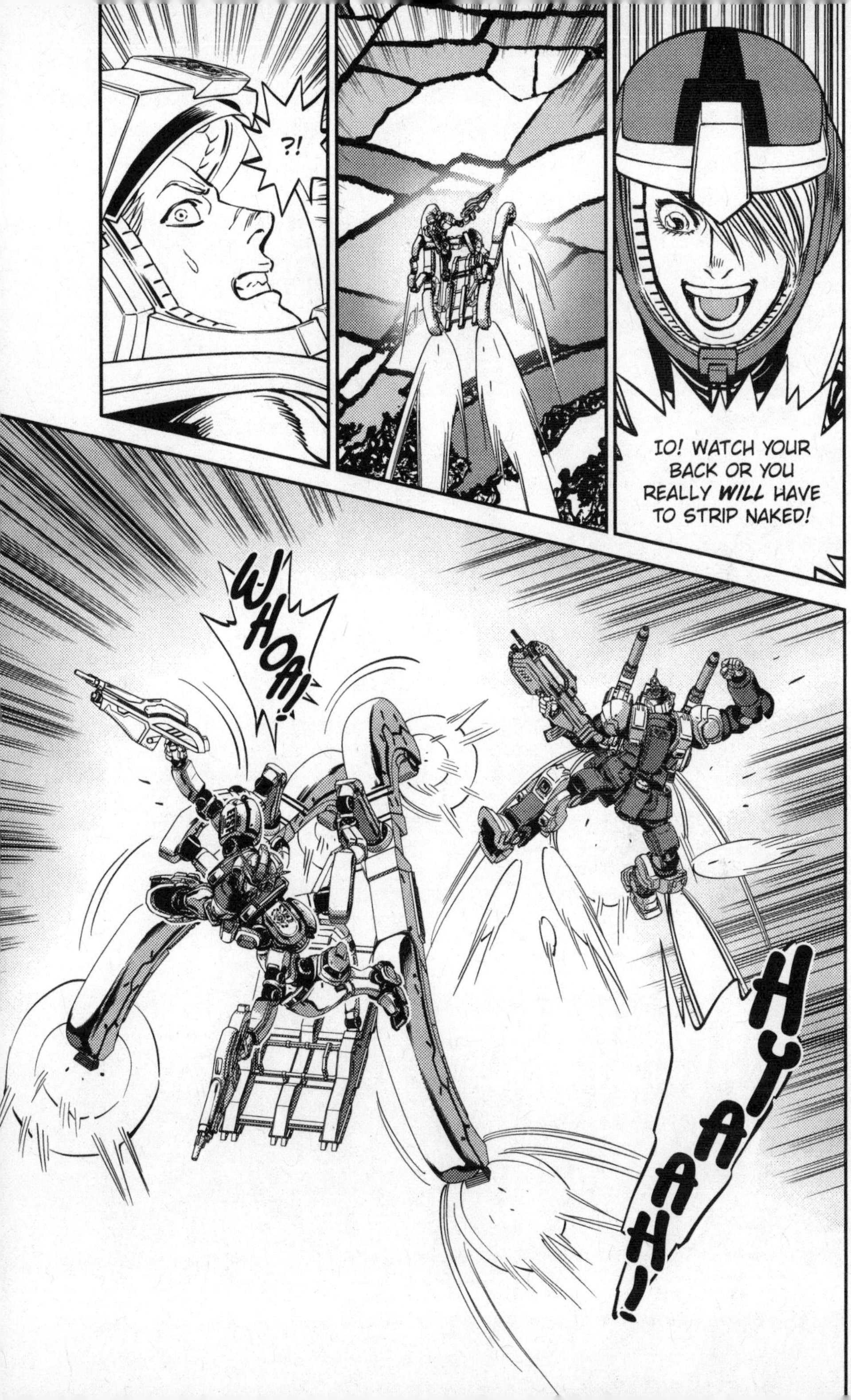
IO! WATCH YOUR BACK OR YOU REALLY *WILL* HAVE TO STRIP NAKED!
?!
WHOA!
HYAAAH!

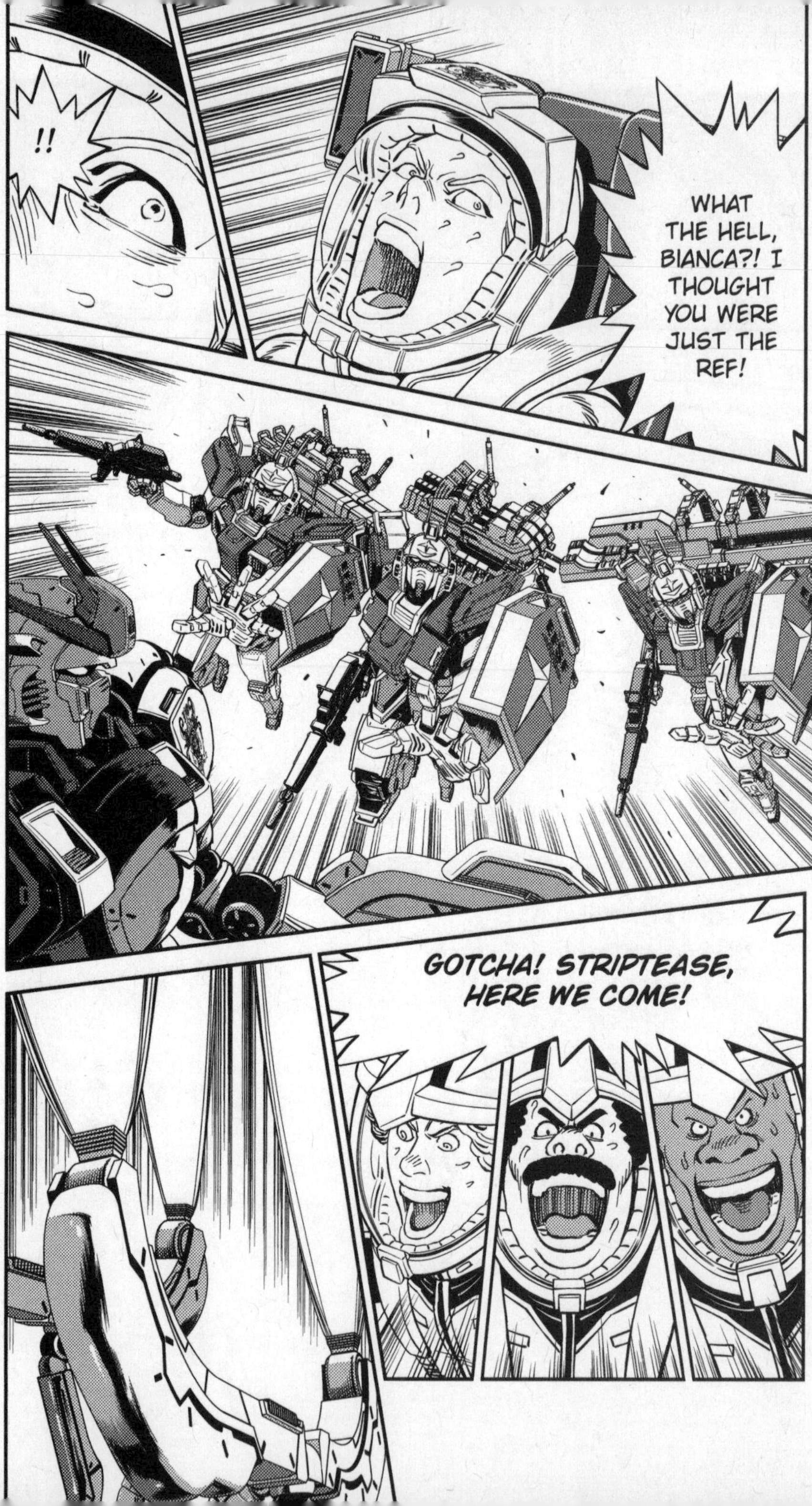
WHAT THE HELL, BIANCA?! I THOUGHT YOU WERE JUST THE REF!
!!
GOTCHA! STRIPTEASE, HERE WE COME!

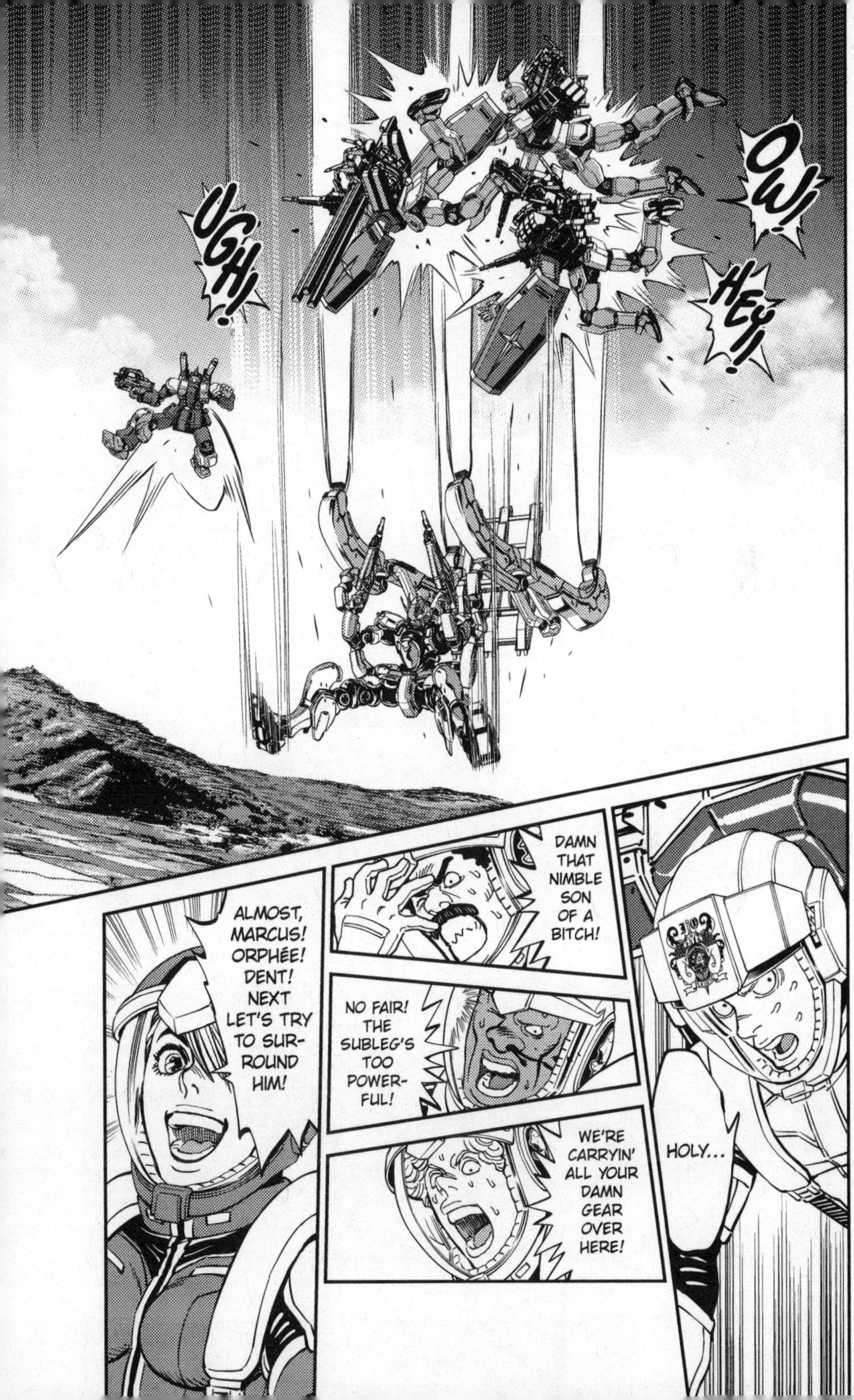
OW!
HEY!
UGH!
HOLY...
DAMN THAT NIMBLE SON OF A BITCH!
NO FAIR! THE SUBLEG'S TOO POWERFUL!
WE'RE CARRYIN' ALL YOUR DAMN GEAR OVER HERE!
ALMOST, MARCUS! ORPHÉE! DENT! NEXT LET'S TRY TO SURROUND HIM!

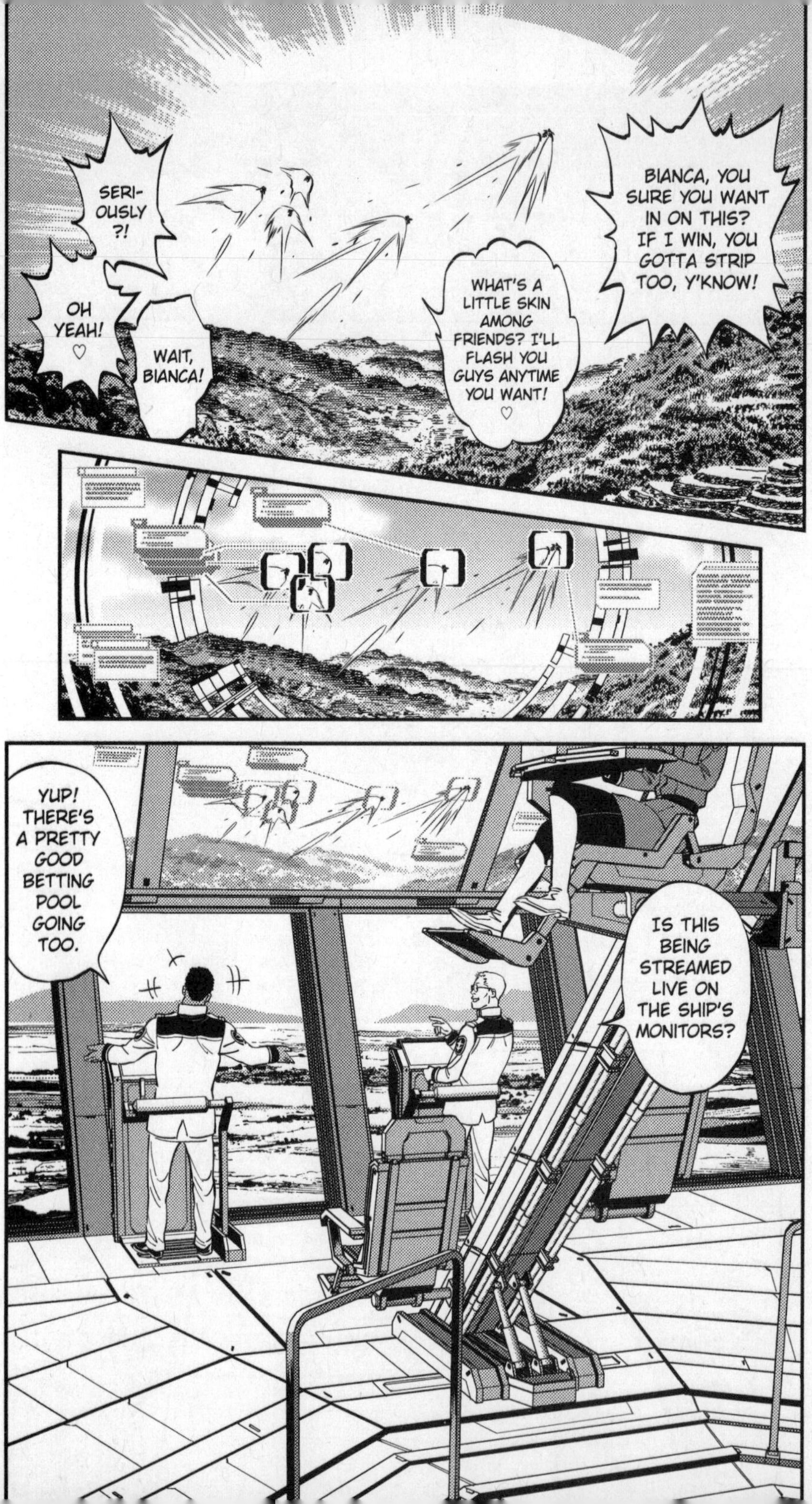
BIANCA, YOU SURE YOU WANT IN ON THIS? IF I WIN, YOU GOTTA STRIP TOO, Y'KNOW!
WHAT'S A LITTLE SKIN AMONG FRIENDS? I'LL FLASH YOU GUYS ANYTIME YOU WANT! ♡
SERI-OUSLY ?!
WAIT, BIANCA!
OH YEAH! ♡
IS THIS BEING STREAMED LIVE ON THE SHIP'S MONITORS?
YUP! THERE'S A PRETTY GOOD BETTING POOL GOING TOO.

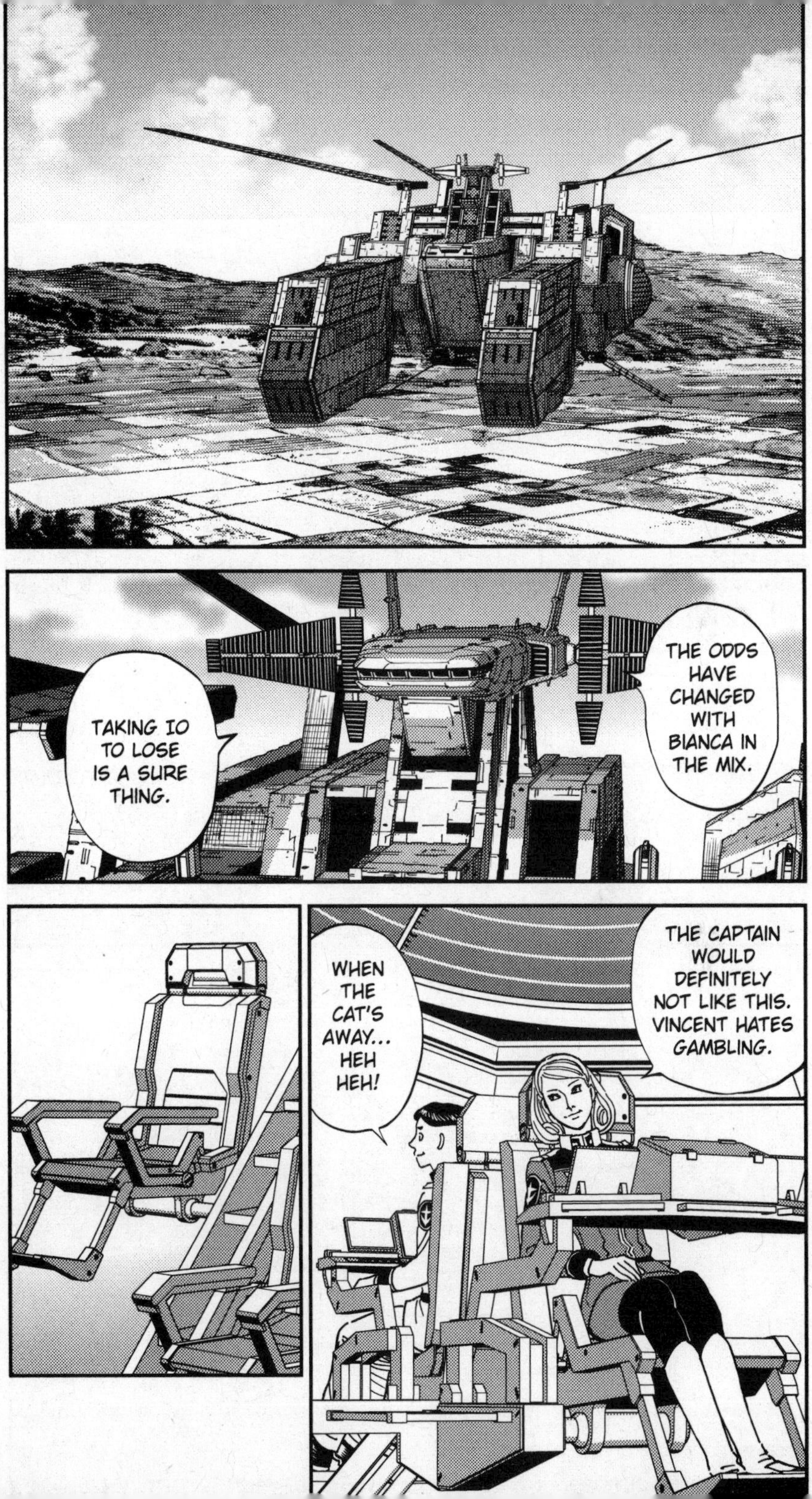
THE ODDS HAVE CHANGED WITH BIANCA IN THE MIX.
TAKING IO TO LOSE IS A SURE THING.
THE CAPTAIN WOULD DEFINITELY NOT LIKE THIS. VINCENT HATES GAMBLING.
WHEN THE CAT'S AWAY... HEH HEH!

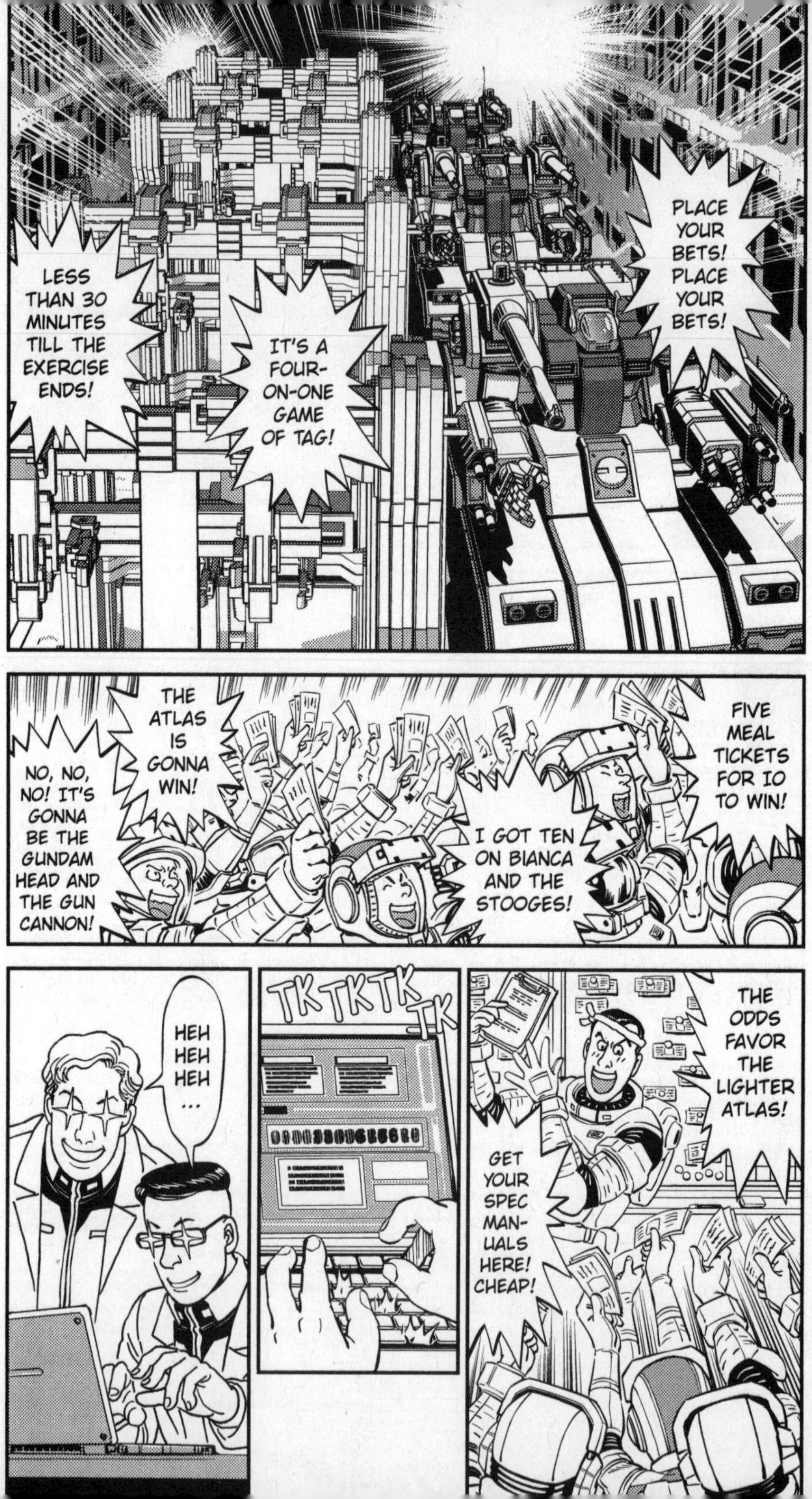
PLACE YOUR BETS! PLACE YOUR BETS!
IT'S A FOUR-ON-ONE GAME OF TAG!
LESS THAN 30 MINUTES TILL THE EXERCISE ENDS!
FIVE MEAL TICKETS FOR IO TO WIN!
I GOT TEN ON BIANCA AND THE STOOGES!
THE ATLAS IS GONNA WIN!
NO, NO, NO! IT'S GONNA BE THE GUNDAM HEAD AND THE GUN CANNON!
THE ODDS FAVOR THE LIGHTER ATLAS!
GET YOUR SPEC MAN-UALS HERE! CHEAP!
TKTKTK TK
HEH HEH HEH ...

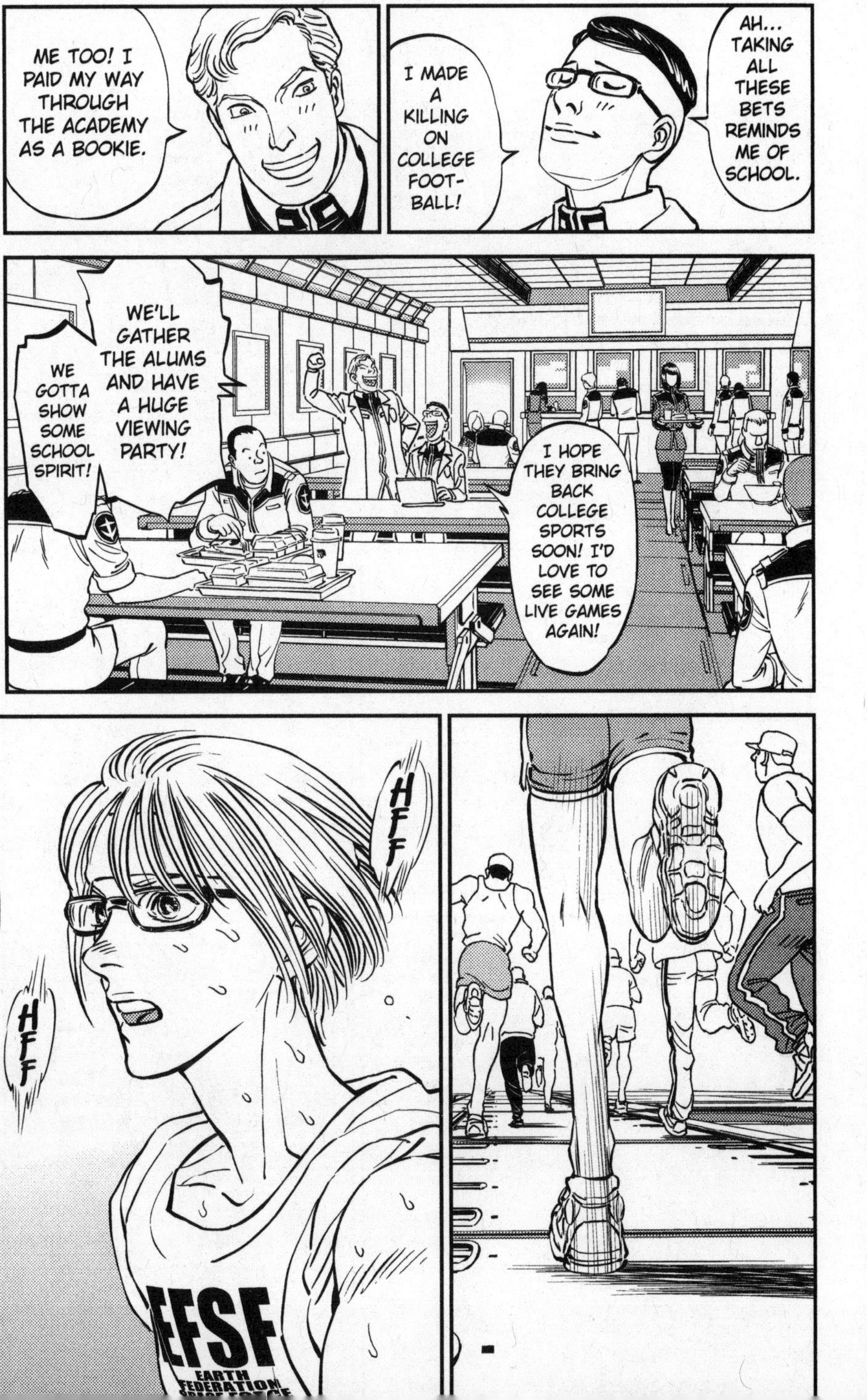
AH... TAKING ALL THESE BETS REMINDS ME OF SCHOOL.
I MADE A KILLING ON COLLEGE FOOT-BALL!
ME TOO! I PAID MY WAY THROUGH THE ACADEMY AS A BOOKIE.
I HOPE THEY BRING BACK COLLEGE SPORTS SOON! I'D LOVE TO SEE SOME LIVE GAMES AGAIN!
WE'LL GATHER THE ALUMS AND HAVE A HUGE VIEWING PARTY!
WE GOTTA SHOW SOME SCHOOL SPIRIT!
HFF
HFF
HFF
EFSF
EARTH FEDERATION

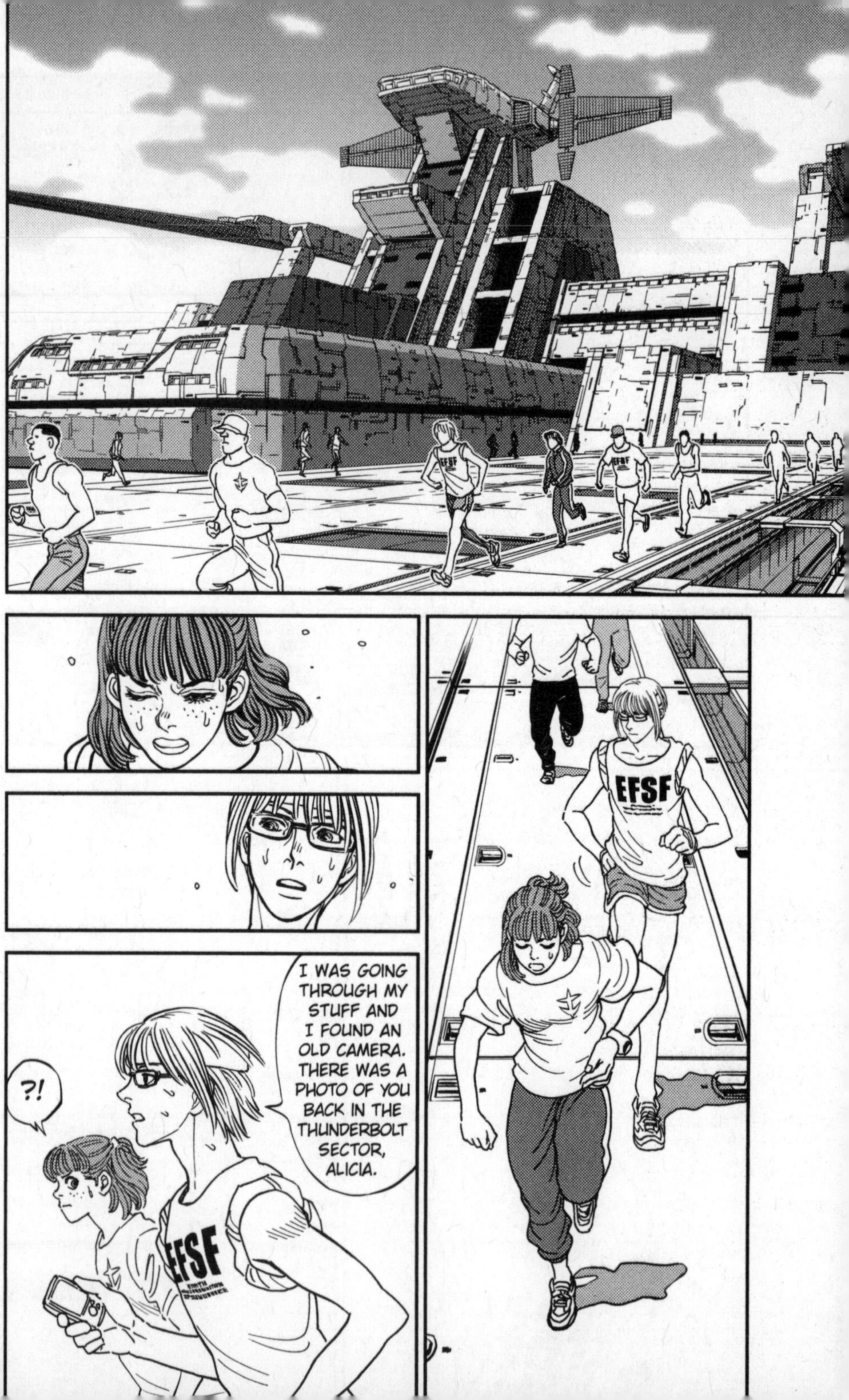
EFSF
EFSF
I WAS GOING THROUGH MY STUFF AND I FOUND AN OLD CAMERA. THERE WAS A PHOTO OF YOU BACK IN THE THUNDERBOLT SECTOR, ALICIA.
?!

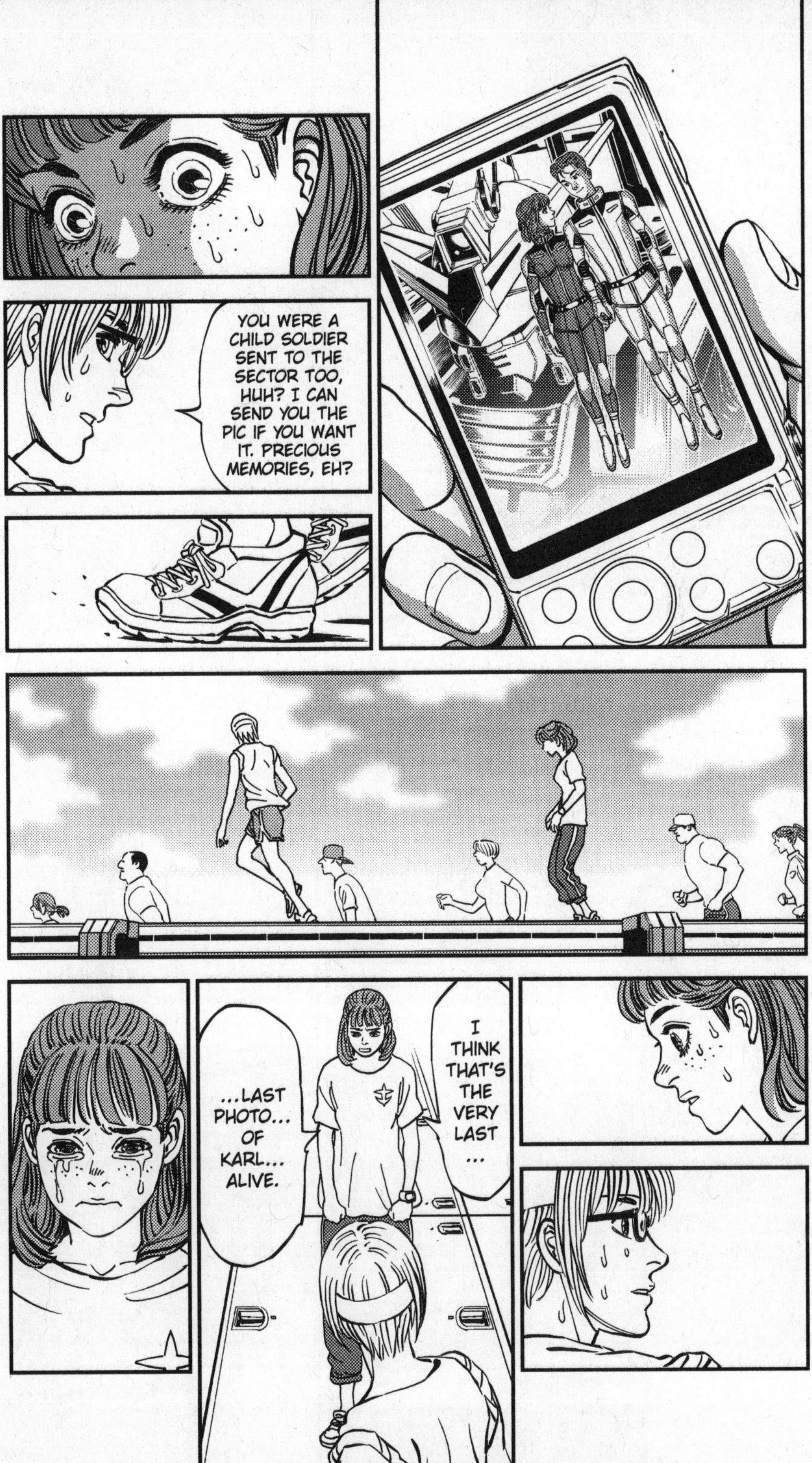
YOU WERE A CHILD SOLDIER SENT TO THE SECTOR TOO, HUH? I CAN SEND YOU THE PIC IF YOU WANT IT. PRECIOUS MEMORIES, EH?
I THINK THAT'S THE VERY LAST ...
...LAST PHOTO... OF KARL... ALIVE.

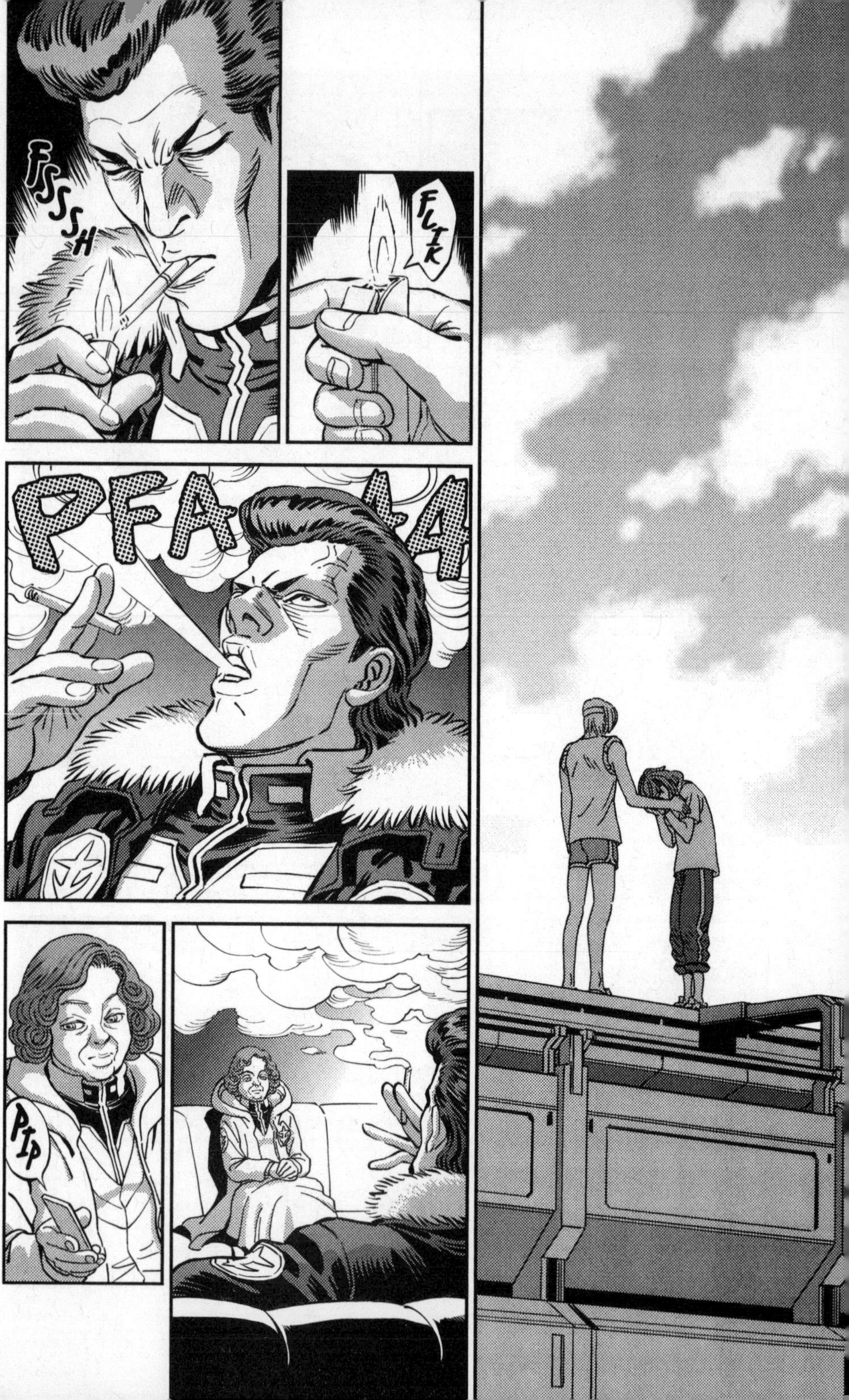
FLIK
FSSSH
PFAAA
PIP

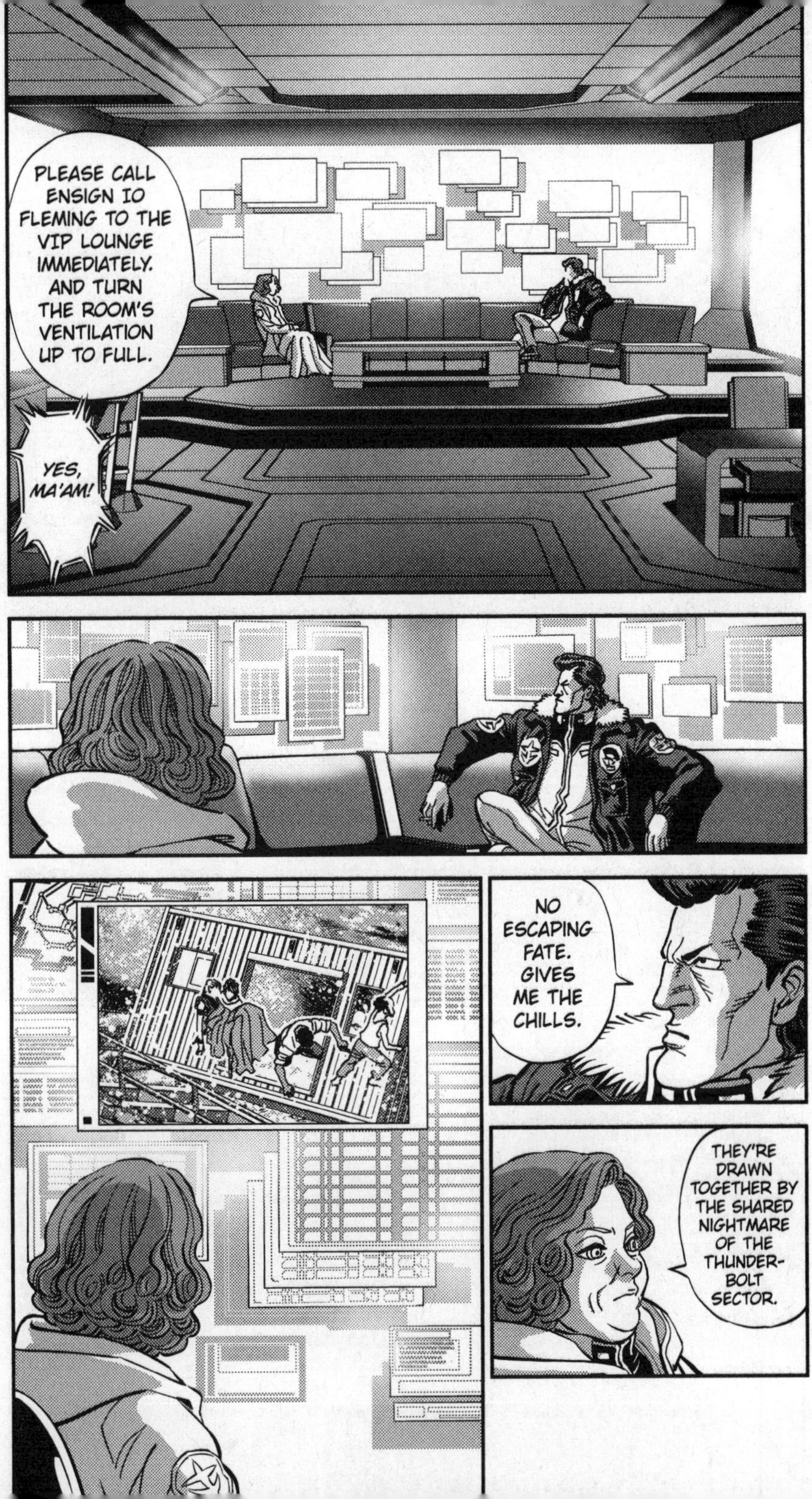
PLEASE CALL ENSIGN IO FLEMING TO THE VIP LOUNGE IMMEDIATELY. AND TURN THE ROOM'S VENTILATION UP TO FULL.
YES, MA'AM!
NO ESCAPING FATE. GIVES ME THE CHILLS.
THEY'RE DRAWN TOGETHER BY THE SHARED NIGHTMARE OF THE THUNDER-BOLT SECTOR.

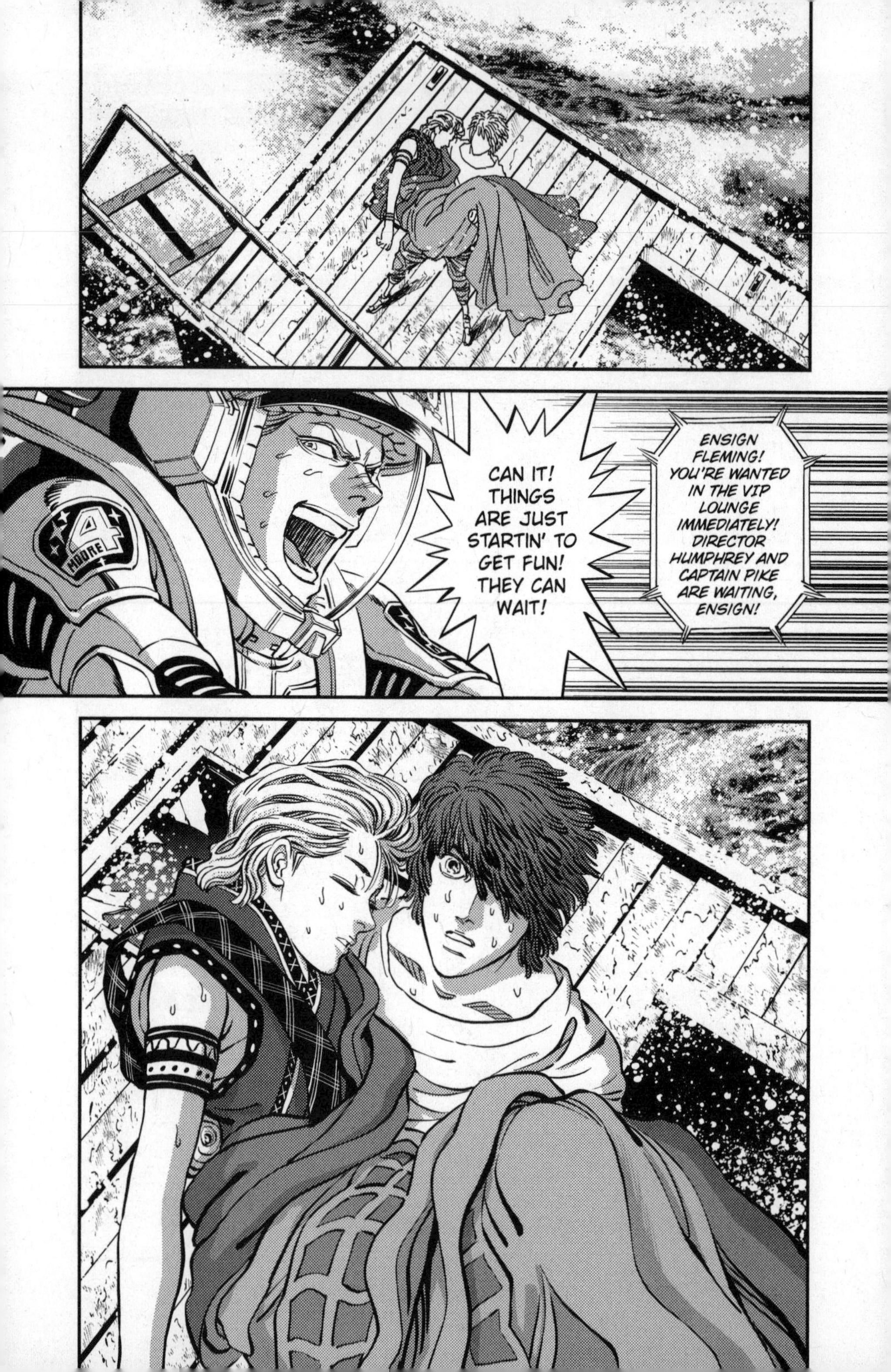
ENSIGN FLEMING! YOU'RE WANTED IN THE VIP LOUNGE IMMEDIATELY! DIRECTOR HUMPHREY AND CAPTAIN PIKE ARE WAITING, ENSIGN!
CAN IT! THINGS ARE JUST STARTIN' TO GET FUN! THEY CAN WAIT!

MOBILE SUIT GUNDAM
THUNDERBOLT
CHAPTER
83

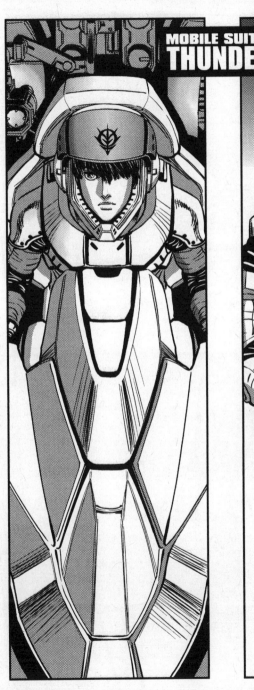

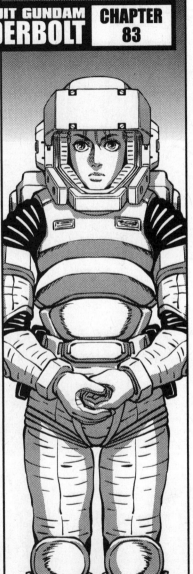

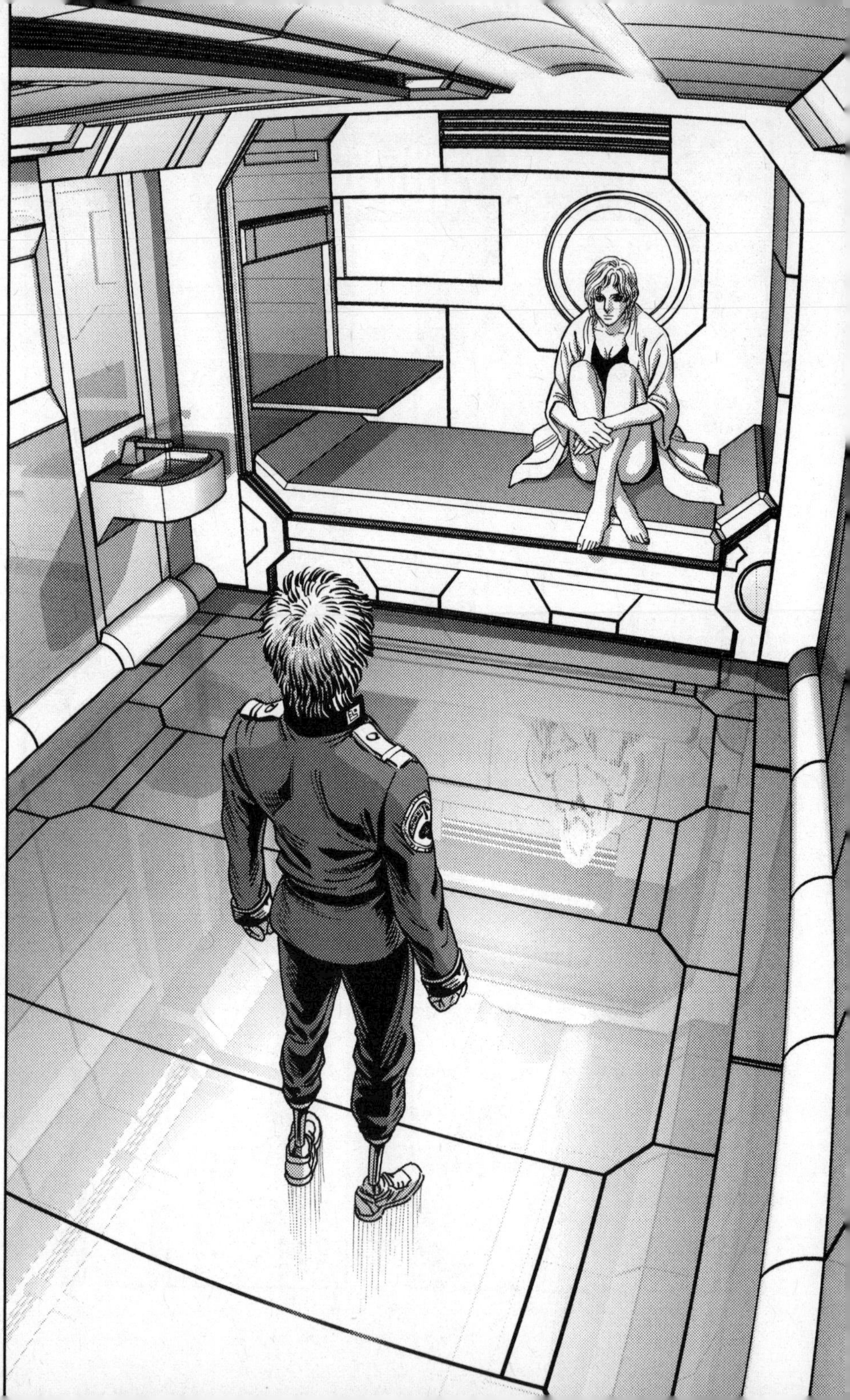

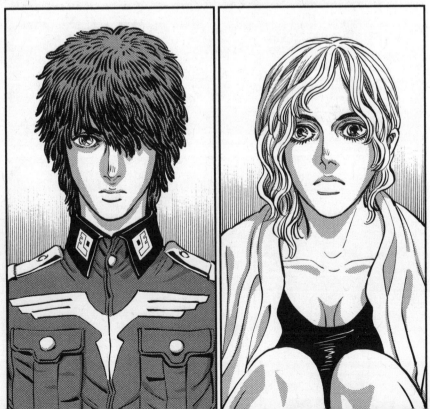

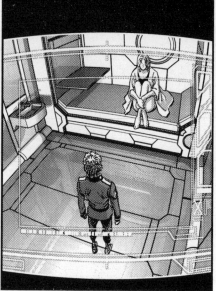

ALL RIGHT, THE AUDIO'S OFF. THEY CAN TALK FREELY NOW.

WHEN SOMEONE GOES TO SEE A PRISON-ER...

...THEY RECORD EVERY-THING. SHUTTING THE CAMERAS DOWN WOULD ALARM SECURITY.

GOOD JOB.

WE BAGGED HER, BUT THIS IS OUR ONLY CHANCE TO QUESTION HER OUR-SELVES!

TELL ME ABOUT IT.

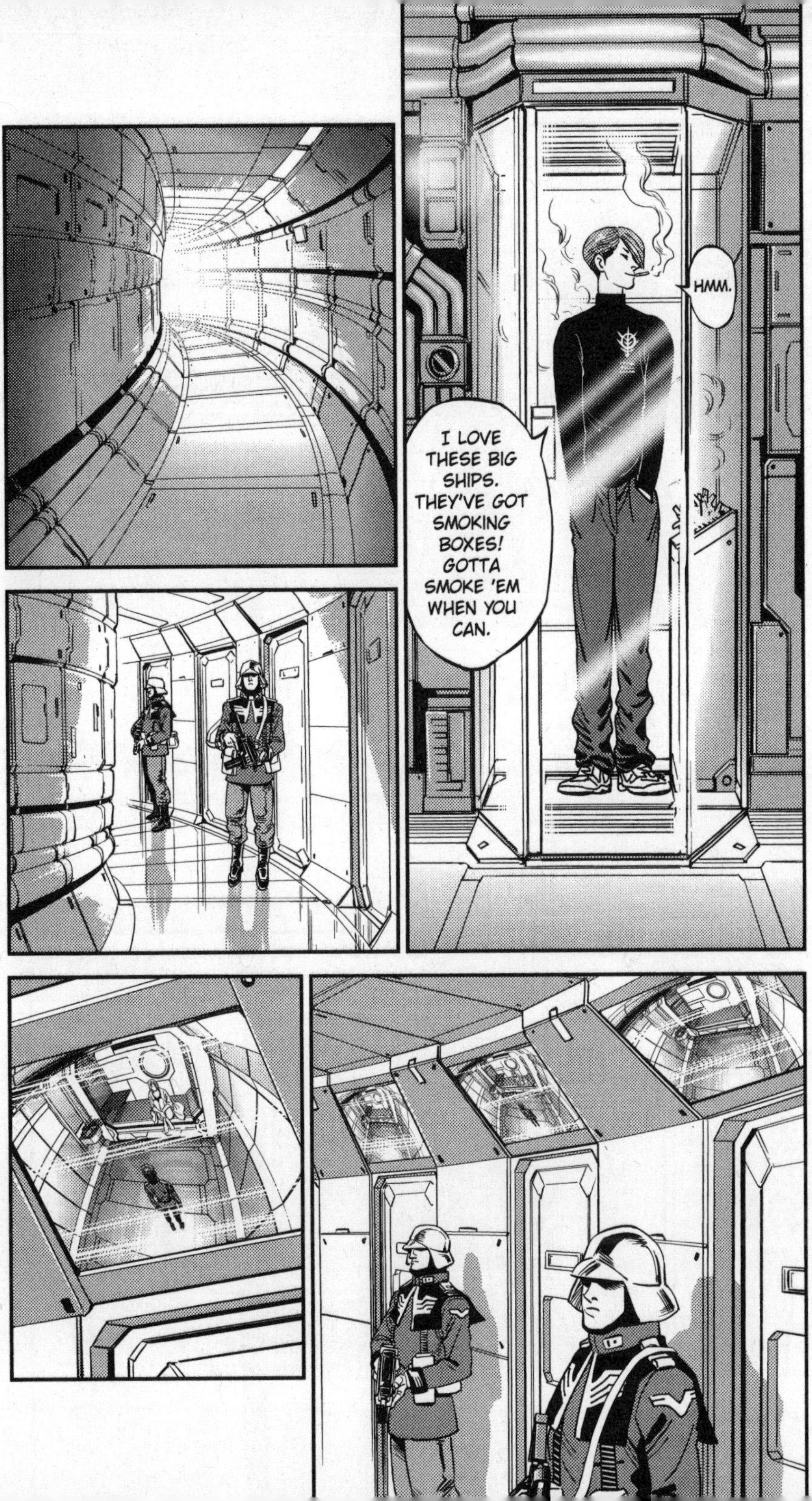
HMM.
I LOVE THESE BIG SHIPS. THEY'VE GOT SMOKING BOXES! GOTTA SMOKE 'EM WHEN YOU CAN.

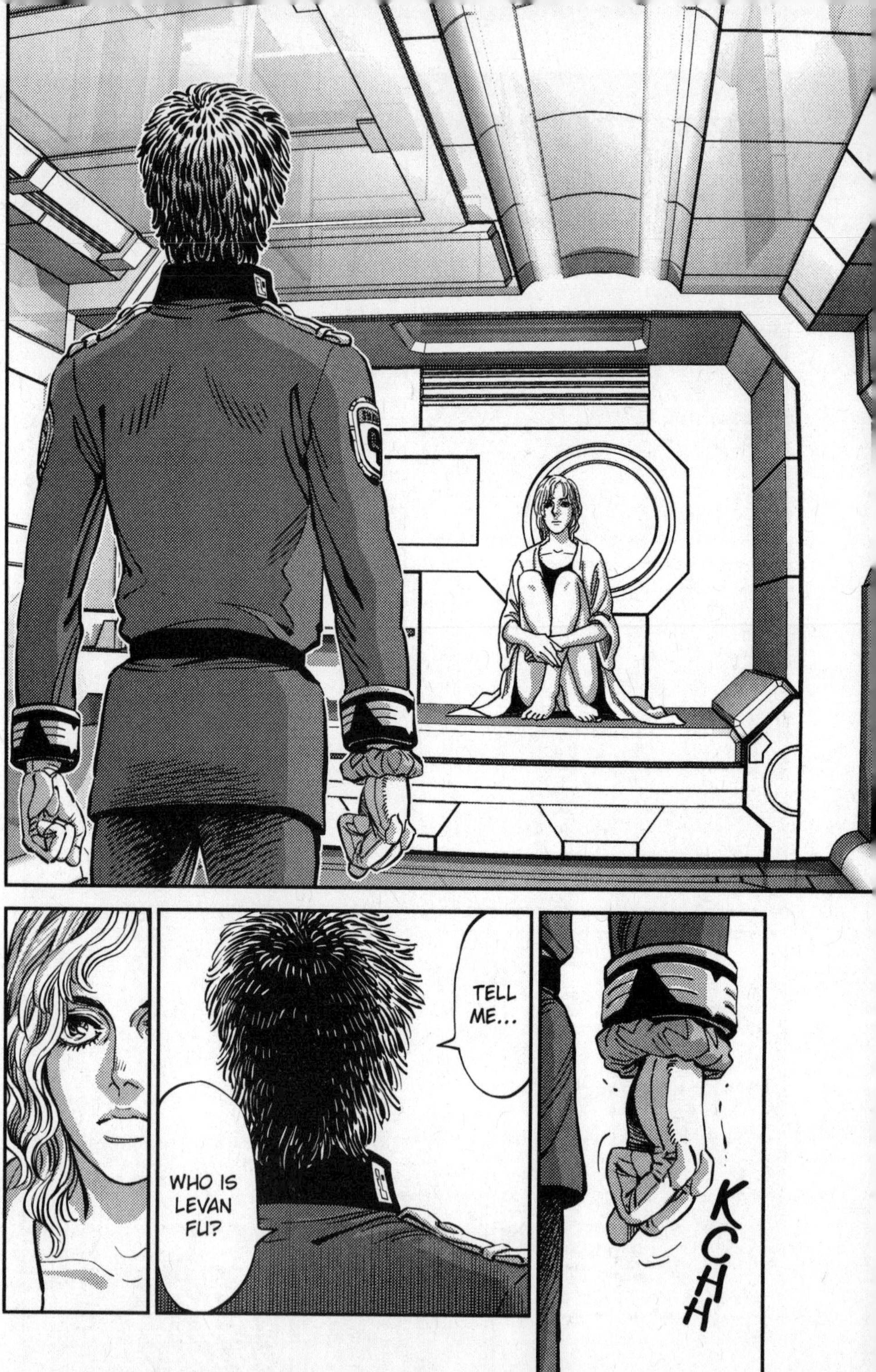
KCHH
TELL ME...
WHO IS LEVAN FU?

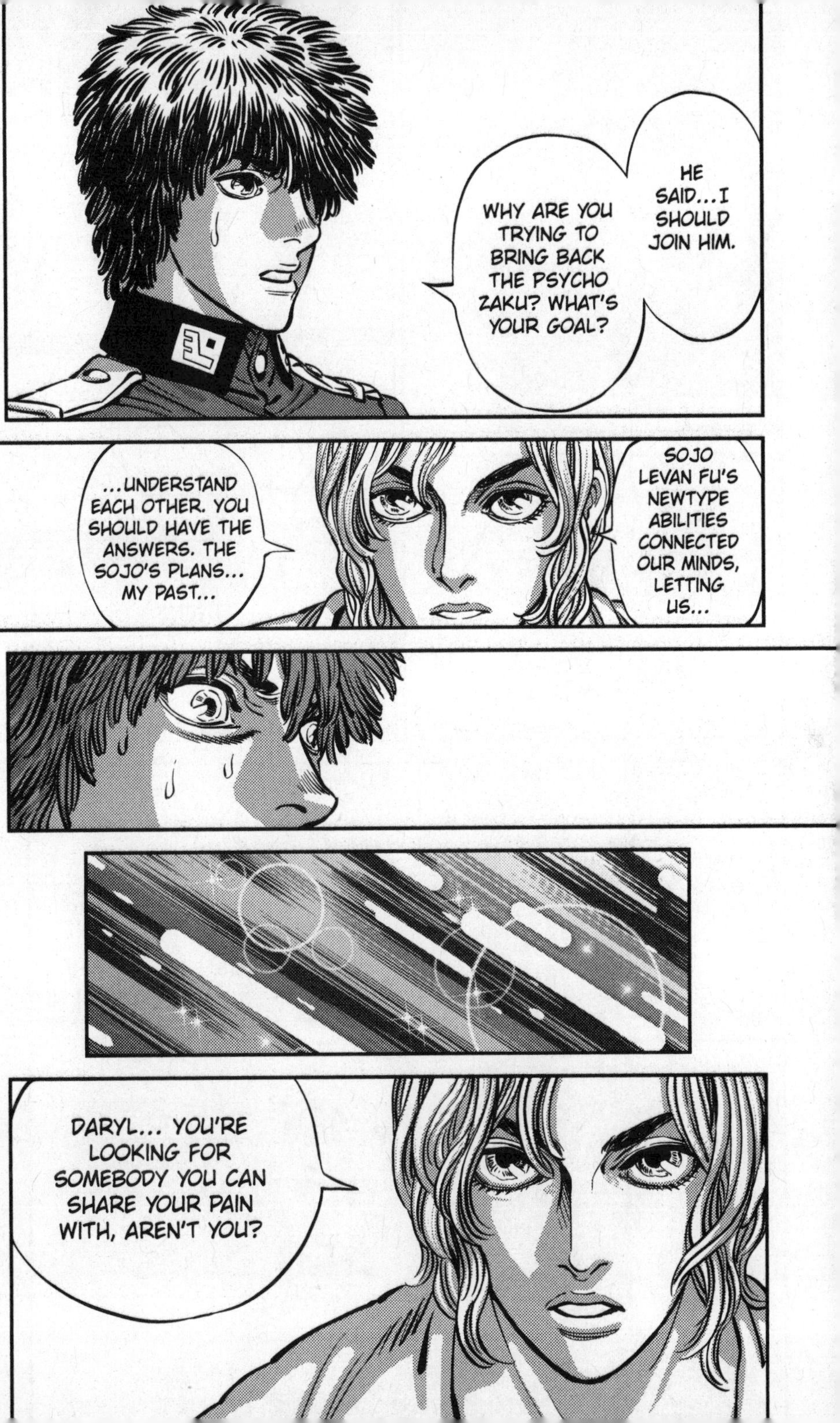
HE SAID...I SHOULD JOIN HIM.
WHY ARE YOU TRYING TO BRING BACK THE PSYCHO ZAKU? WHAT'S YOUR GOAL?
SOJO LEVAN FU'S NEWTYPE ABILITIES CONNECTED OUR MINDS, LETTING US...
...UNDERSTAND EACH OTHER. YOU SHOULD HAVE THE ANSWERS. THE SOJO'S PLANS... MY PAST...
DARYL... YOU'RE LOOKING FOR SOMEBODY YOU CAN SHARE YOUR PAIN WITH, AREN'T YOU?

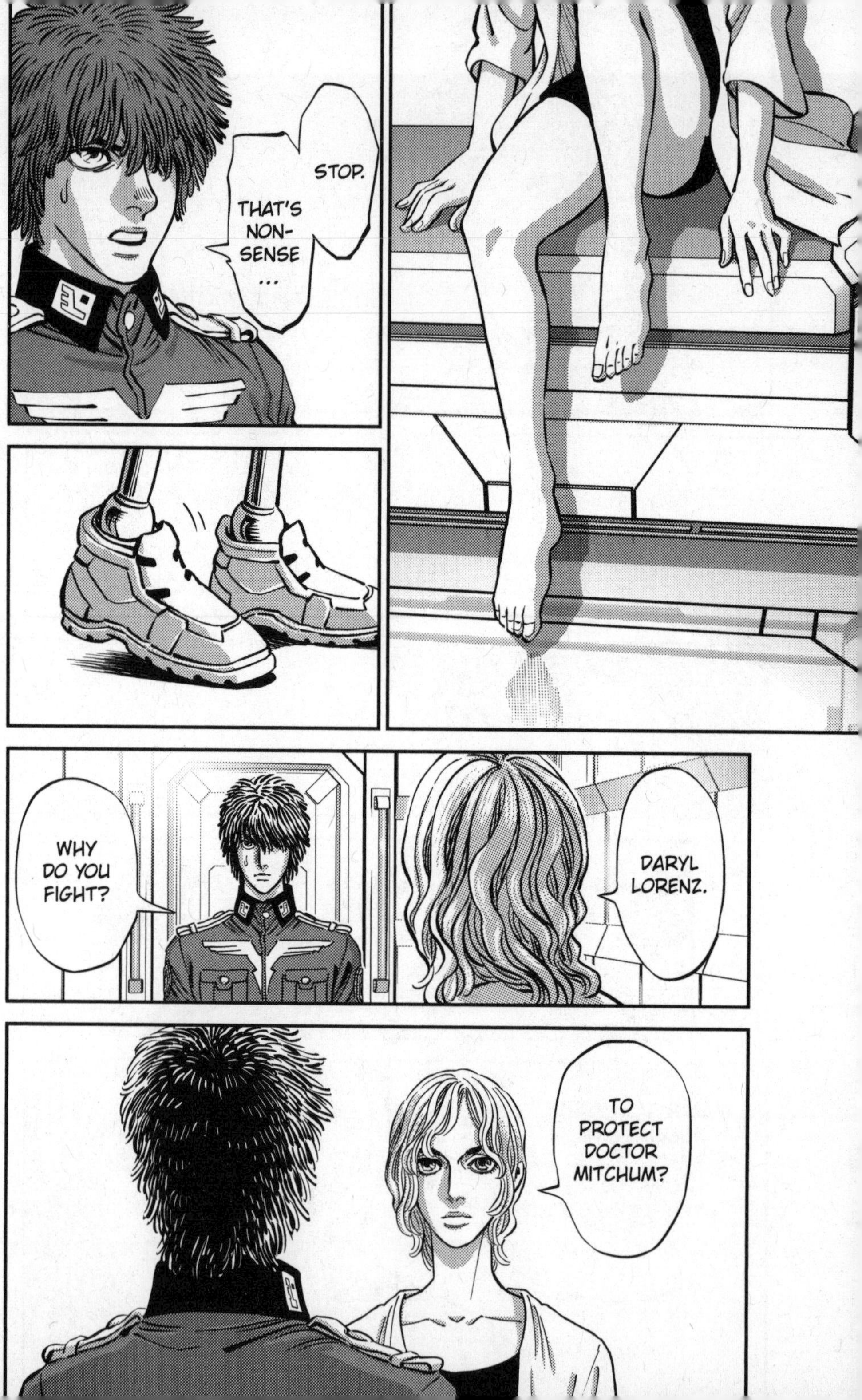
STOP.
THAT'S NON-SENSE ...
DARYL LORENZ.
WHY DO YOU FIGHT?
TO PROTECT DOCTOR MITCHUM?

THE ZEON REMNANT FORCES WILL KEEP HER DETAINED. AND WHEN SHE RECOVERS, THEY'LL ORDER HER TO DEVELOP THE REUSE P. DEVICE ONCE AGAIN.

IF THE TREATMENT IS A SUCCESS AND HER MIND IS RESTORED, ALL THAT AWAITS HER IS A *NEW* HELL!

SHE'LL BE FORCED TO DEVELOP A WEAPON THAT SHE DOESN'T EVEN BELIEVE IN!

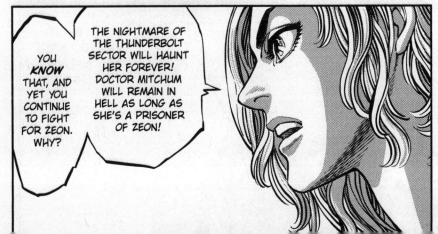

THE NIGHTMARE OF THE THUNDERBOLT SECTOR WILL HAUNT HER FOREVER! DOCTOR MITCHUM WILL REMAIN IN HELL AS LONG AS SHE'S A PRISONER OF ZEON!

YOU *KNOW* THAT, AND YET YOU CONTINUE TO FIGHT FOR ZEON. WHY?

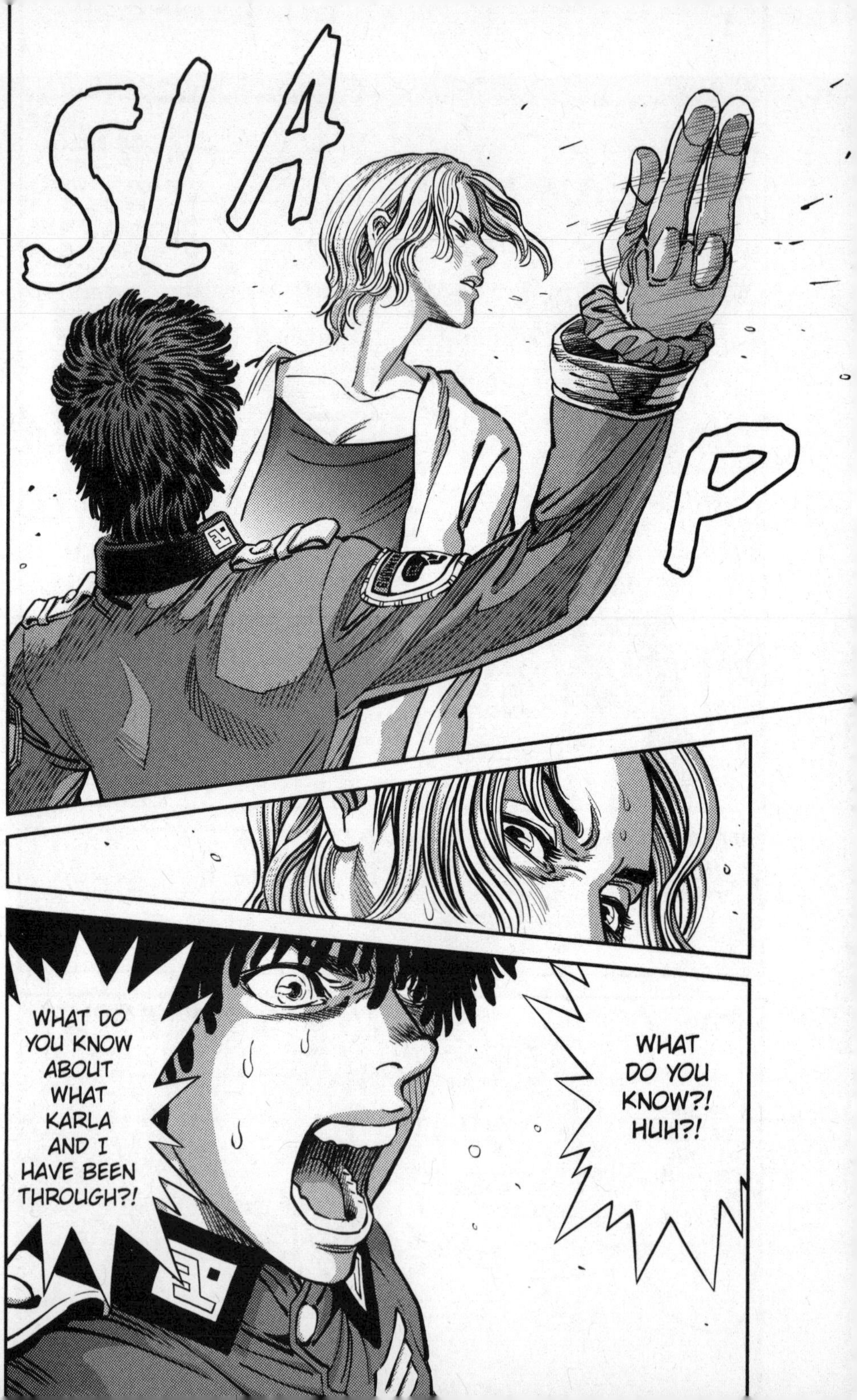
SLAP
WHAT DO YOU KNOW?! HUH?!
WHAT DO YOU KNOW ABOUT WHAT KARLA AND I HAVE BEEN THROUGH?!

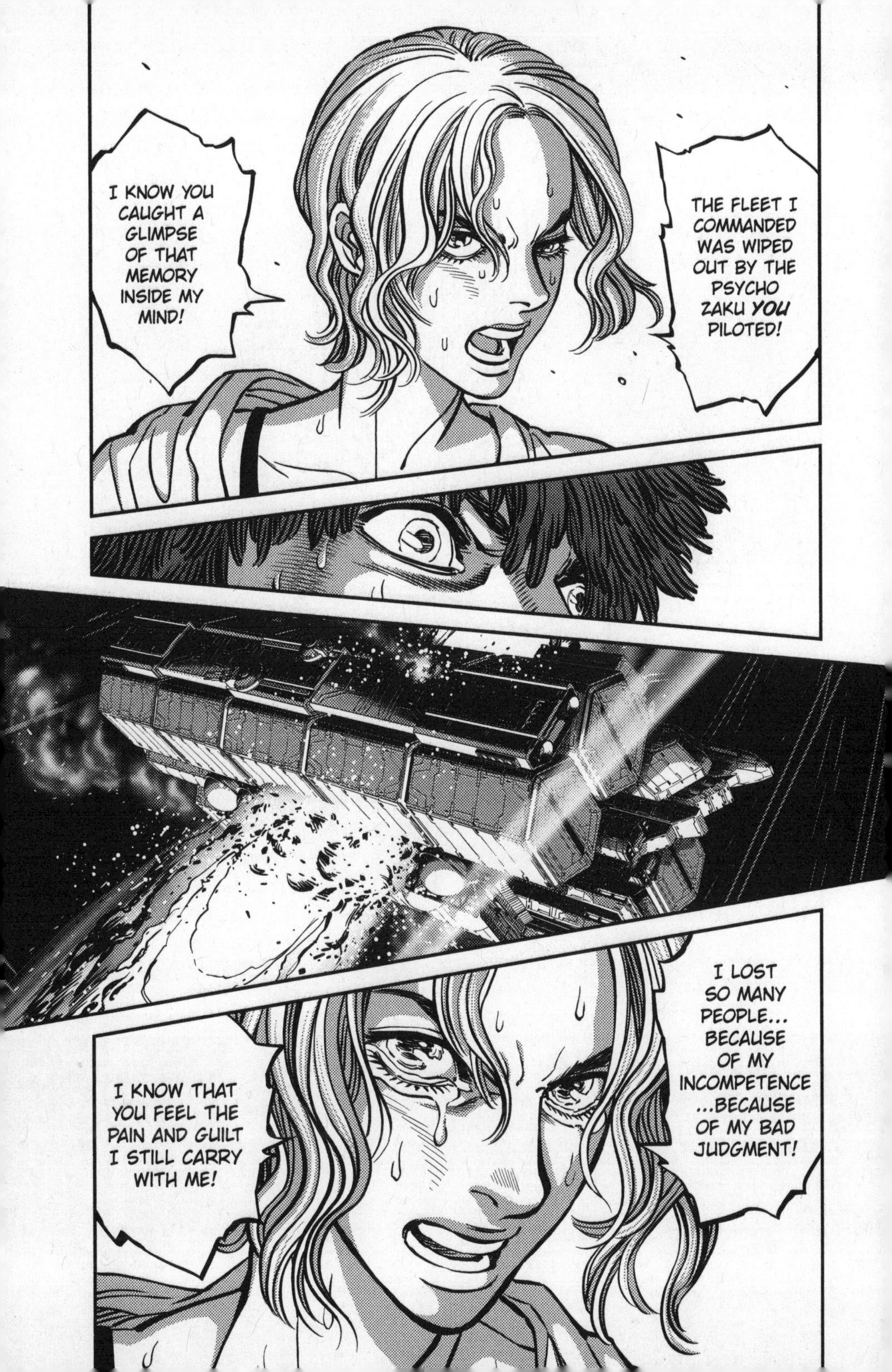
THE FLEET I COMMANDED WAS WIPED OUT BY THE PSYCHO ZAKU *YOU* PILOTED!
I KNOW YOU CAUGHT A GLIMPSE OF THAT MEMORY INSIDE MY MIND!
I LOST SO MANY PEOPLE... BECAUSE OF MY INCOMPETENCE ...BECAUSE OF MY BAD JUDGMENT!
I KNOW THAT YOU FEEL THE PAIN AND GUILT I STILL CARRY WITH ME!

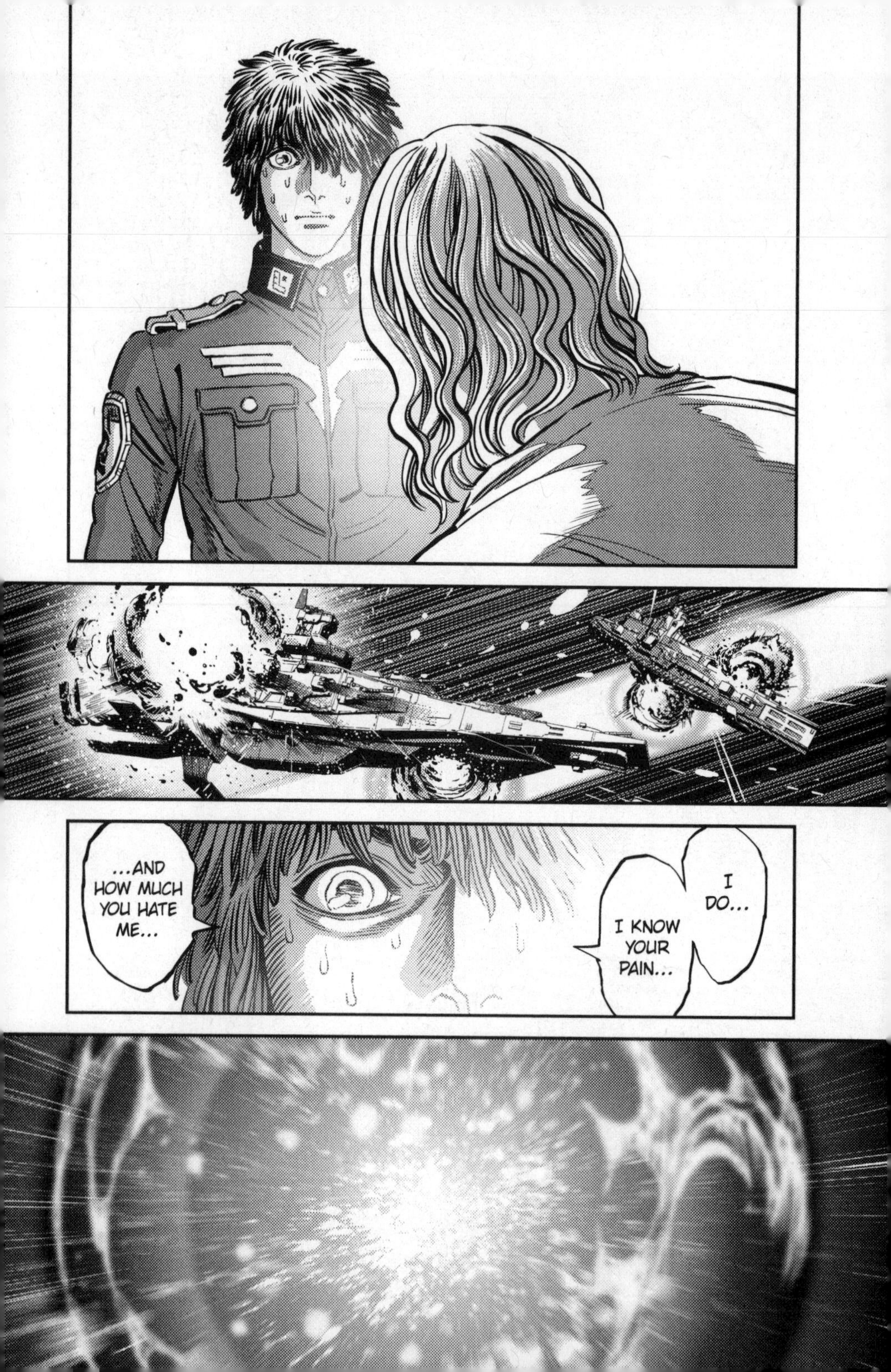
I DO... I KNOW YOUR PAIN...
...AND HOW MUCH YOU HATE ME...

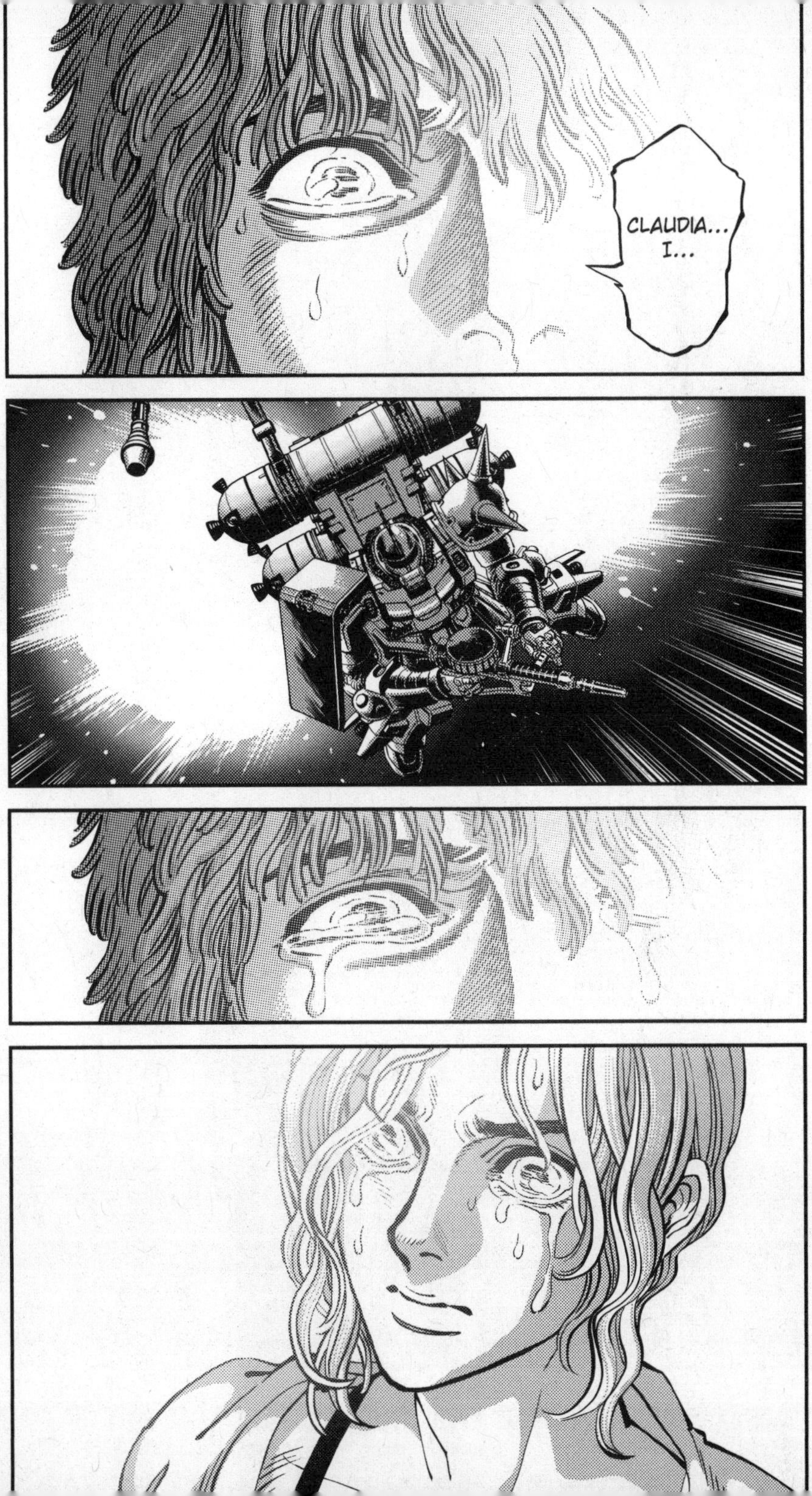
CLAUDIA... I...

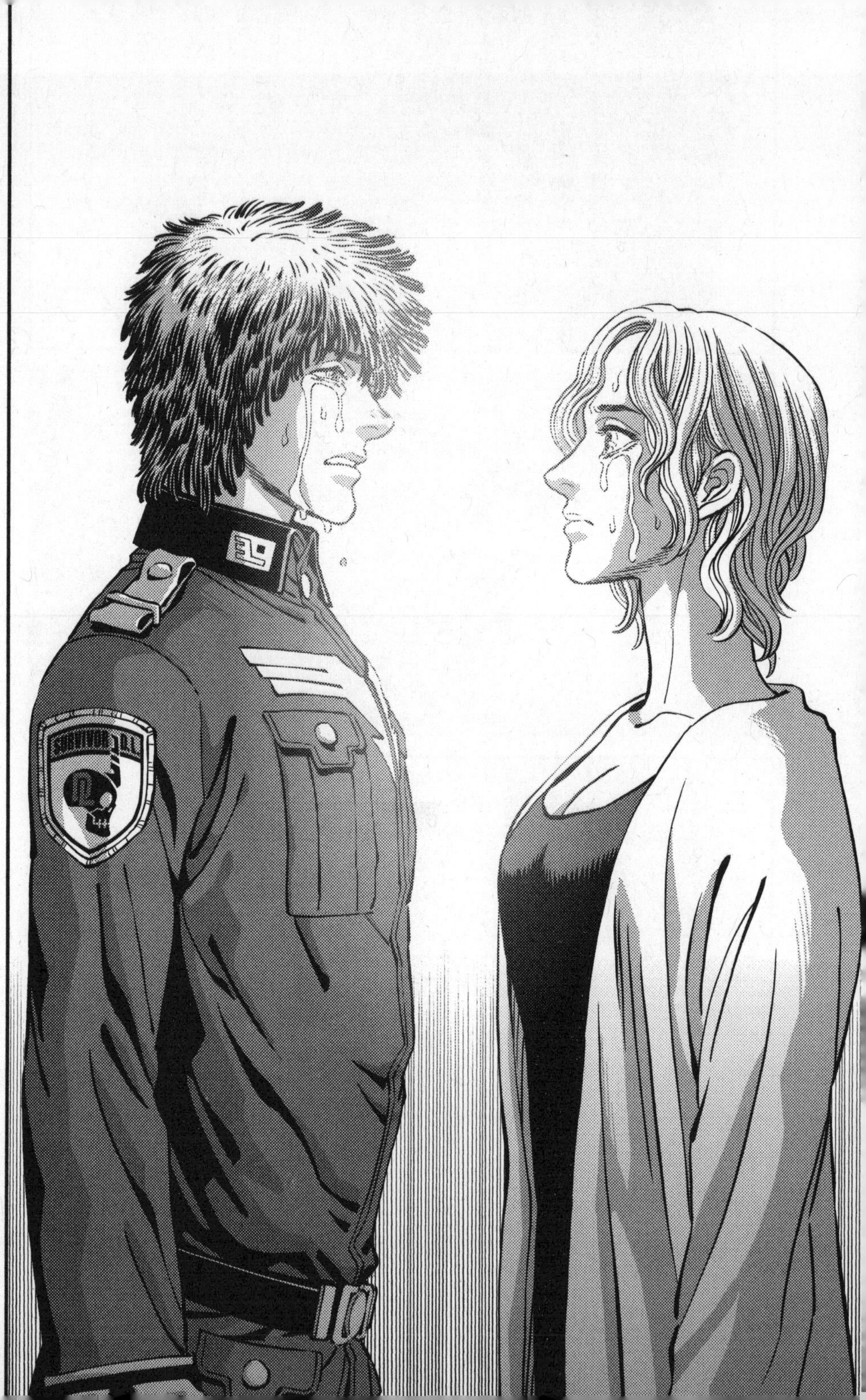
SURVIVOR D.L.

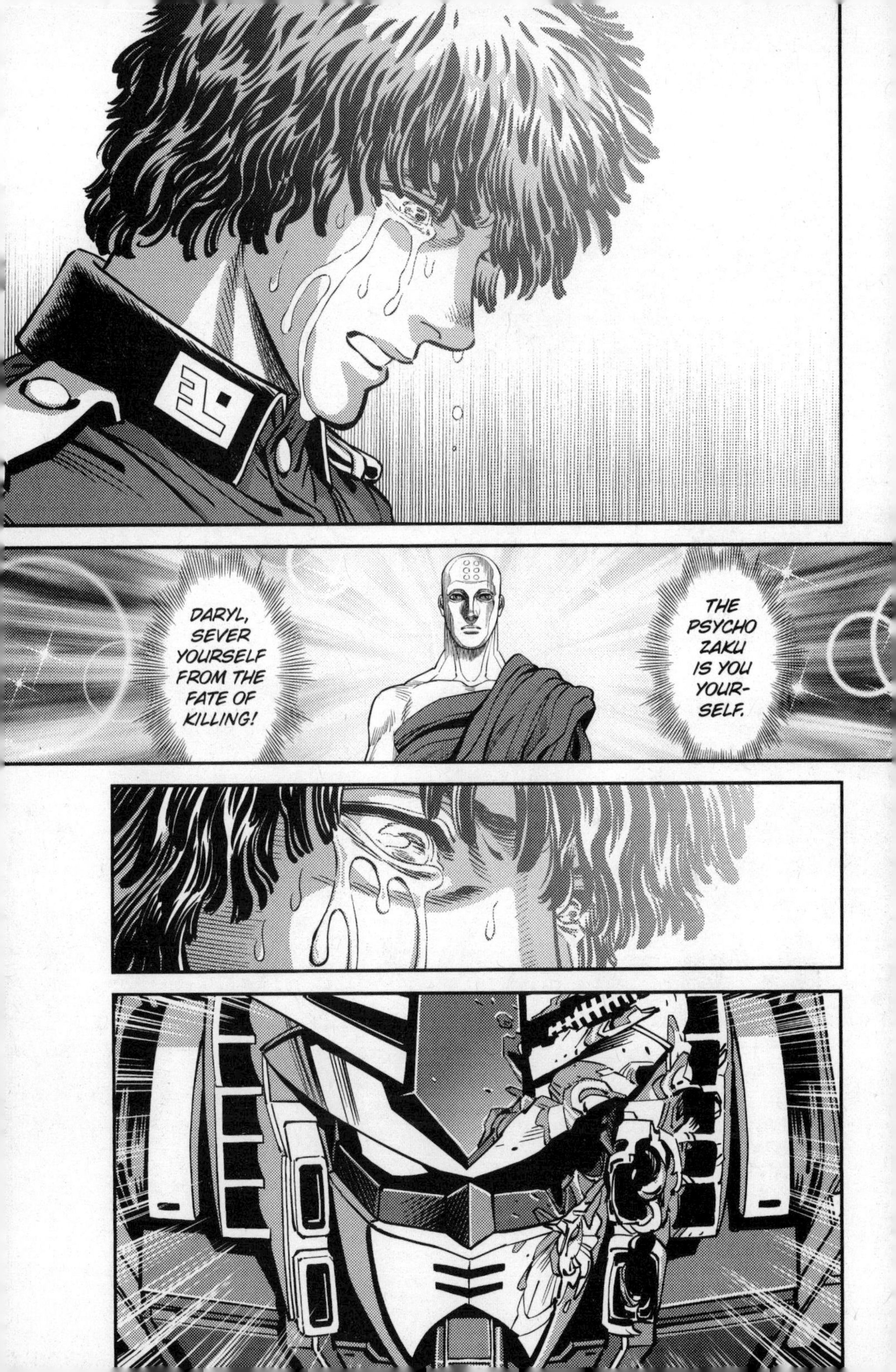
THE PSYCHO ZAKU IS YOU YOUR-SELF.
DARYL, SEVER YOURSELF FROM THE FATE OF KILLING!

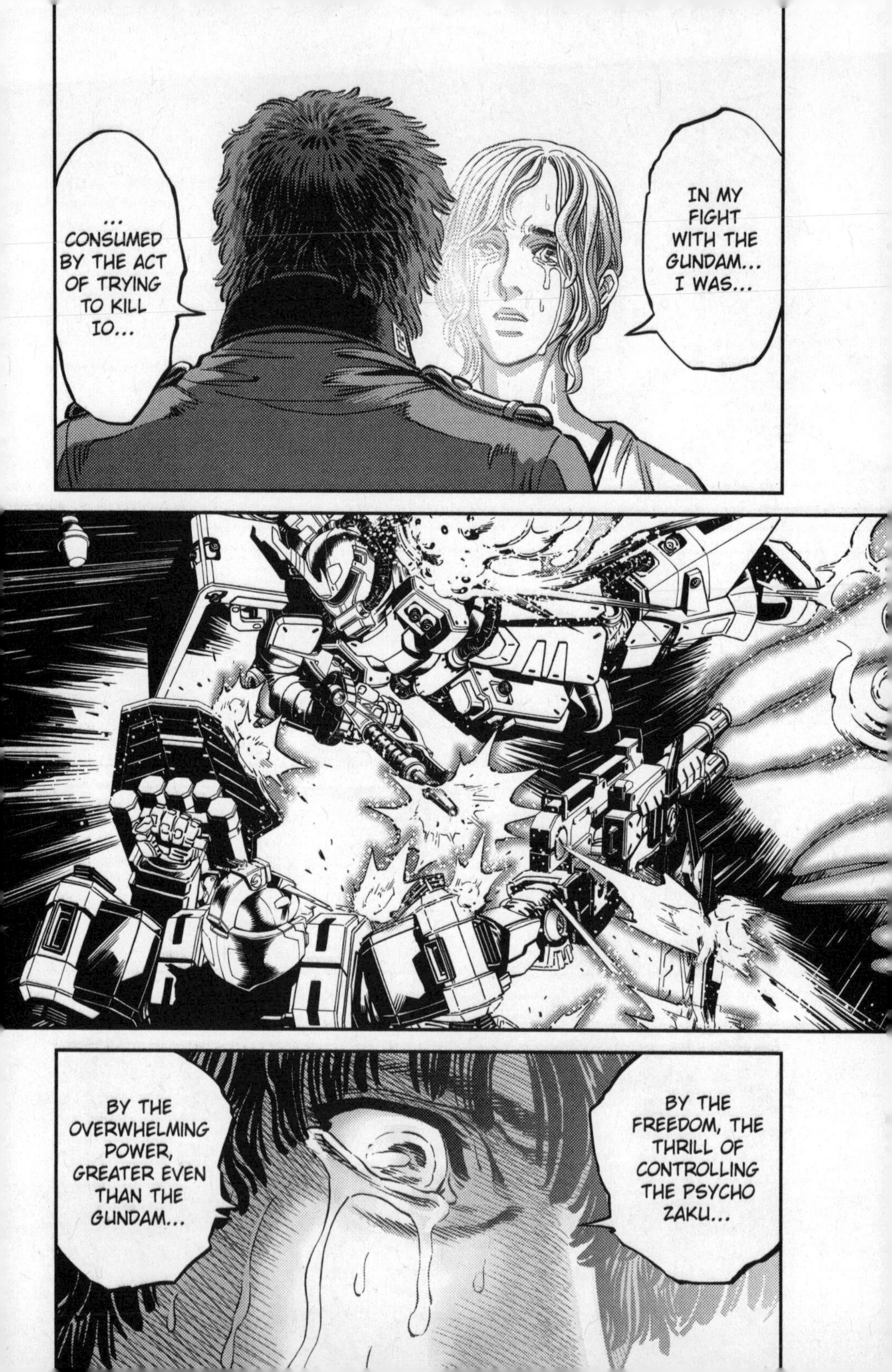
IN MY FIGHT WITH THE GUNDAM... I WAS...
... CONSUMED BY THE ACT OF TRYING TO KILL IO...
BY THE FREEDOM, THE THRILL OF CONTROLLING THE PSYCHO ZAKU...
BY THE OVERWHELMING POWER, GREATER EVEN THAN THE GUNDAM...

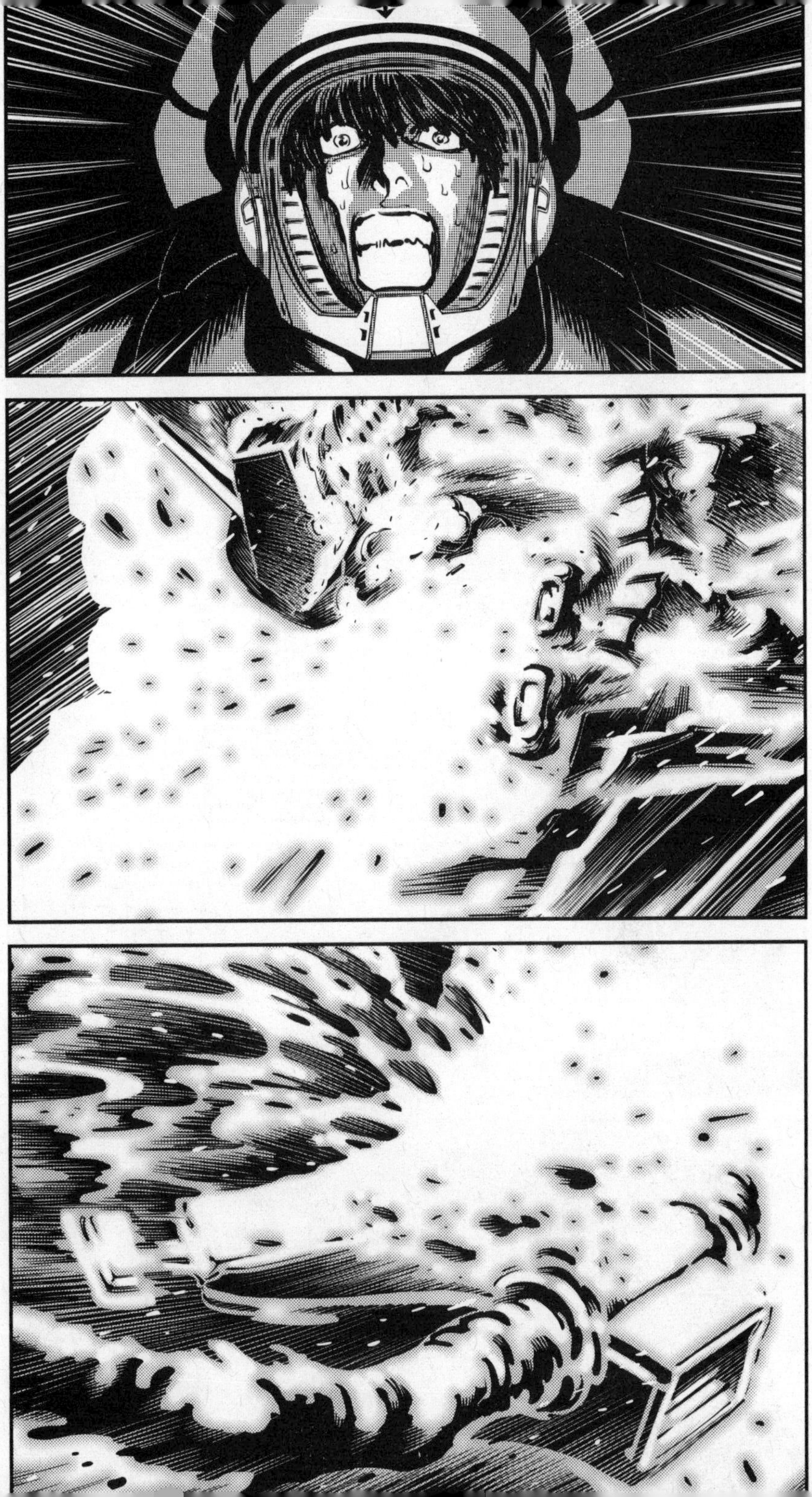

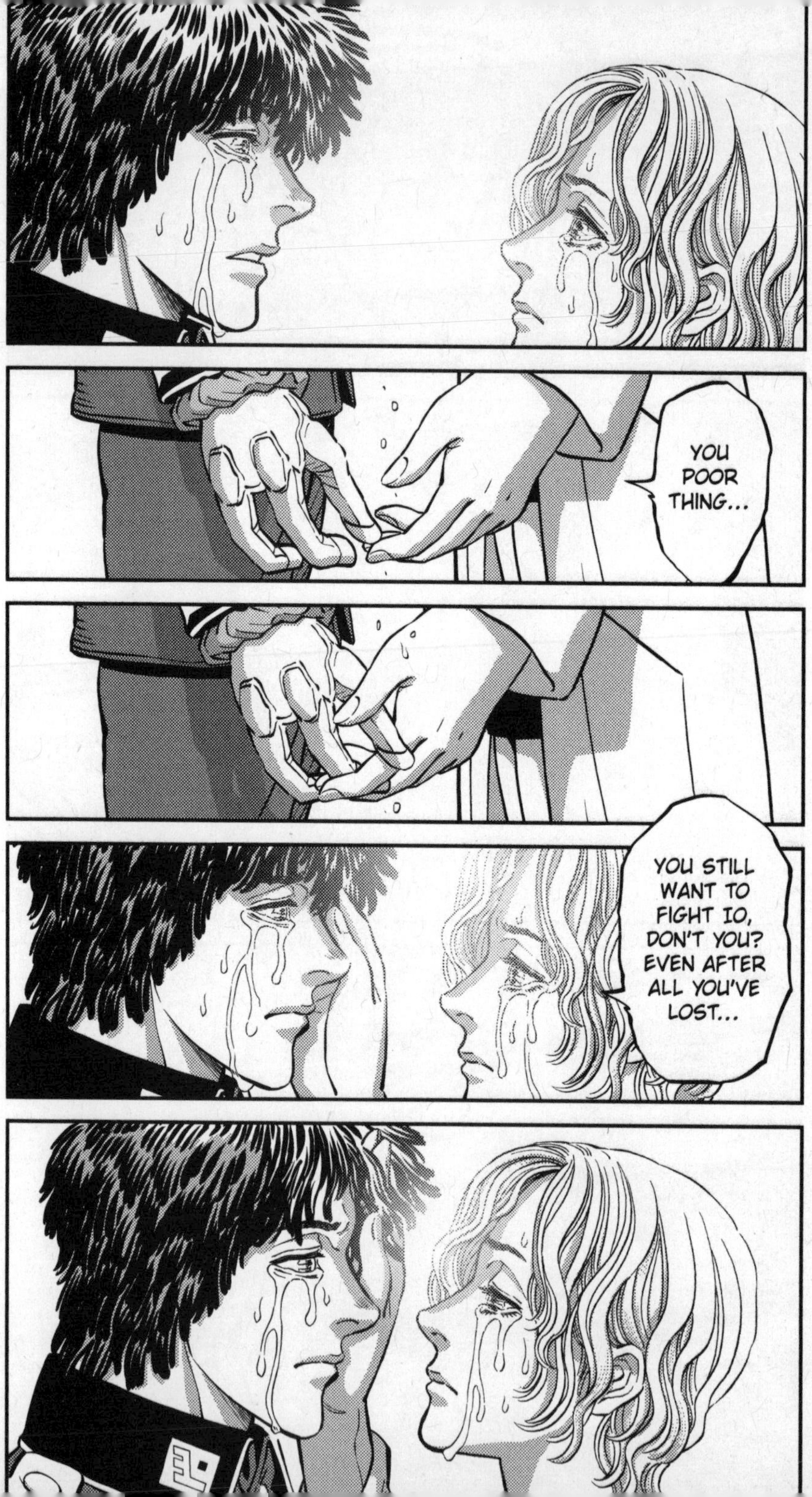
YOU POOR THING...
YOU STILL WANT TO FIGHT IO, DON'T YOU? EVEN AFTER ALL YOU'VE LOST...

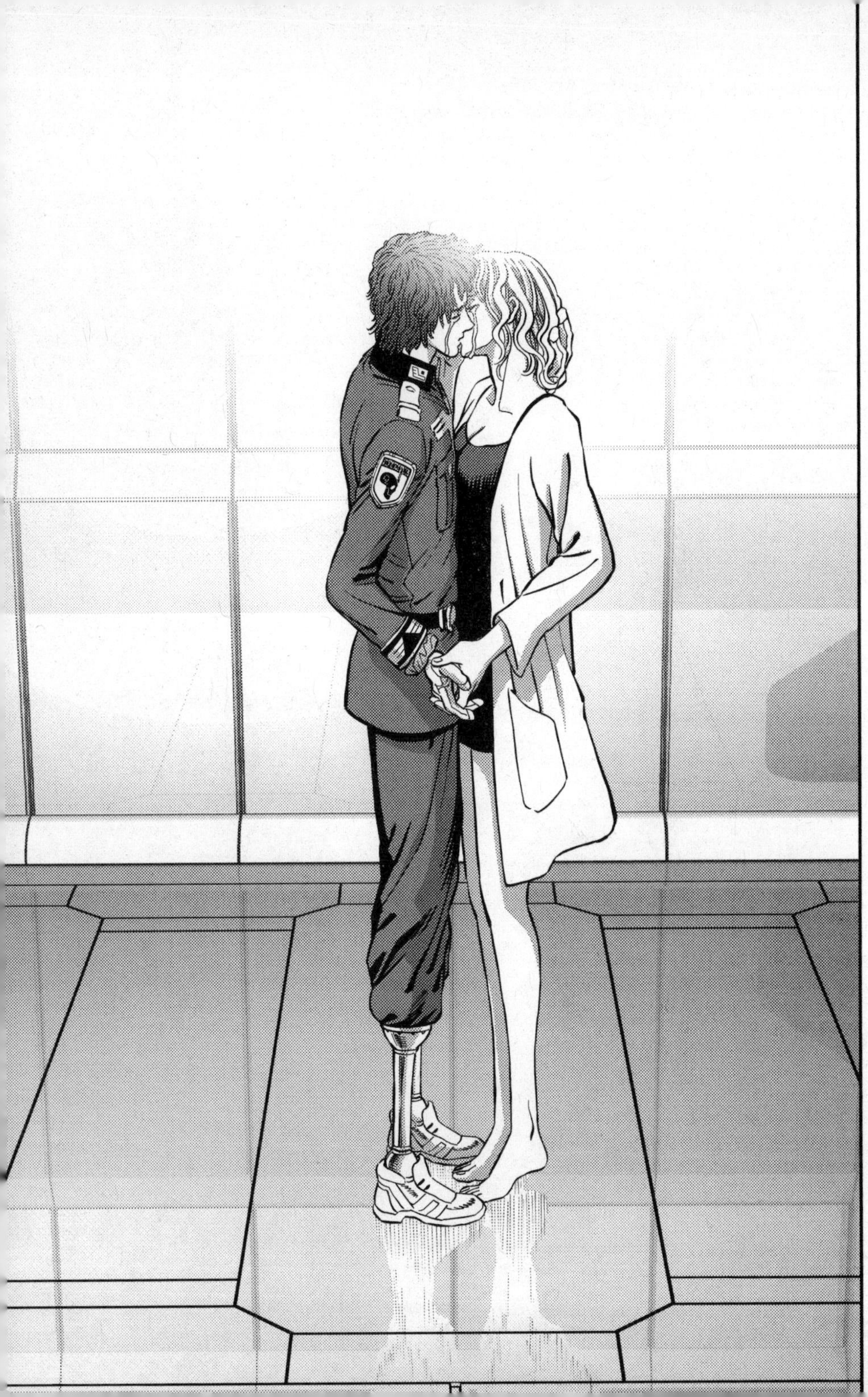

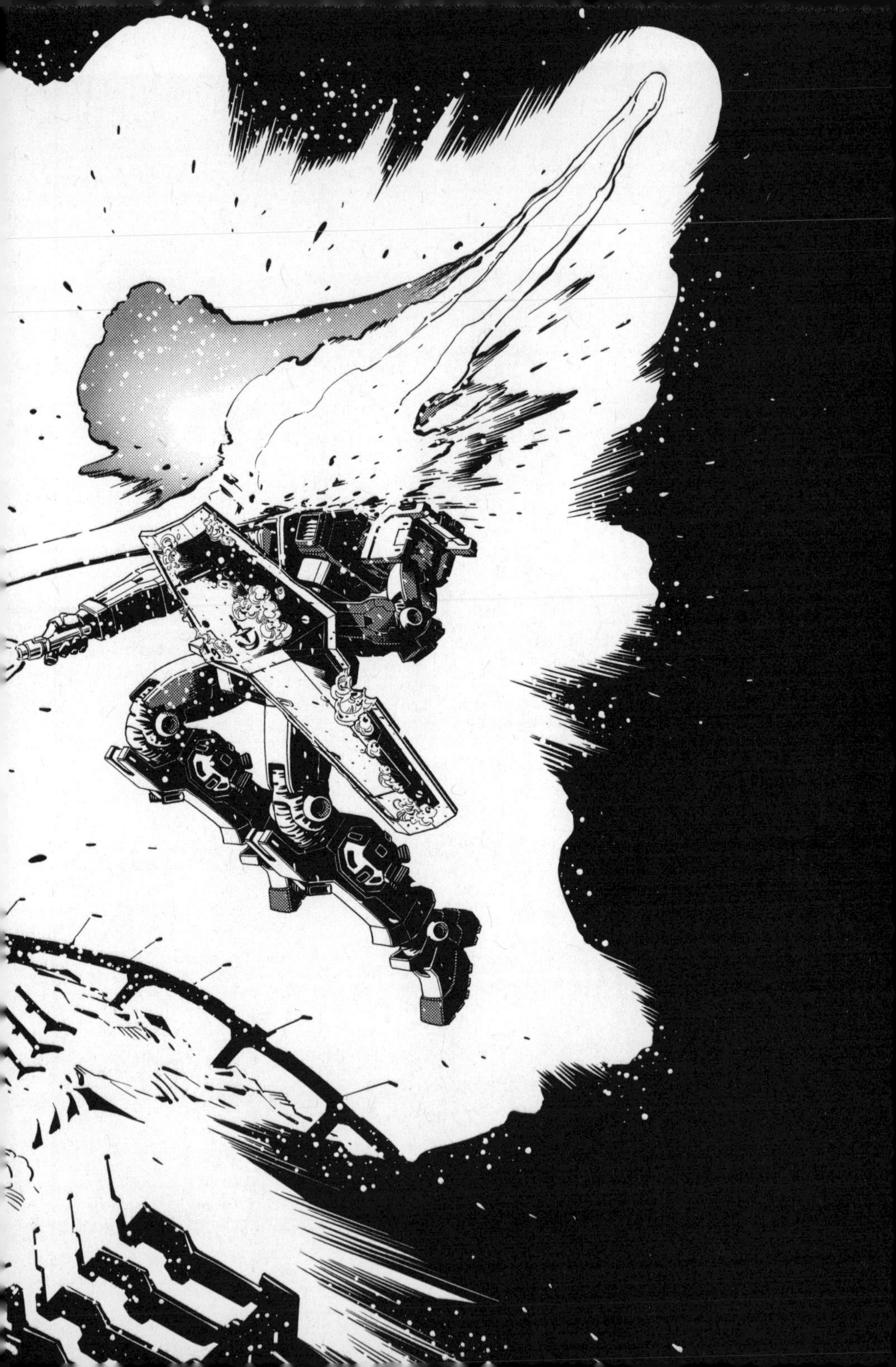

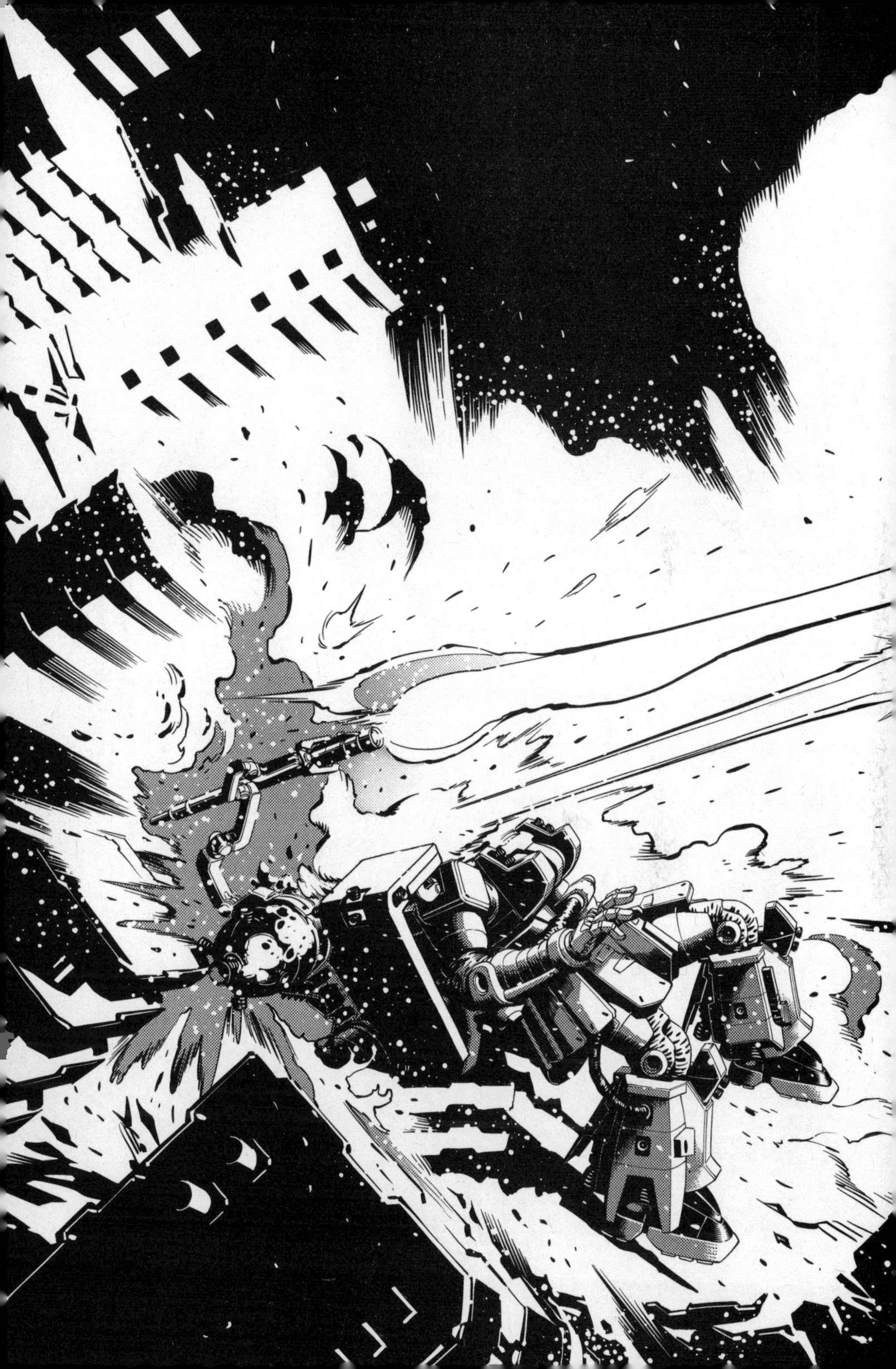

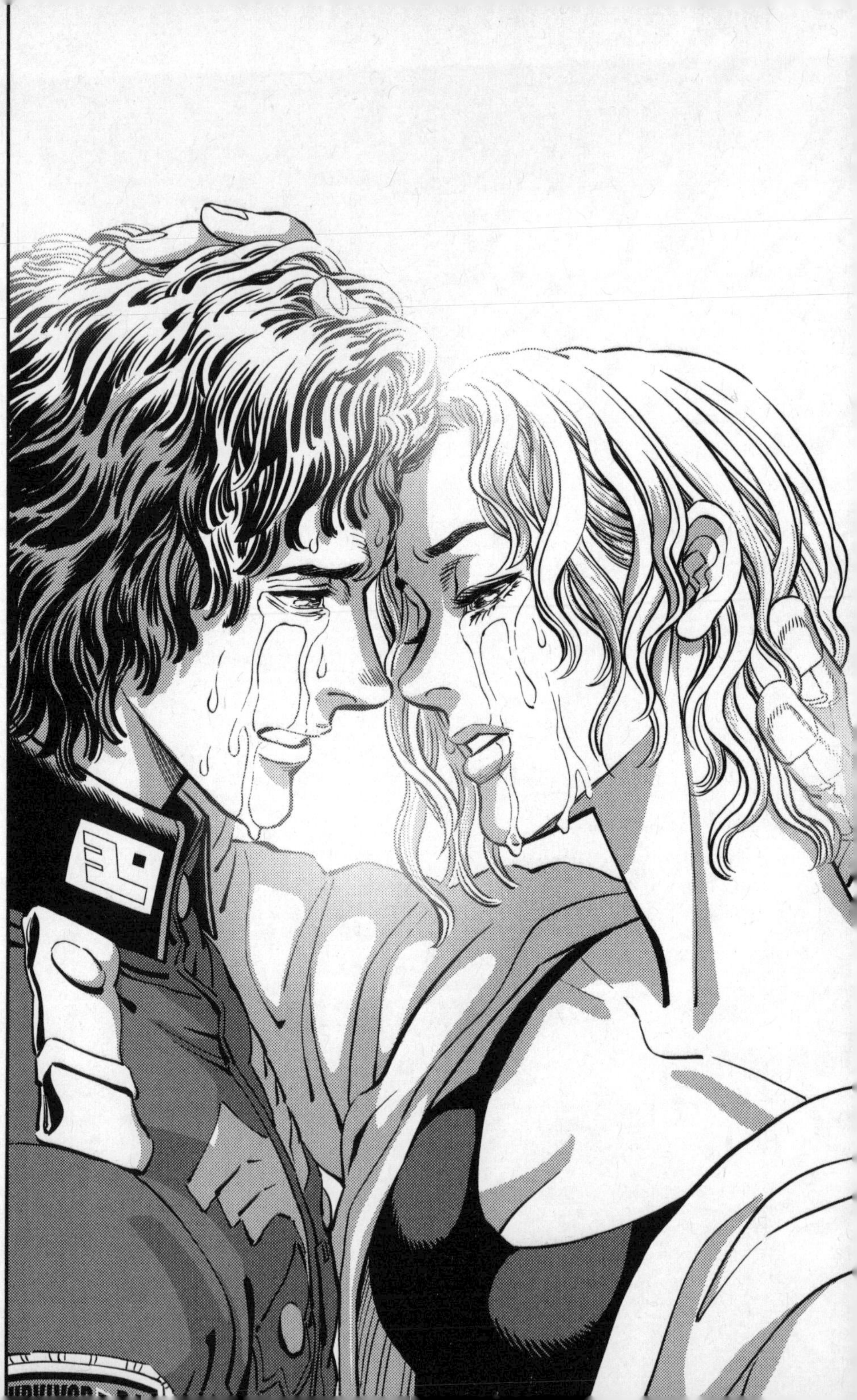

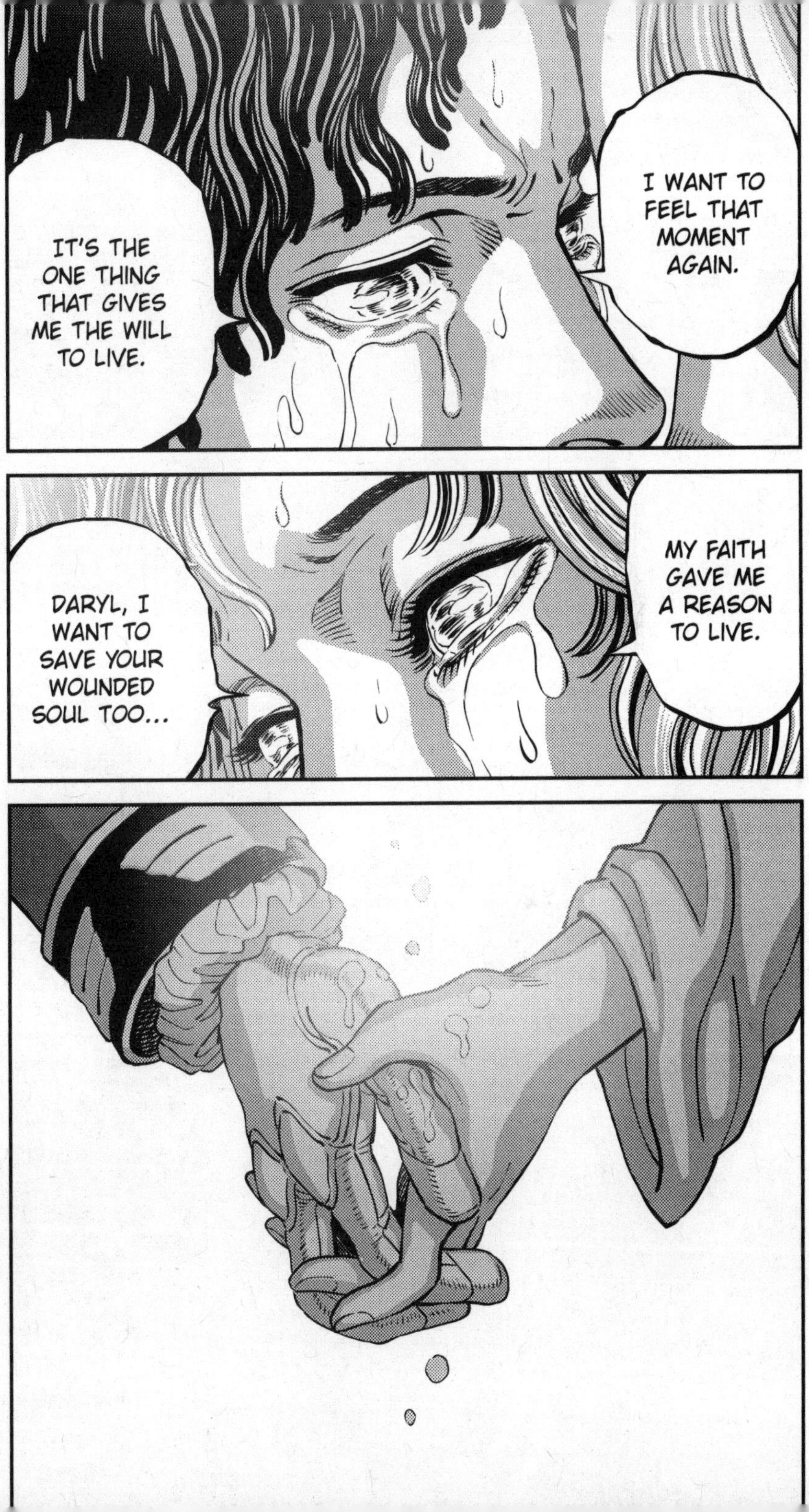
I WANT TO FEEL THAT MOMENT AGAIN.
IT'S THE ONE THING THAT GIVES ME THE WILL TO LIVE.
MY FAITH GAVE ME A REASON TO LIVE.
DARYL, I WANT TO SAVE YOUR WOUNDED SOUL TOO...

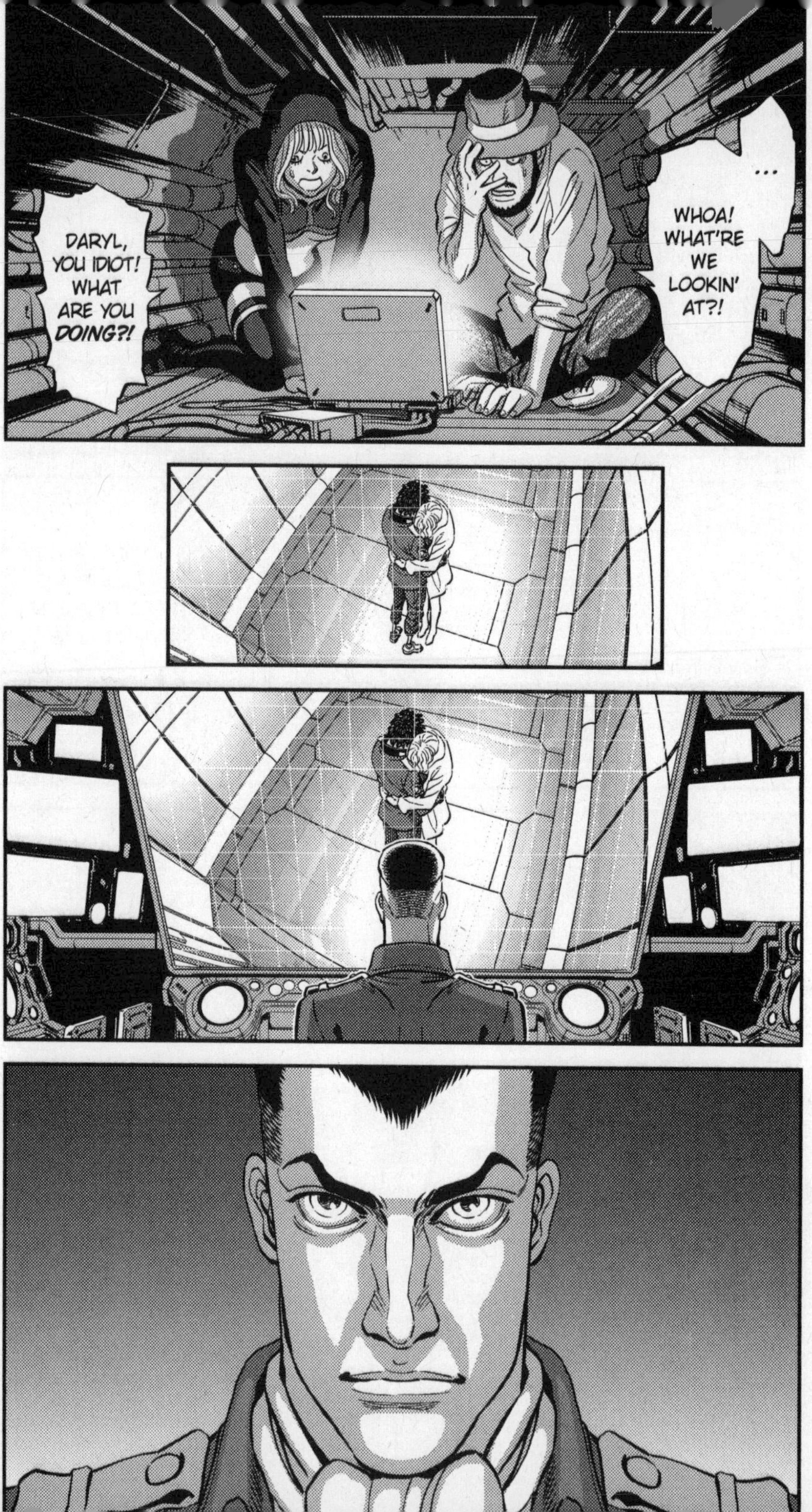
...
WHOA! WHAT'RE WE LOOKIN' AT?!
DARYL, YOU IDIOT! WHAT ARE YOU *DOING?!*

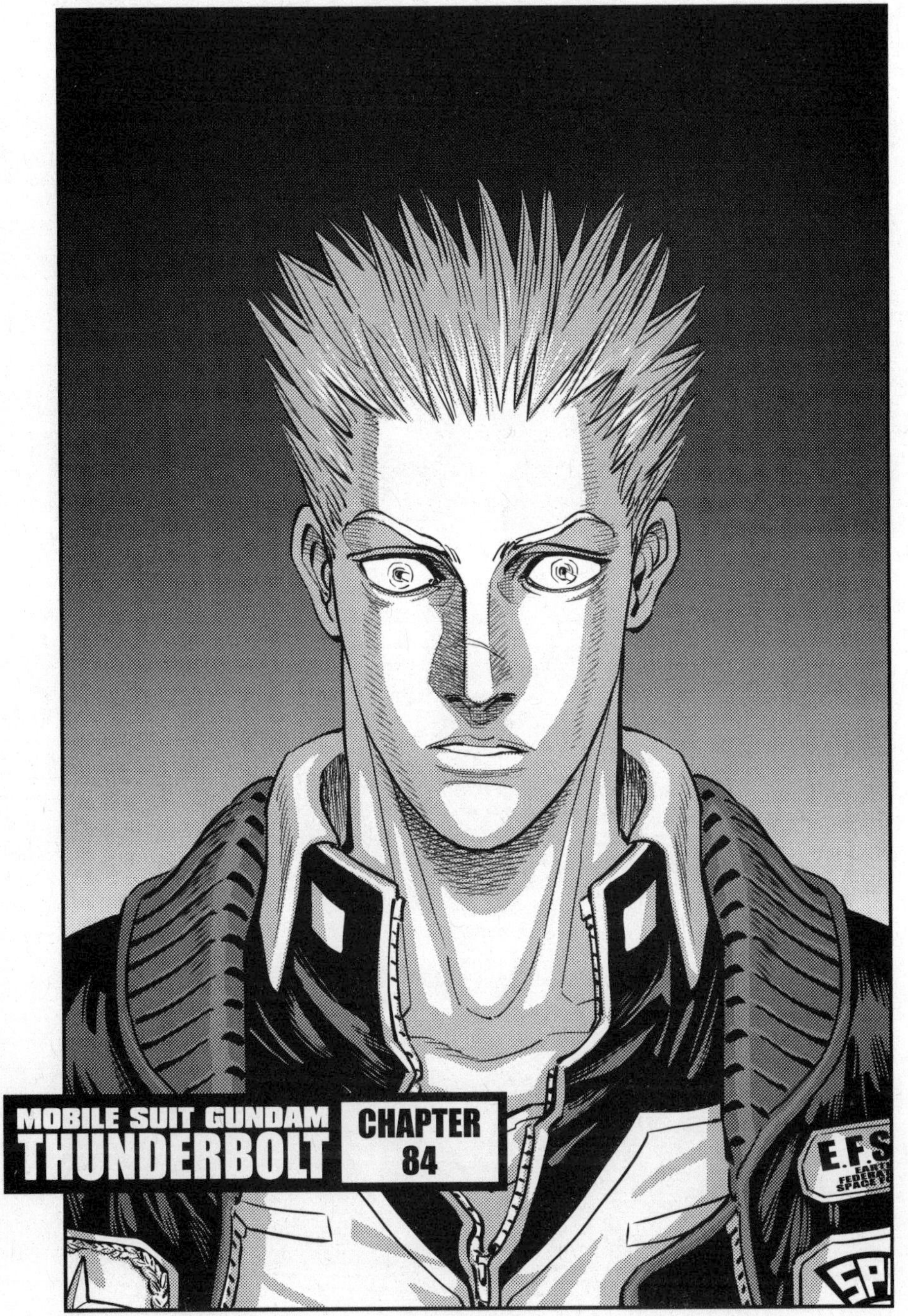
MOBILE SUIT GUNDAM
THUNDERBOLT
CHAPTER
84
E.F.S

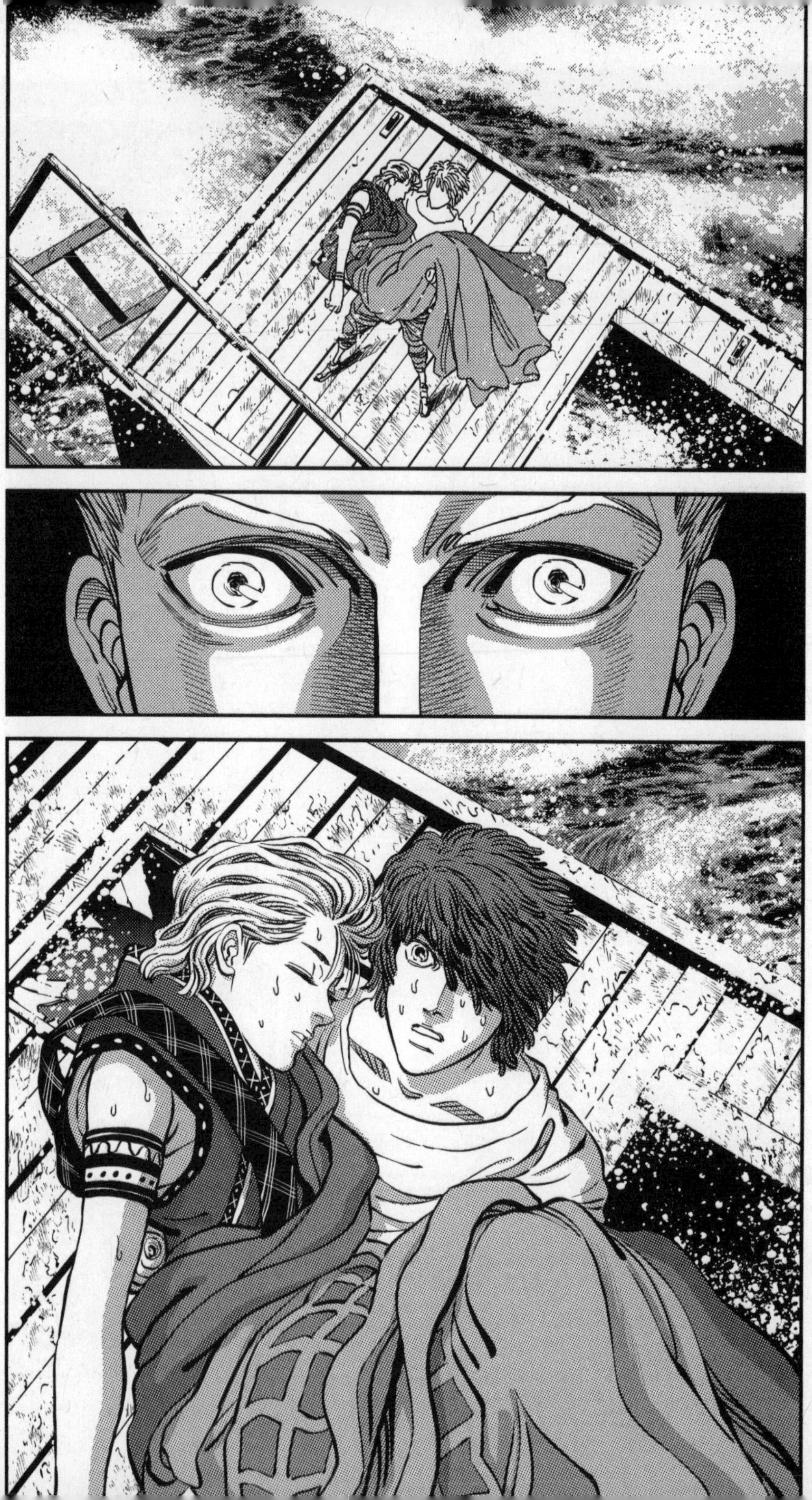

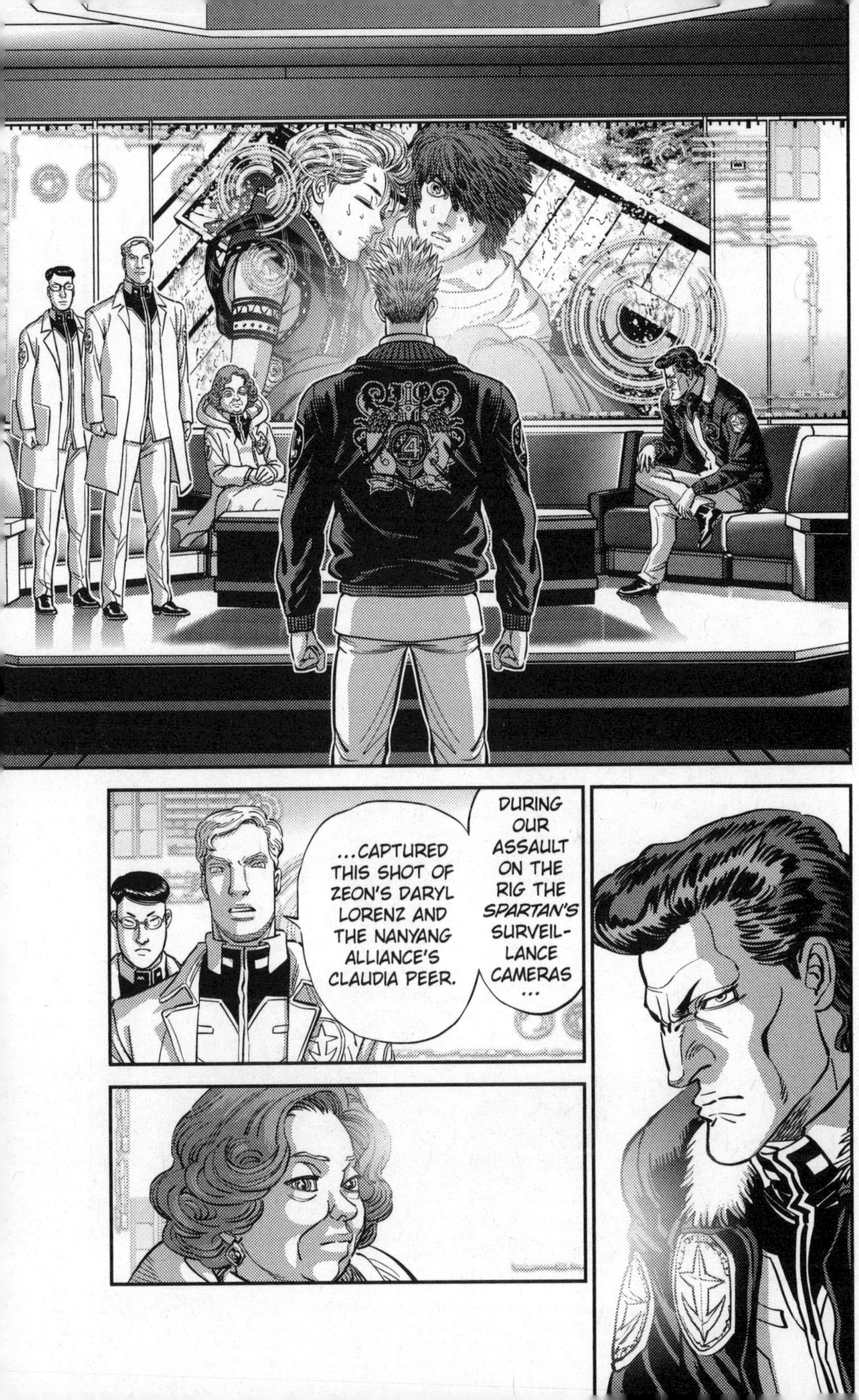
DURING OUR ASSAULT ON THE RIG THE *SPARTAN'S* SURVEIL-LANCE CAMERAS ...
...CAPTURED THIS SHOT OF ZEON'S DARYL LORENZ AND THE NANYANG ALLIANCE'S CLAUDIA PEER.

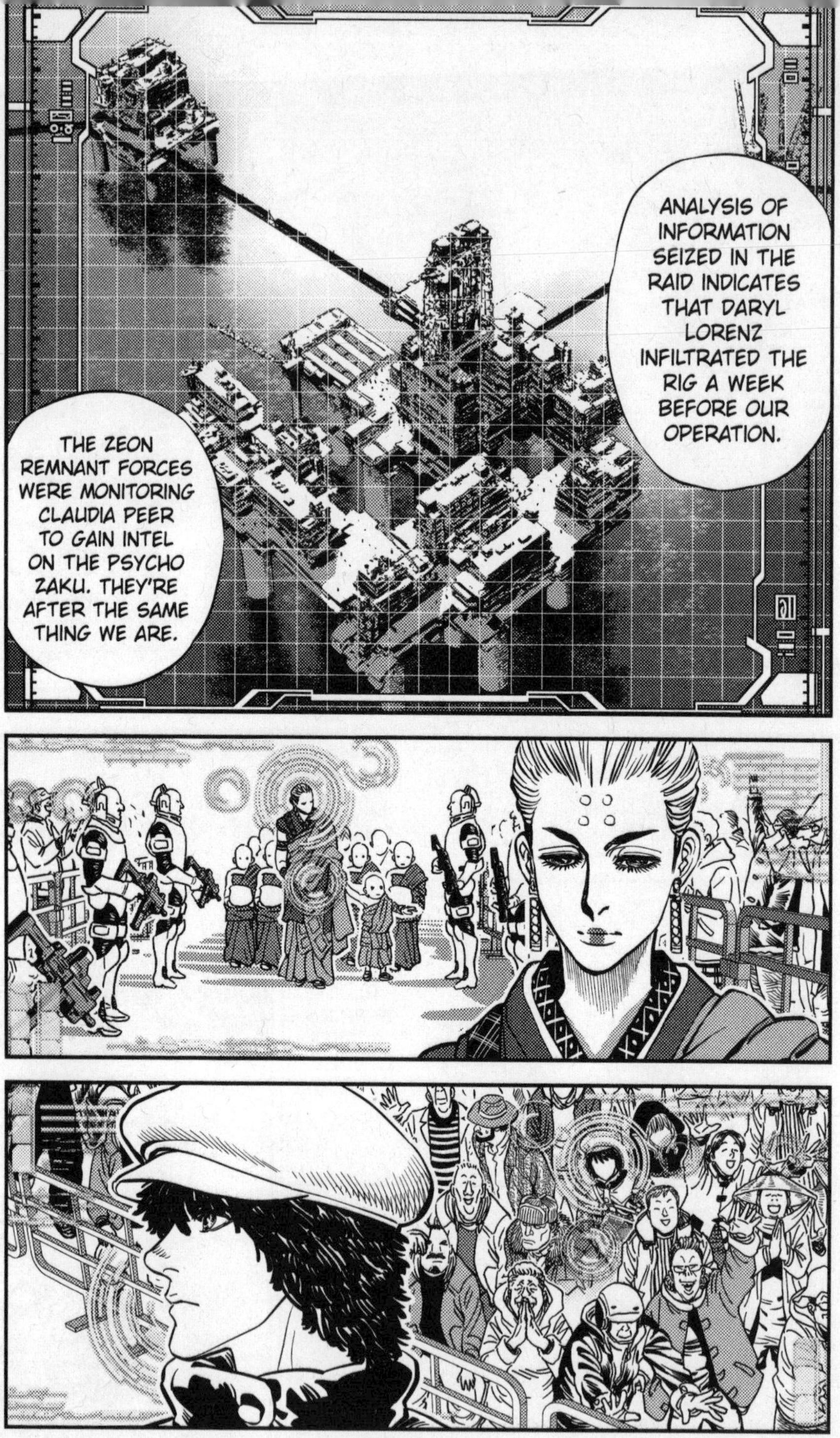
ANALYSIS OF INFORMATION SEIZED IN THE RAID INDICATES THAT DARYL LORENZ INFILTRATED THE RIG A WEEK BEFORE OUR OPERATION.
THE ZEON REMNANT FORCES WERE MONITORING CLAUDIA PEER TO GAIN INTEL ON THE PSYCHO ZAKU. THEY'RE AFTER THE SAME THING WE ARE.

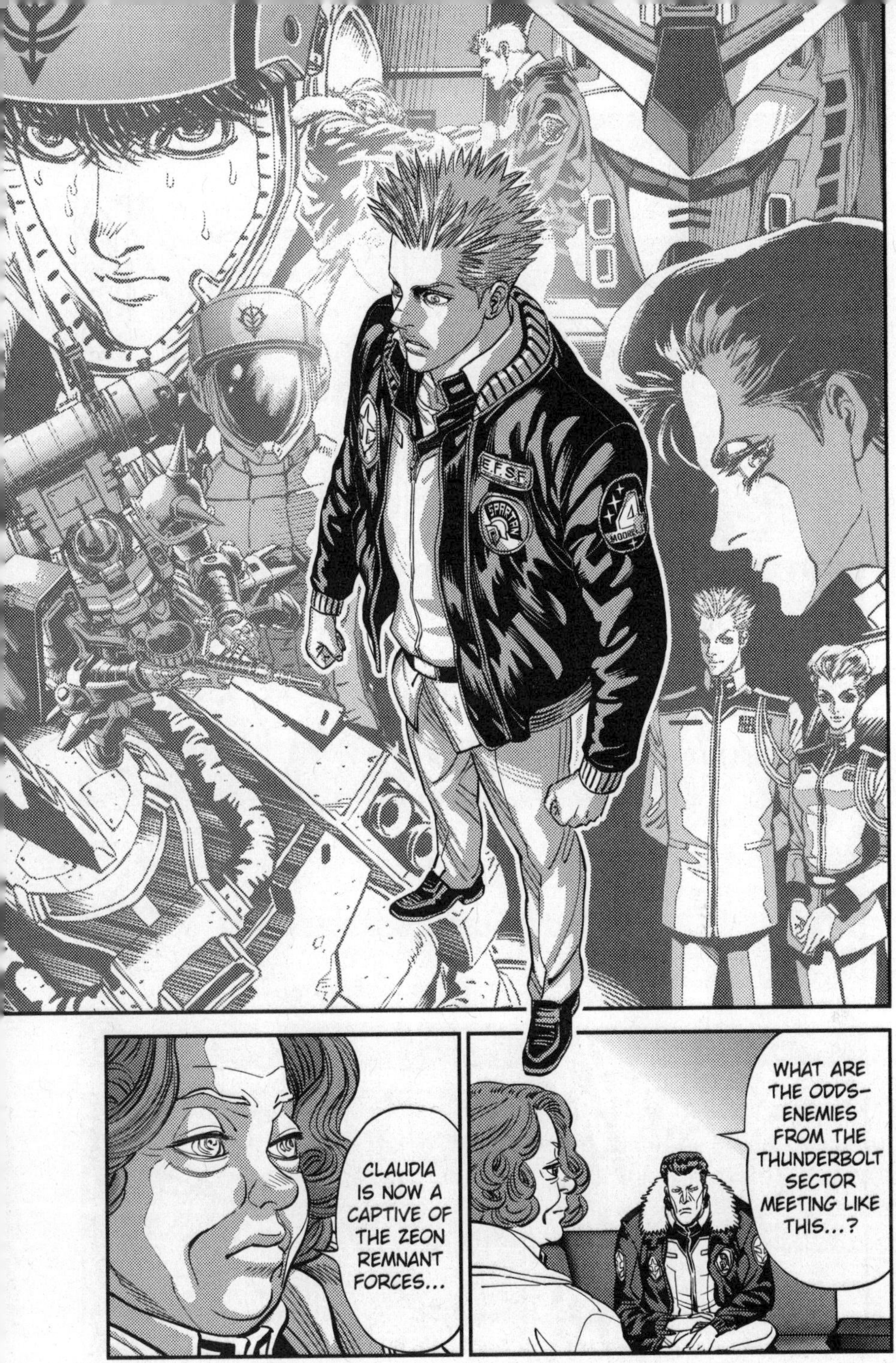
E.F.S.F.
SPARTAN
WHAT ARE THE ODDS—ENEMIES FROM THE THUNDERBOLT SECTOR MEETING LIKE THIS...?
CLAUDIA IS NOW A CAPTIVE OF THE ZEON REMNANT FORCES...

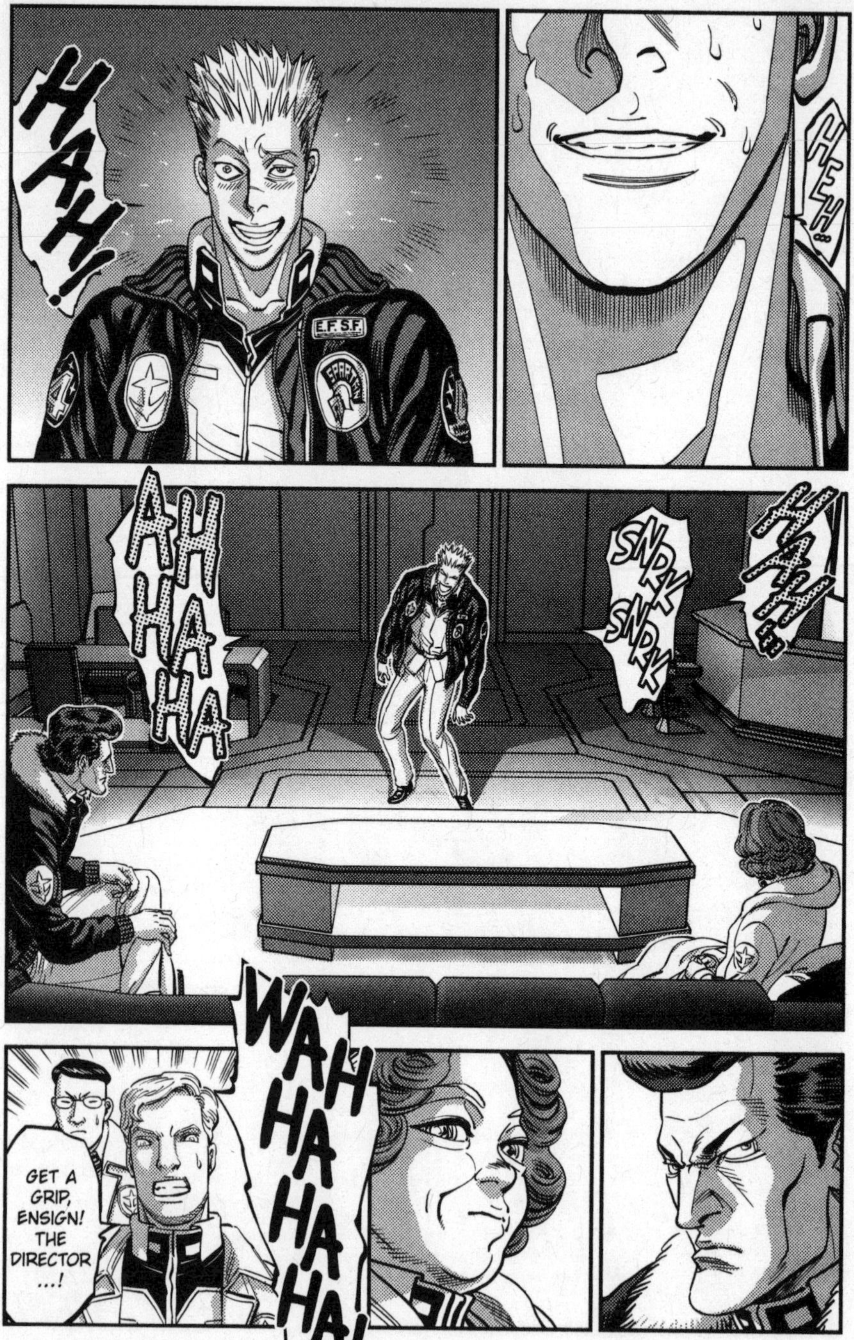
HEH...
HAH!
SNRK SNRK
AH HA HA HA
WAH HA HA HA HA!
GET A GRIP, ENSIGN! THE DIRECTOR ...!

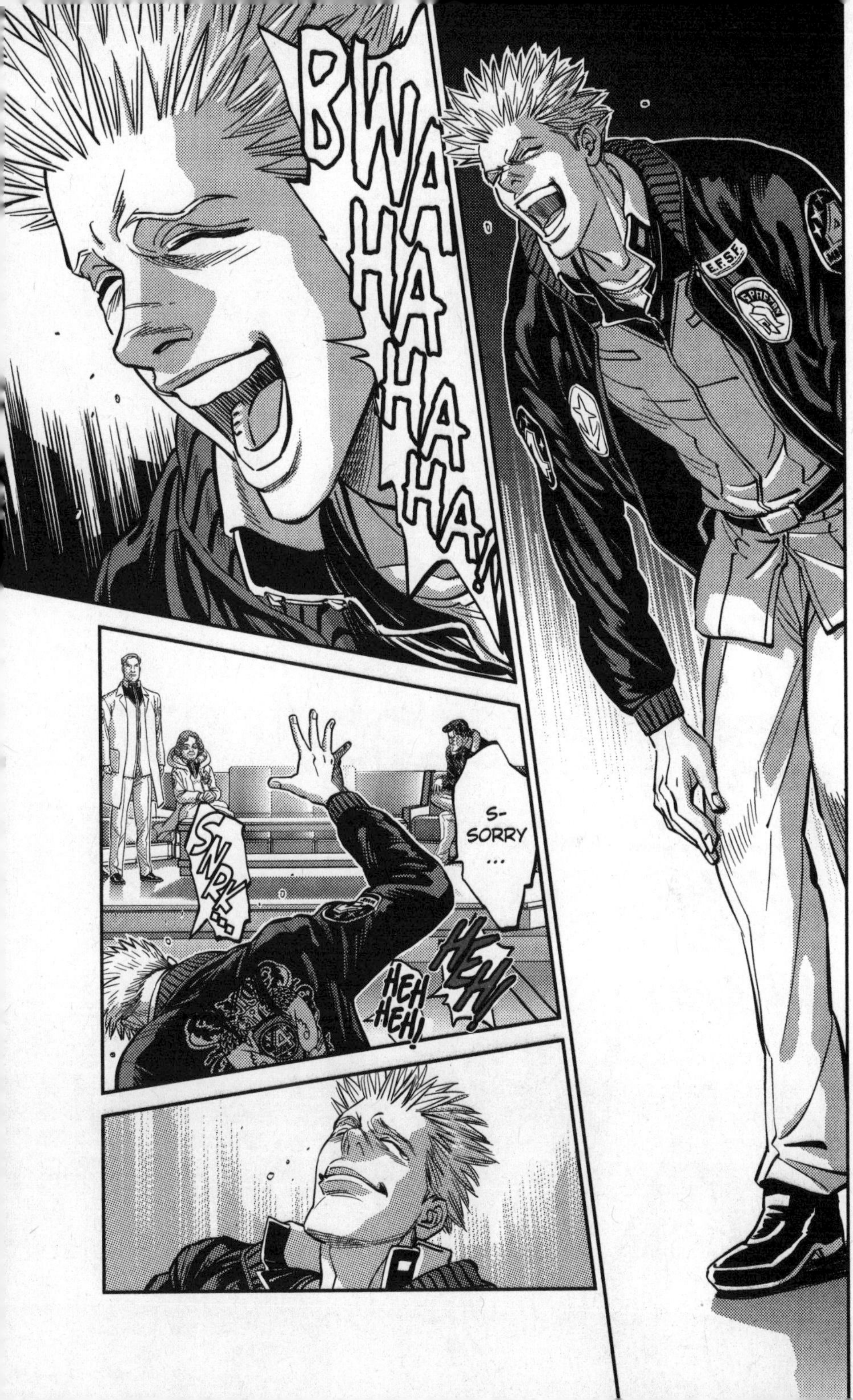
BWAHAHAHAHAHA!
S-SORRY...
SNRK...
HEH!
HEH HEH!

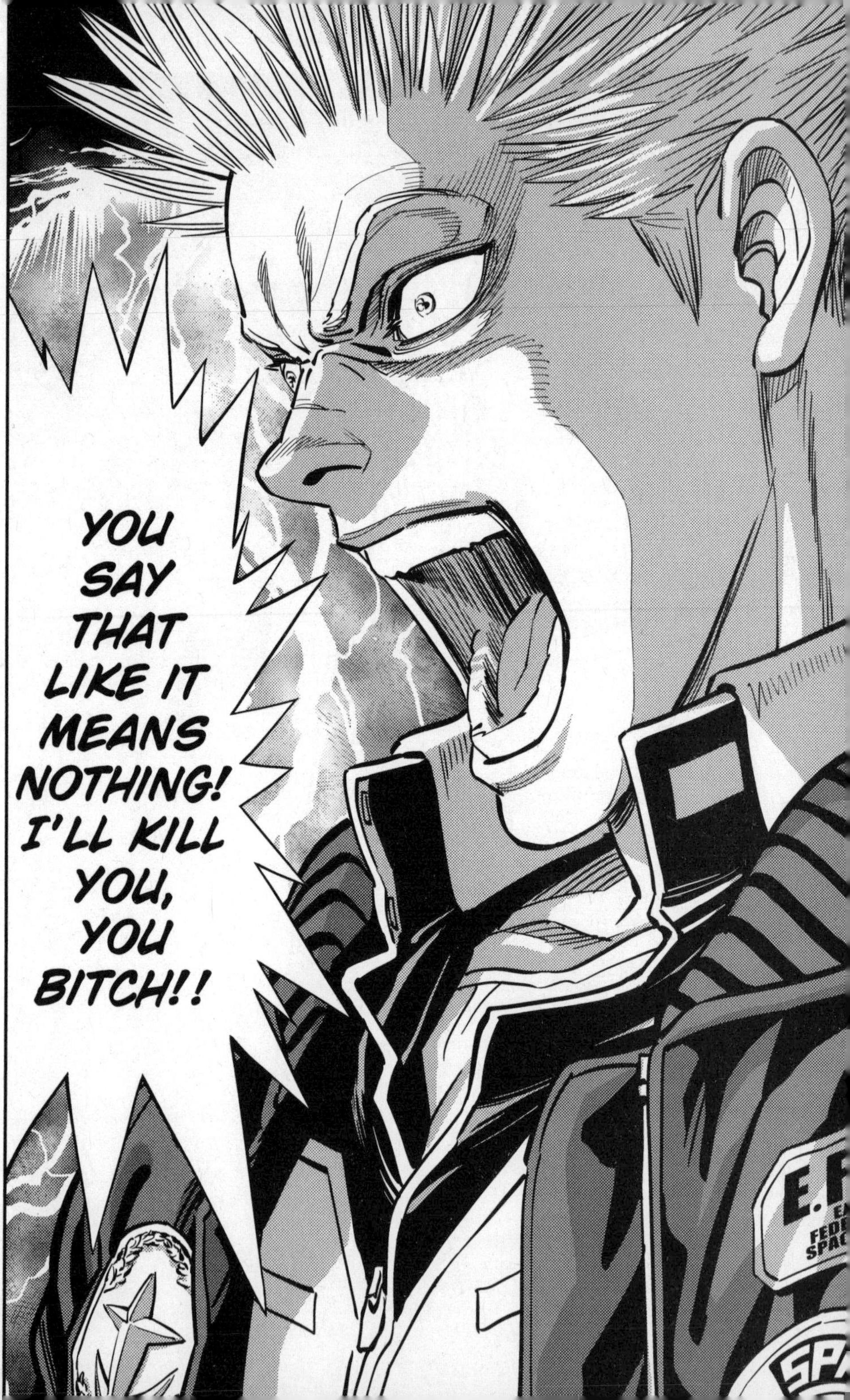
YOU SAY THAT LIKE IT MEANS NOTHING! I'LL KILL YOU, YOU BITCH!!

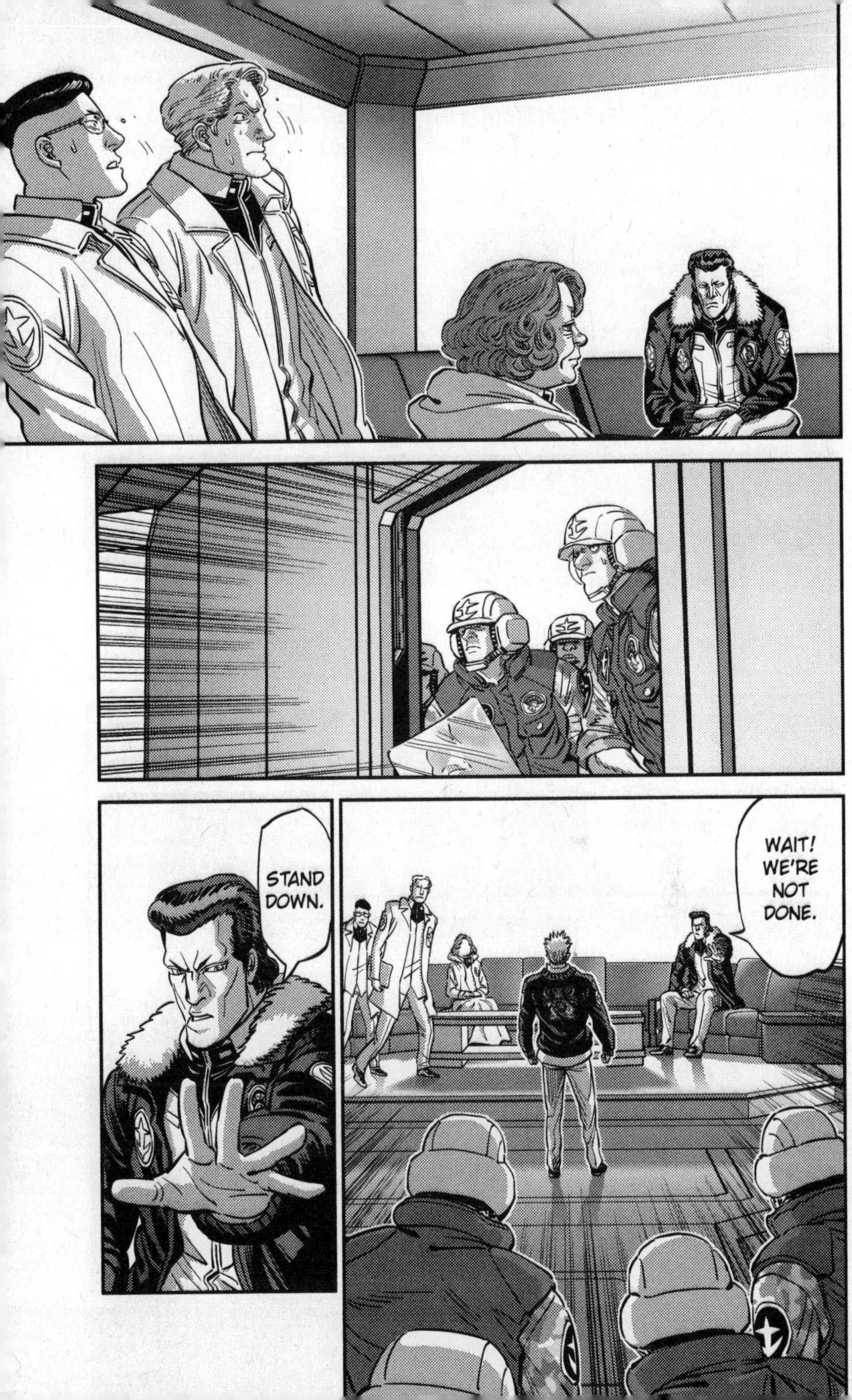
WAIT! WE'RE NOT DONE.
STAND DOWN.

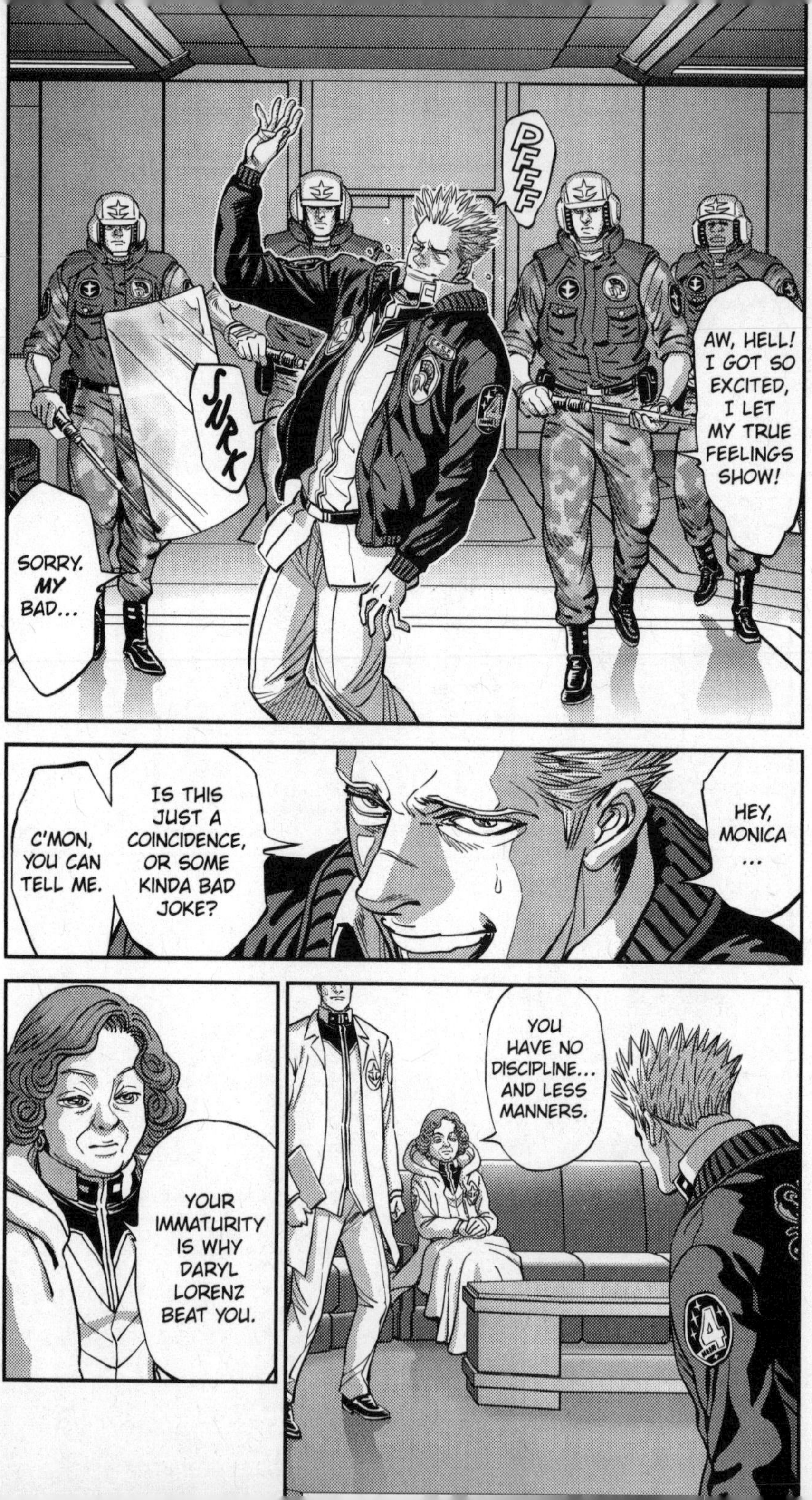
PFFF
AW, HELL! I GOT SO EXCITED, I LET MY TRUE FEELINGS SHOW!
SNRK
SORRY. MY BAD...
HEY, MONICA ...
IS THIS JUST A COINCIDENCE, OR SOME KINDA BAD JOKE?
C'MON, YOU CAN TELL ME.
YOU HAVE NO DISCIPLINE... AND LESS MANNERS.
YOUR IMMATURITY IS WHY DARYL LORENZ BEAT YOU.

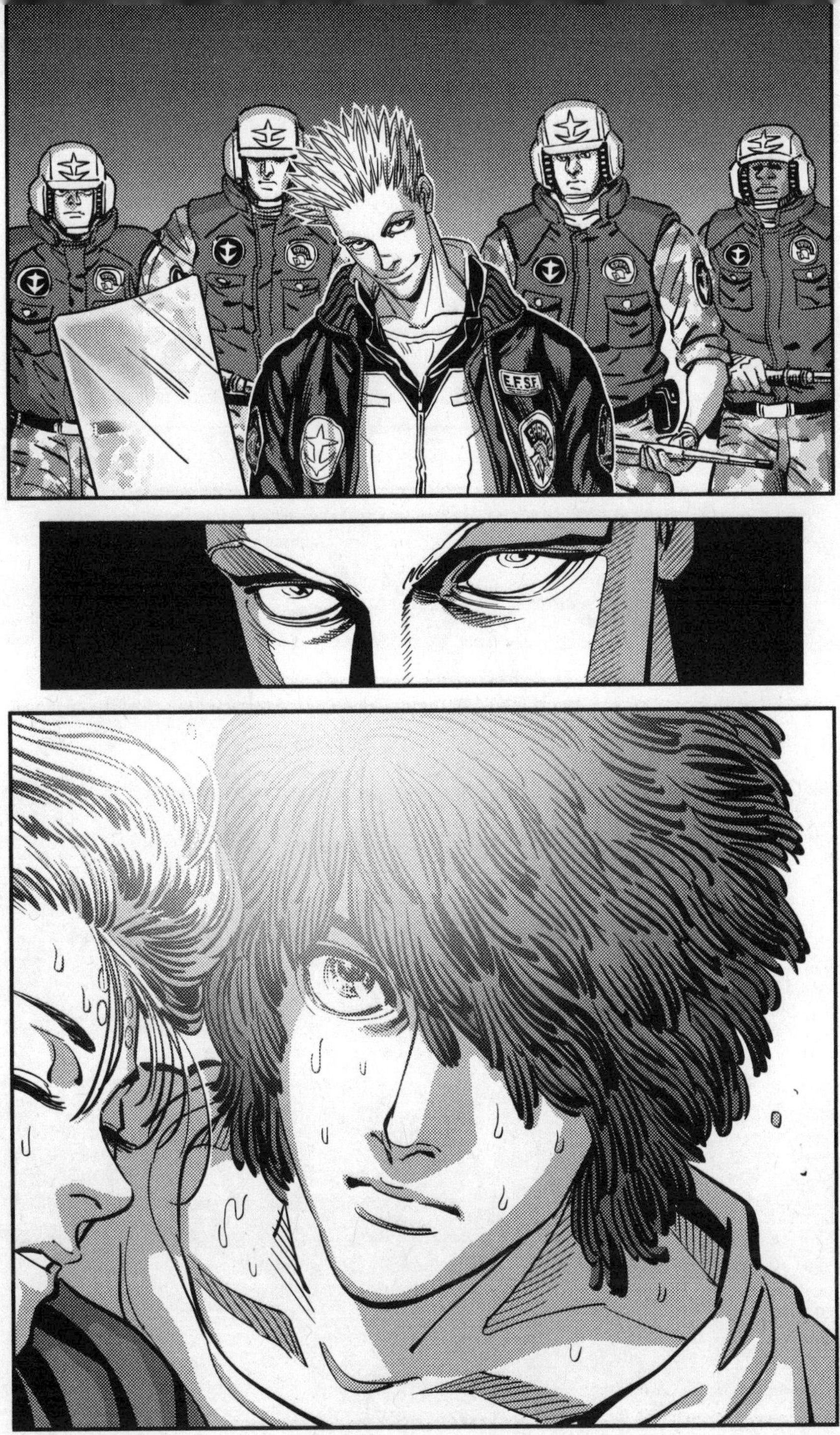
E.F.S.F.

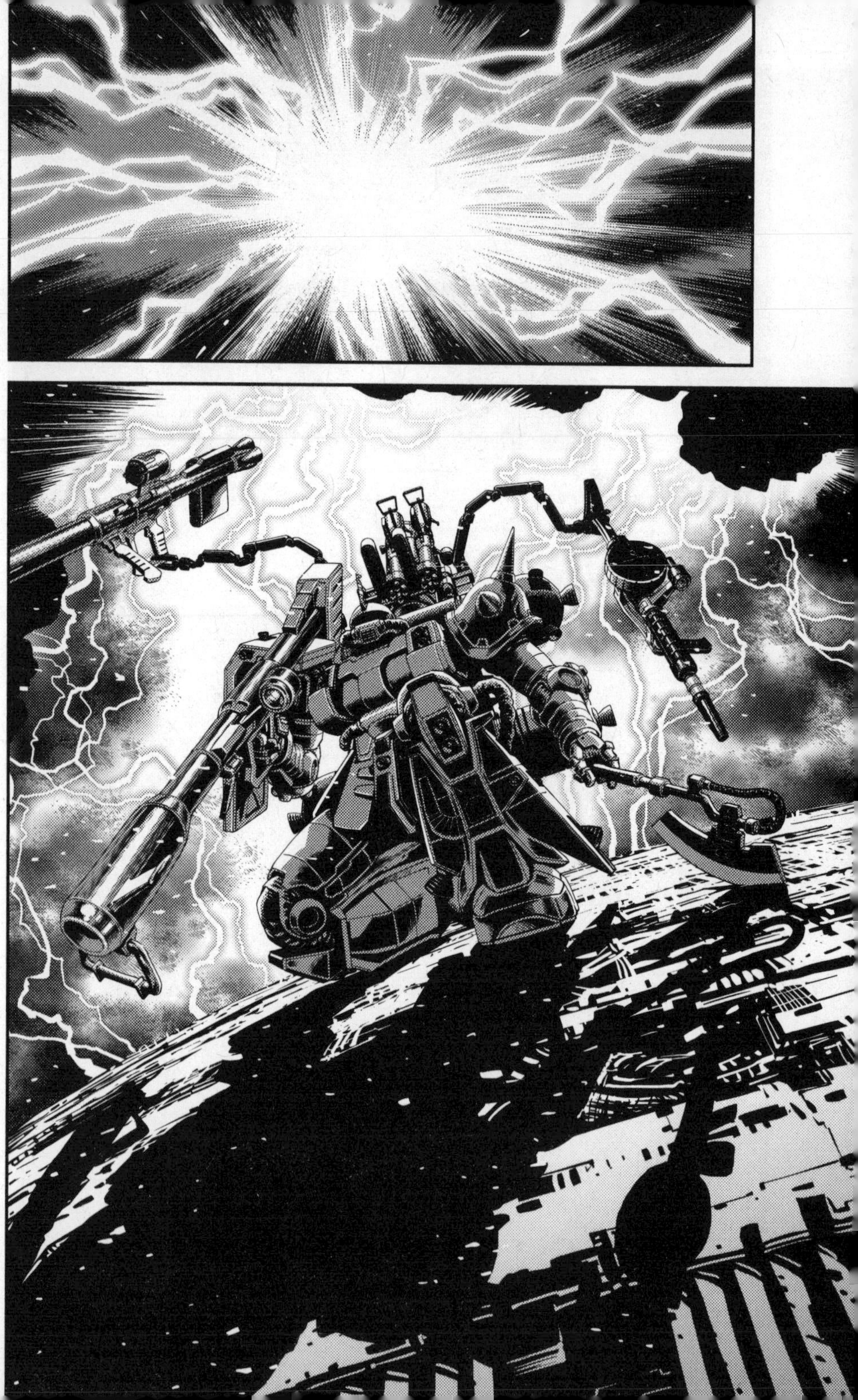

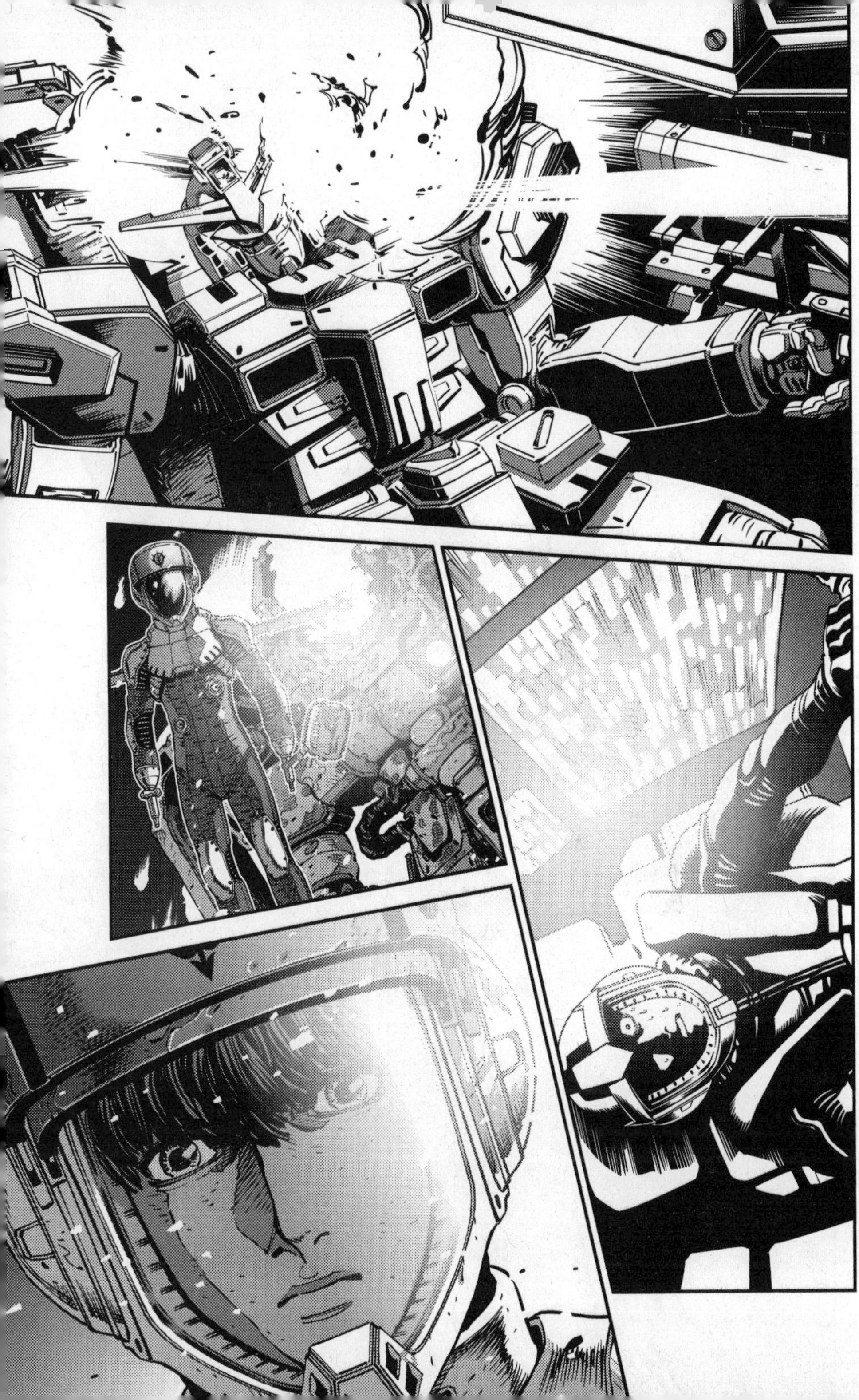

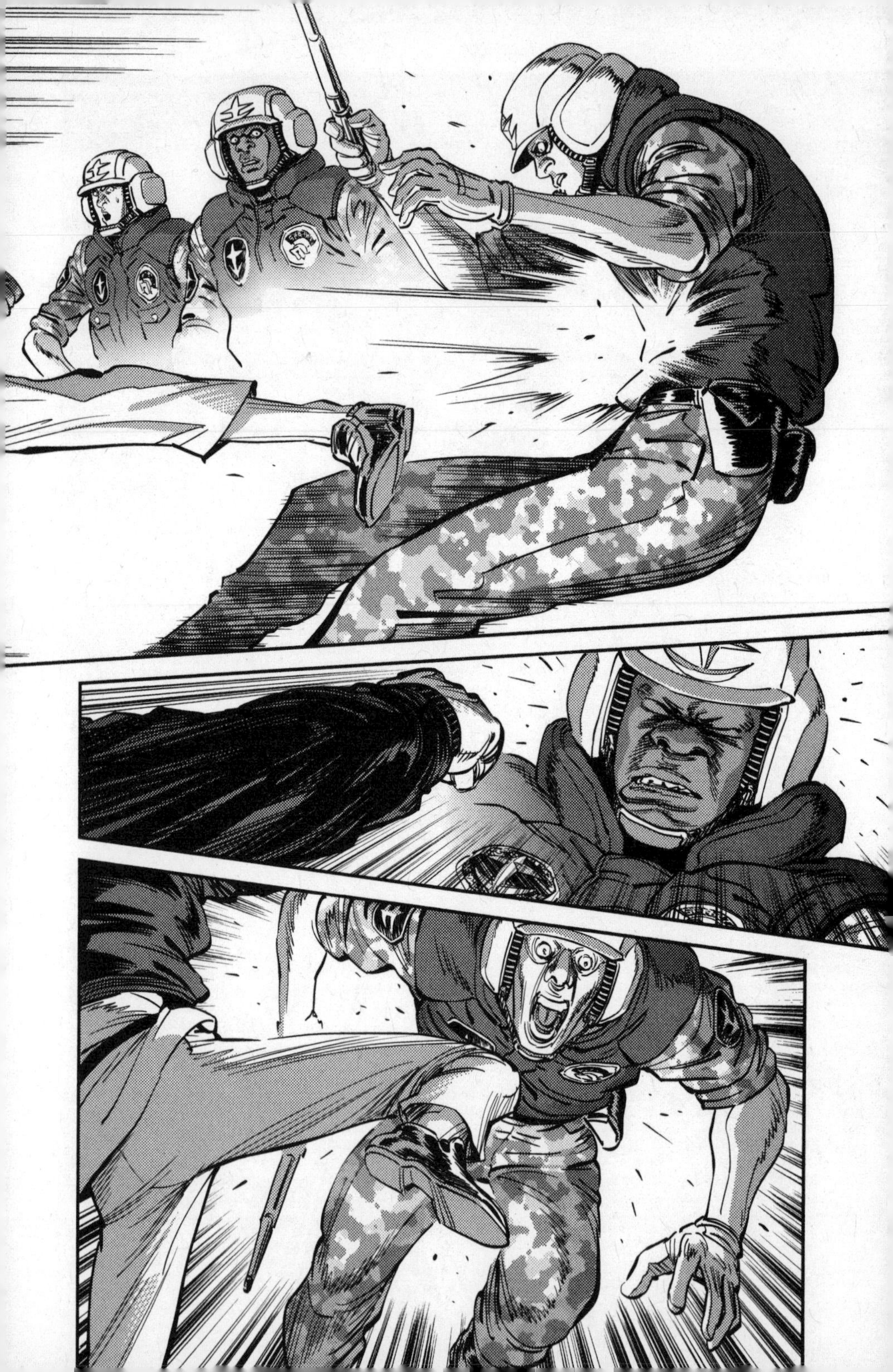

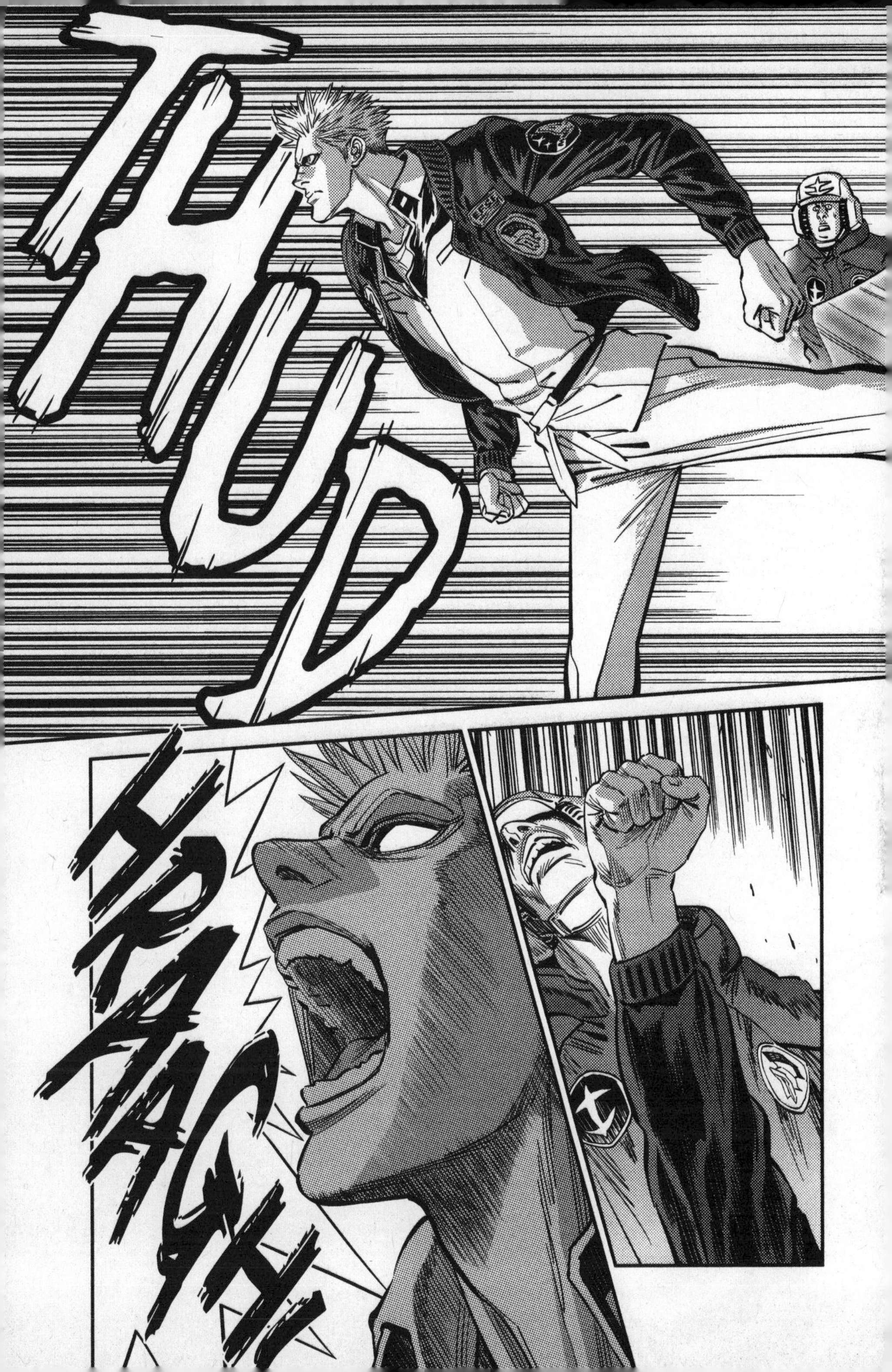
THUD
HRAAGH!

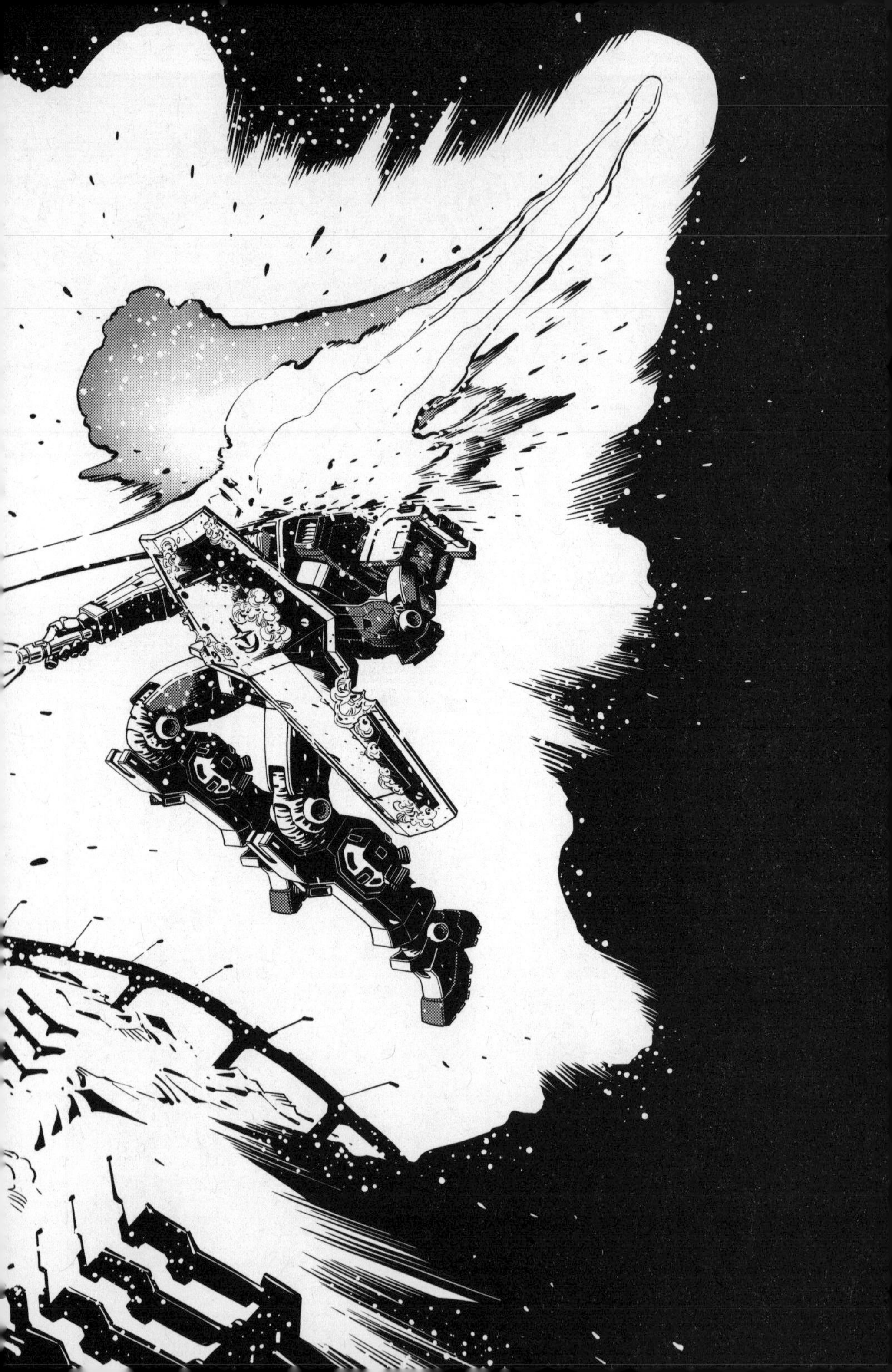

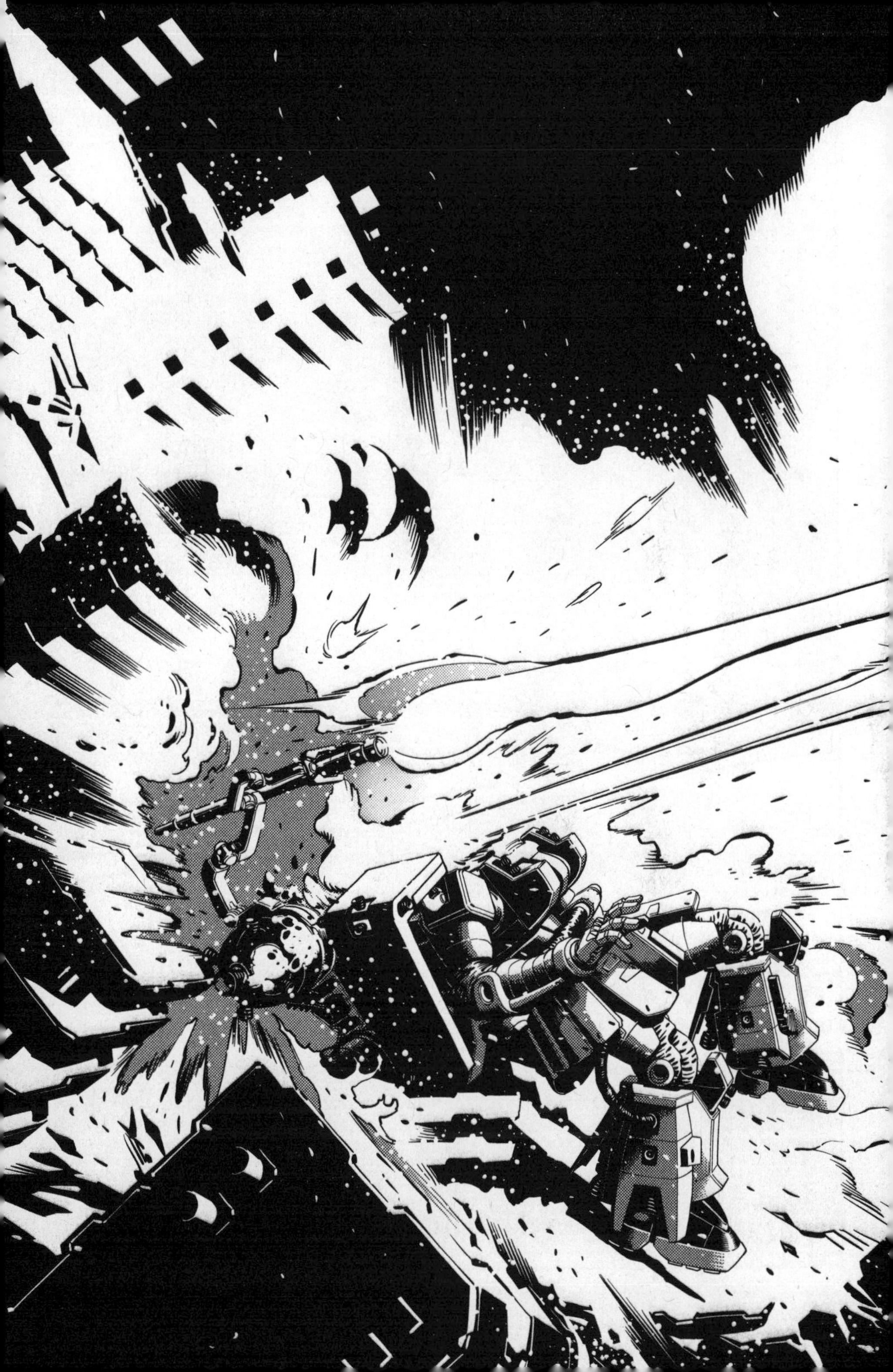

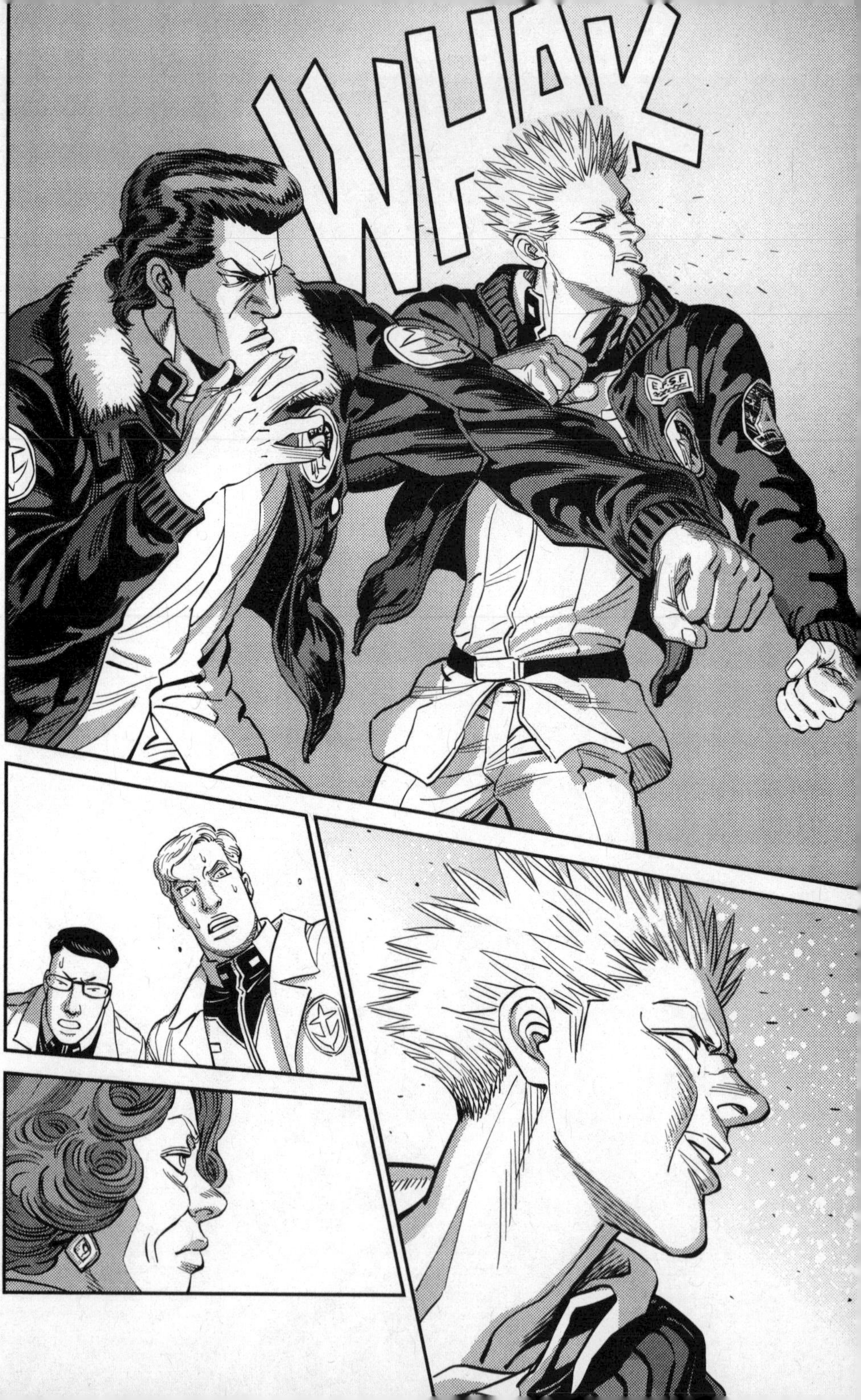
WHAK
E.F.S.F

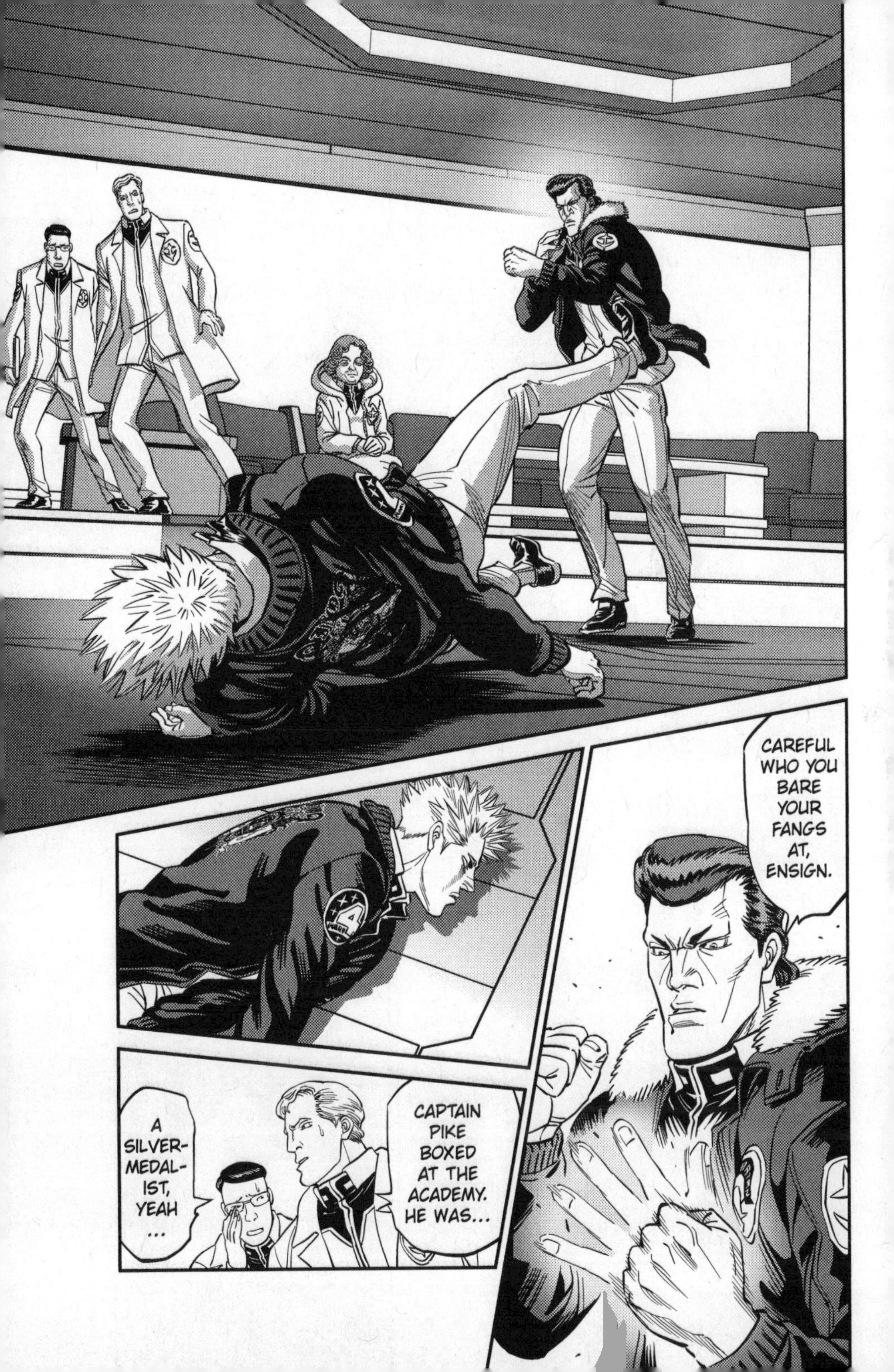
CAREFUL WHO YOU BARE YOUR FANGS AT, ENSIGN.
CAPTAIN PIKE BOXED AT THE ACADEMY. HE WAS...
A SILVER-MEDALIST, YEAH...

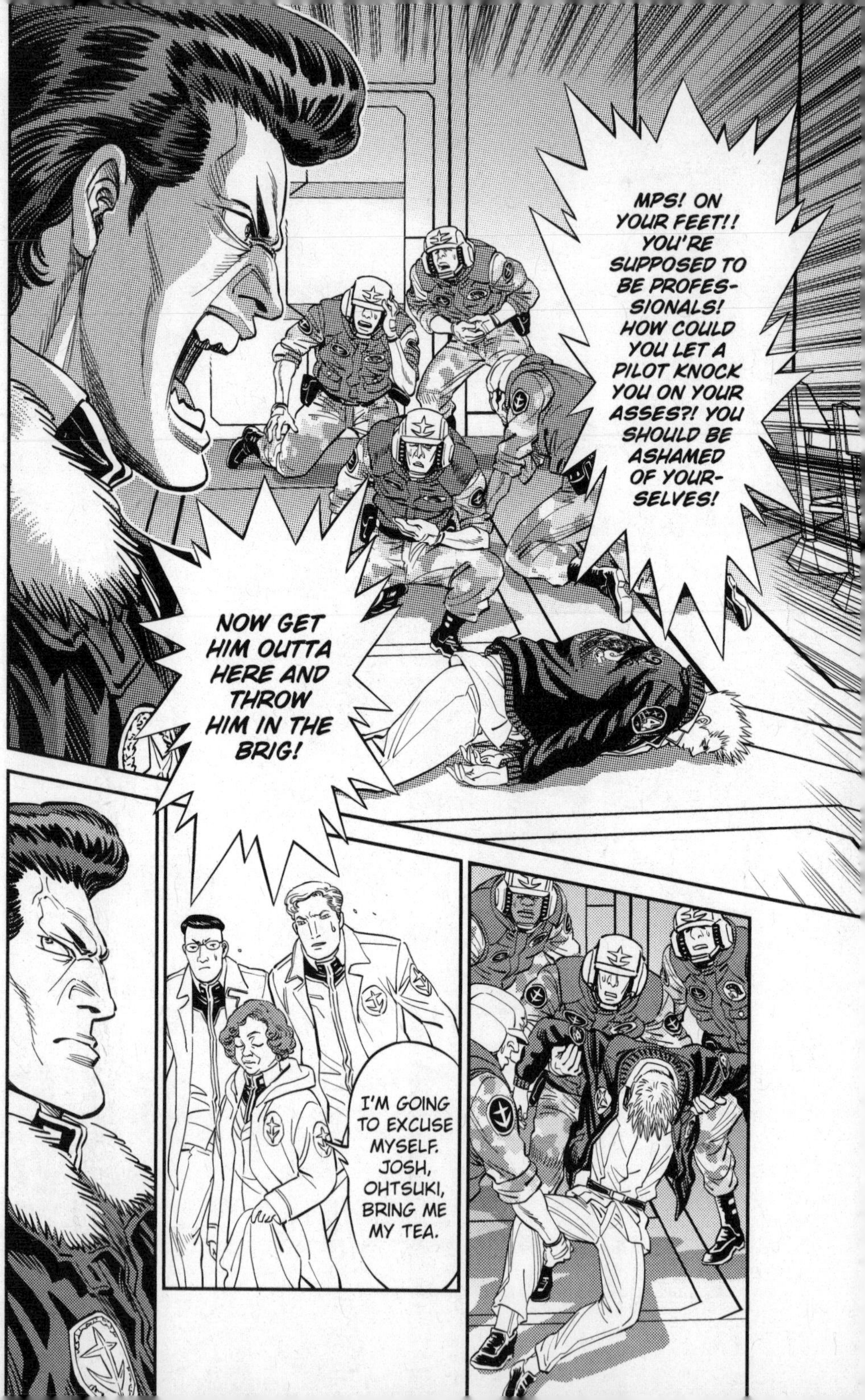
MPS! ON YOUR FEET!! YOU'RE SUPPOSED TO BE PROFES-SIONALS! HOW COULD YOU LET A PILOT KNOCK YOU ON YOUR ASSES?! YOU SHOULD BE ASHAMED OF YOUR-SELVES!
NOW GET HIM OUTTA HERE AND THROW HIM IN THE BRIG!
I'M GOING TO EXCUSE MYSELF. JOSH, OHTSUKI, BRING ME MY TEA.

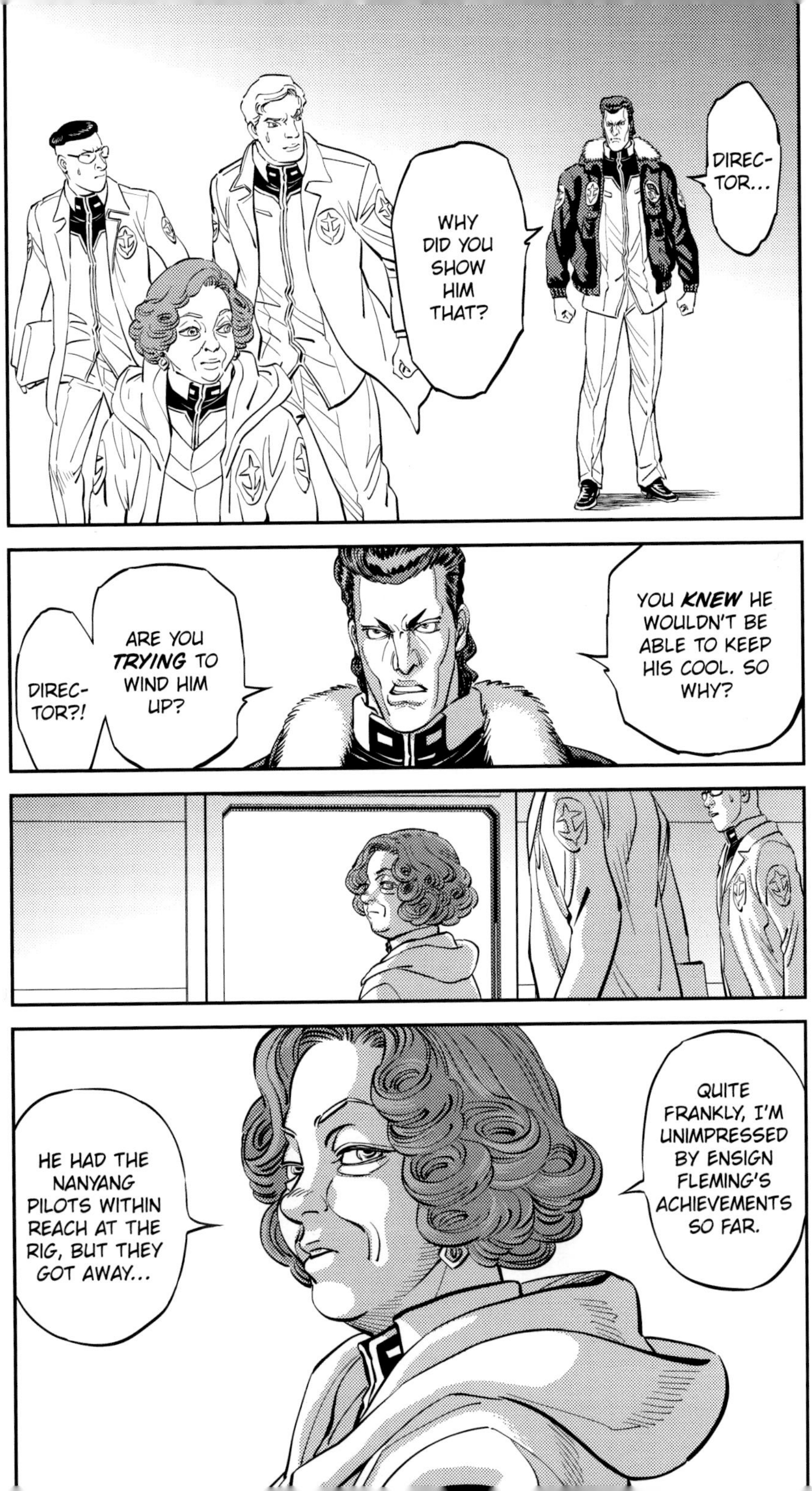
DIREC-TOR...
WHY DID YOU SHOW HIM THAT?
YOU KNEW HE WOULDN'T BE ABLE TO KEEP HIS COOL. SO WHY?
ARE YOU TRYING TO WIND HIM UP?
DIREC-TOR?!
QUITE FRANKLY, I'M UNIMPRESSED BY ENSIGN FLEMING'S ACHIEVEMENTS SO FAR.
HE HAD THE NANYANG PILOTS WITHIN REACH AT THE RIG, BUT THEY GOT AWAY...

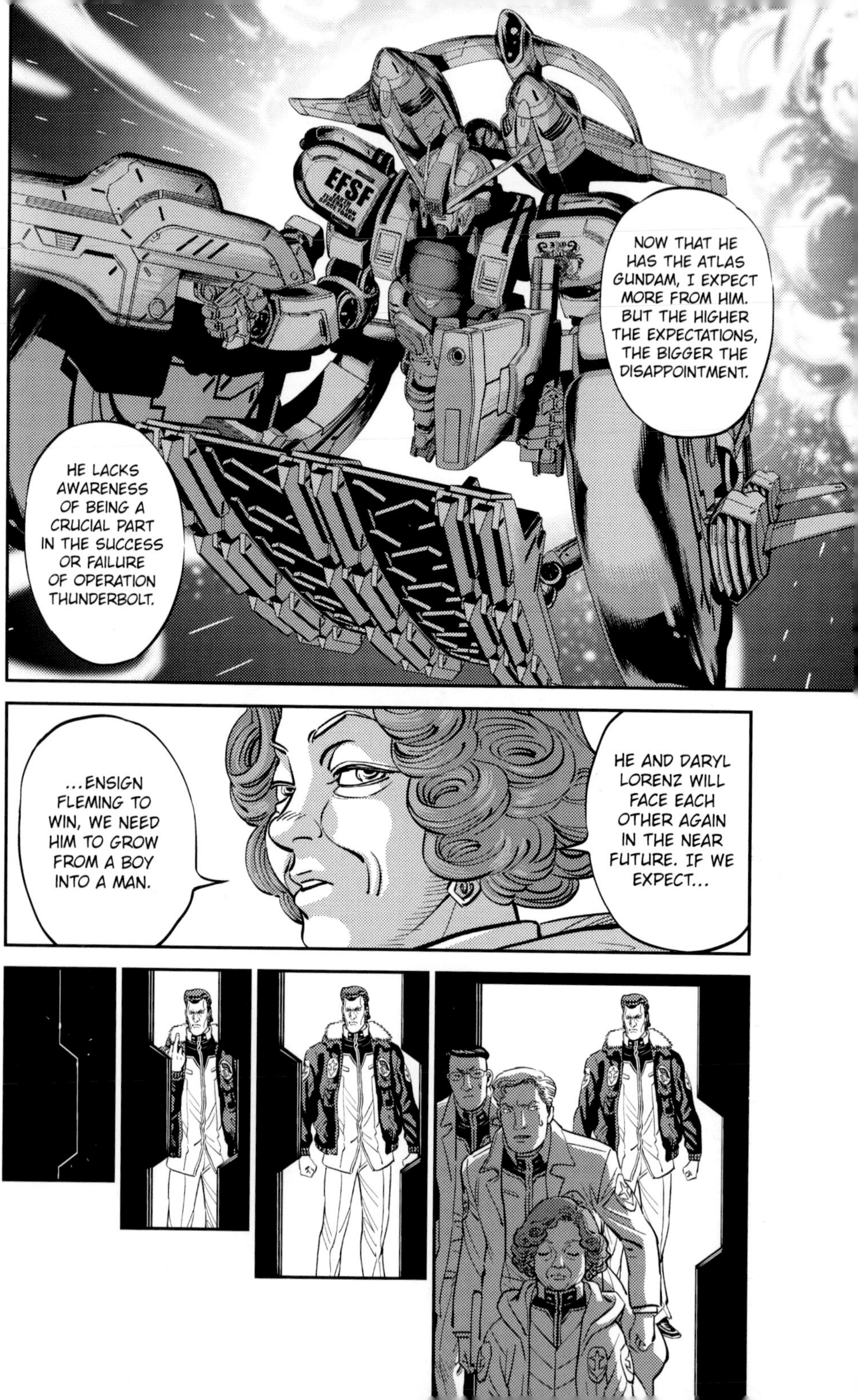
NOW THAT HE HAS THE ATLAS GUNDAM, I EXPECT MORE FROM HIM. BUT THE HIGHER THE EXPECTATIONS, THE BIGGER THE DISAPPOINTMENT.
HE LACKS AWARENESS OF BEING A CRUCIAL PART IN THE SUCCESS OR FAILURE OF OPERATION THUNDERBOLT.
HE AND DARYL LORENZ WILL FACE EACH OTHER AGAIN IN THE NEAR FUTURE. IF WE EXPECT...
...ENSIGN FLEMING TO WIN, WE NEED HIM TO GROW FROM A BOY INTO A MAN.

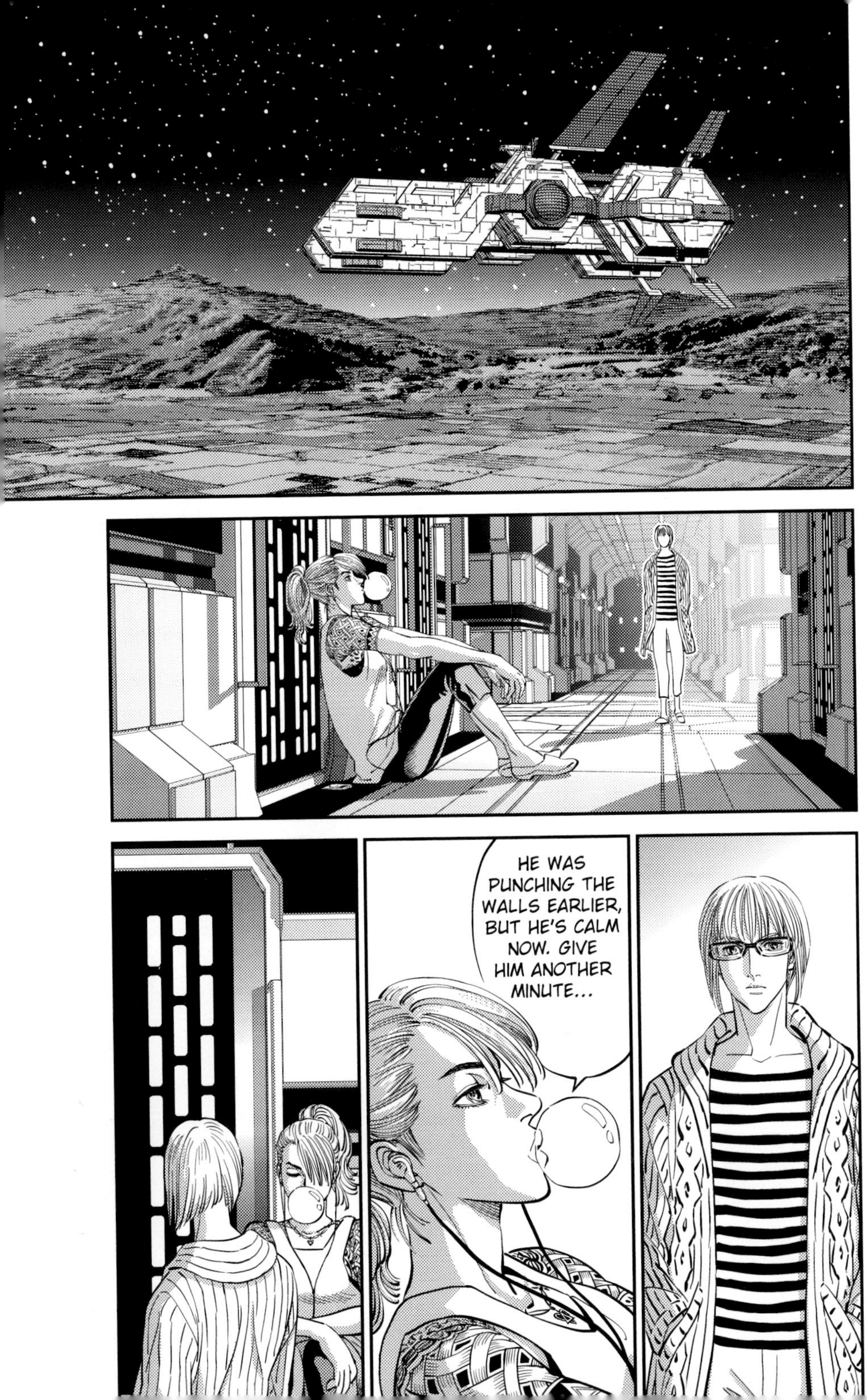
HE WAS PUNCHING THE WALLS EARLIER, BUT HE'S CALM NOW. GIVE HIM ANOTHER MINUTE...

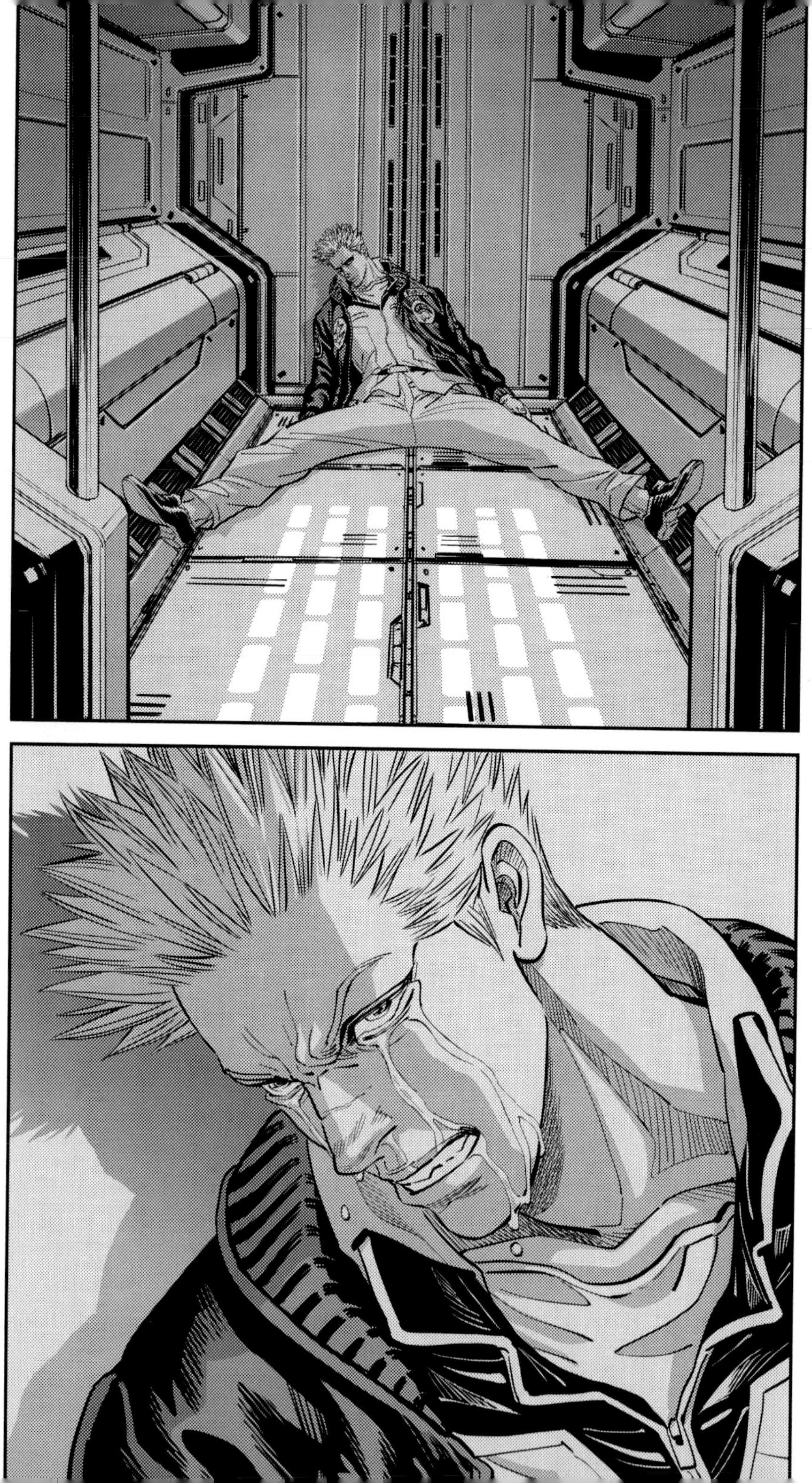

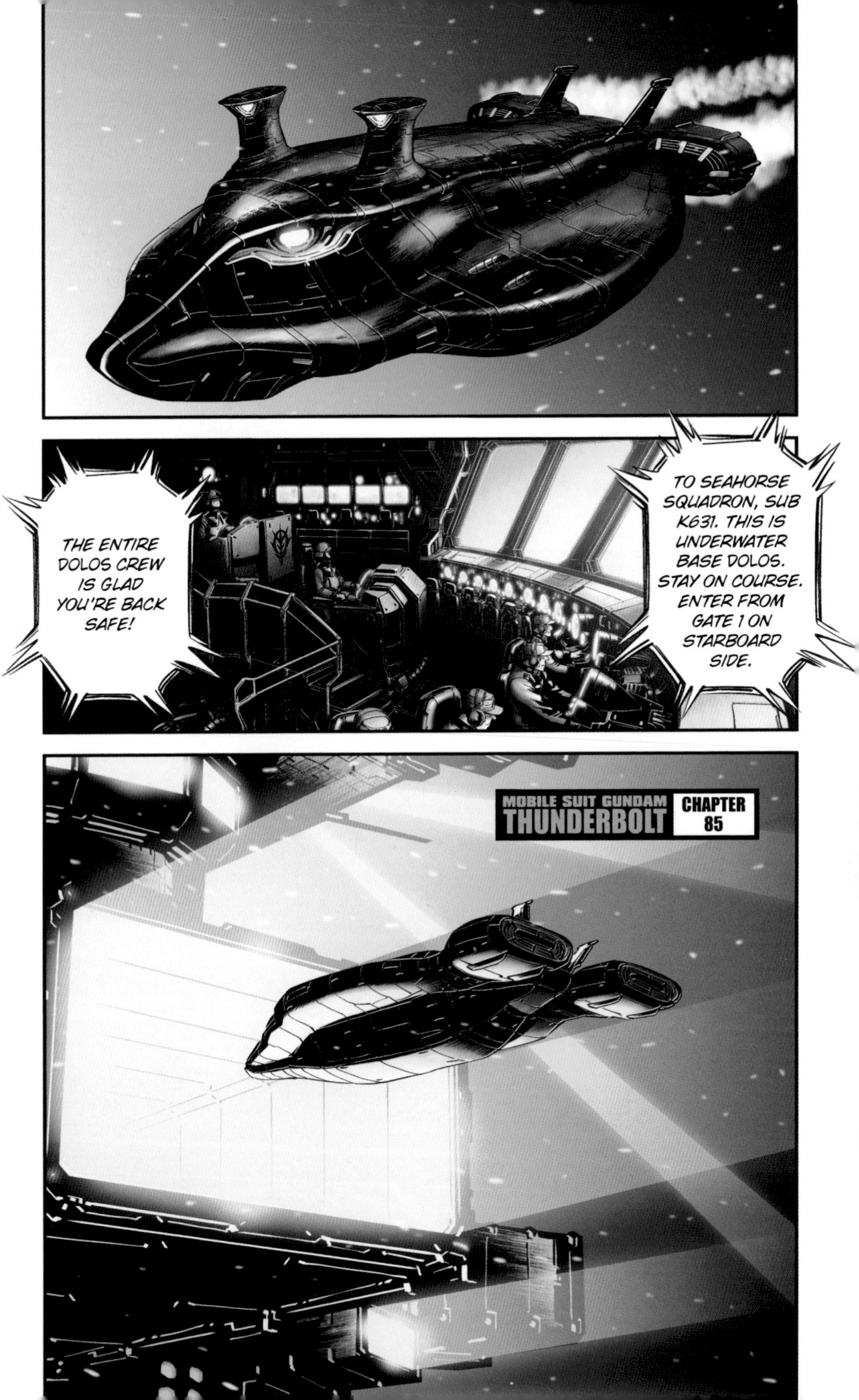
TO SEAHORSE SQUADRON, SUB K631. THIS IS UNDERWATER BASE DOLOS. STAY ON COURSE. ENTER FROM GATE 1 ON STARBOARD SIDE.
THE ENTIRE DOLOS CREW IS GLAD YOU'RE BACK SAFE!
MOBILE SUIT GUNDAM THUNDERBOLT
CHAPTER 85

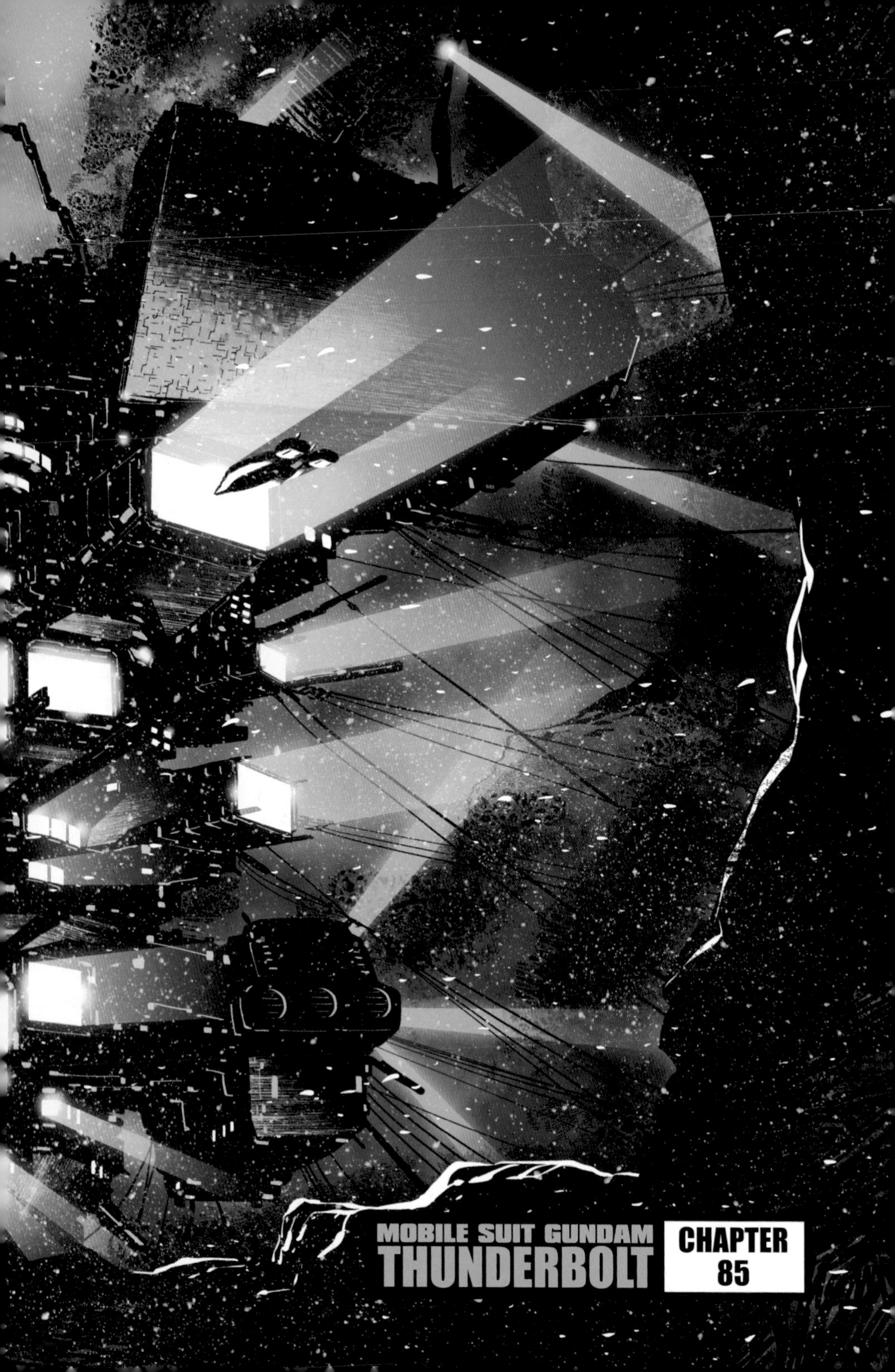
MOBILE SUIT GUNDAM
THUNDERBOLT
CHAPTER
85

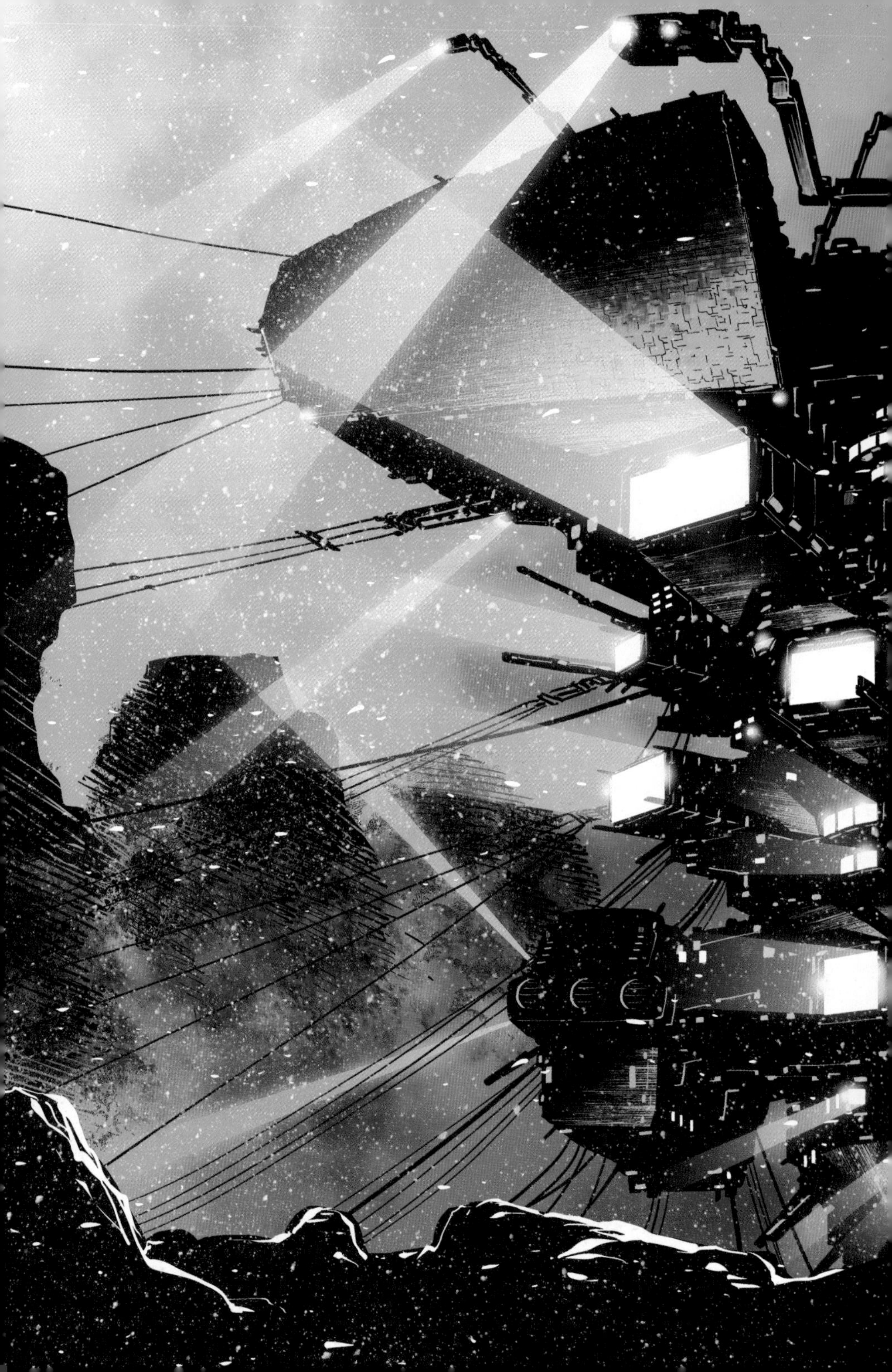

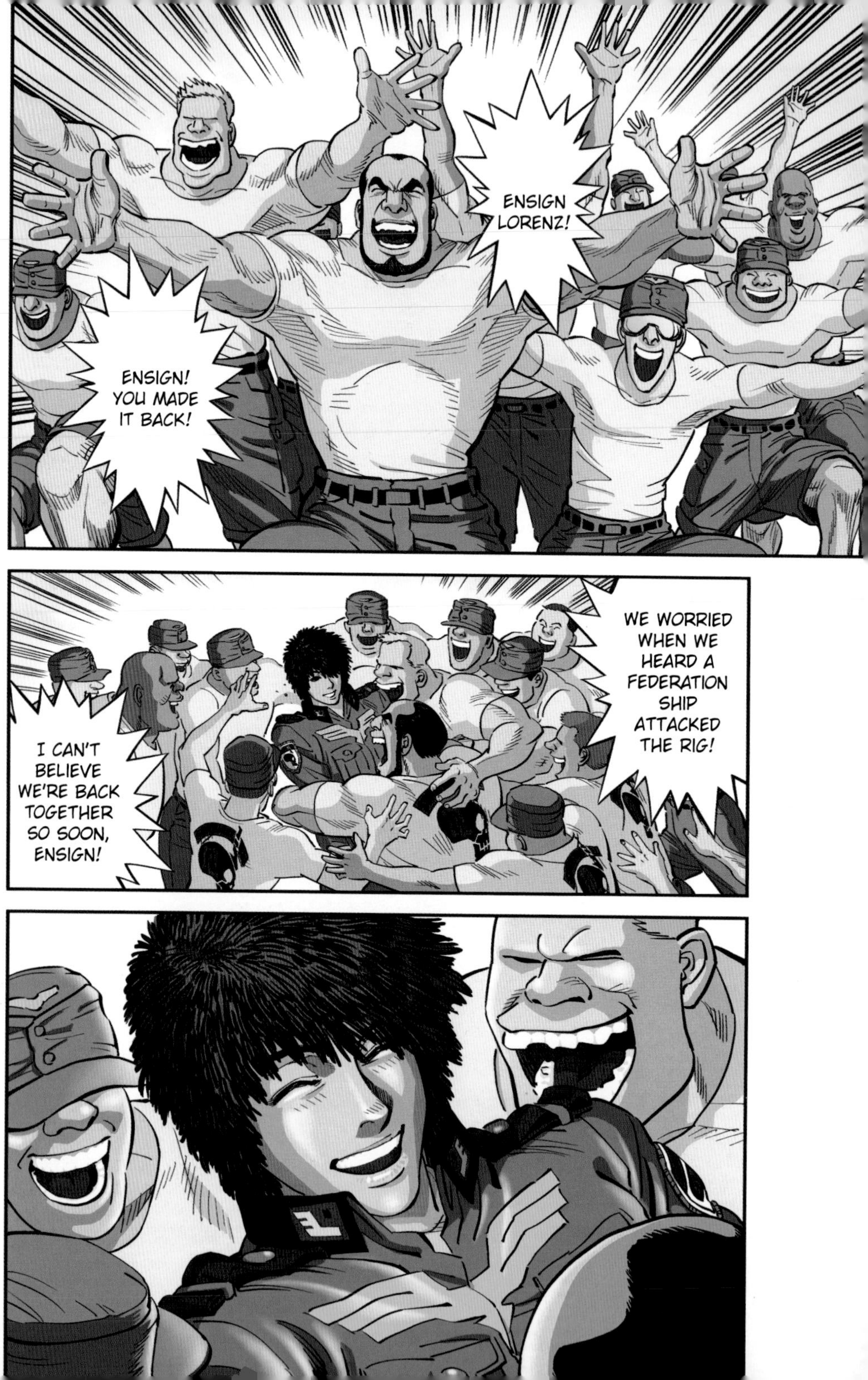
ENSIGN LORENZ!
ENSIGN! YOU MADE IT BACK!
WE WORRIED WHEN WE HEARD A FEDERATION SHIP ATTACKED THE RIG!
I CAN'T BELIEVE WE'RE BACK TOGETHER SO SOON, ENSIGN!

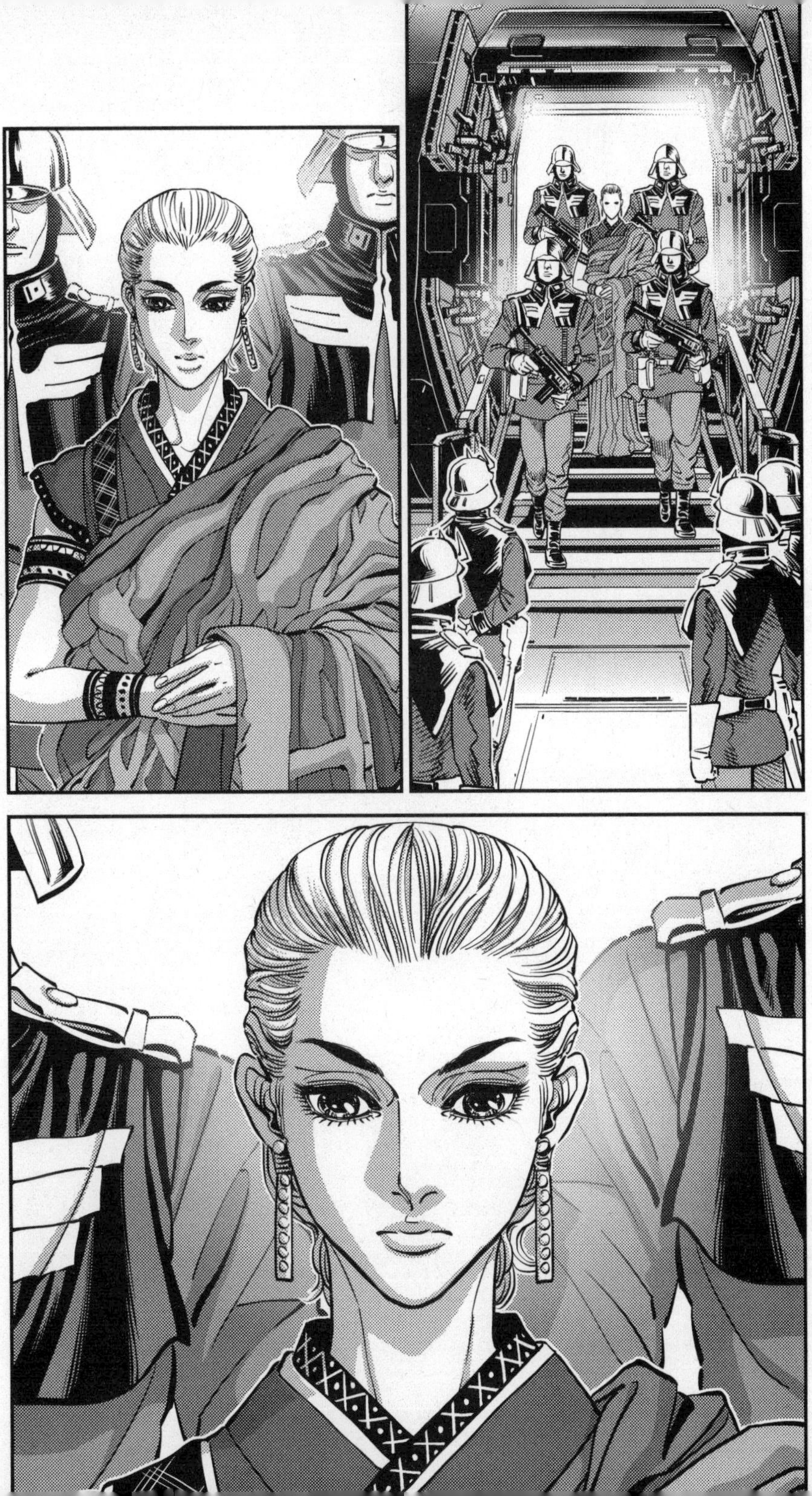

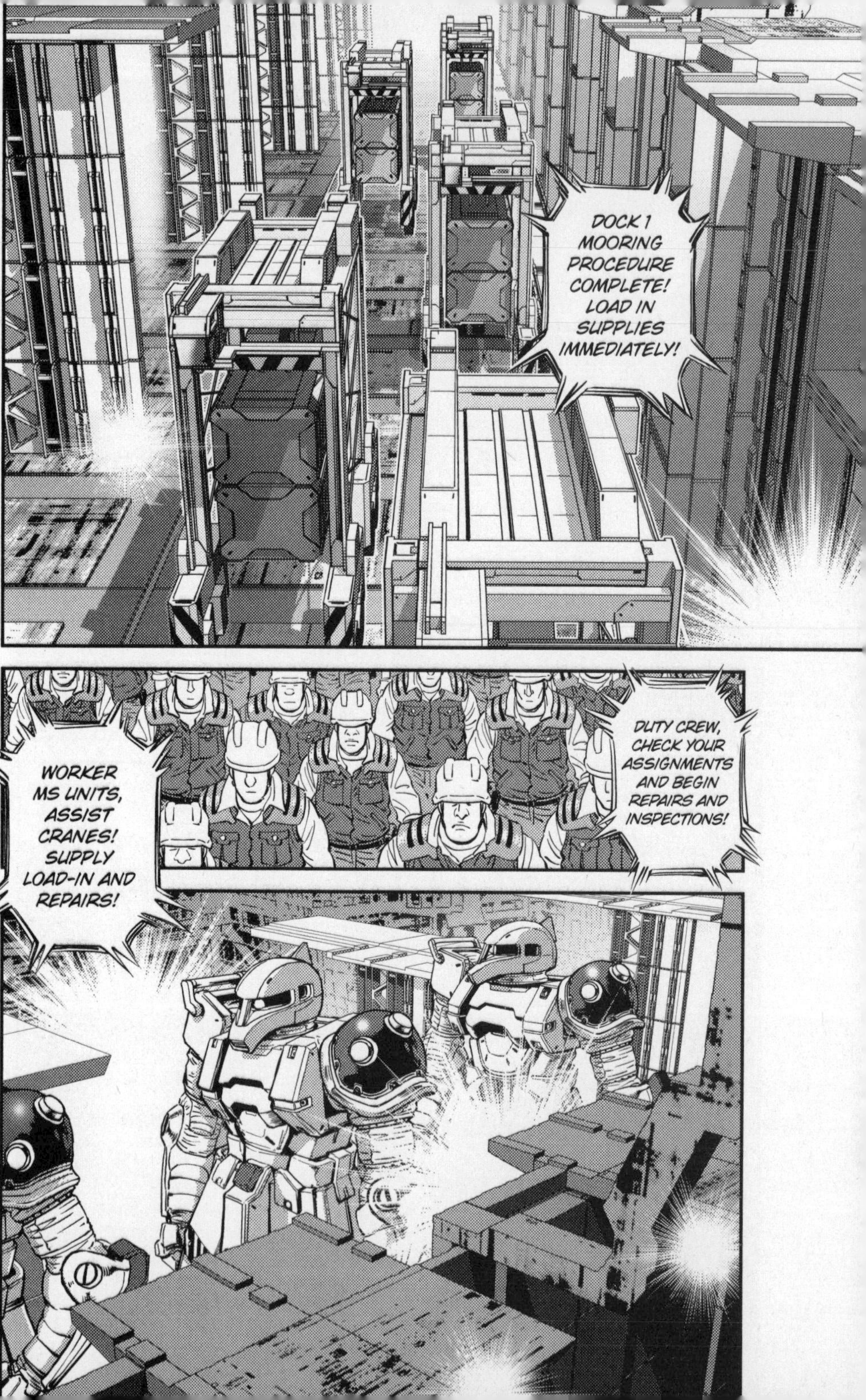
DOCK 1 MOORING PROCEDURE COMPLETE! LOAD IN SUPPLIES IMMEDIATELY!
DUTY CREW, CHECK YOUR ASSIGNMENTS AND BEGIN REPAIRS AND INSPECTIONS!
WORKER MS UNITS, ASSIST CRANES! SUPPLY LOAD-IN AND REPAIRS!

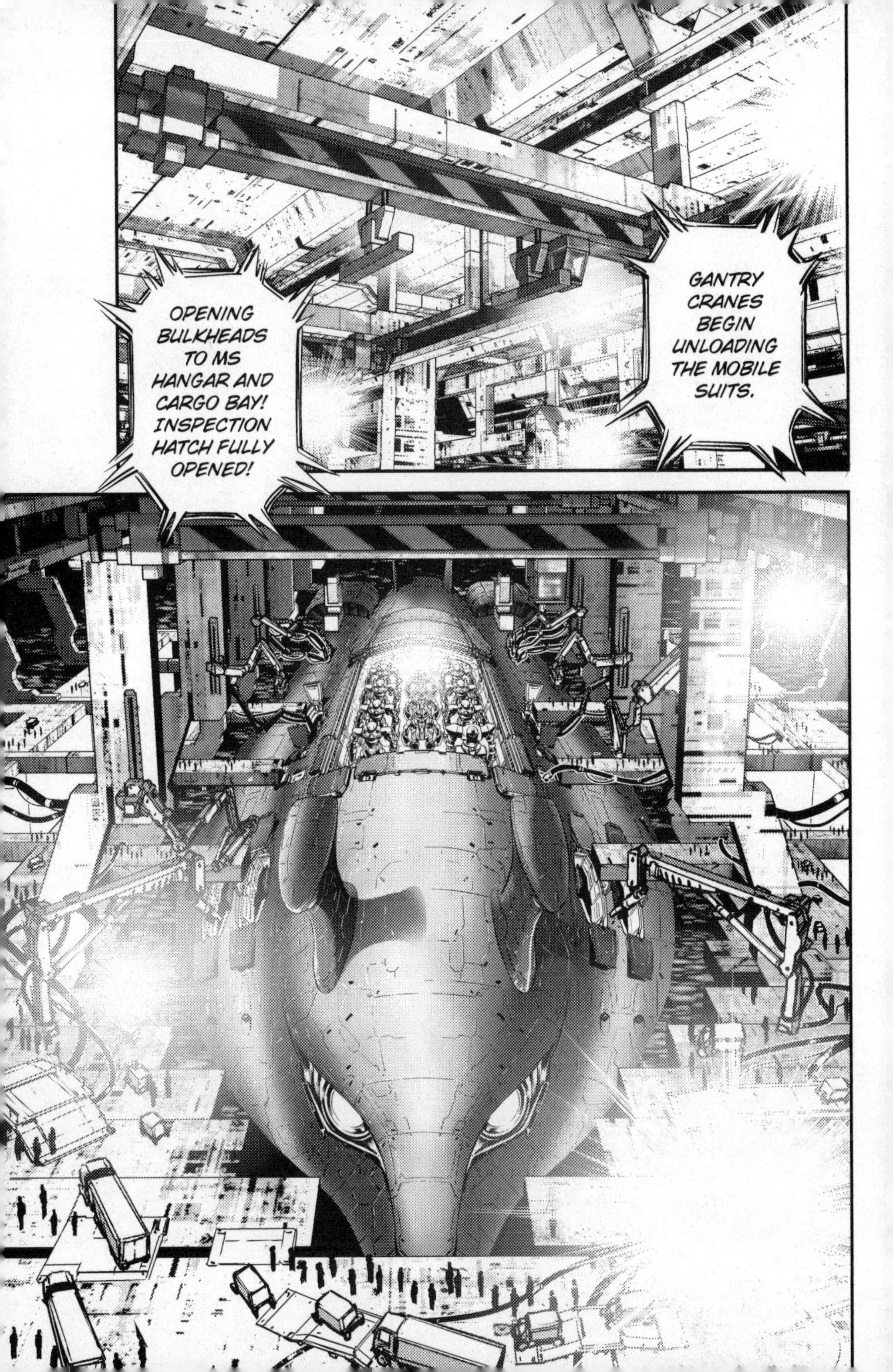
GANTRY CRANES BEGIN UNLOADING THE MOBILE SUITS.
OPENING BULKHEADS TO MS HANGAR AND CARGO BAY! INSPECTION HATCH FULLY OPENED!

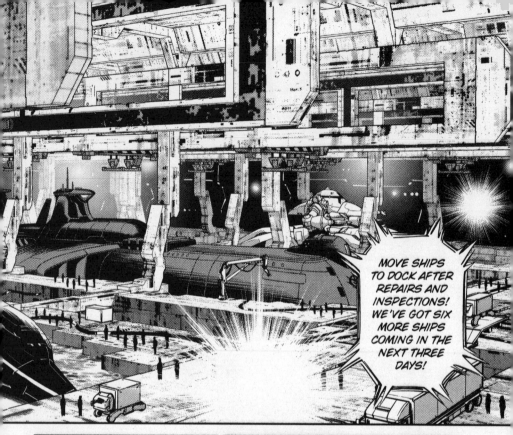

MOVE SHIPS TO DOCK AFTER REPAIRS AND INSPECTIONS! WE'VE GOT SIX MORE SHIPS COMING IN THE NEXT THREE DAYS!

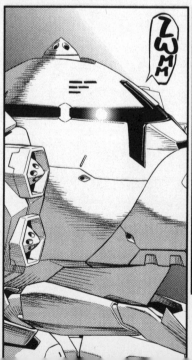

ZWMM

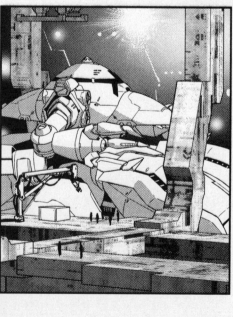

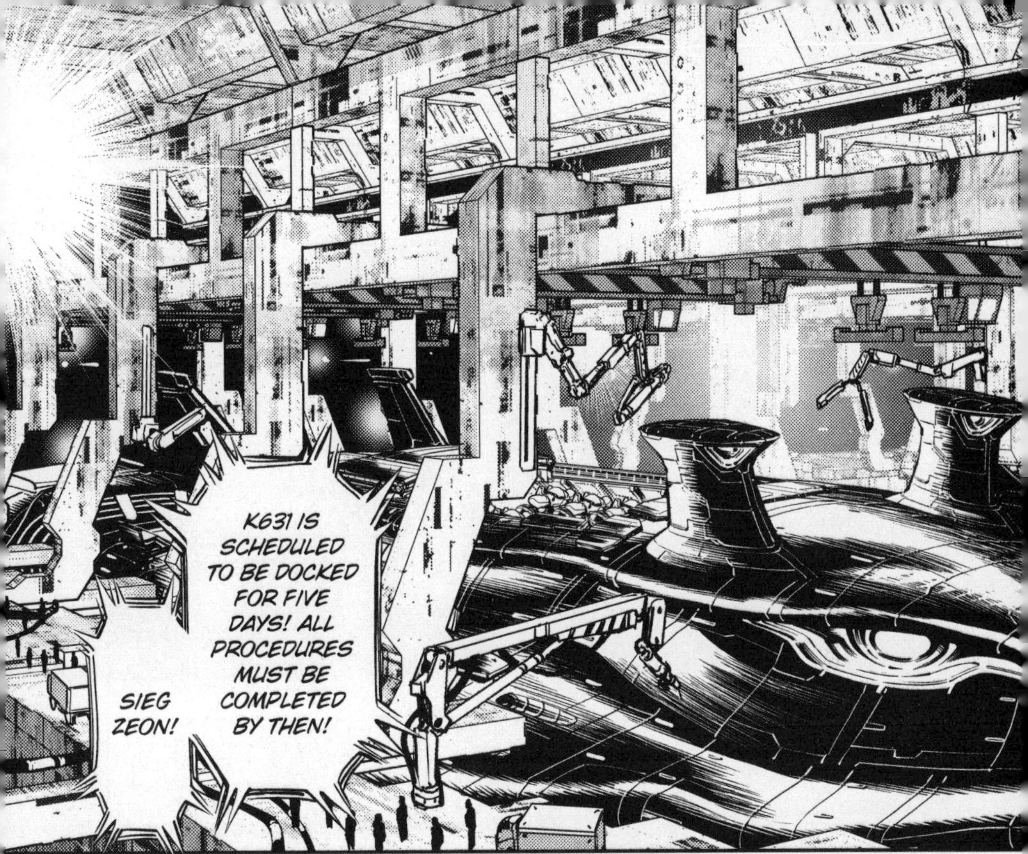
K631 IS SCHEDULED TO BE DOCKED FOR FIVE DAYS! ALL PROCEDURES MUST BE COMPLETED BY THEN!
SIEG ZEON!
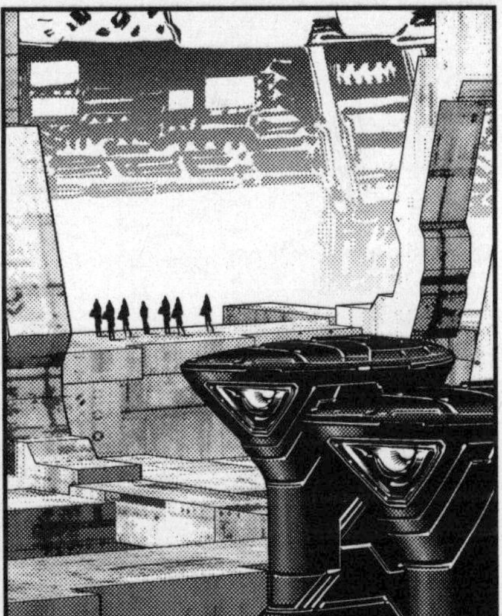
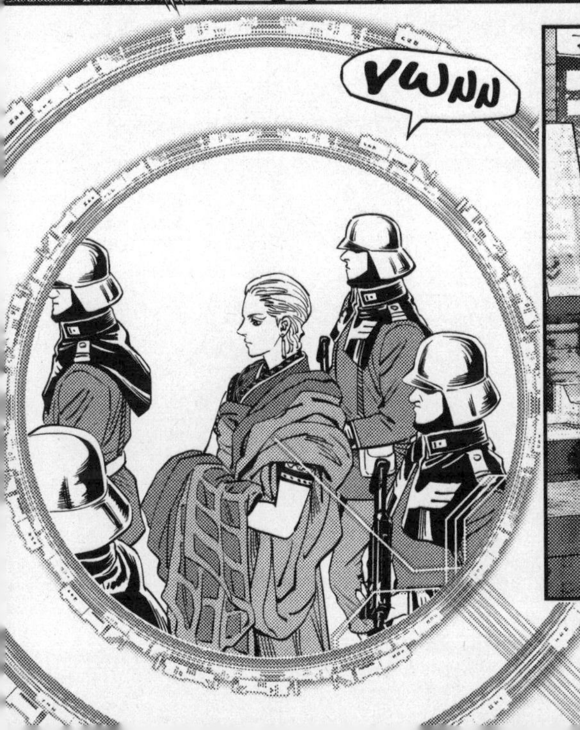
VWNN

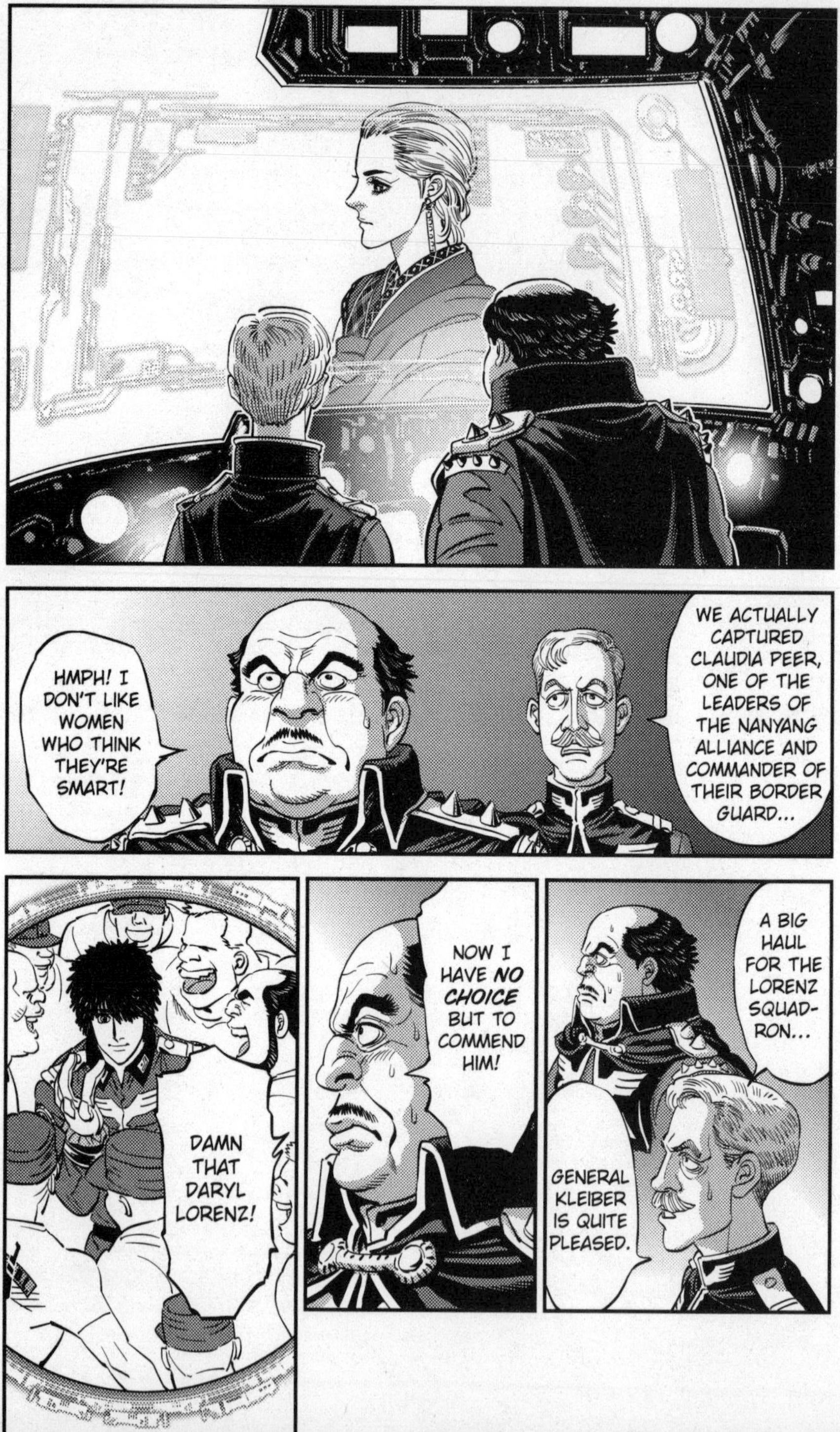
WE ACTUALLY CAPTURED CLAUDIA PEER, ONE OF THE LEADERS OF THE NANYANG ALLIANCE AND COMMANDER OF THEIR BORDER GUARD...
HMPH! I DON'T LIKE WOMEN WHO THINK THEY'RE SMART!
A BIG HAUL FOR THE LORENZ SQUAD-RON...
GENERAL KLEIBER IS QUITE PLEASED.
NOW I HAVE NO CHOICE BUT TO COMMEND HIM!
DAMN THAT DARYL LORENZ!

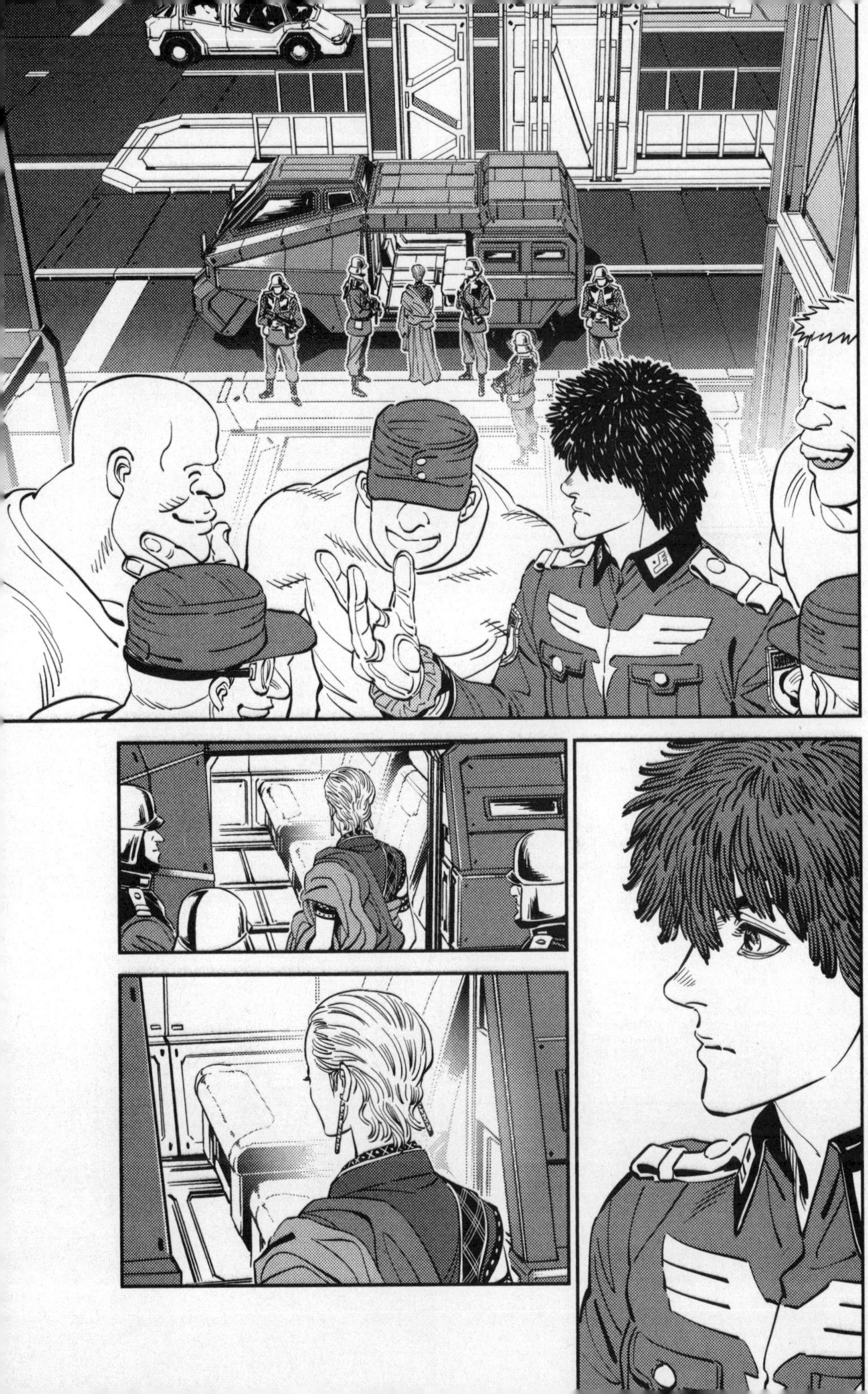

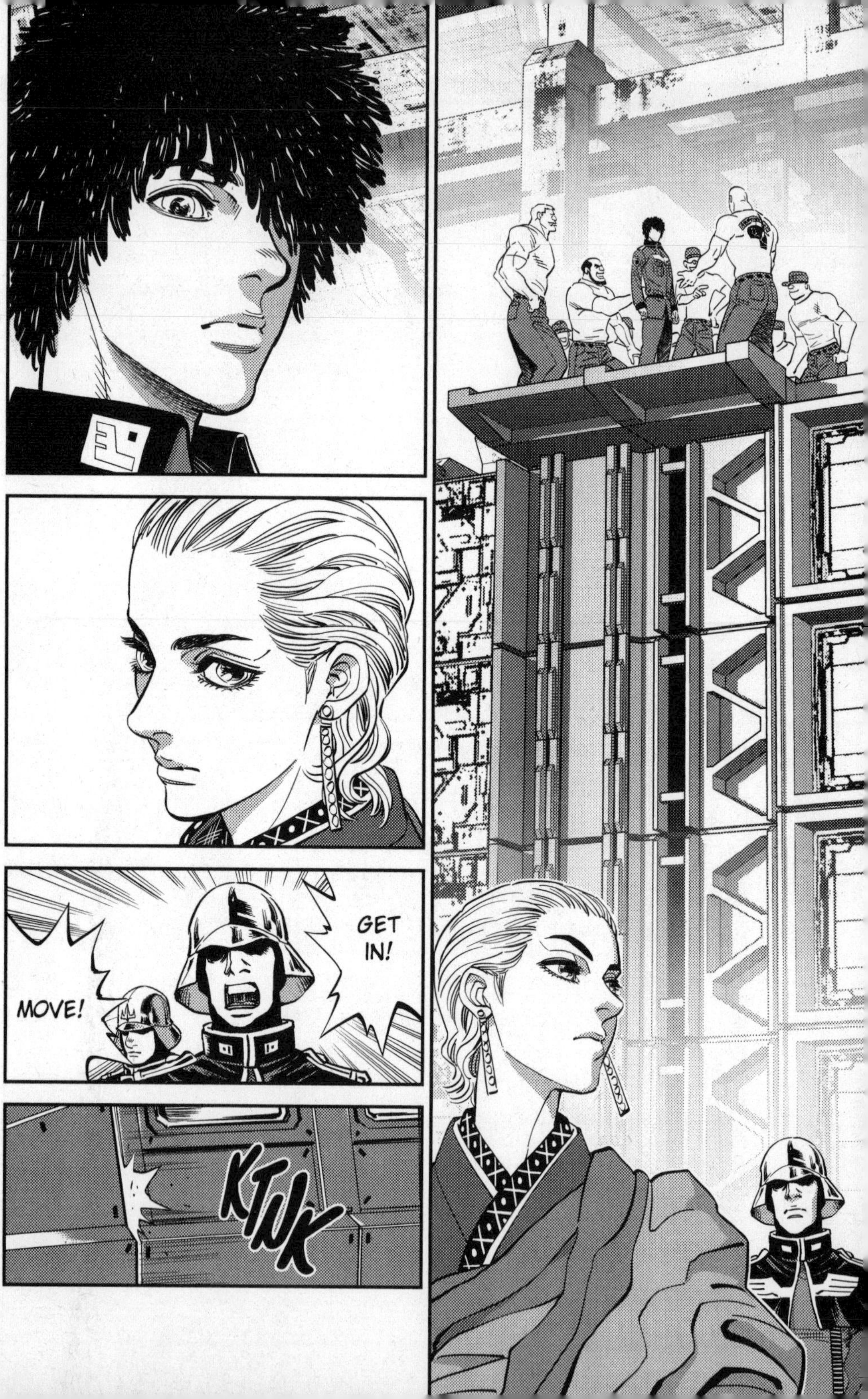
GET IN!
MOVE!
KTUK

VRRRZZZZ

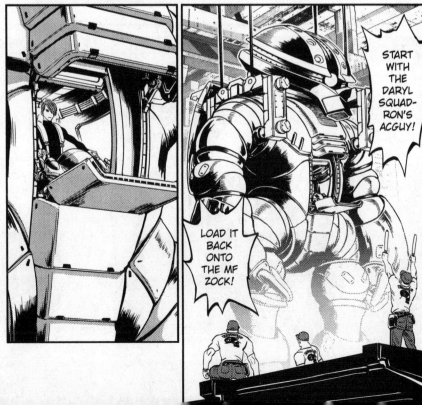

START WITH THE DARYL SQUADRON'S ACGUY!

LOAD IT BACK ONTO THE MF ZOCK!

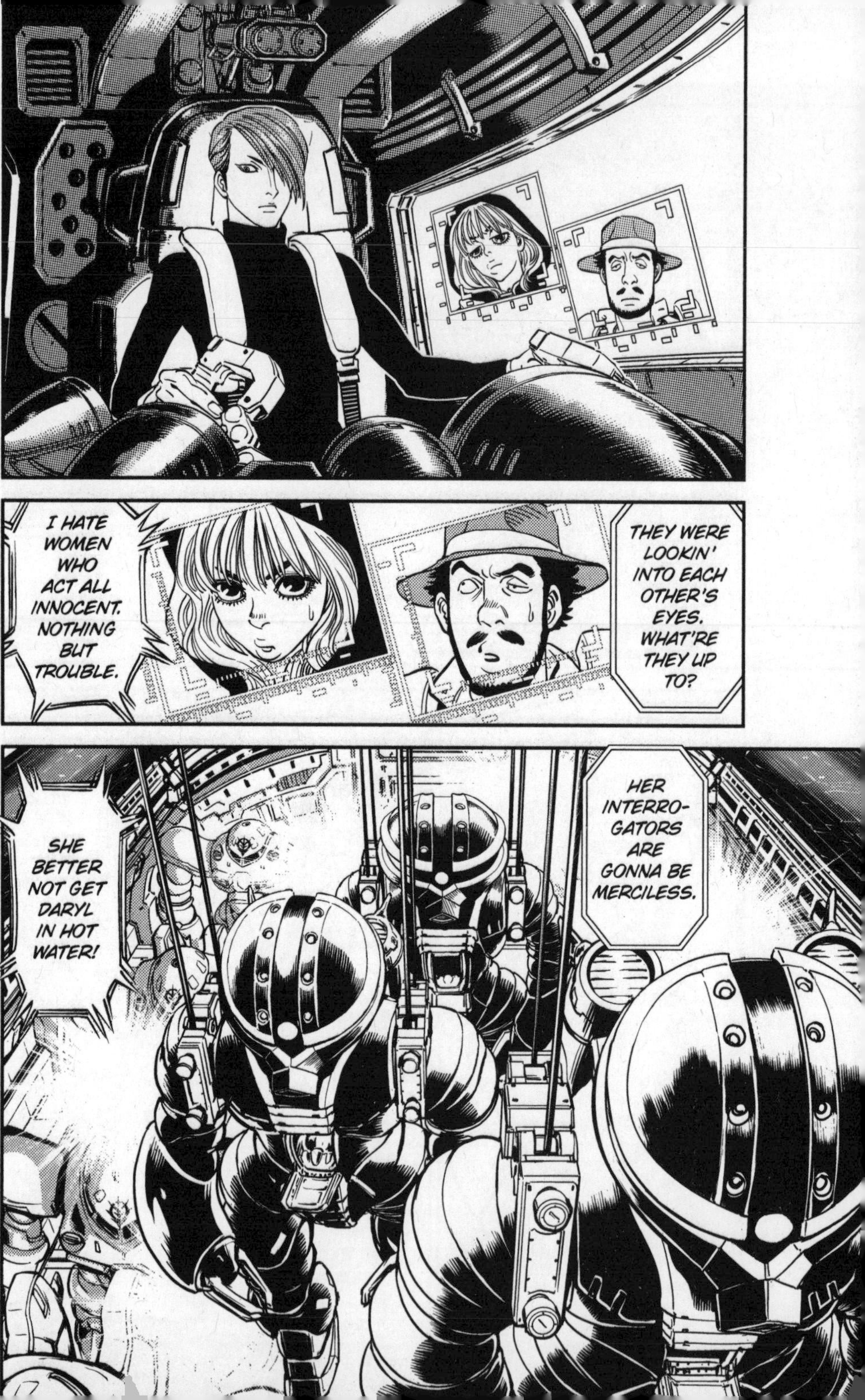
THEY WERE LOOKIN' INTO EACH OTHER'S EYES. WHAT'RE THEY UP TO?
I HATE WOMEN WHO ACT ALL INNOCENT. NOTHING BUT TROUBLE.
HER INTERRO-GATORS ARE GONNA BE MERCILESS.
SHE BETTER NOT GET DARYL IN HOT WATER!

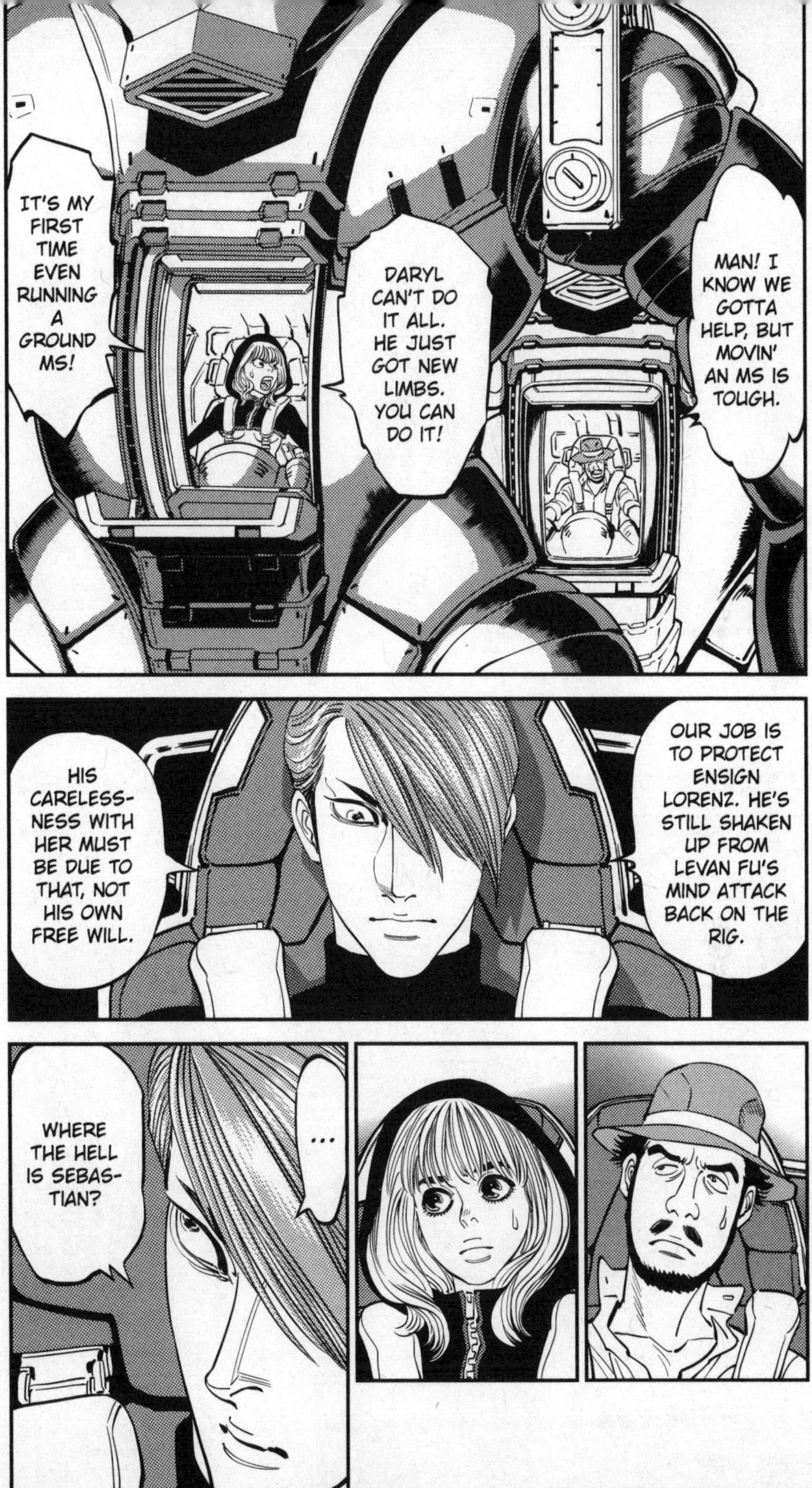
MAN! I KNOW WE GOTTA HELP, BUT MOVIN' AN MS IS TOUGH.
DARYL CAN'T DO IT ALL. HE JUST GOT NEW LIMBS. YOU CAN DO IT!
IT'S MY FIRST TIME EVEN RUNNING A GROUND MS!
OUR JOB IS TO PROTECT ENSIGN LORENZ. HE'S STILL SHAKEN UP FROM LEVAN FU'S MIND ATTACK BACK ON THE RIG.
HIS CARELESS-NESS WITH HER MUST BE DUE TO THAT, NOT HIS OWN FREE WILL.
...
WHERE THE HELL IS SEBAS-TIAN?

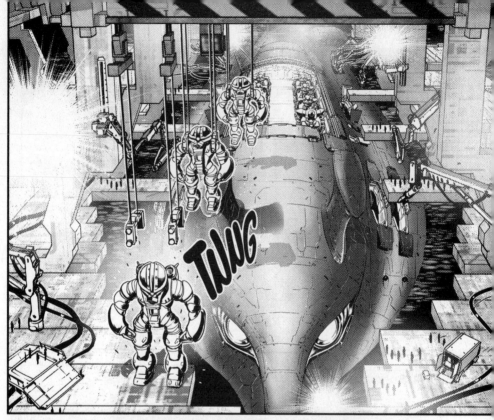

TWANG

OKAY!

FOLLOW THE LEAD CAR!

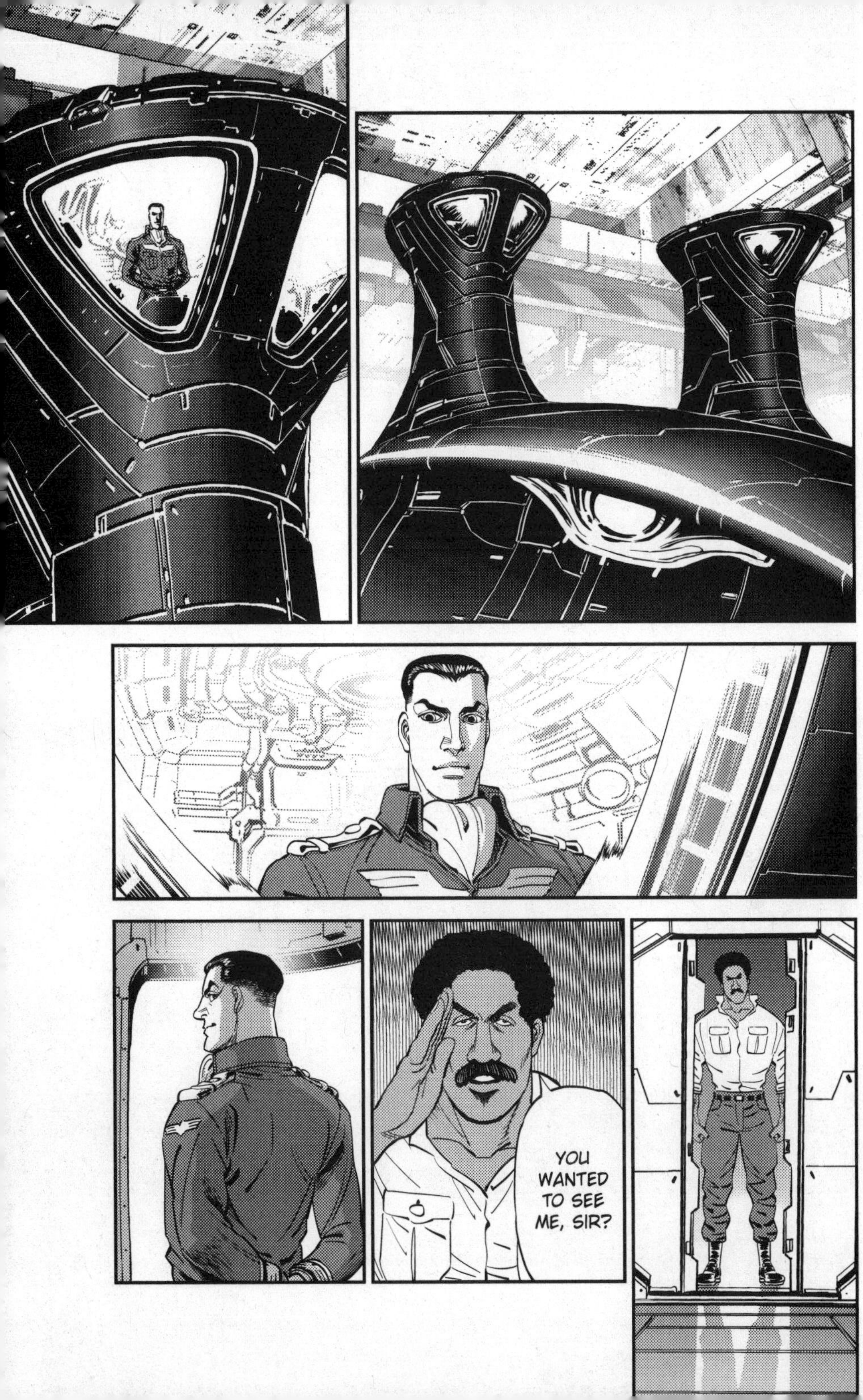
YOU WANTED TO SEE ME, SIR?

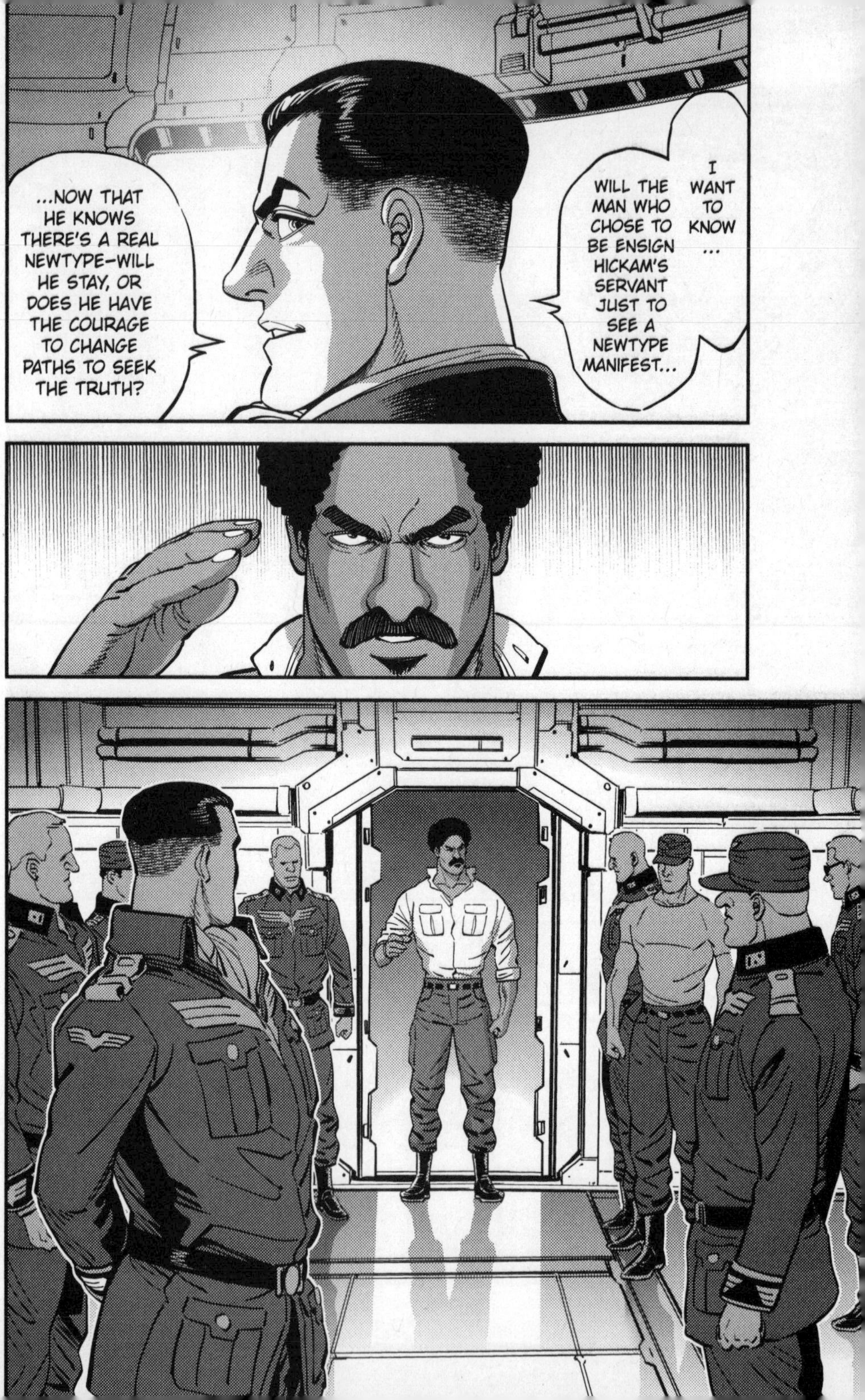
I WANT TO KNOW... WILL THE MAN WHO CHOSE TO BE ENSIGN HICKAM'S SERVANT JUST TO SEE A NEWTYPE MANIFEST...
...NOW THAT HE KNOWS THERE'S A REAL NEWTYPE–WILL HE STAY, OR DOES HE HAVE THE COURAGE TO CHANGE PATHS TO SEEK THE TRUTH?

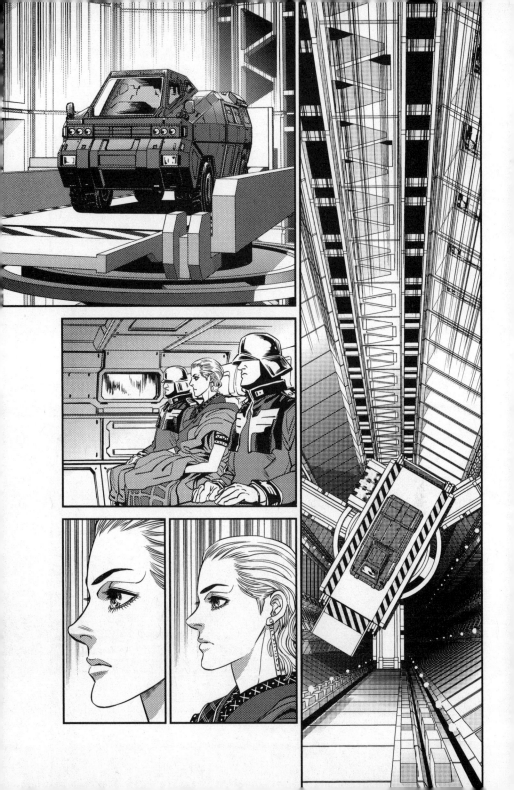

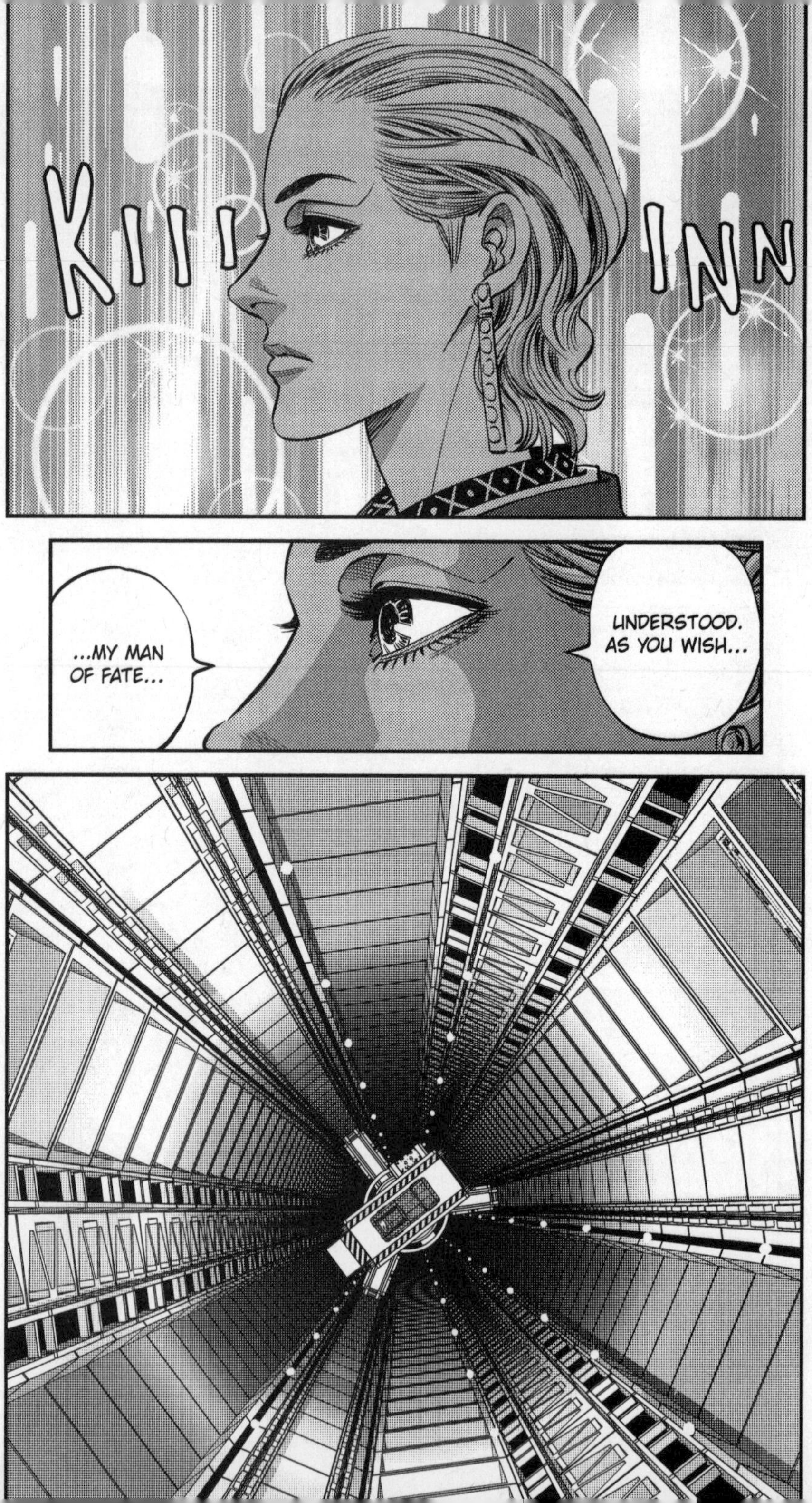
KIII
INN
UNDERSTOOD. AS YOU WISH...
...MY MAN OF FATE...

KARLA, I'M HOME.

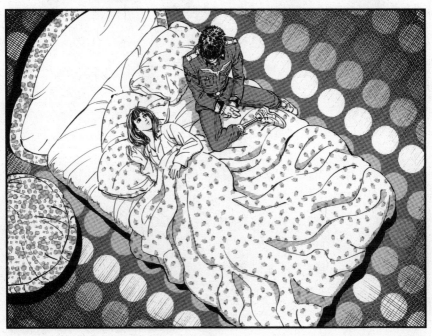

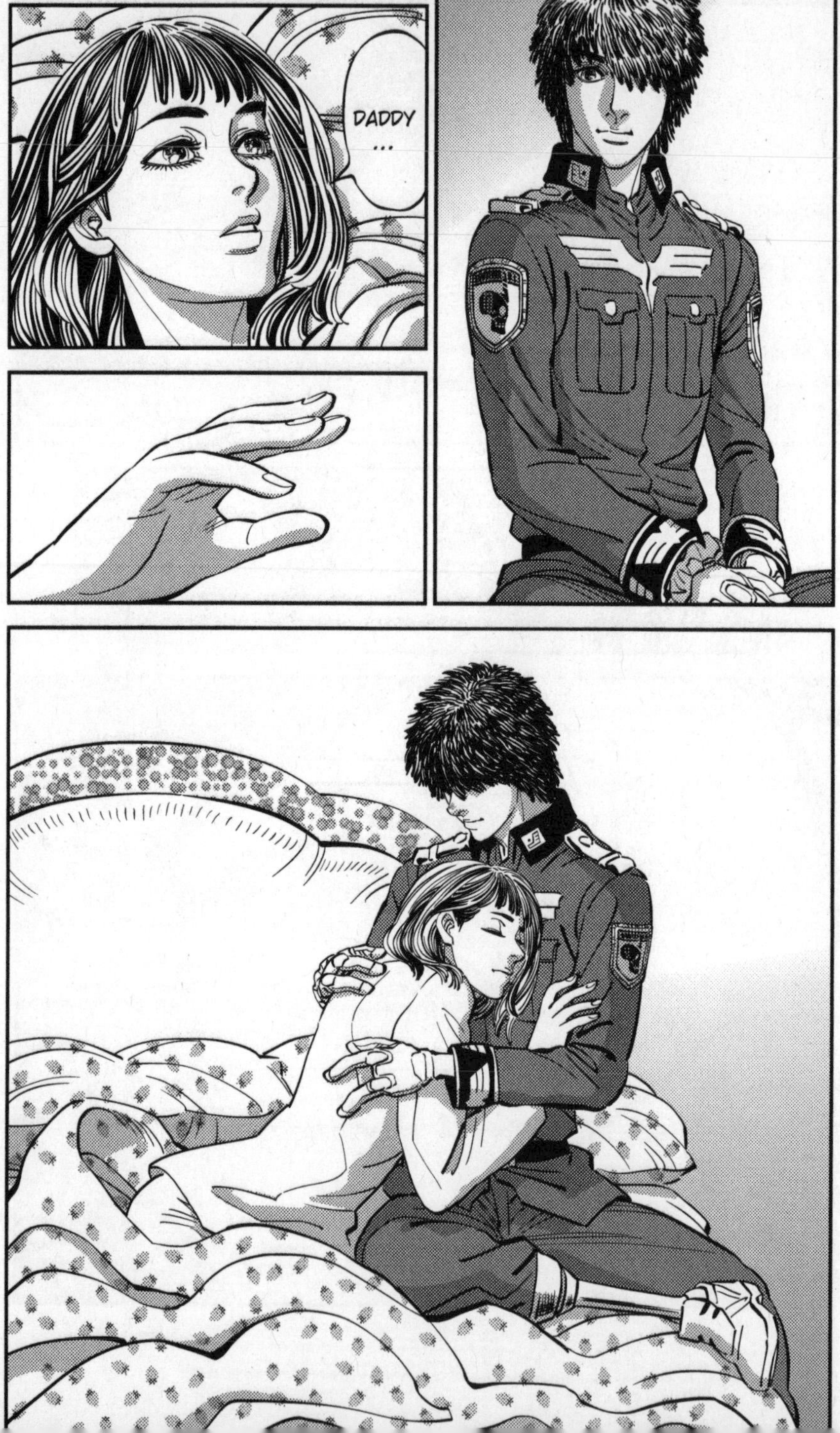
DADDY ...

I KEEP HAVING NIGHTMARES. I'M ON A SPACESHIP AND THERE'S A WAR GOING ON AND I SEE LOTS OF PEOPLE DYING...

YOU'RE IN IT TOO, DADDY. YOU GO OUT ALONE AND FIGHT TO PROTECT EVERYONE. ON A BIG, SCARY RED DEVIL...

DADDY ...?

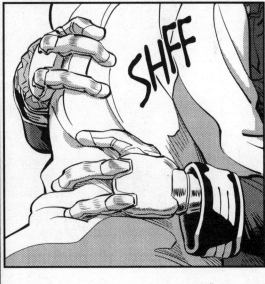

SHFF

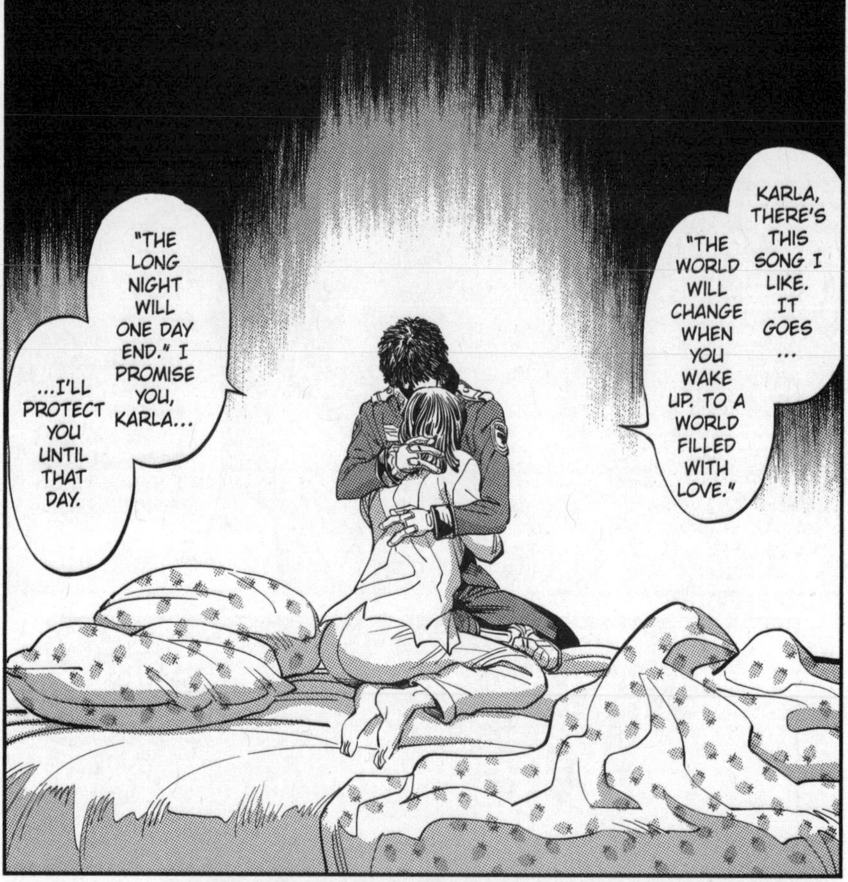
KARLA, THERE'S THIS SONG I LIKE. IT GOES ... "THE WORLD WILL CHANGE WHEN YOU WAKE UP. TO A WORLD FILLED WITH LOVE."
"THE LONG NIGHT WILL ONE DAY END." I PROMISE YOU, KARLA... ...I'LL PROTECT YOU UNTIL THAT DAY.
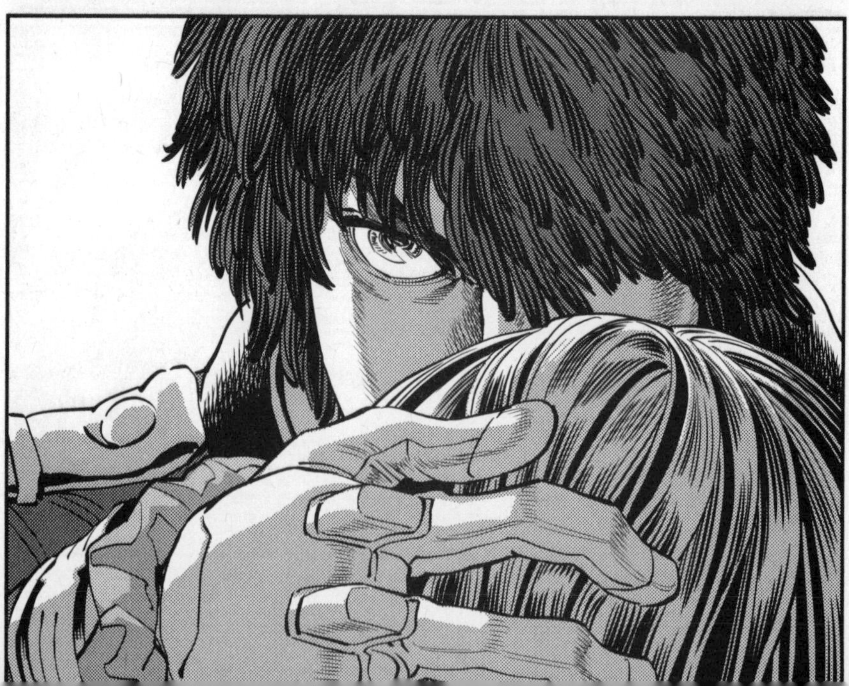

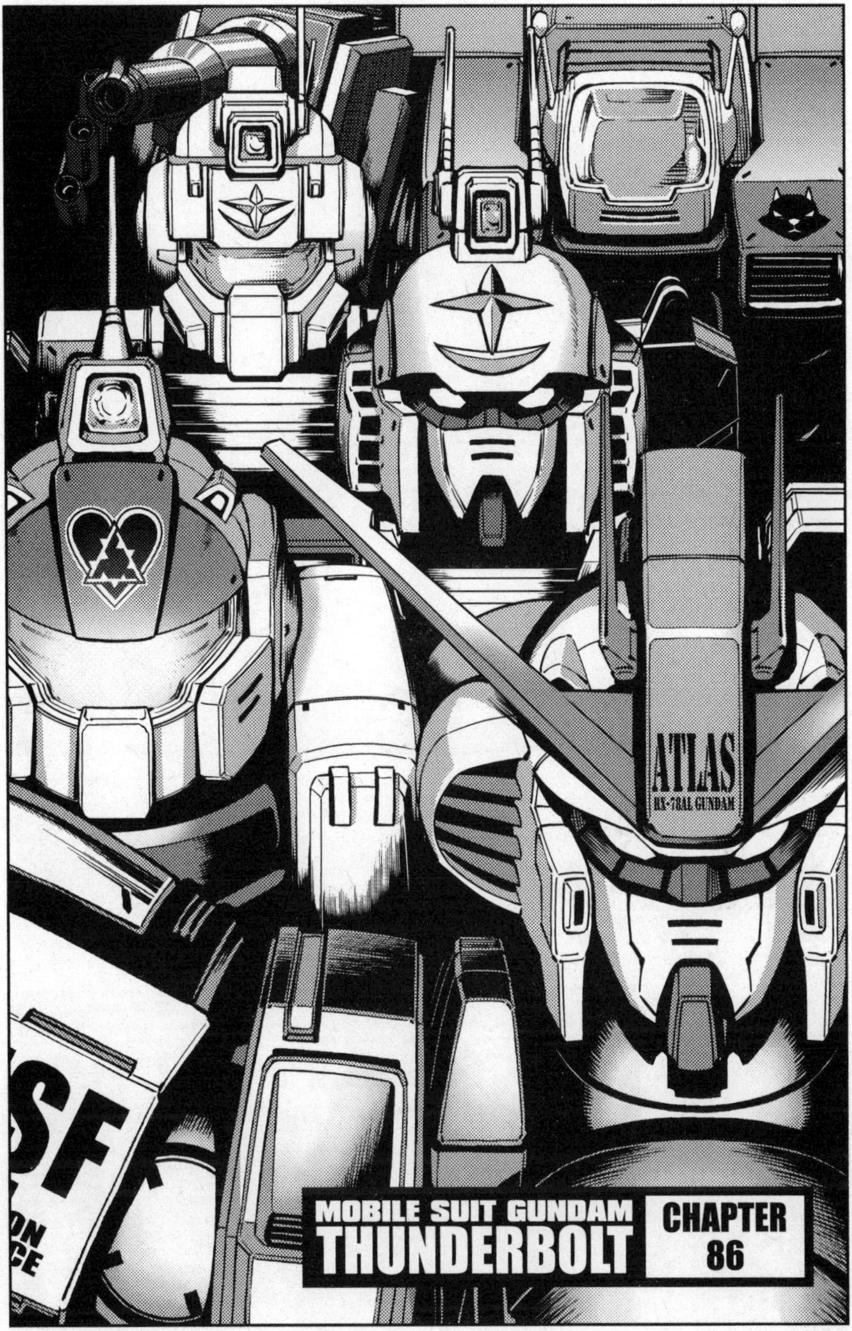
ATLAS
RX-78AL GUNDAM
MOBILE SUIT GUNDAM
THUNDERBOLT
CHAPTER
86

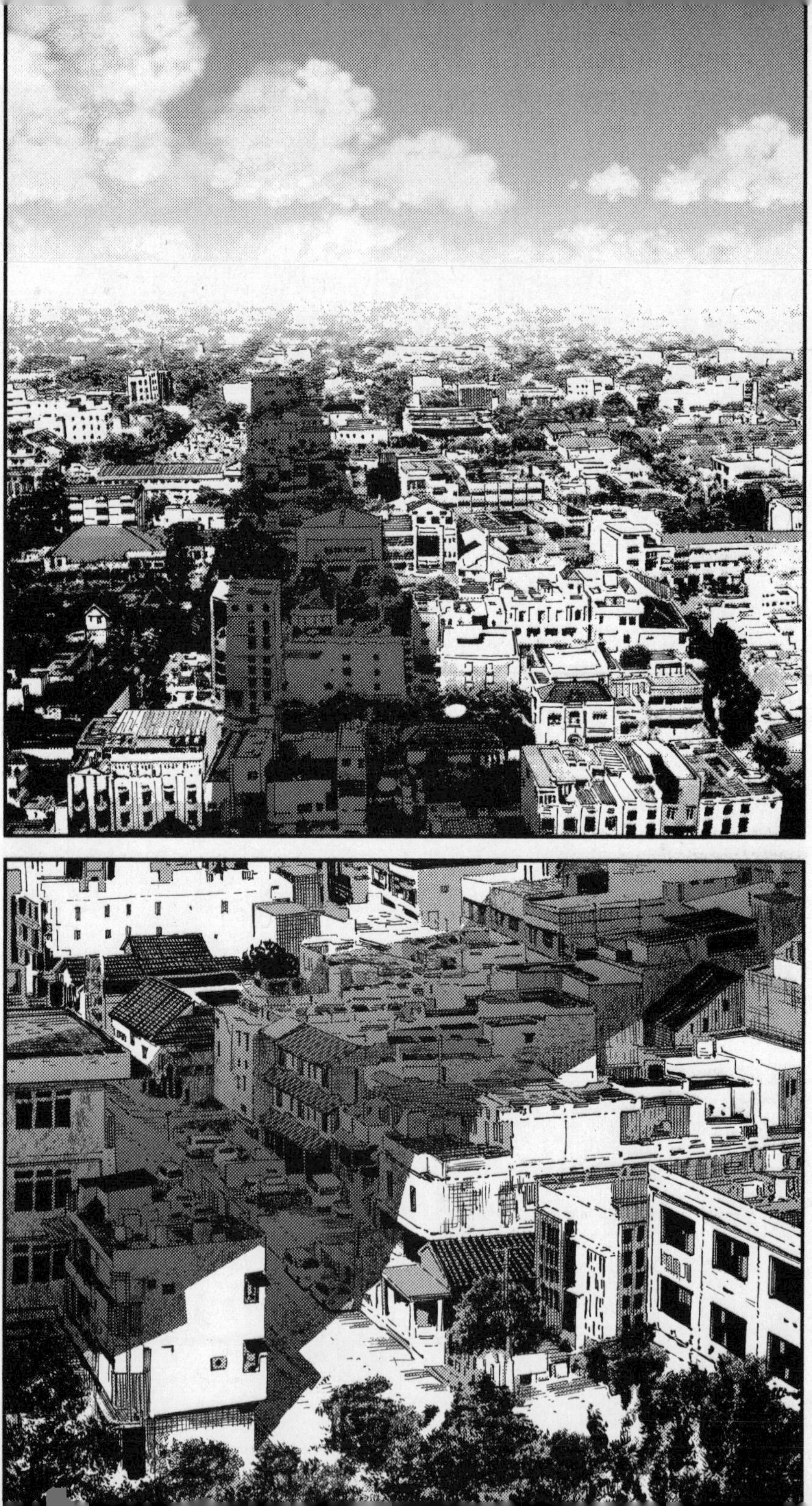

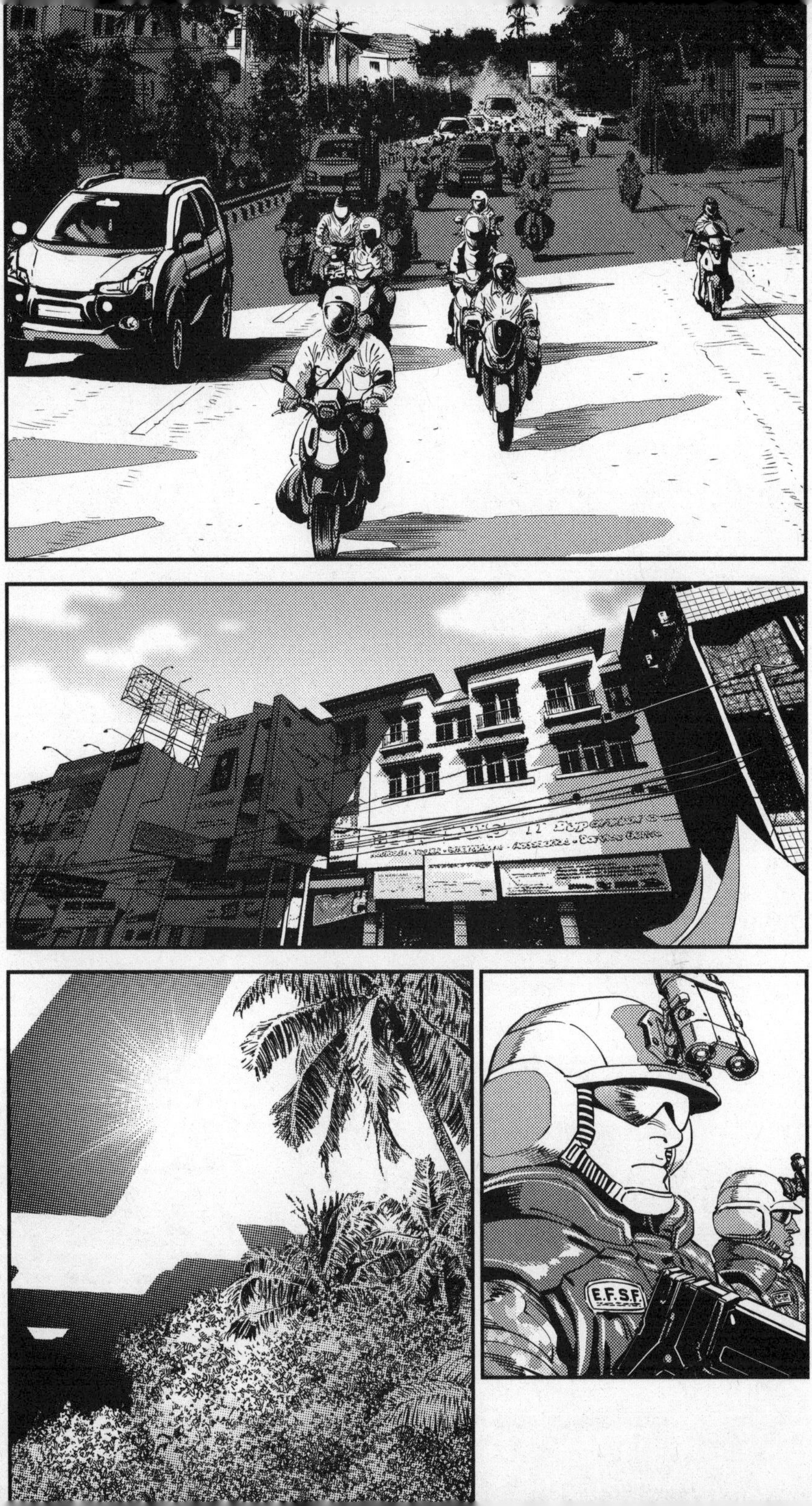
E.F.S.F.

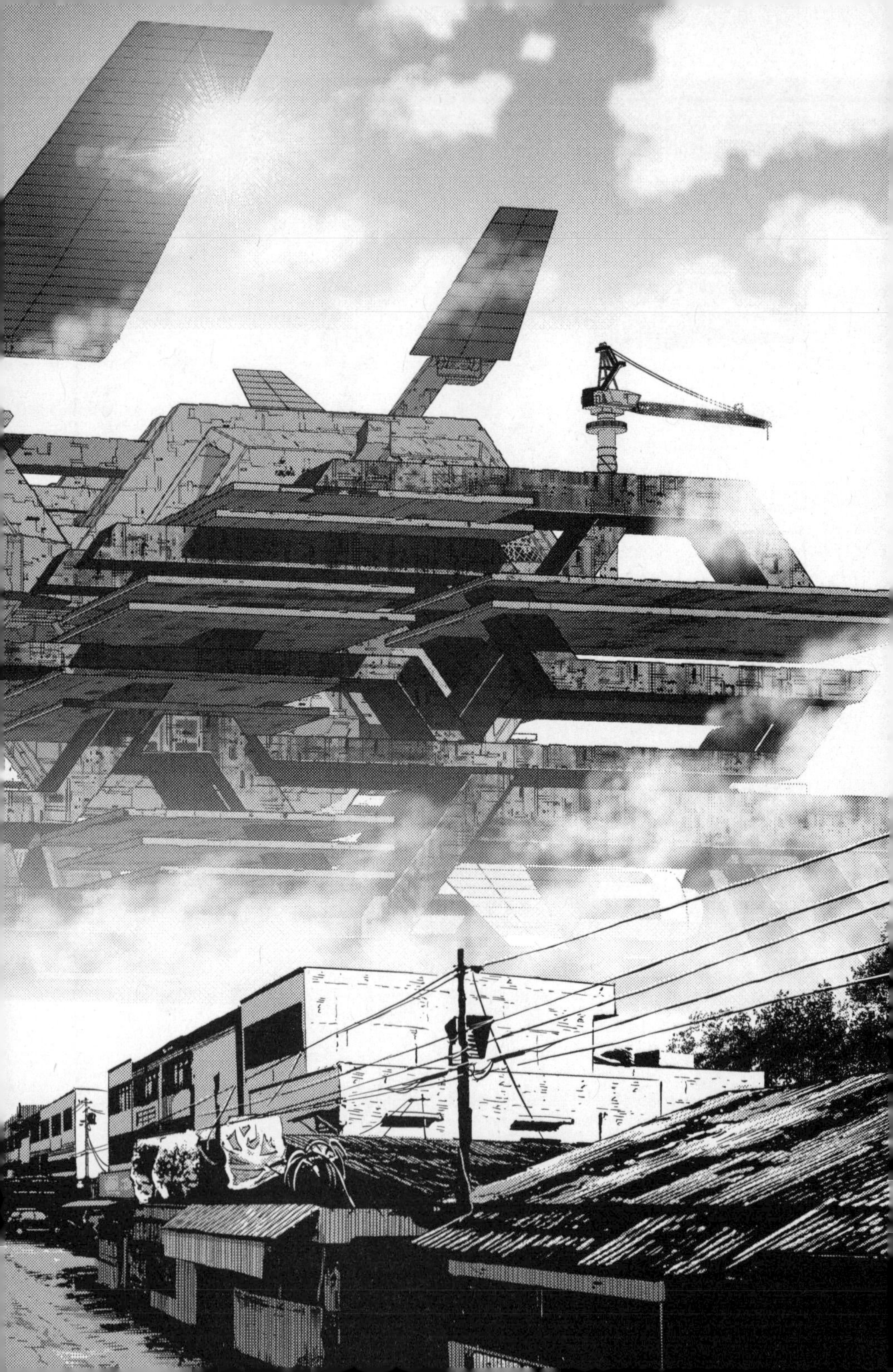

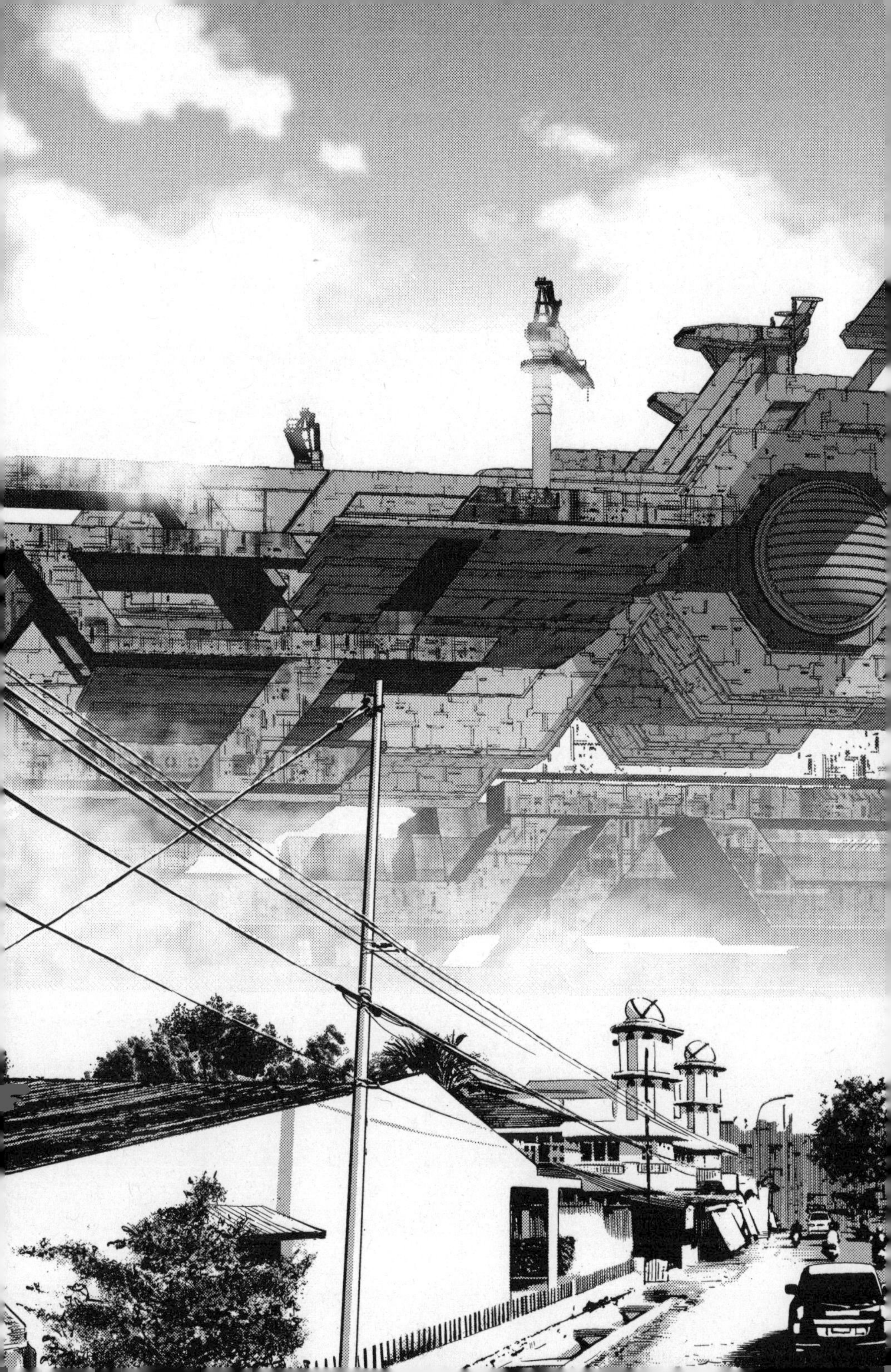

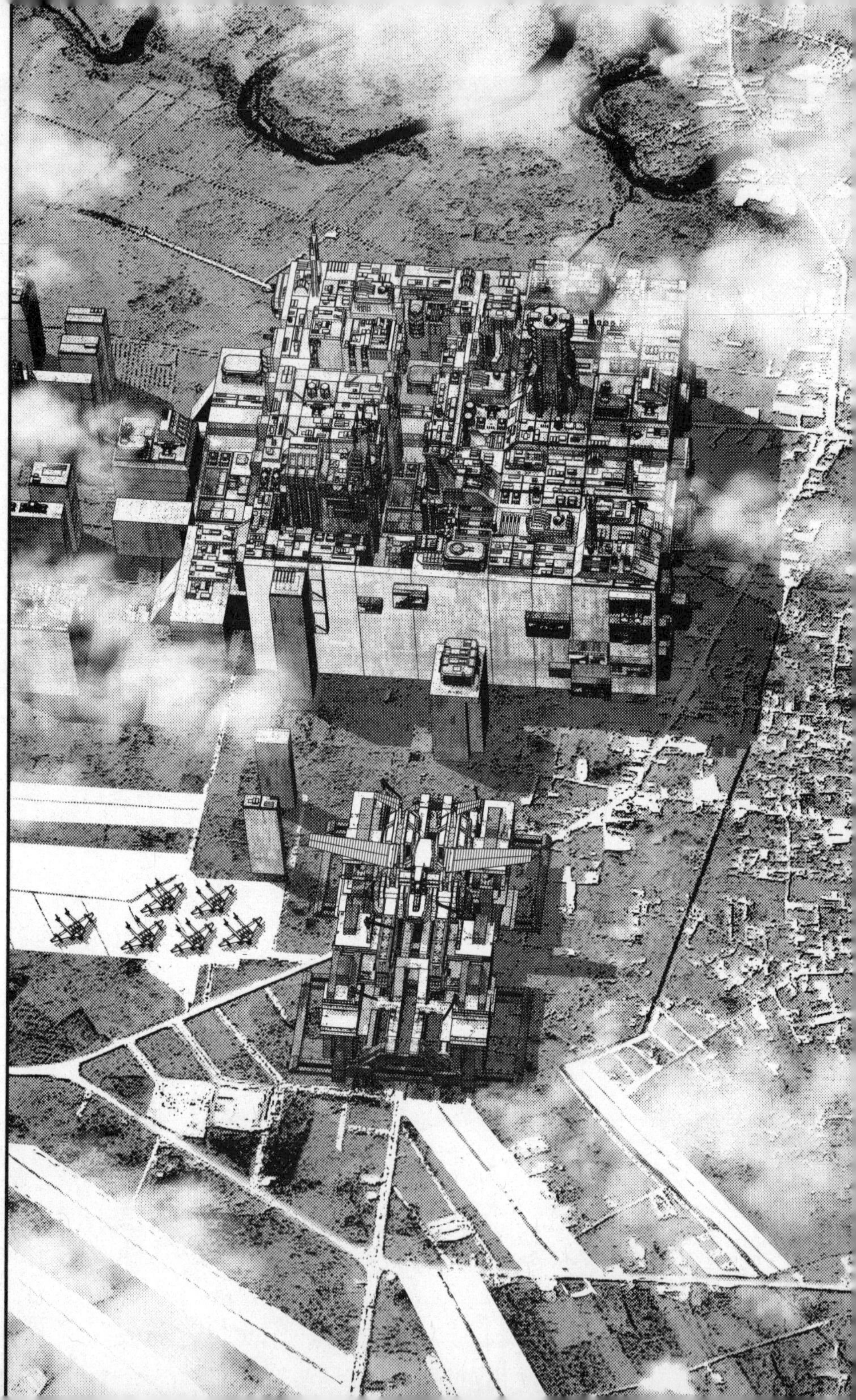

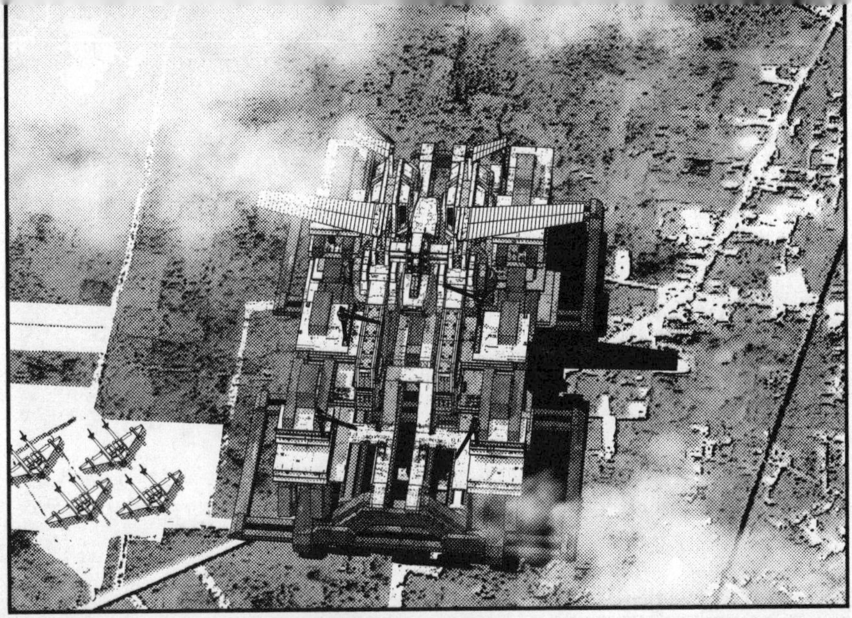
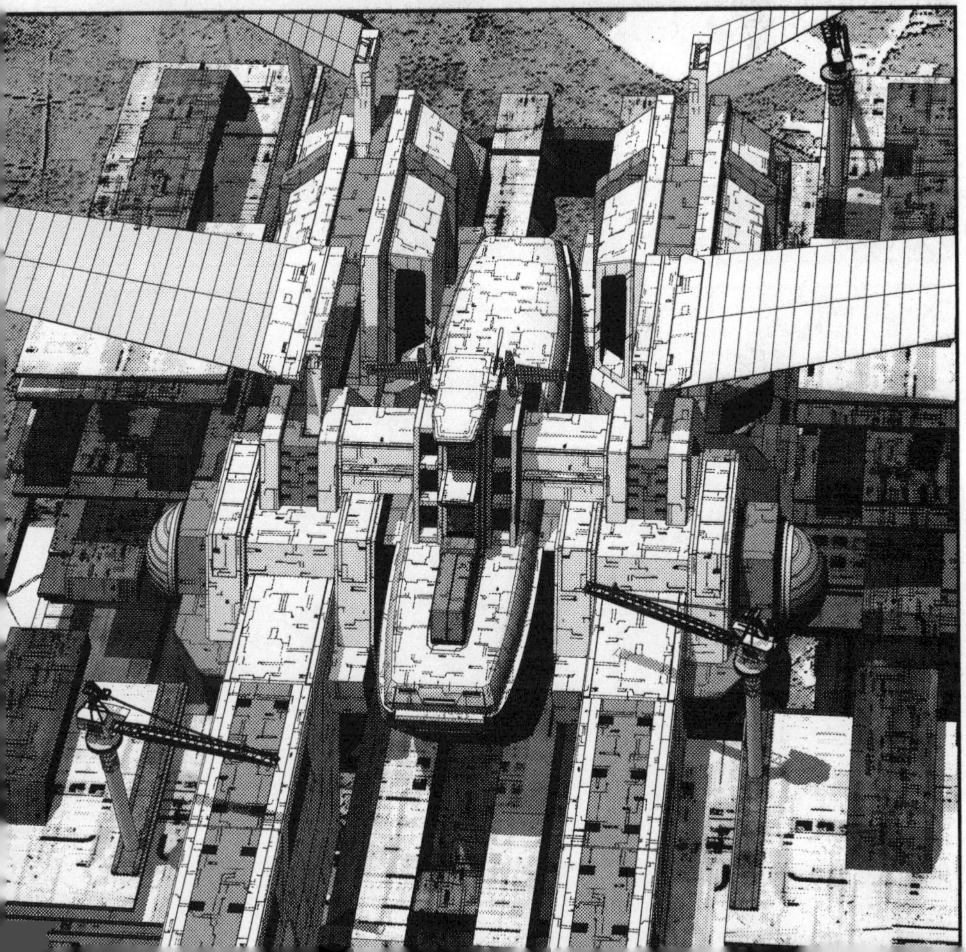

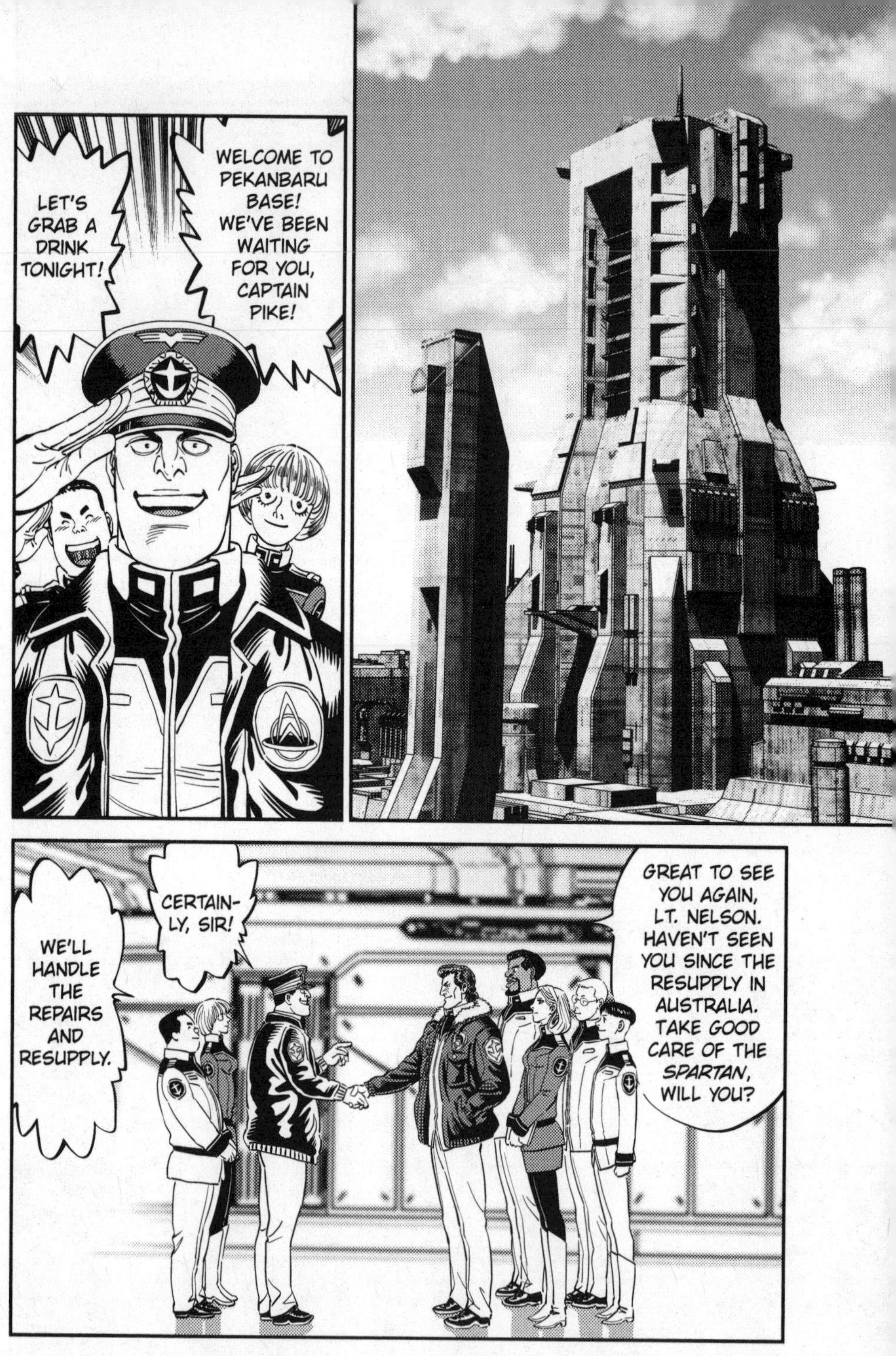
WELCOME TO PEKANBARU BASE! WE'VE BEEN WAITING FOR YOU, CAPTAIN PIKE!
LET'S GRAB A DRINK TONIGHT!
GREAT TO SEE YOU AGAIN, LT. NELSON. HAVEN'T SEEN YOU SINCE THE RESUPPLY IN AUSTRALIA. TAKE GOOD CARE OF THE *SPARTAN*, WILL YOU?
CERTAIN-LY, SIR!
WE'LL HANDLE THE REPAIRS AND RESUPPLY.

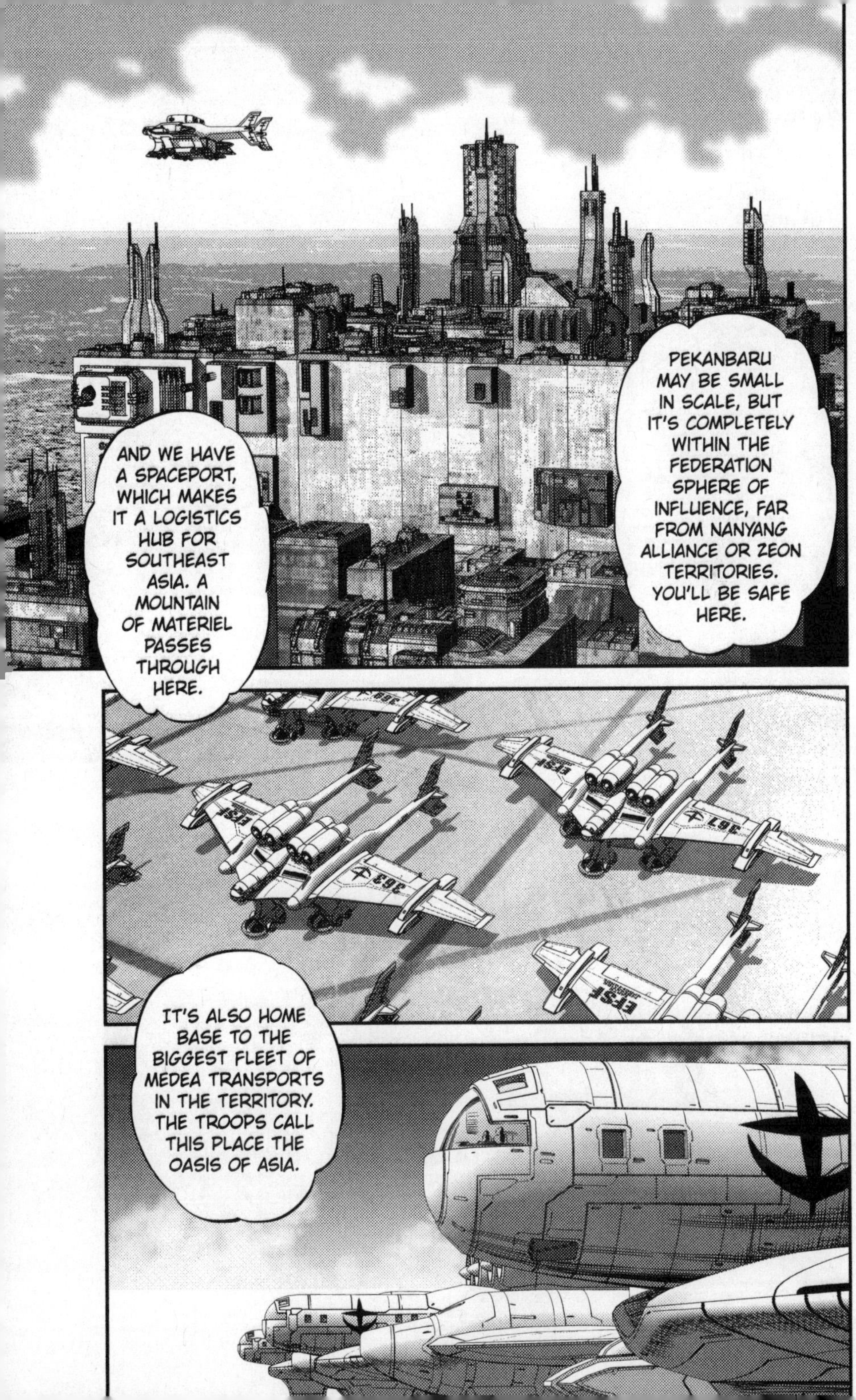
PEKANBARU MAY BE SMALL IN SCALE, BUT IT'S COMPLETELY WITHIN THE FEDERATION SPHERE OF INFLUENCE, FAR FROM NANYANG ALLIANCE OR ZEON TERRITORIES. YOU'LL BE SAFE HERE.
AND WE HAVE A SPACEPORT, WHICH MAKES IT A LOGISTICS HUB FOR SOUTHEAST ASIA. A MOUNTAIN OF MATERIEL PASSES THROUGH HERE.
IT'S ALSO HOME BASE TO THE BIGGEST FLEET OF MEDEA TRANSPORTS IN THE TERRITORY. THE TROOPS CALL THIS PLACE THE OASIS OF ASIA.

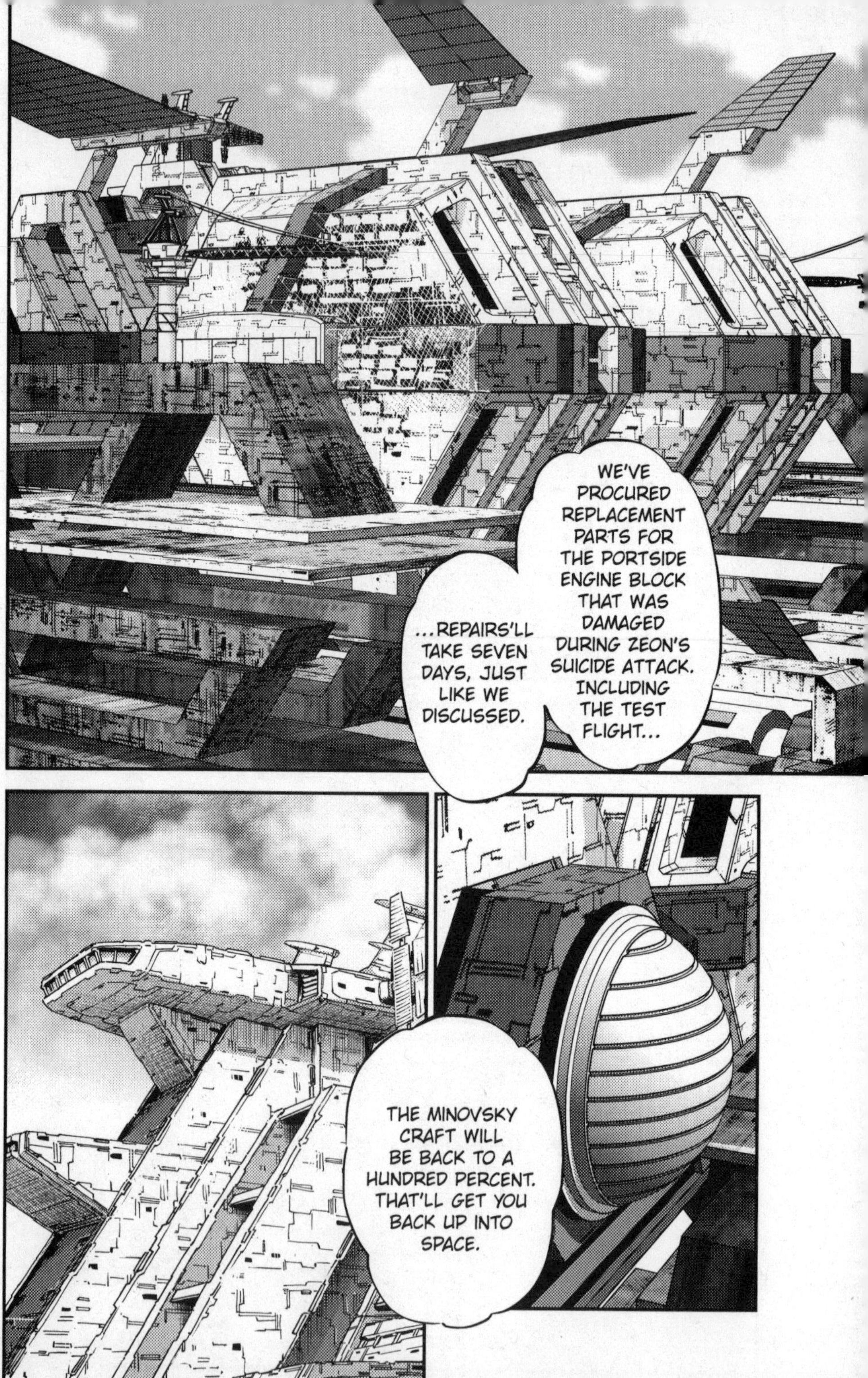
WE'VE PROCURED REPLACEMENT PARTS FOR THE PORTSIDE ENGINE BLOCK THAT WAS DAMAGED DURING ZEON'S SUICIDE ATTACK. INCLUDING THE TEST FLIGHT...
...REPAIRS'LL TAKE SEVEN DAYS, JUST LIKE WE DISCUSSED.
THE MINOVSKY CRAFT WILL BE BACK TO A HUNDRED PERCENT. THAT'LL GET YOU BACK UP INTO SPACE.

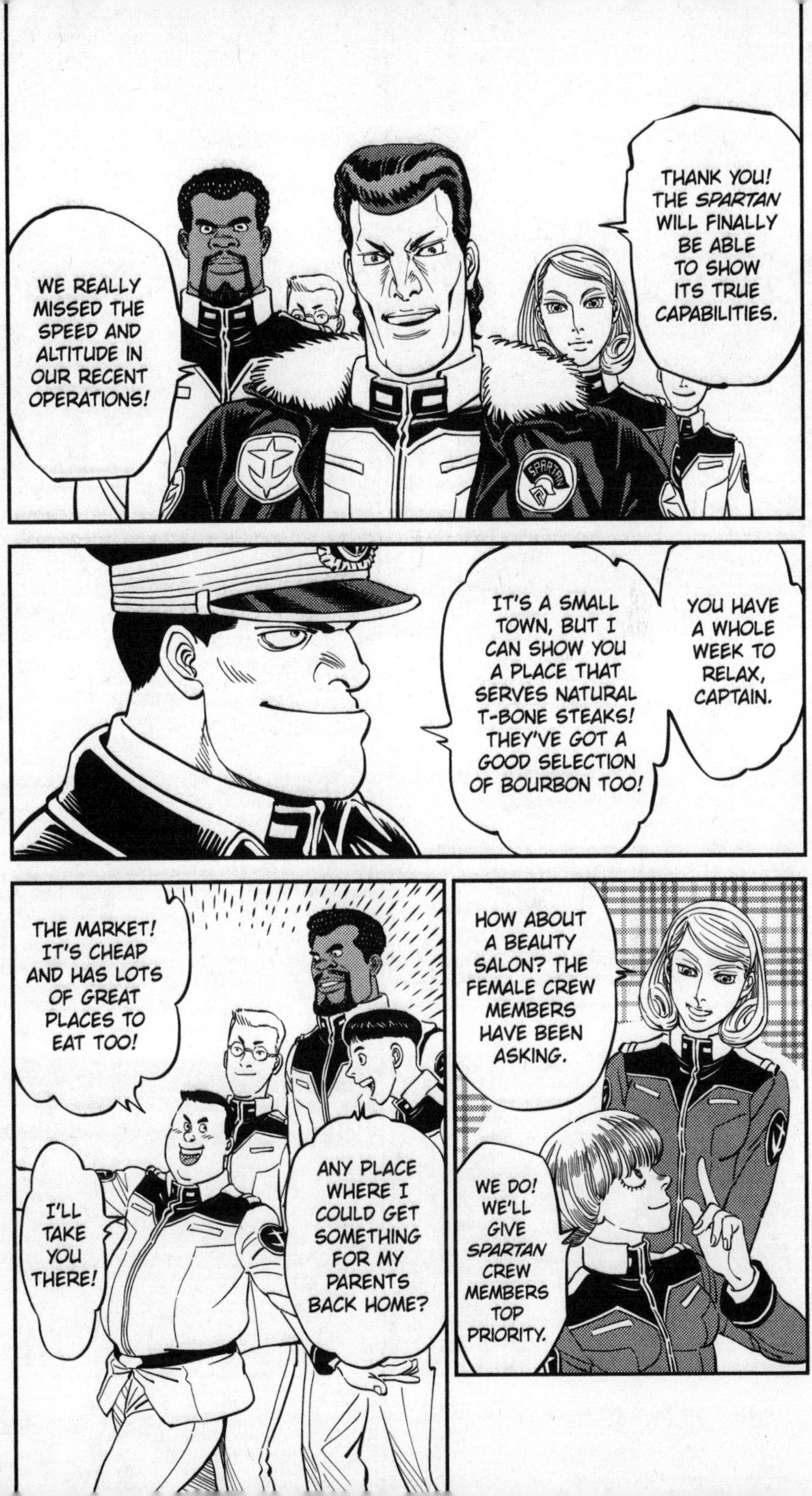
THANK YOU! THE SPARTAN WILL FINALLY BE ABLE TO SHOW ITS TRUE CAPABILITIES.
WE REALLY MISSED THE SPEED AND ALTITUDE IN OUR RECENT OPERATIONS!
YOU HAVE A WHOLE WEEK TO RELAX, CAPTAIN.
IT'S A SMALL TOWN, BUT I CAN SHOW YOU A PLACE THAT SERVES NATURAL T-BONE STEAKS! THEY'VE GOT A GOOD SELECTION OF BOURBON TOO!
HOW ABOUT A BEAUTY SALON? THE FEMALE CREW MEMBERS HAVE BEEN ASKING.
WE DO! WE'LL GIVE SPARTAN CREW MEMBERS TOP PRIORITY.
THE MARKET! IT'S CHEAP AND HAS LOTS OF GREAT PLACES TO EAT TOO!
ANY PLACE WHERE I COULD GET SOMETHING FOR MY PARENTS BACK HOME?
I'LL TAKE YOU THERE!

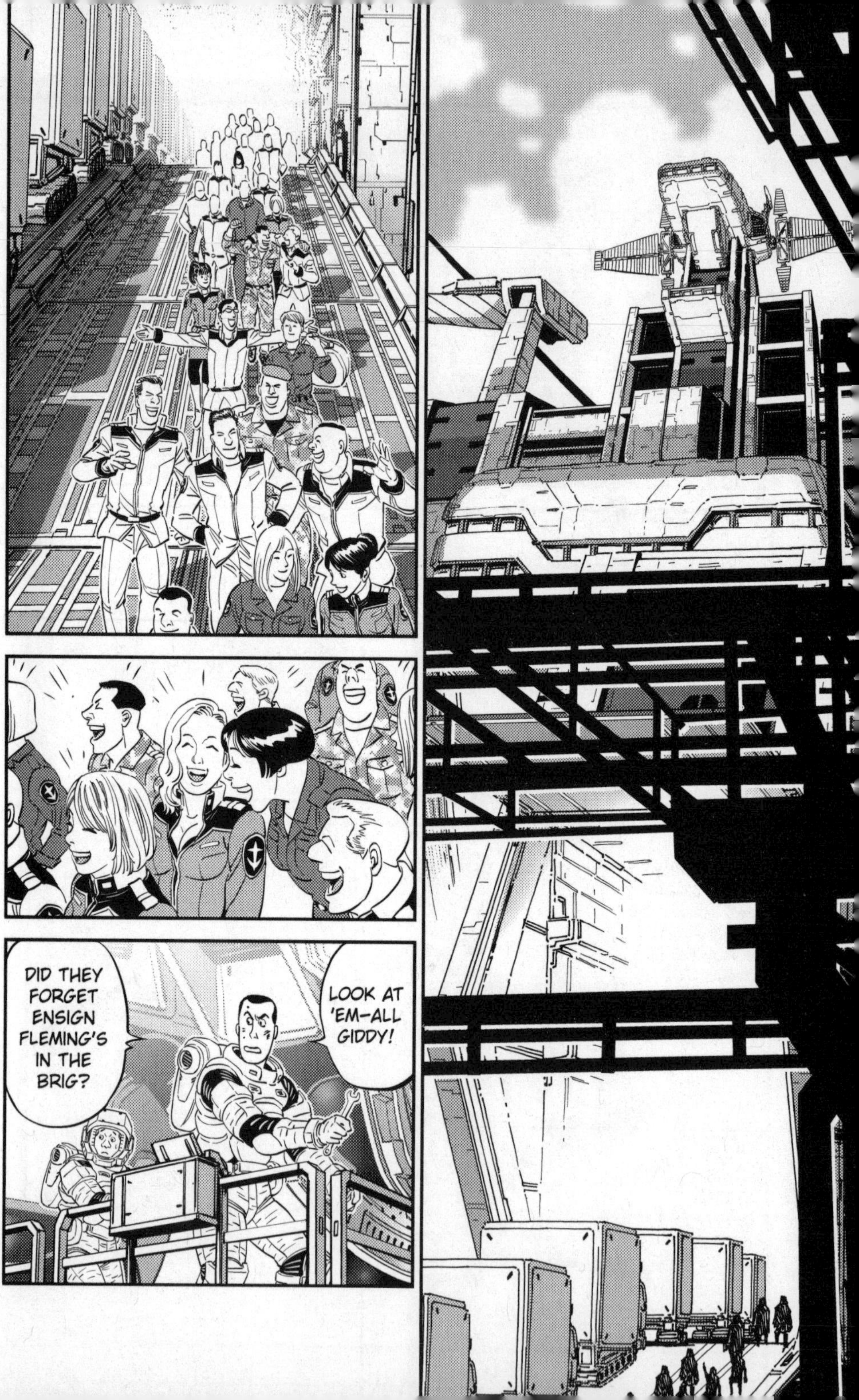
LOOK AT 'EM—ALL GIDDY!
DID THEY FORGET ENSIGN FLEMING'S IN THE BRIG?

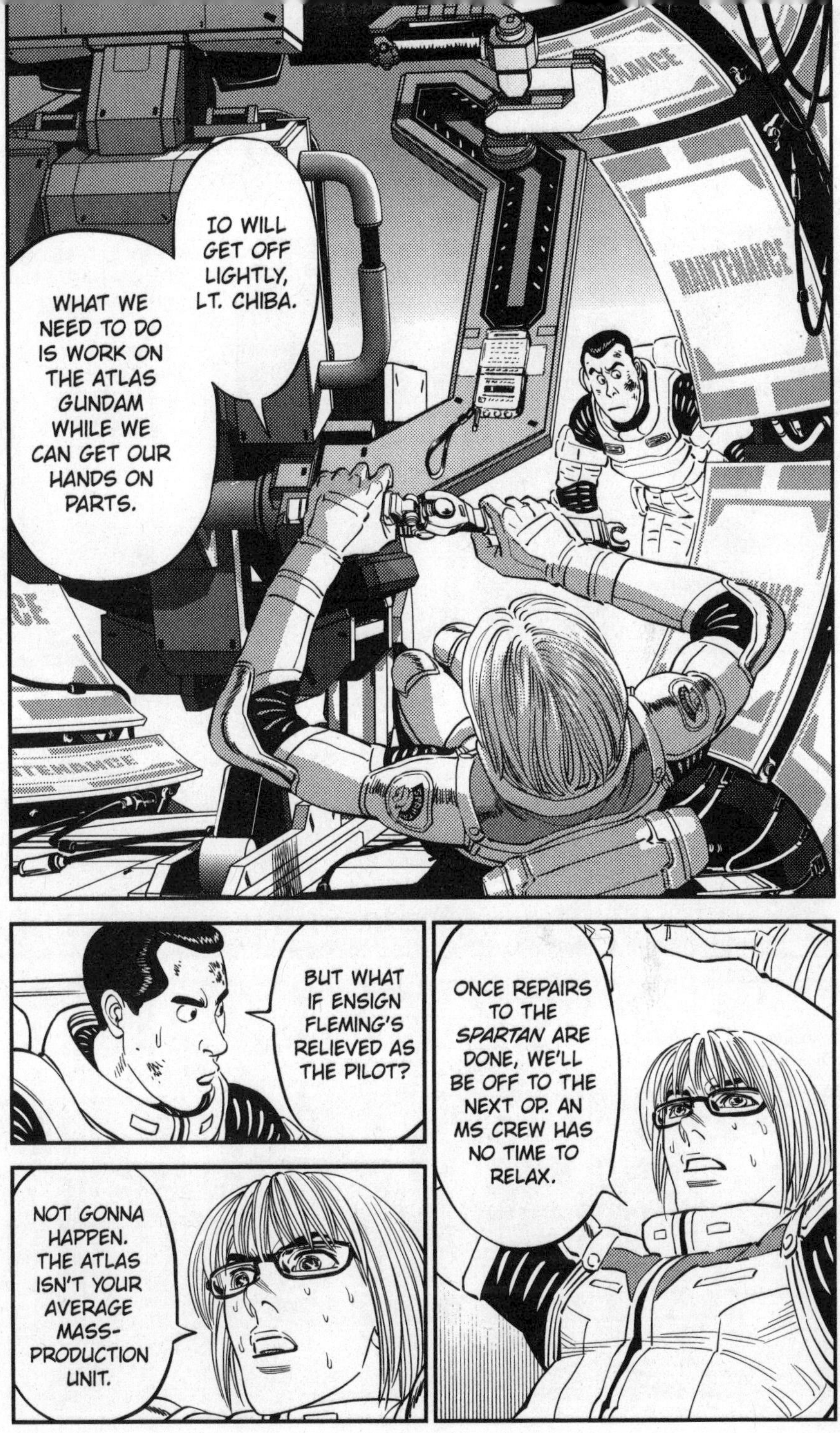
MAINTENANCE
IO WILL GET OFF LIGHTLY, LT. CHIBA.
WHAT WE NEED TO DO IS WORK ON THE ATLAS GUNDAM WHILE WE CAN GET OUR HANDS ON PARTS.
ONCE REPAIRS TO THE *SPARTAN* ARE DONE, WE'LL BE OFF TO THE NEXT OP. AN MS CREW HAS NO TIME TO RELAX.
BUT WHAT IF ENSIGN FLEMING'S RELIEVED AS THE PILOT?
NOT GONNA HAPPEN. THE ATLAS ISN'T YOUR AVERAGE MASS-PRODUCTION UNIT.

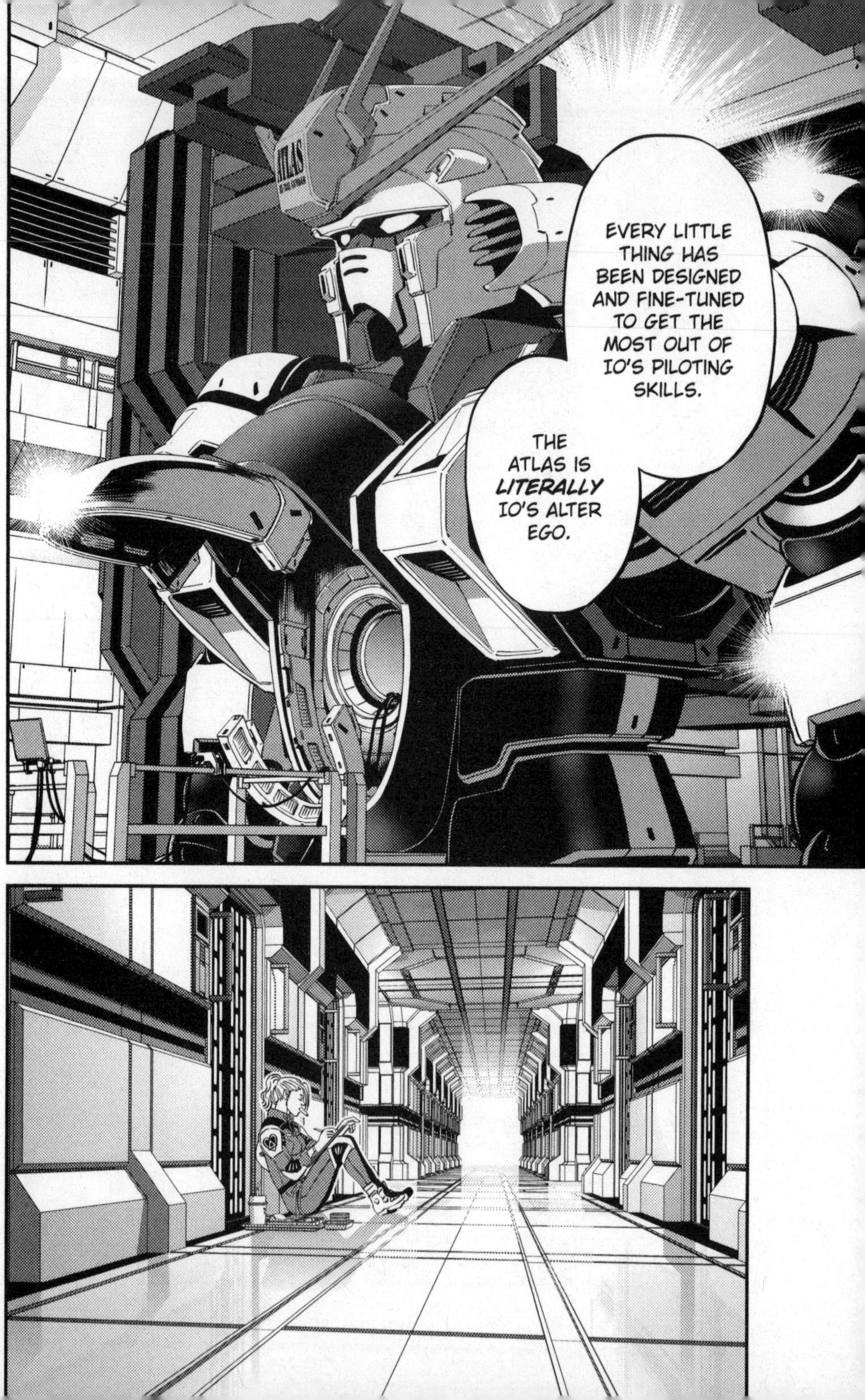
ATLAS
EVERY LITTLE THING HAS BEEN DESIGNED AND FINE-TUNED TO GET THE MOST OUT OF IO'S PILOTING SKILLS.
THE ATLAS IS *LITERALLY* IO'S ALTER EGO.

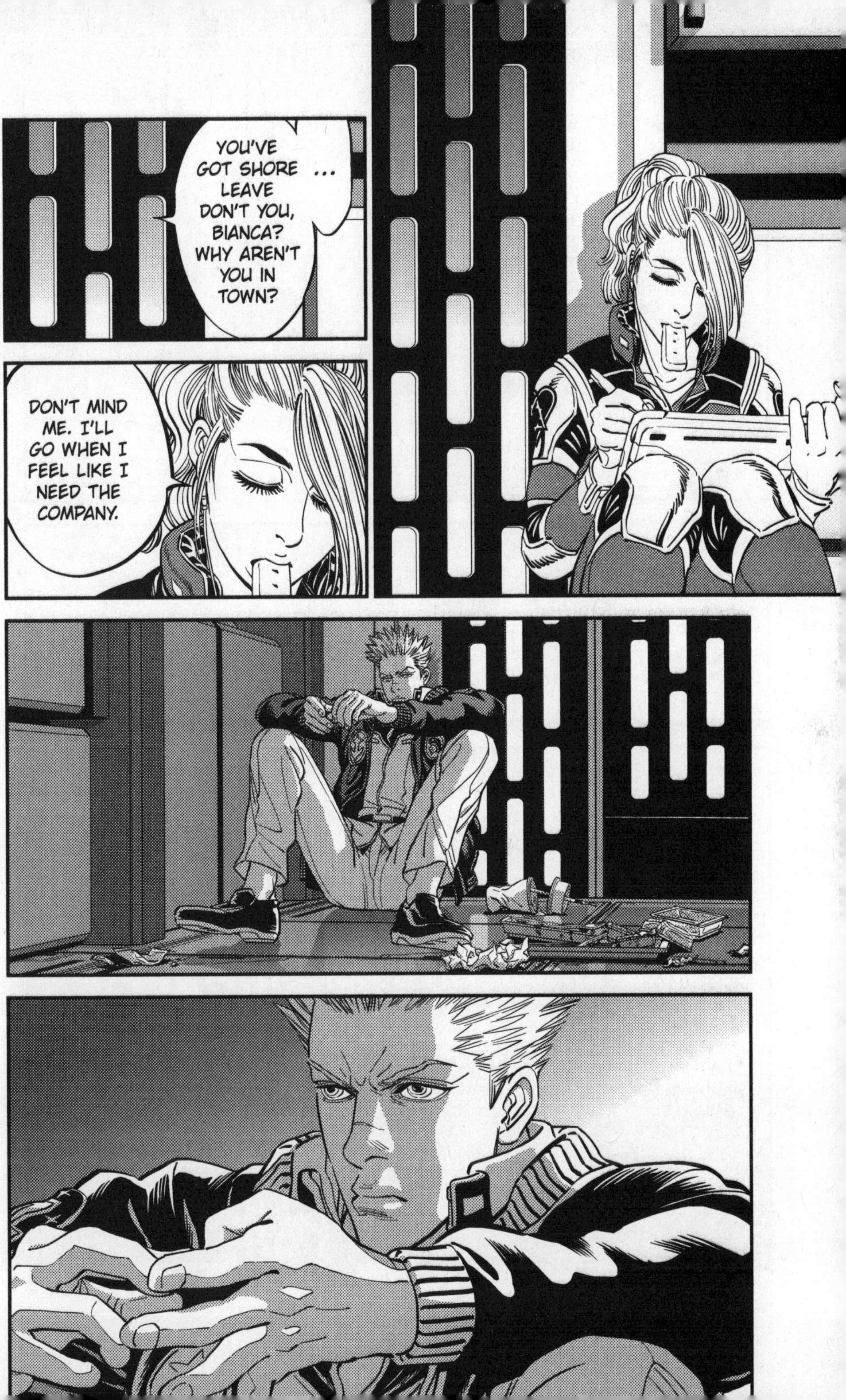
YOU'VE GOT SHORE LEAVE ... DON'T YOU, BIANCA? WHY AREN'T YOU IN TOWN?
DON'T MIND ME. I'LL GO WHEN I FEEL LIKE I NEED THE COMPANY.

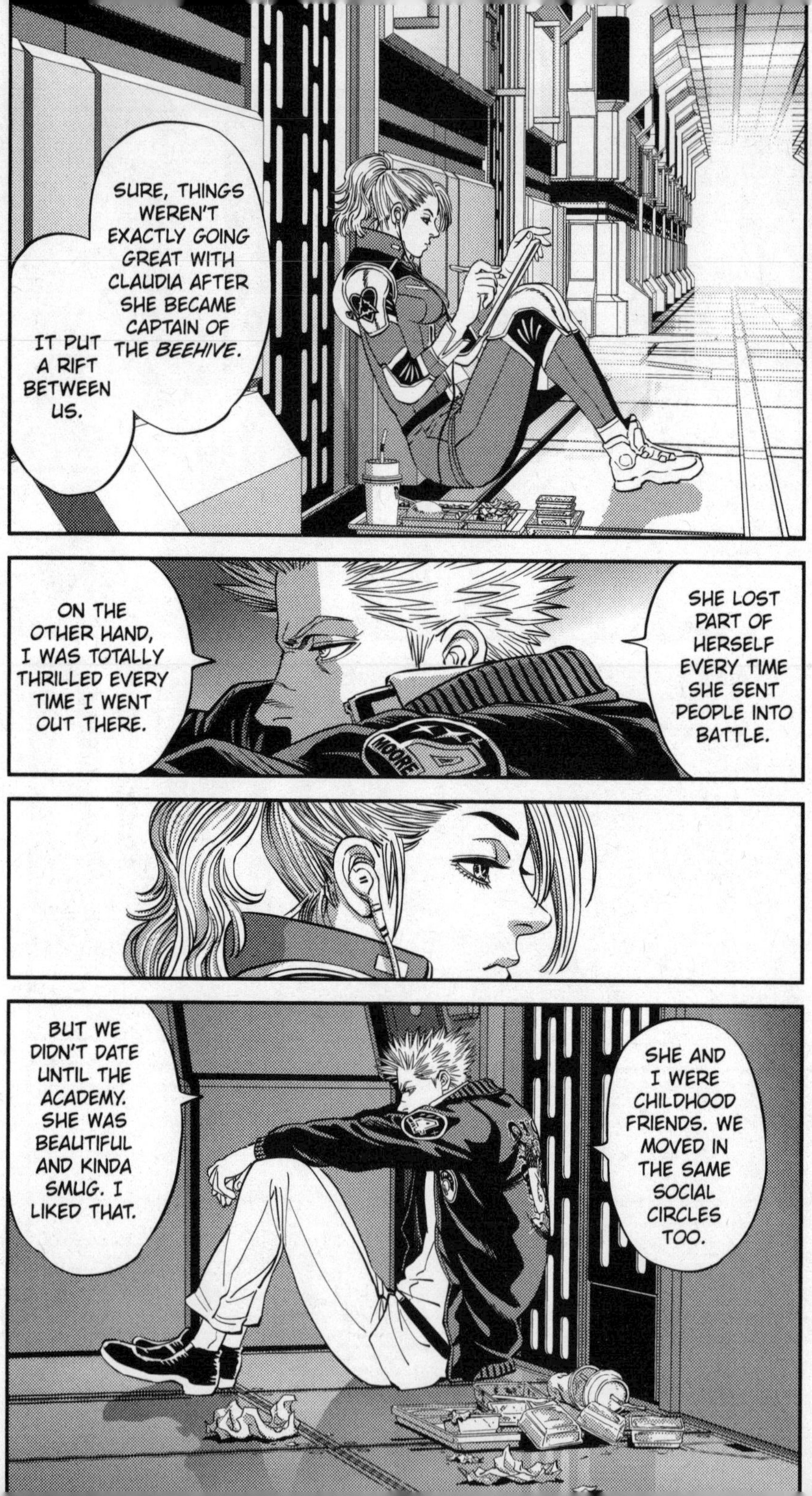
SURE, THINGS WEREN'T EXACTLY GOING GREAT WITH CLAUDIA AFTER SHE BECAME CAPTAIN OF THE *BEEHIVE*.
IT PUT A RIFT BETWEEN US.
SHE LOST PART OF HERSELF EVERY TIME SHE SENT PEOPLE INTO BATTLE.
ON THE OTHER HAND, I WAS TOTALLY THRILLED EVERY TIME I WENT OUT THERE.
MOORE
SHE AND I WERE CHILDHOOD FRIENDS. WE MOVED IN THE SAME SOCIAL CIRCLES TOO.
BUT WE DIDN'T DATE UNTIL THE ACADEMY. SHE WAS BEAUTIFUL AND KINDA SMUG. I LIKED THAT.

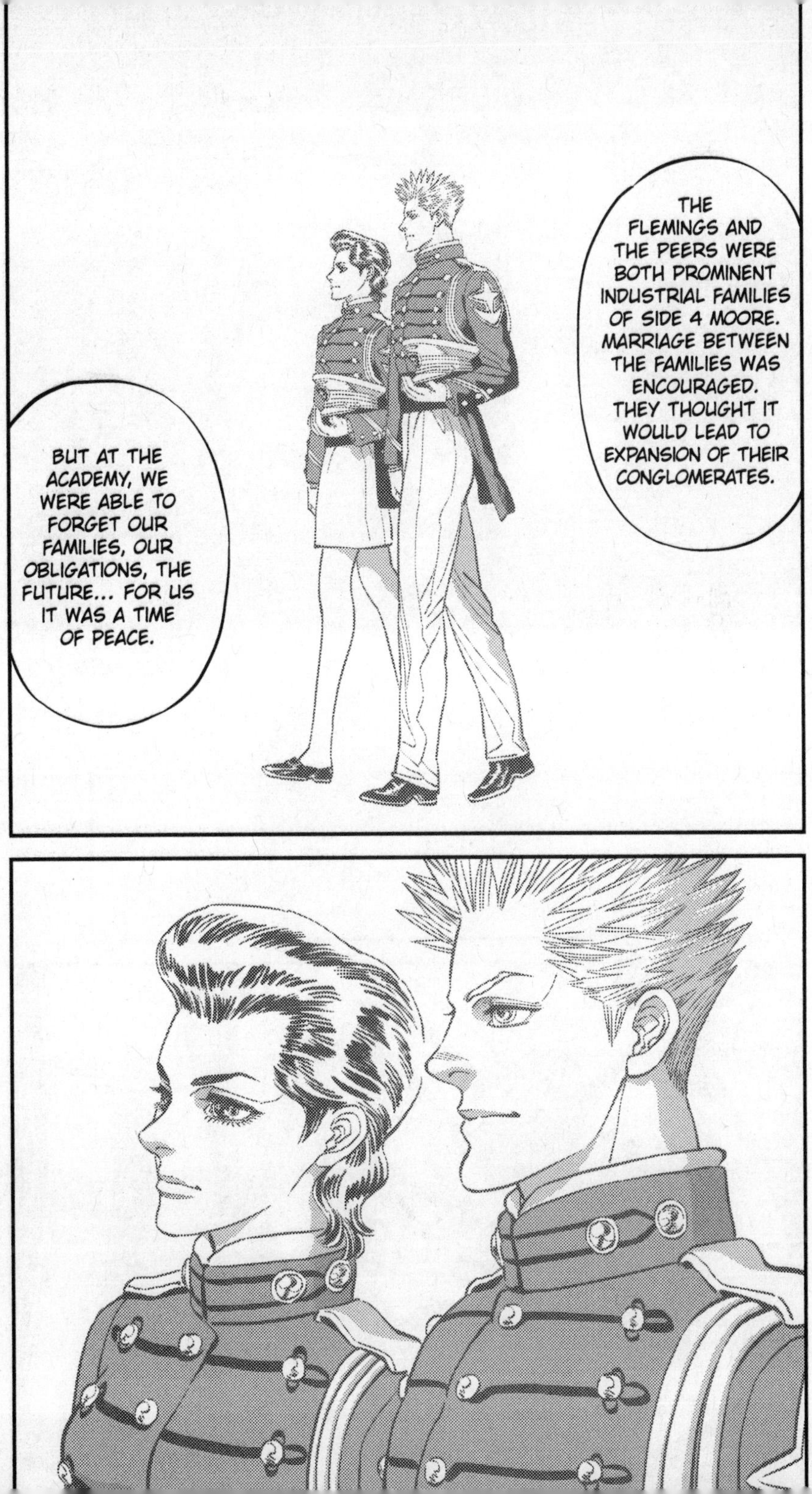
THE FLEMINGS AND THE PEERS WERE BOTH PROMINENT INDUSTRIAL FAMILIES OF SIDE 4 MOORE. MARRIAGE BETWEEN THE FAMILIES WAS ENCOURAGED. THEY THOUGHT IT WOULD LEAD TO EXPANSION OF THEIR CONGLOMERATES.
BUT AT THE ACADEMY, WE WERE ABLE TO FORGET OUR FAMILIES, OUR OBLIGATIONS, THE FUTURE... FOR US IT WAS A TIME OF PEACE.

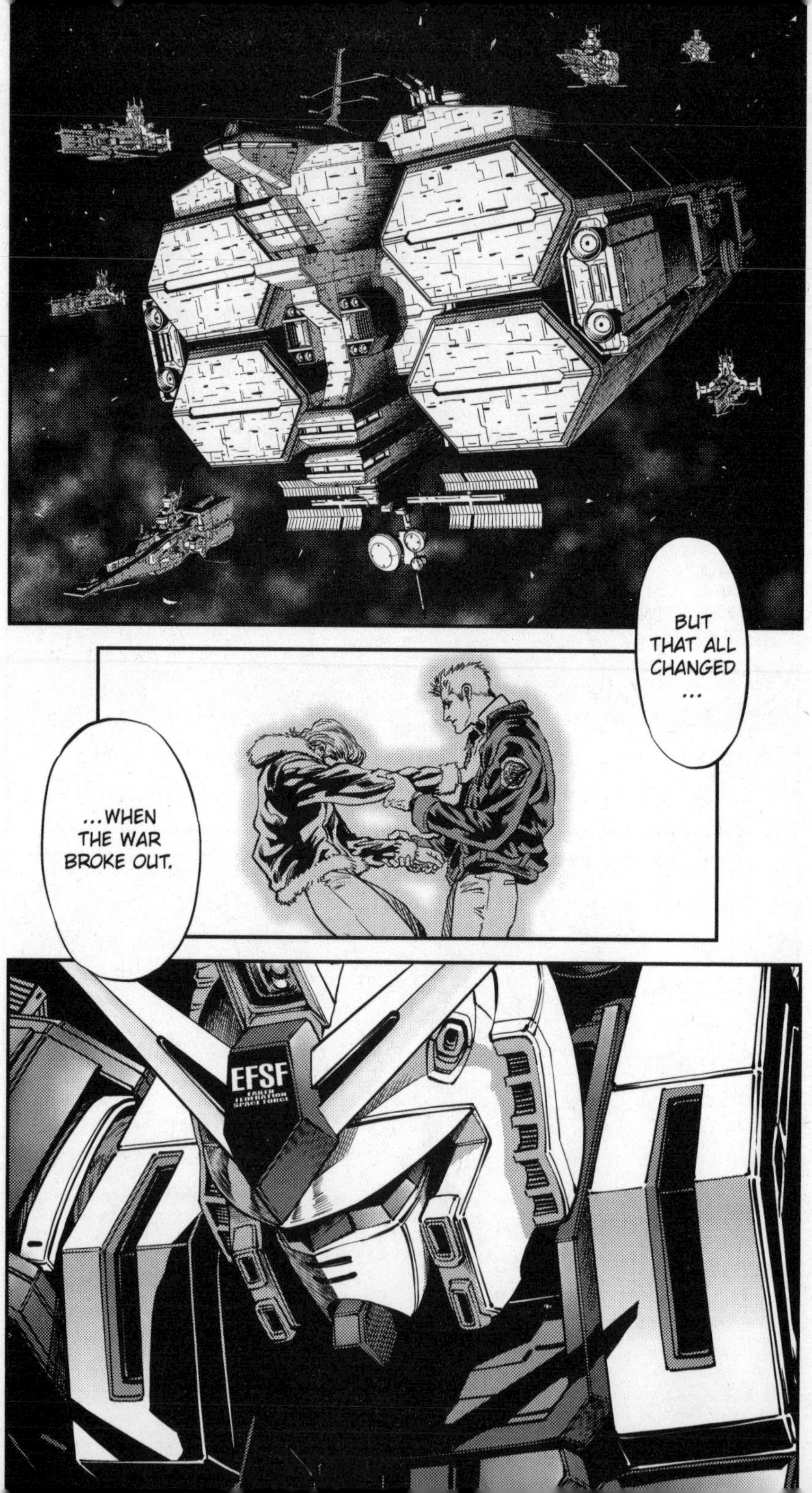
BUT THAT ALL CHANGED ...
...WHEN THE WAR BROKE OUT.
EFSF

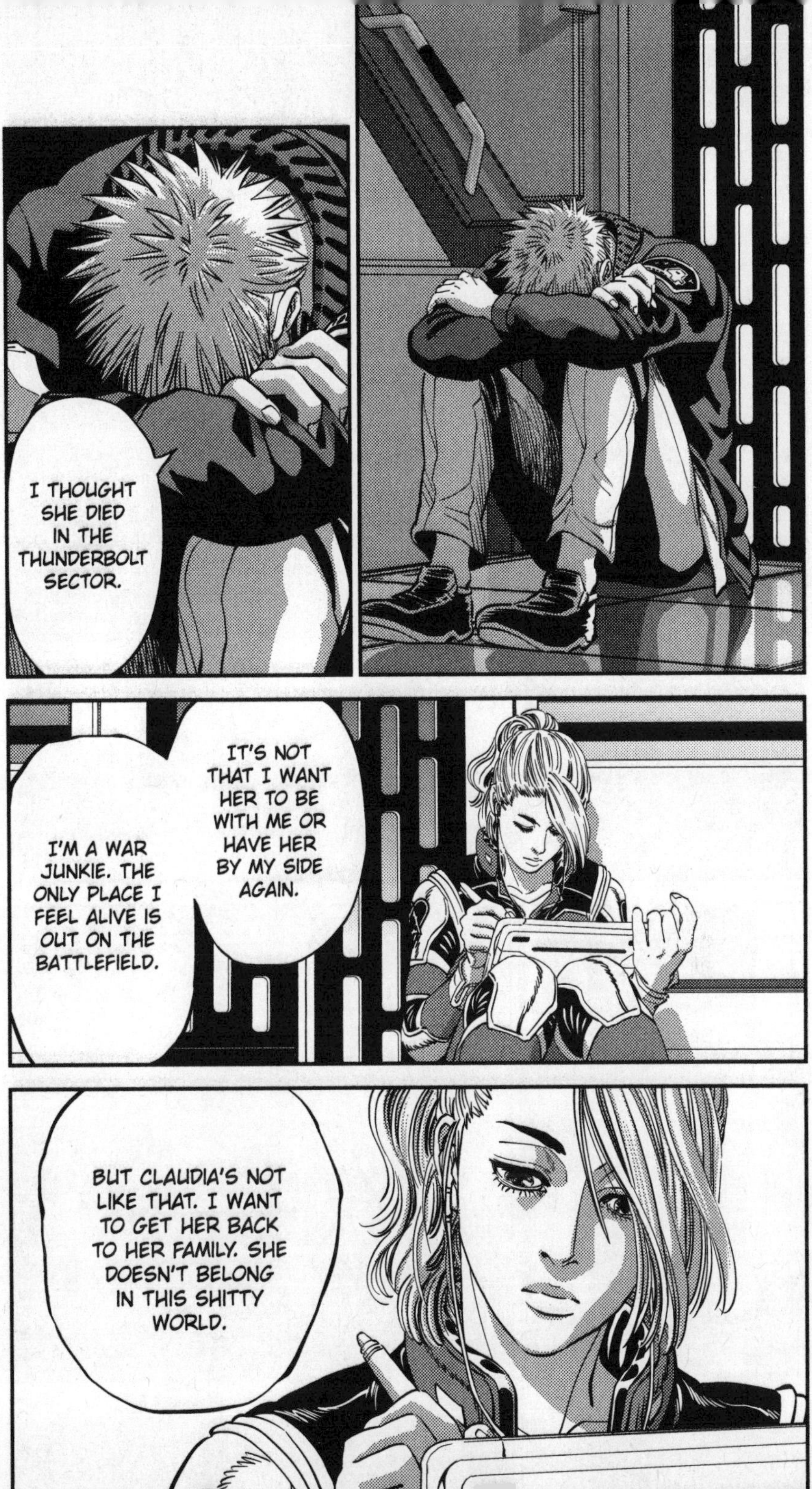
I THOUGHT SHE DIED IN THE THUNDERBOLT SECTOR.
IT'S NOT THAT I WANT HER TO BE WITH ME OR HAVE HER BY MY SIDE AGAIN.
I'M A WAR JUNKIE. THE ONLY PLACE I FEEL ALIVE IS OUT ON THE BATTLEFIELD.
BUT CLAUDIA'S NOT LIKE THAT. I WANT TO GET HER BACK TO HER FAMILY. SHE DOESN'T BELONG IN THIS SHITTY WORLD.

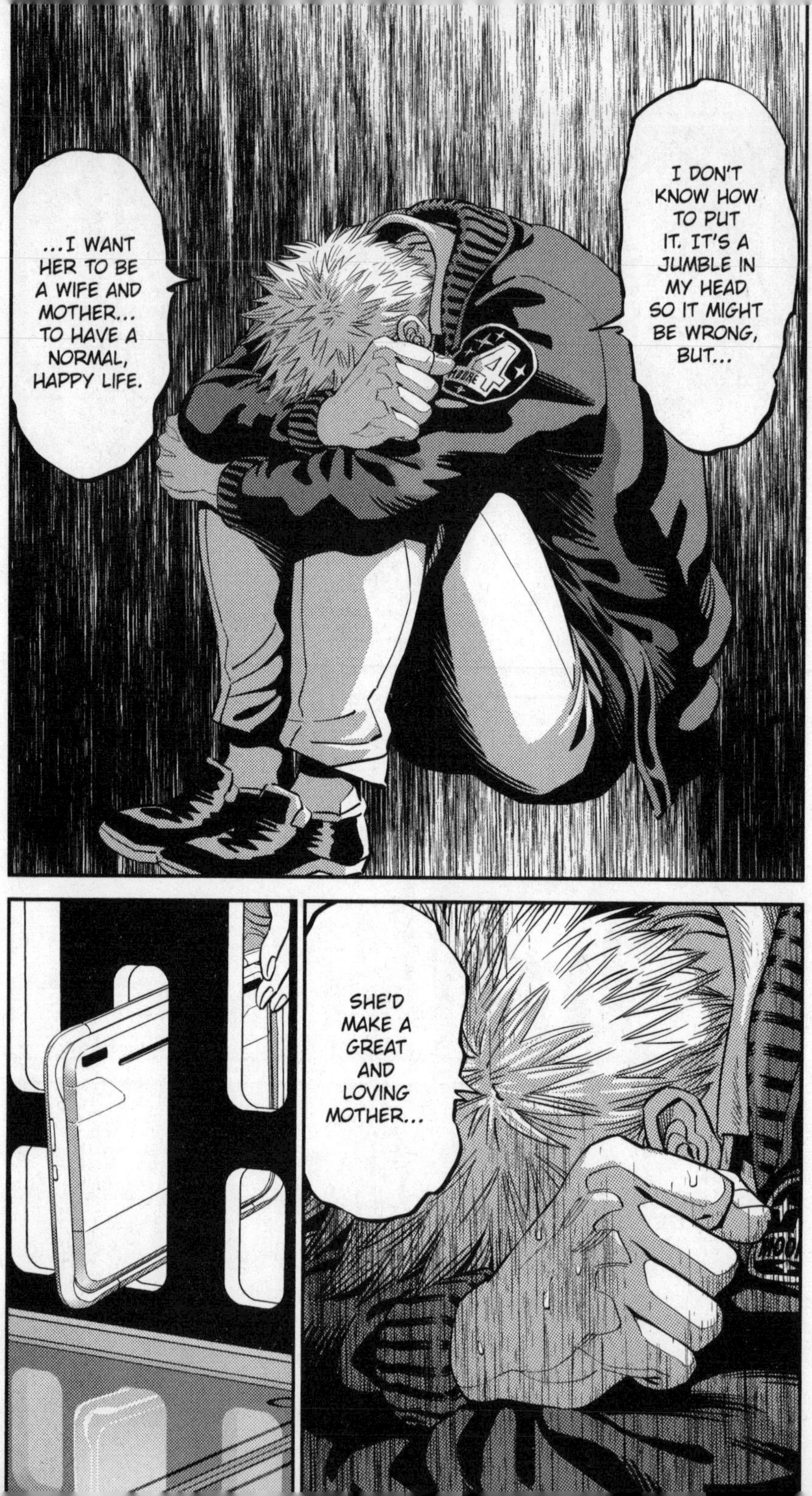
I DON'T KNOW HOW TO PUT IT. IT'S A JUMBLE IN MY HEAD SO IT MIGHT BE WRONG, BUT...
...I WANT HER TO BE A WIFE AND MOTHER... TO HAVE A NORMAL, HAPPY LIFE.
SHE'D MAKE A GREAT AND LOVING MOTHER...

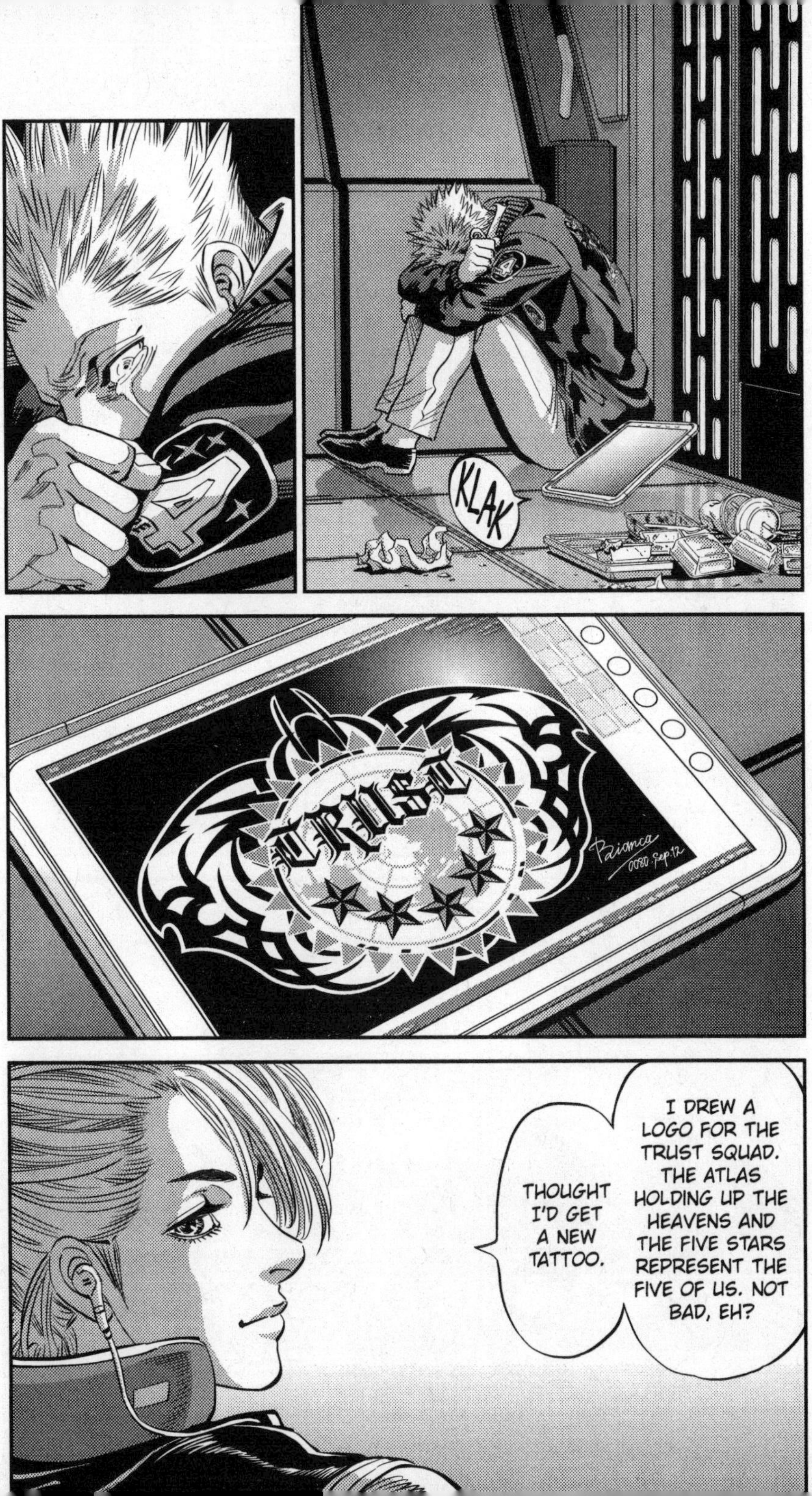
KLAK
TRUST
Bianca 0080 Sep.12
I DREW A LOGO FOR THE TRUST SQUAD. THE ATLAS HOLDING UP THE HEAVENS AND THE FIVE STARS REPRESENT THE FIVE OF US. NOT BAD, EH?
THOUGHT I'D GET A NEW TATTOO.

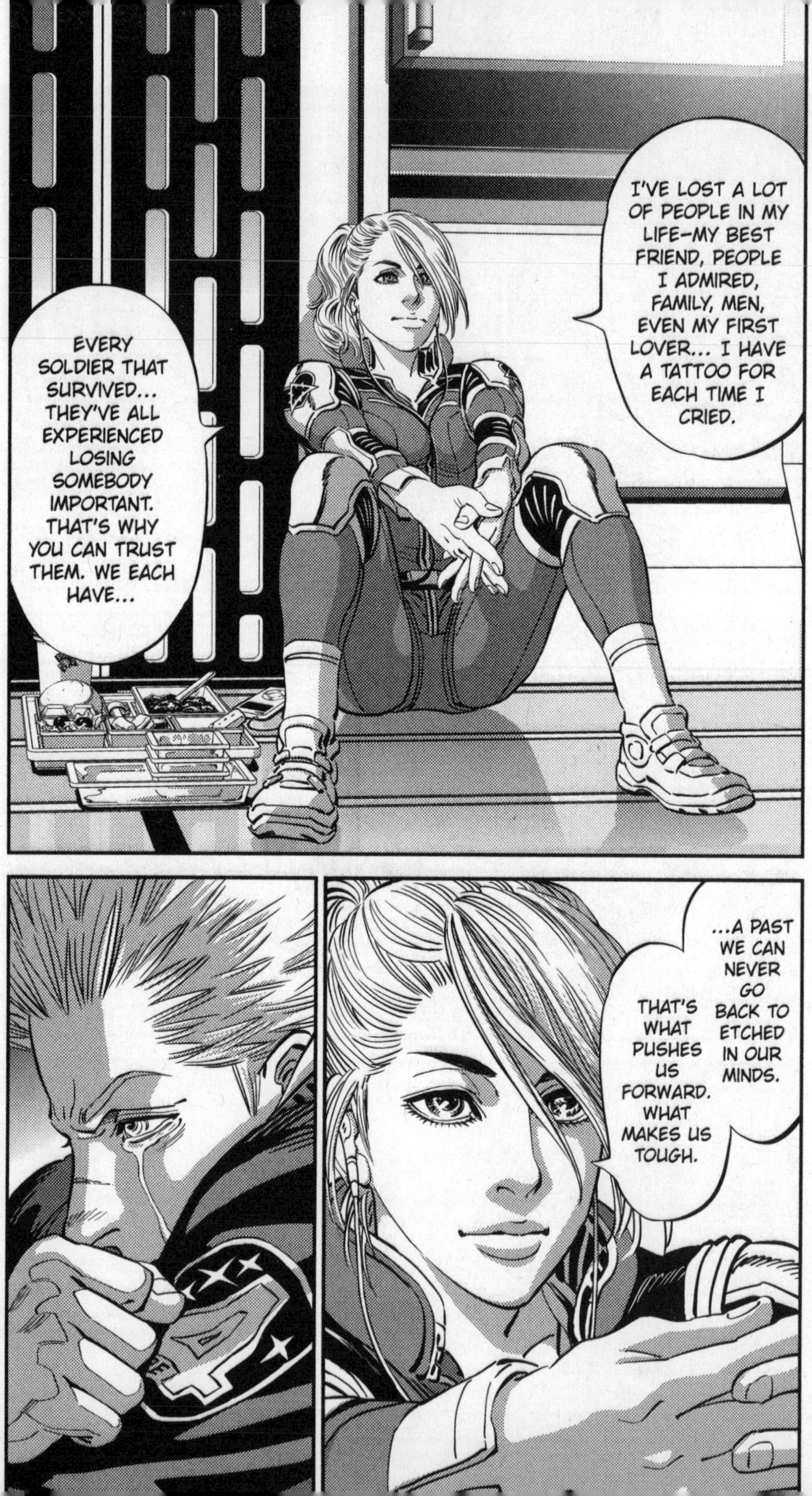
I'VE LOST A LOT OF PEOPLE IN MY LIFE—MY BEST FRIEND, PEOPLE I ADMIRED, FAMILY, MEN, EVEN MY FIRST LOVER... I HAVE A TATTOO FOR EACH TIME I CRIED.
EVERY SOLDIER THAT SURVIVED... THEY'VE ALL EXPERIENCED LOSING SOMEBODY IMPORTANT. THAT'S WHY YOU CAN TRUST THEM. WE EACH HAVE...
...A PAST WE CAN NEVER GO BACK TO ETCHED IN OUR MINDS.
THAT'S WHAT PUSHES US FORWARD. WHAT MAKES US TOUGH.

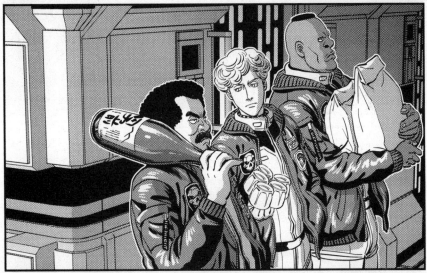

TELL ME ABOUT THE FIRST GUY YOU WERE EVER WITH.

HEY, BIANCA...

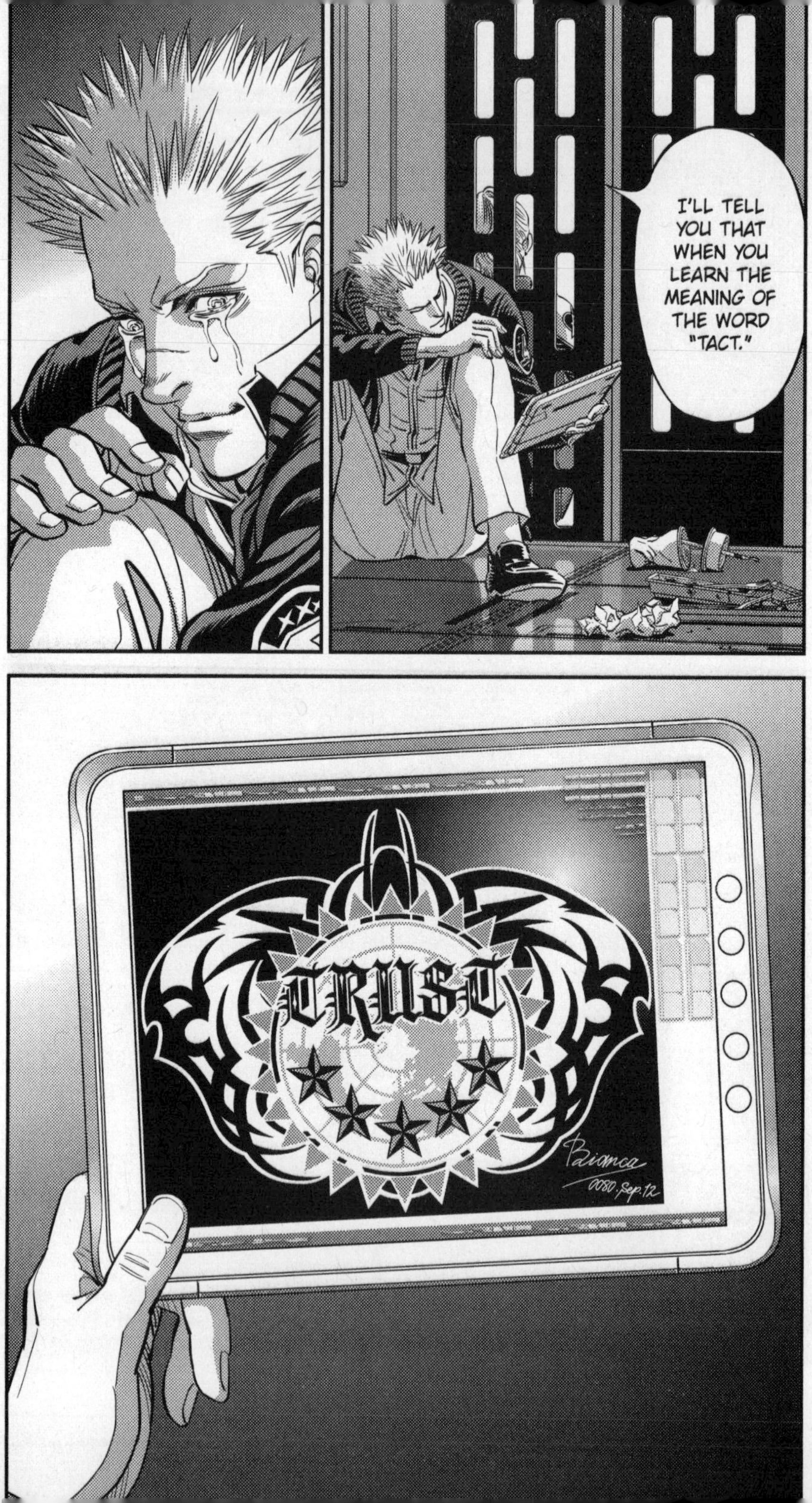
I'LL TELL YOU THAT WHEN YOU LEARN THE MEANING OF THE WORD "TACT."
TRUST
Bianca
0080, Sep. 12

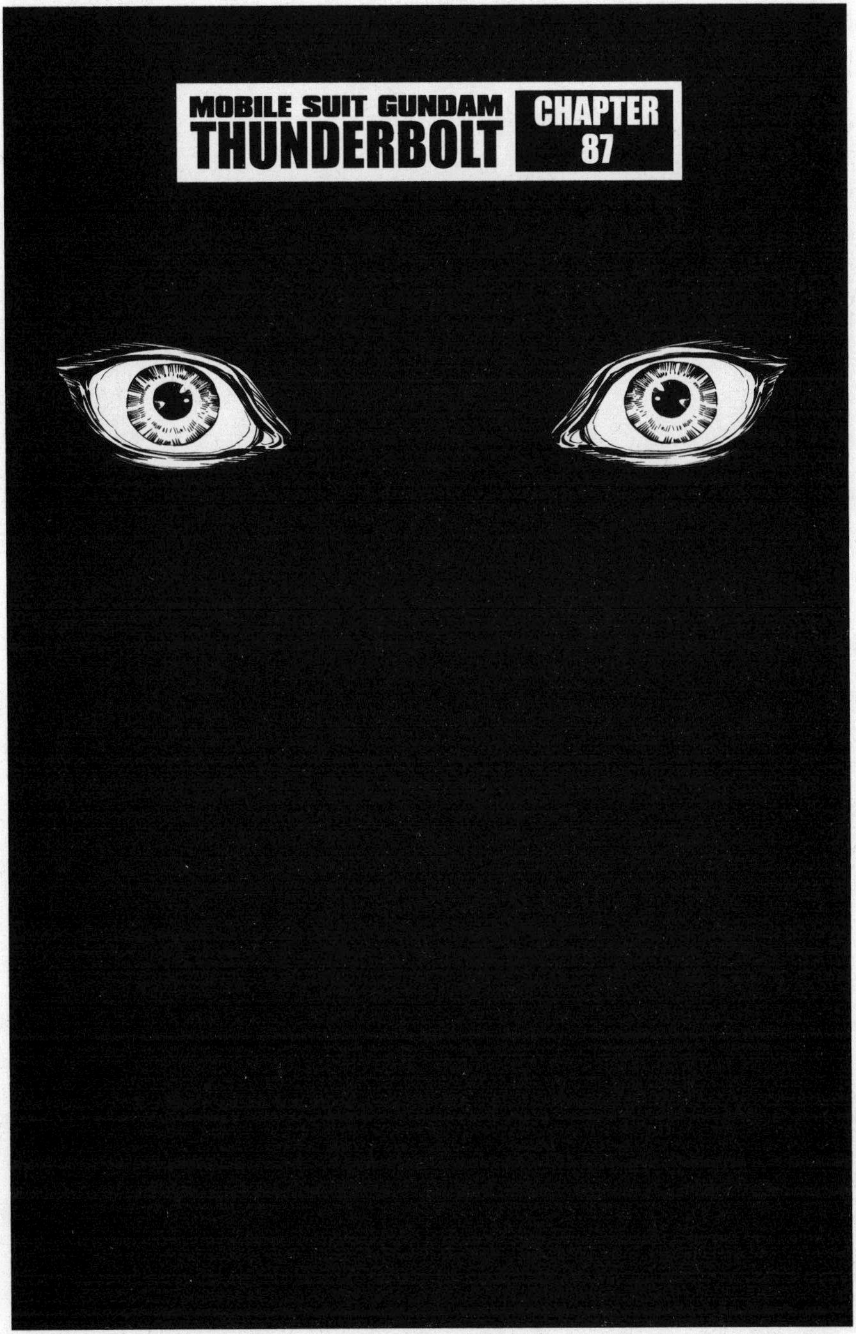
MOBILE SUIT GUNDAM
THUNDERBOLT
CHAPTER
87

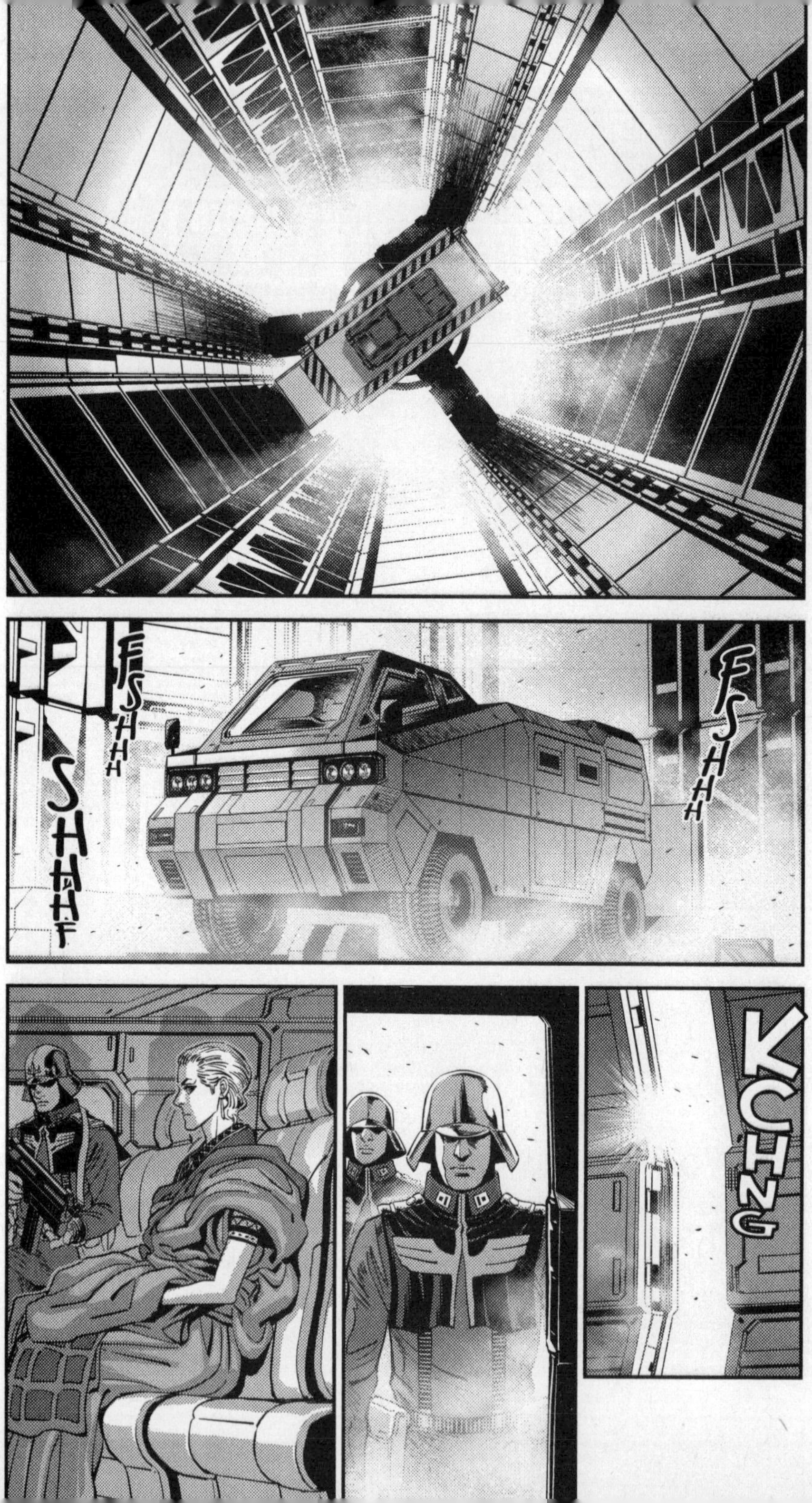
FSHHH
FSHHH
SHHHF
KCHNG

WE'VE BEEN EXPECTING YOU, MS. PEER.

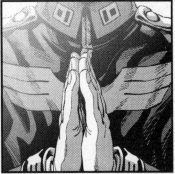

SHHHH HWOO

SHFFFF HWOO

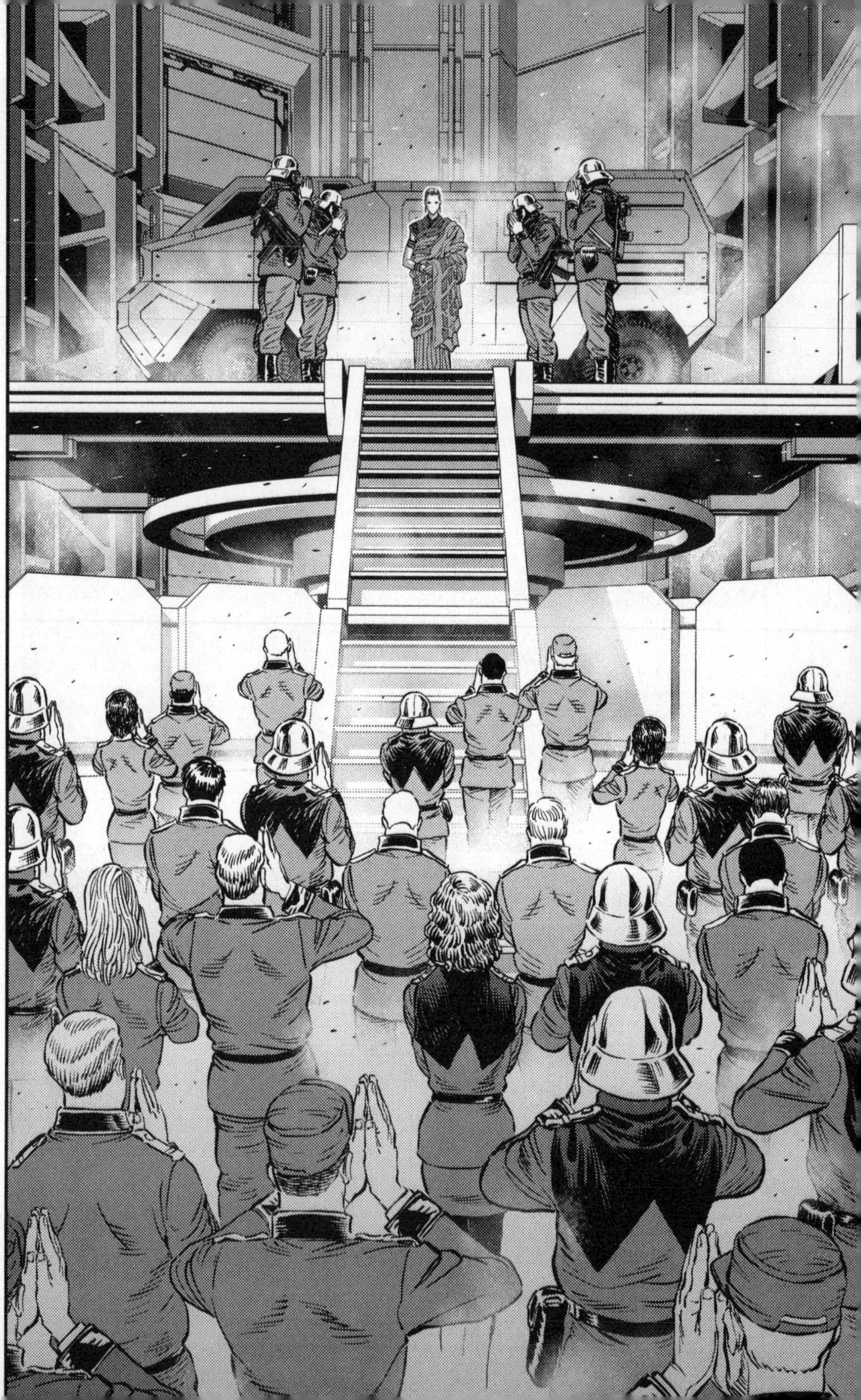

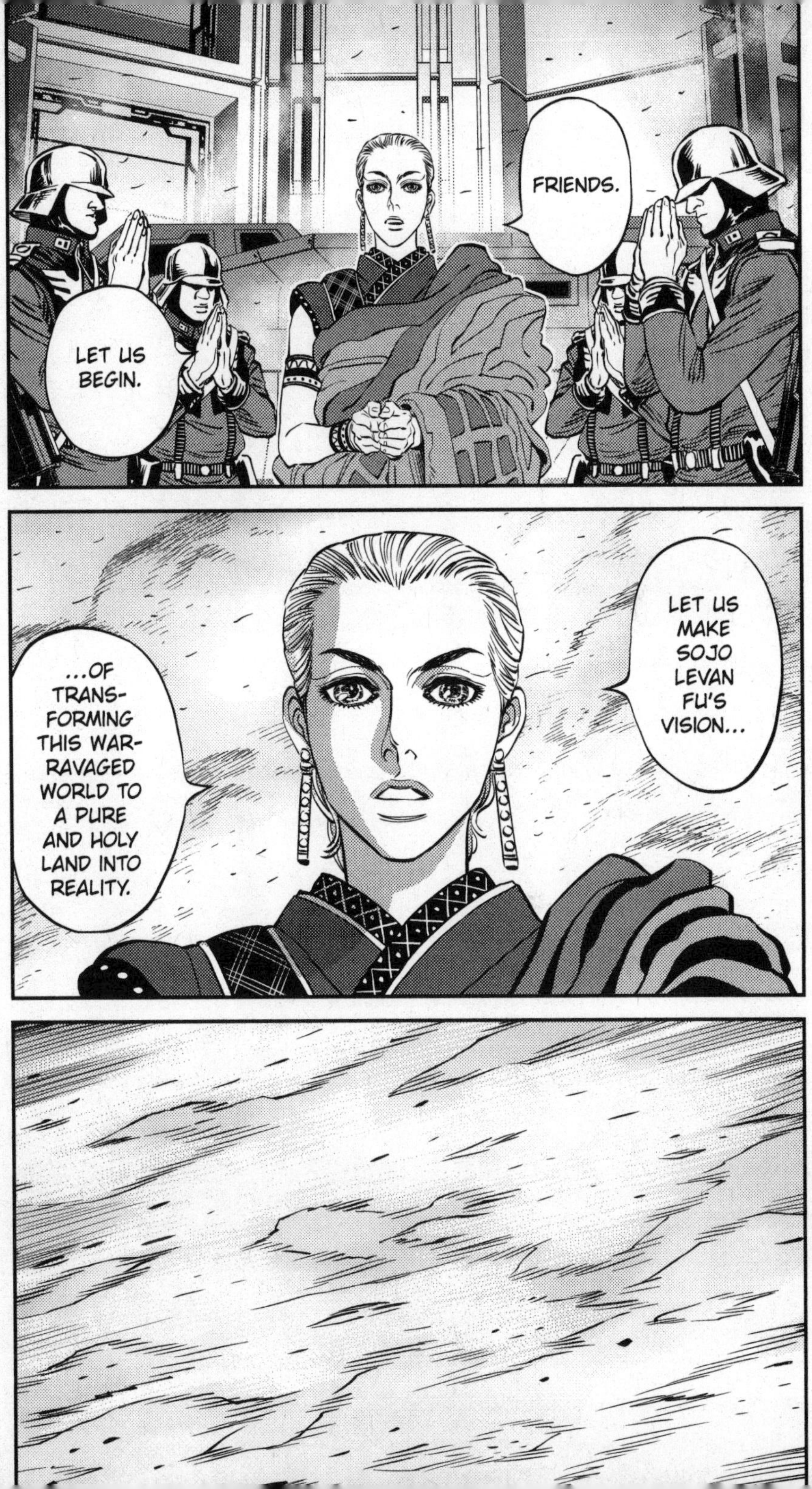
FRIENDS.
LET US BEGIN.
LET US MAKE SOJO LEVAN FU'S VISION...
...OF TRANS-FORMING THIS WAR-RAVAGED WORLD TO A PURE AND HOLY LAND INTO REALITY.

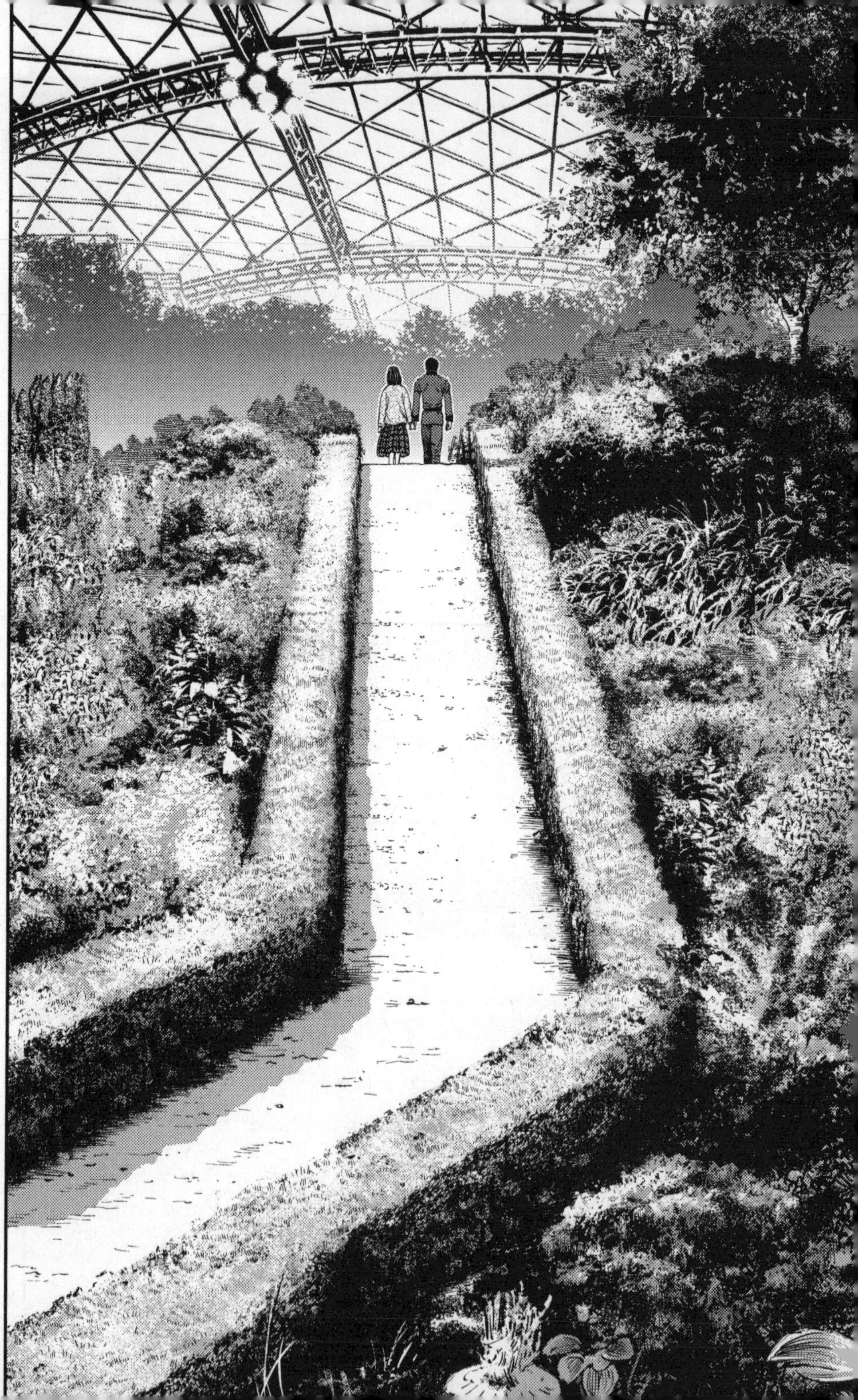

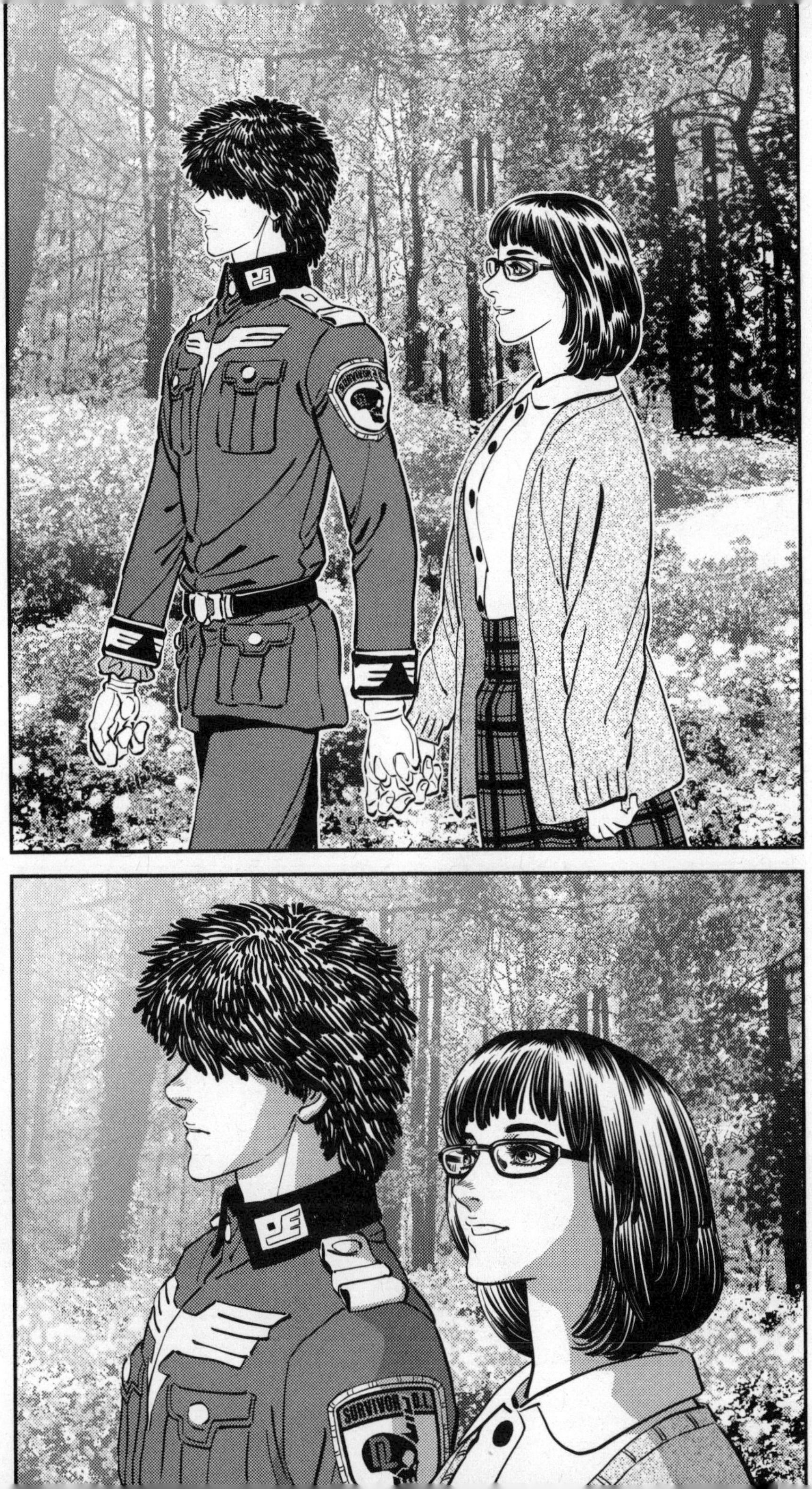

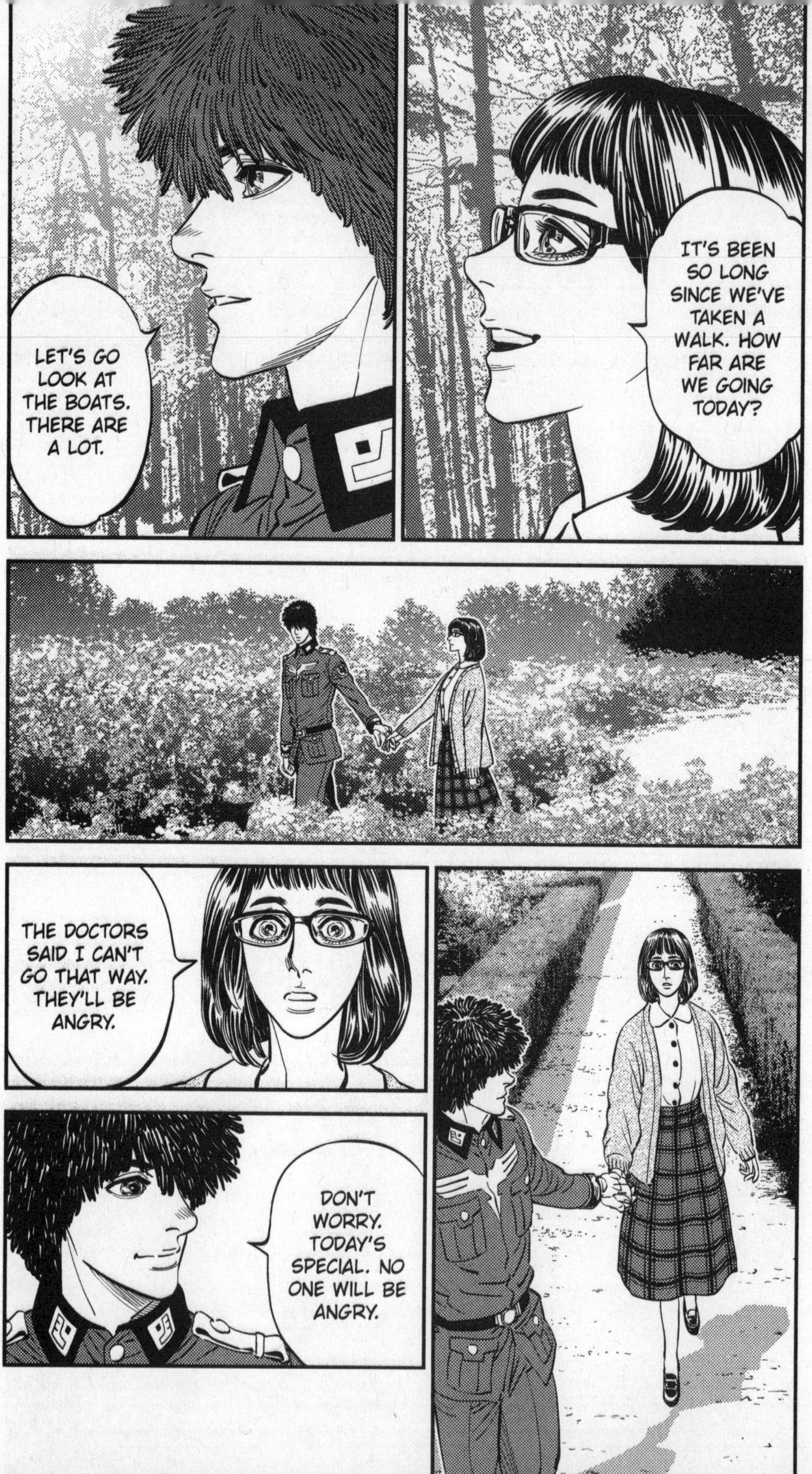
IT'S BEEN SO LONG SINCE WE'VE TAKEN A WALK. HOW FAR ARE WE GOING TODAY?
LET'S GO LOOK AT THE BOATS. THERE ARE A LOT.
THE DOCTORS SAID I CAN'T GO THAT WAY. THEY'LL BE ANGRY.
DON'T WORRY. TODAY'S SPECIAL. NO ONE WILL BE ANGRY.

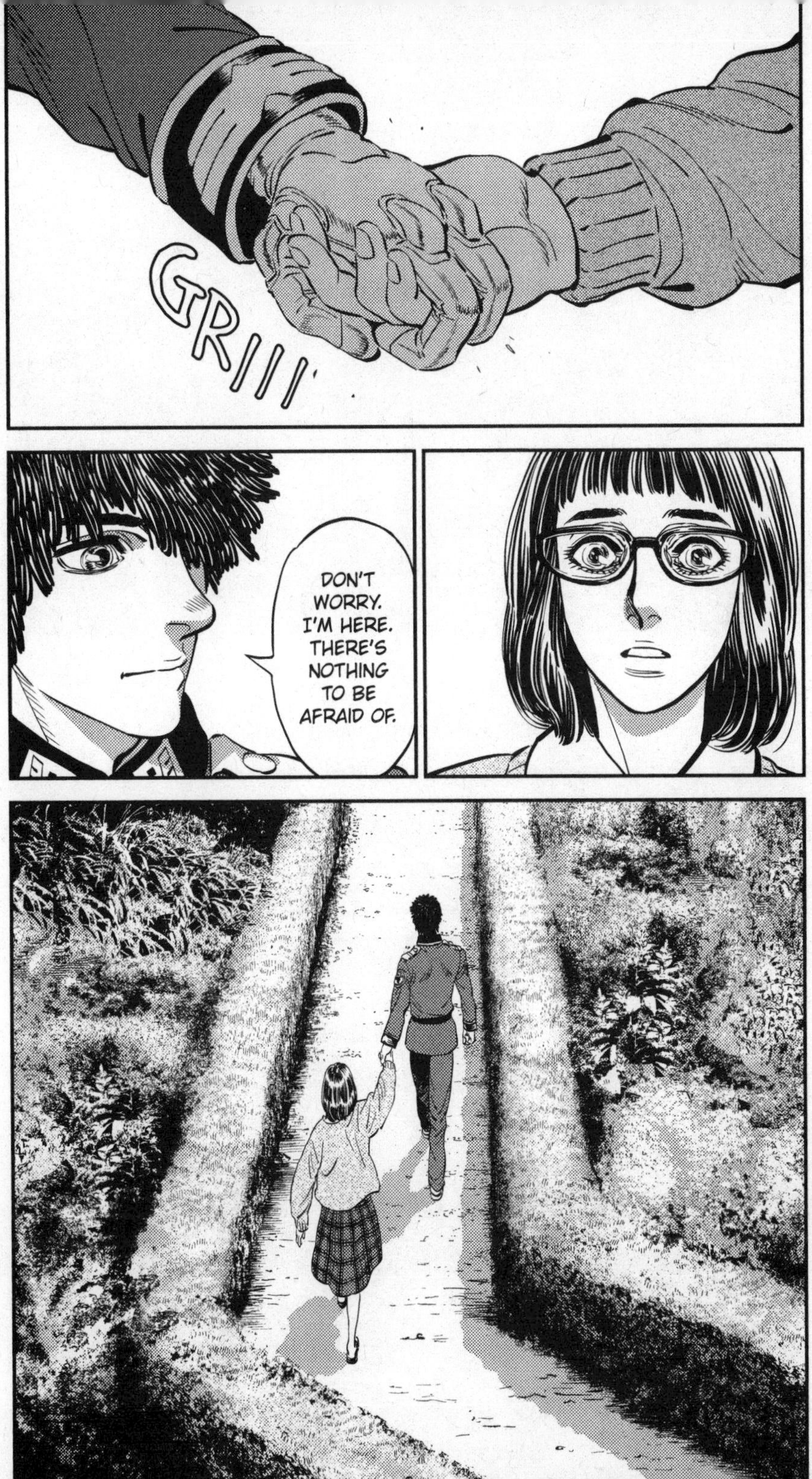
GRIII
DON'T WORRY. I'M HERE. THERE'S NOTHING TO BE AFRAID OF.

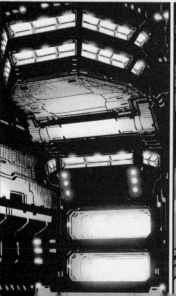

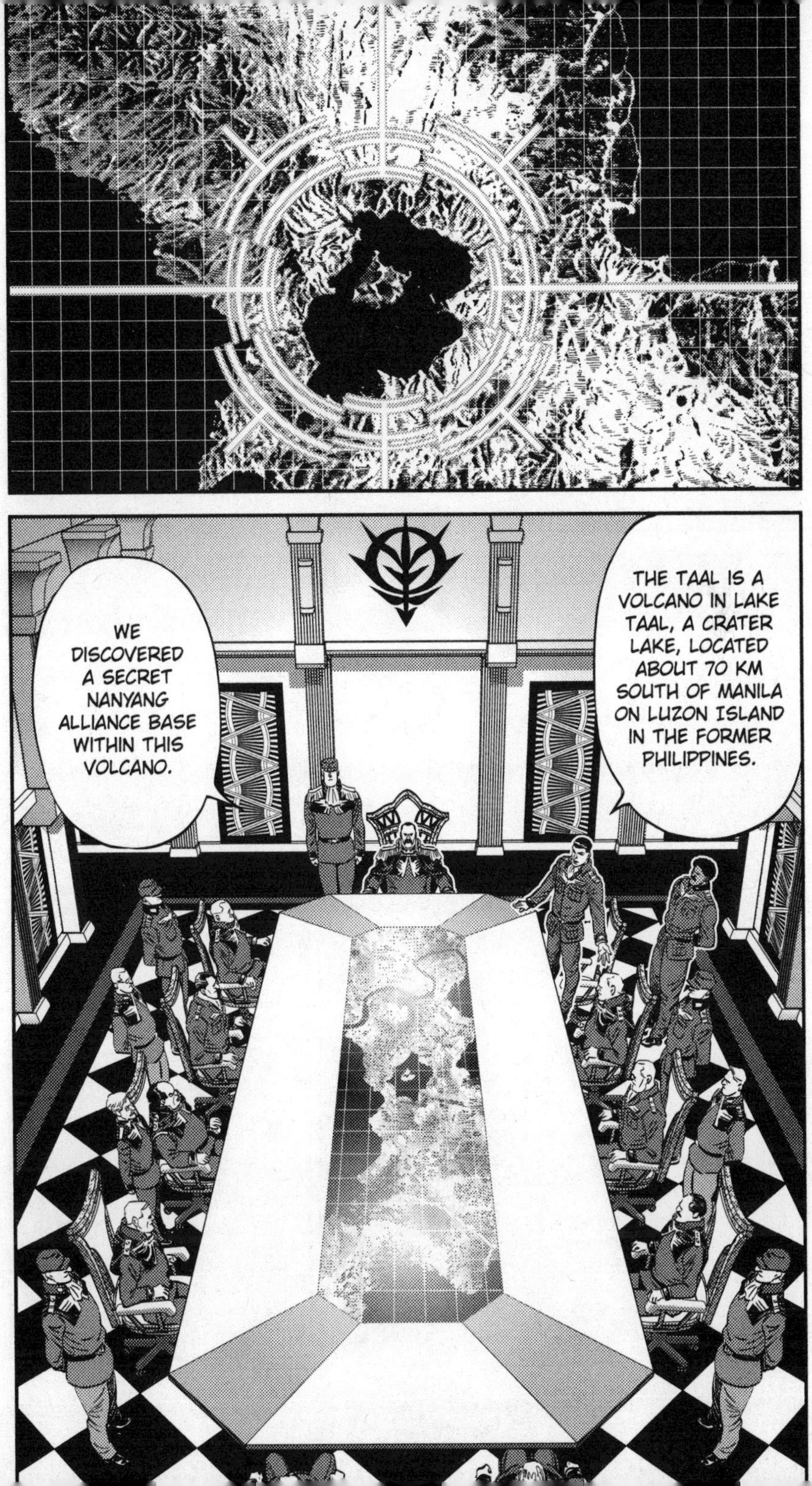
THE TAAL IS A VOLCANO IN LAKE TAAL, A CRATER LAKE, LOCATED ABOUT 70 KM SOUTH OF MANILA ON LUZON ISLAND IN THE FORMER PHILIPPINES.
WE DISCOVERED A SECRET NANYANG ALLIANCE BASE WITHIN THIS VOLCANO.

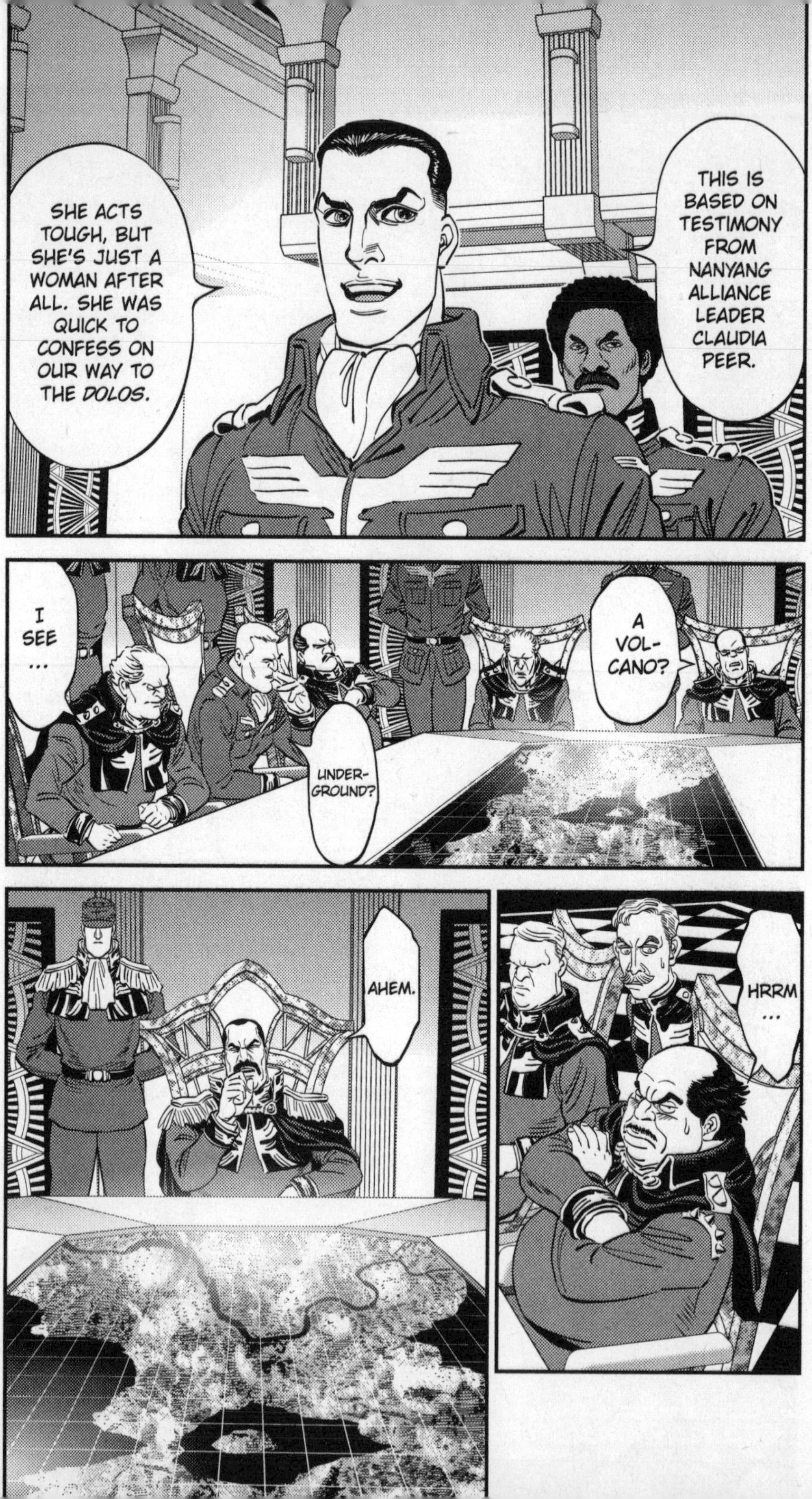
THIS IS BASED ON TESTIMONY FROM NANYANG ALLIANCE LEADER CLAUDIA PEER.
SHE ACTS TOUGH, BUT SHE'S JUST A WOMAN AFTER ALL. SHE WAS QUICK TO CONFESS ON OUR WAY TO THE *DOLOS*.
A VOL-CANO?
UNDER-GROUND?
I SEE ...
HRRM ...
AHEM.

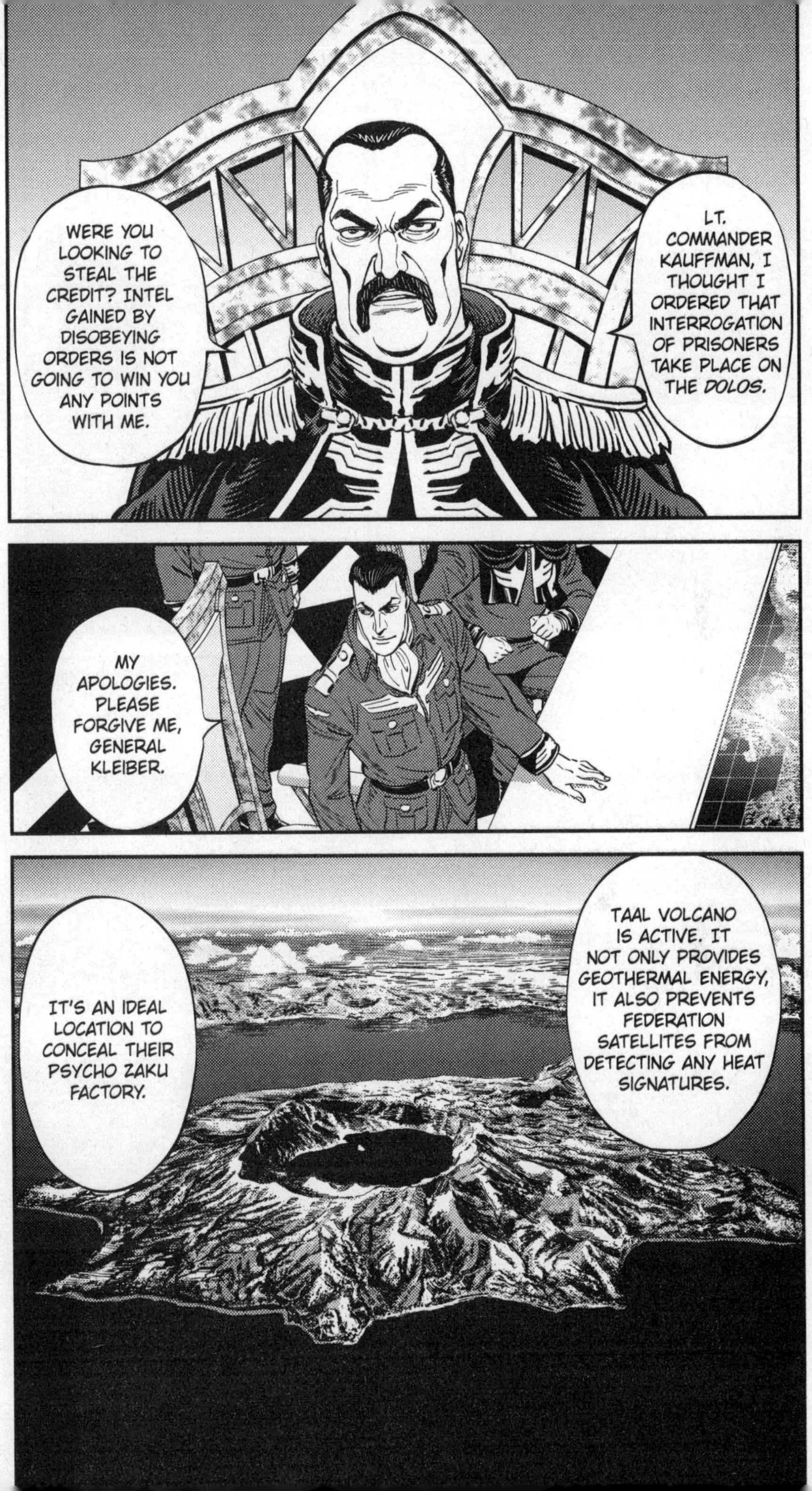
LT. COMMANDER KAUFFMAN, I THOUGHT I ORDERED THAT INTERROGATION OF PRISONERS TAKE PLACE ON THE *DOLOS*.
WERE YOU LOOKING TO STEAL THE CREDIT? INTEL GAINED BY DISOBEYING ORDERS IS NOT GOING TO WIN YOU ANY POINTS WITH ME.
MY APOLOGIES. PLEASE FORGIVE ME, GENERAL KLEIBER.
TAAL VOLCANO IS ACTIVE. IT NOT ONLY PROVIDES GEOTHERMAL ENERGY, IT ALSO PREVENTS FEDERATION SATELLITES FROM DETECTING ANY HEAT SIGNATURES.
IT'S AN IDEAL LOCATION TO CONCEAL THEIR PSYCHO ZAKU FACTORY.

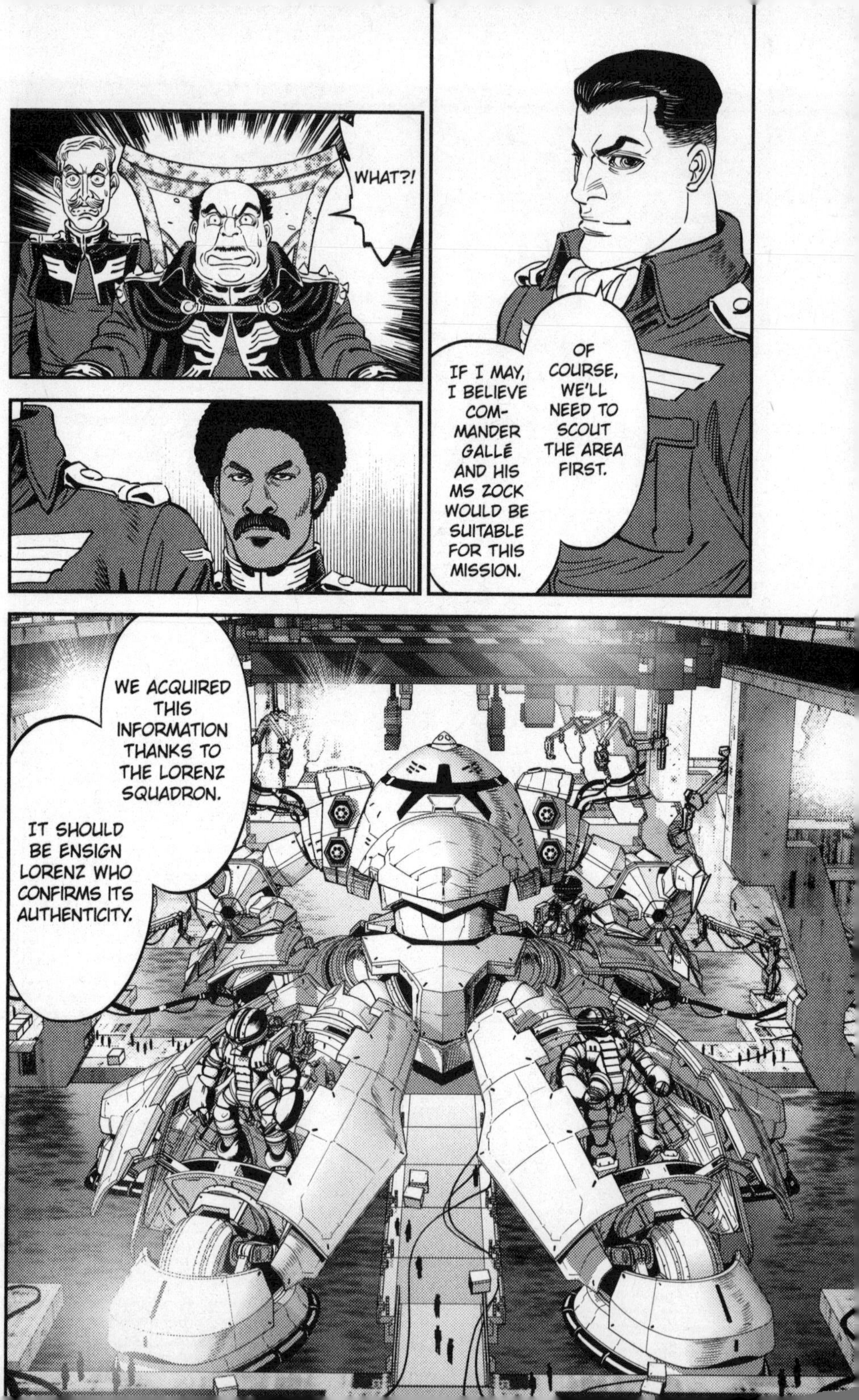
OF COURSE, WE'LL NEED TO SCOUT THE AREA FIRST.
IF I MAY, I BELIEVE COM-MANDER GALLÉ AND HIS MS ZOCK WOULD BE SUITABLE FOR THIS MISSION.
WHAT?!
WE ACQUIRED THIS INFORMATION THANKS TO THE LORENZ SQUADRON.
IT SHOULD BE ENSIGN LORENZ WHO CONFIRMS ITS AUTHENTICITY.

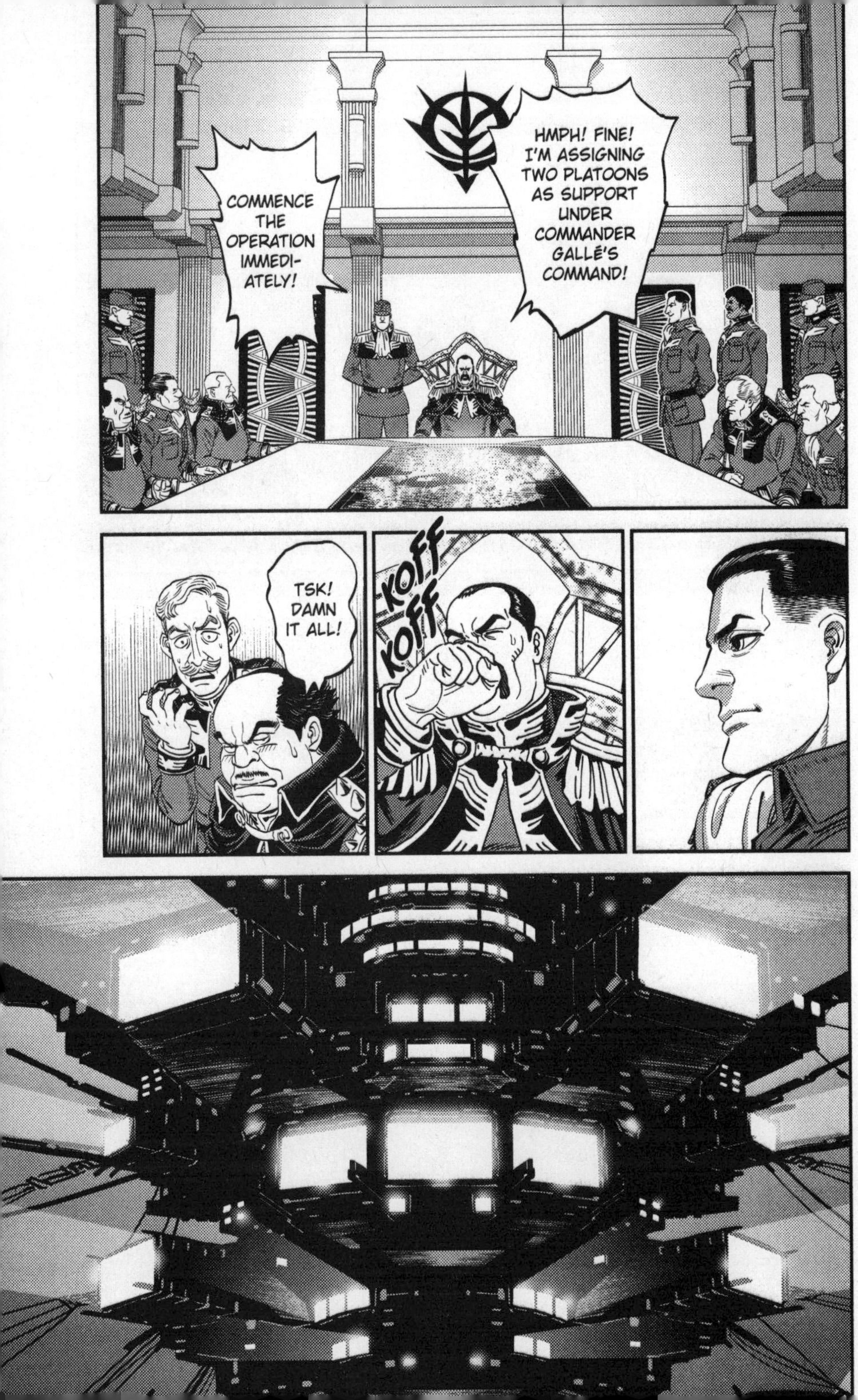
HMPH! FINE! I'M ASSIGNING TWO PLATOONS AS SUPPORT UNDER COMMANDER GALLÉ'S COMMAND!
COMMENCE THE OPERATION IMMEDI-ATELY!
KOFF KOFF
TSK! DAMN IT ALL!

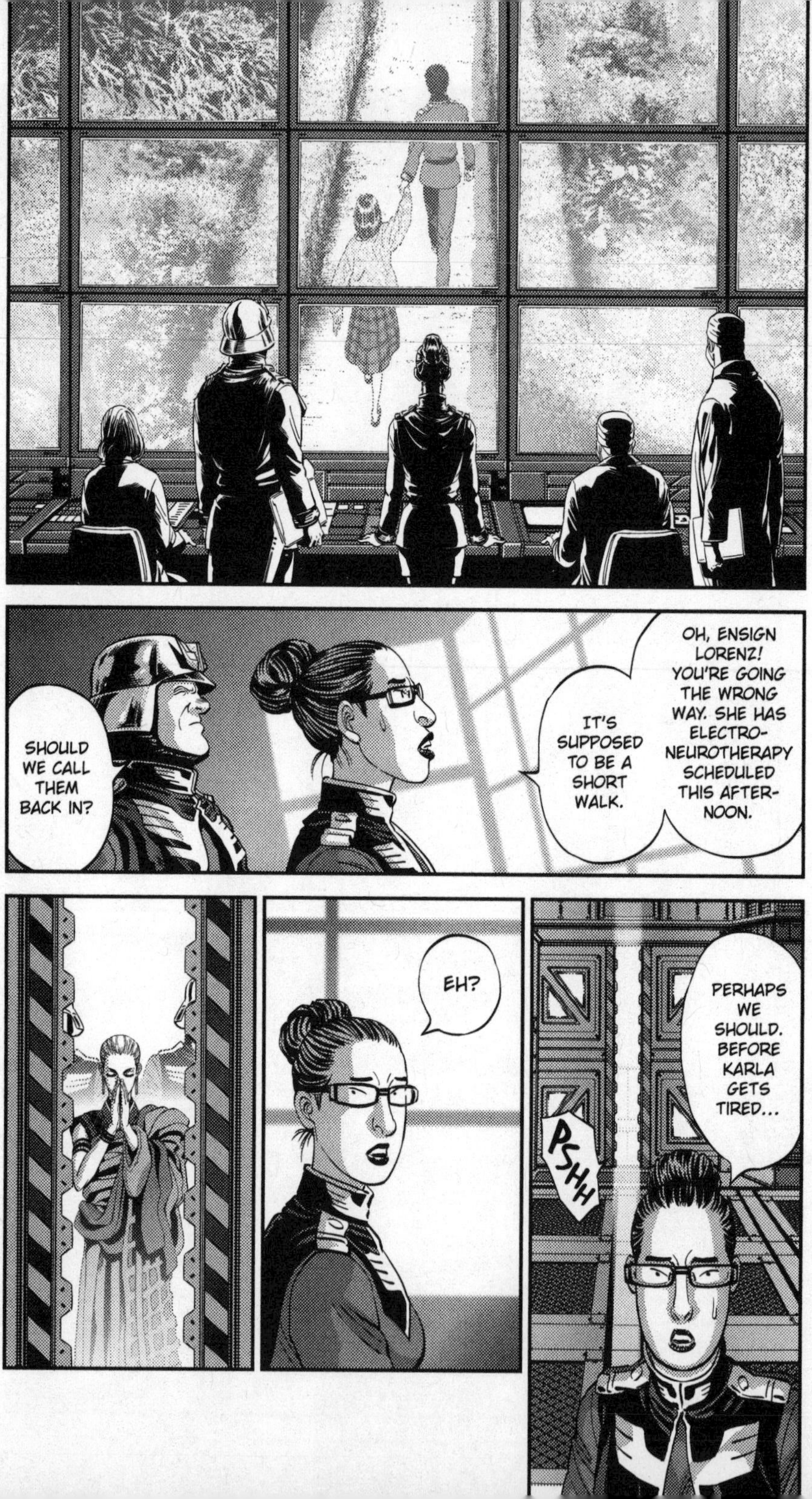
OH, ENSIGN LORENZ! YOU'RE GOING THE WRONG WAY. SHE HAS ELECTRO-NEUROTHERAPY SCHEDULED THIS AFTER-NOON.
IT'S SUPPOSED TO BE A SHORT WALK.
SHOULD WE CALL THEM BACK IN?
PERHAPS WE SHOULD. BEFORE KARLA GETS TIRED...
PSHH
EH?

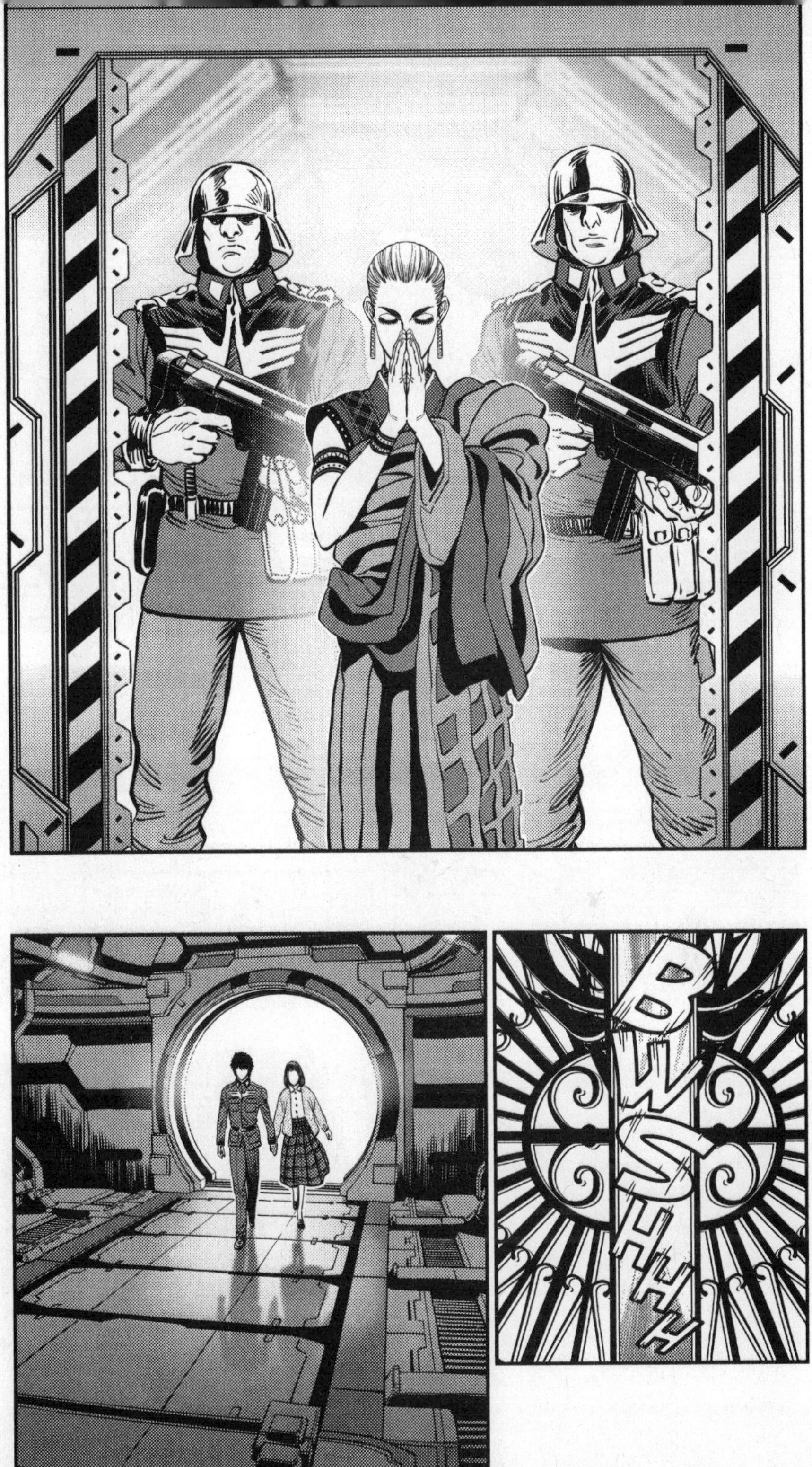
BWSHHHH

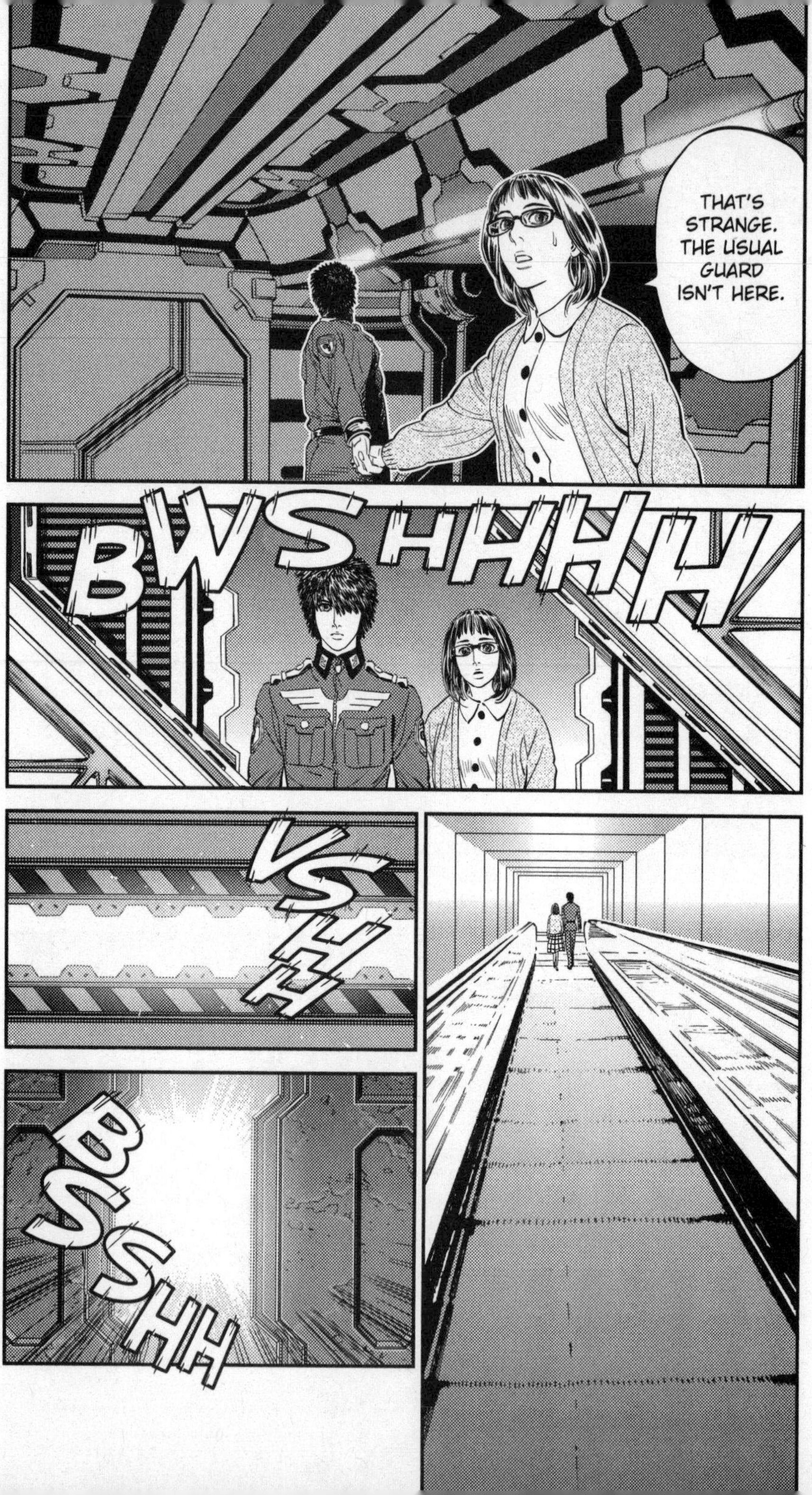
THAT'S STRANGE. THE USUAL GUARD ISN'T HERE.
BWSHHHHH
VSHHH
BSSHH

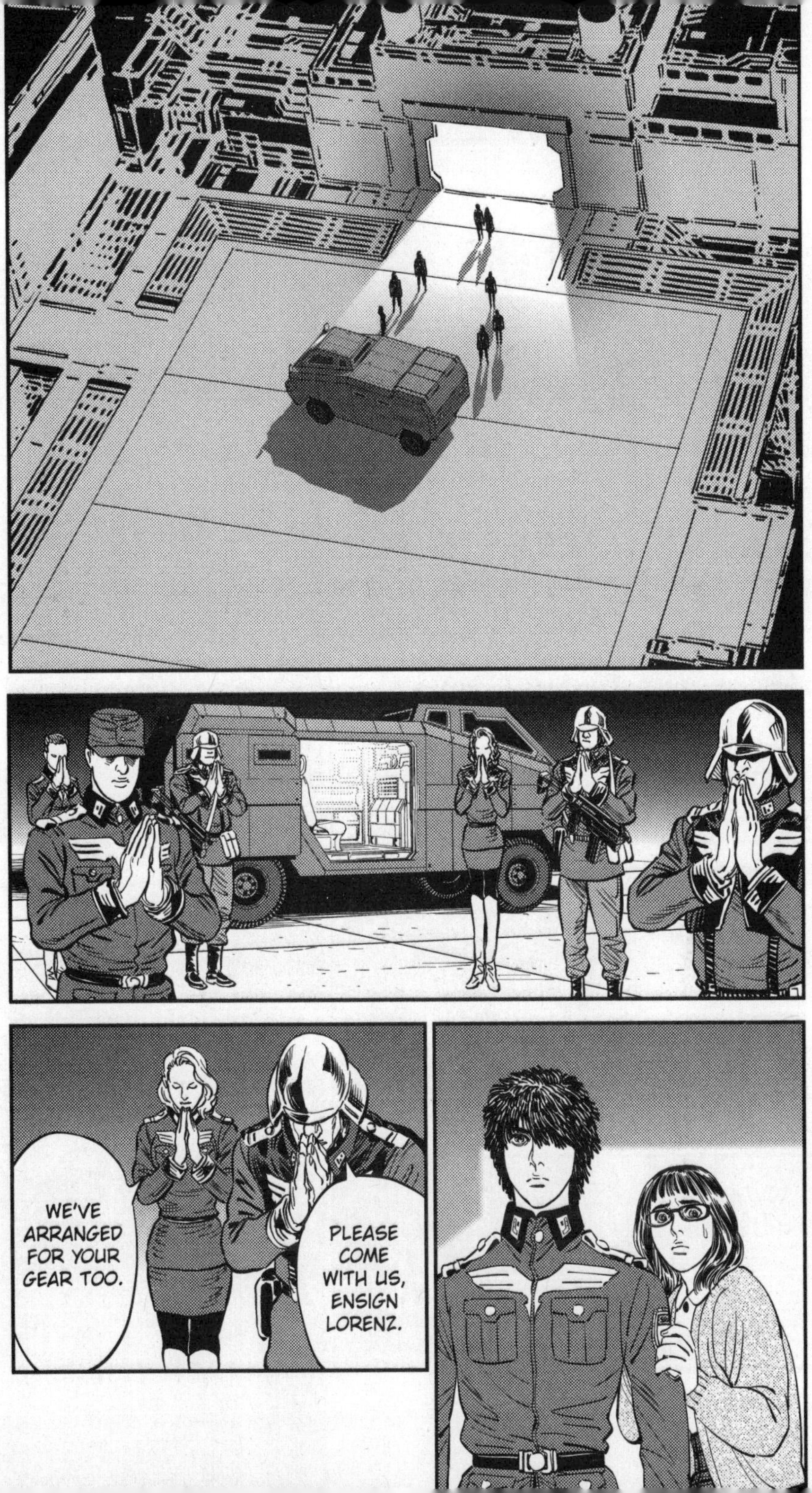
PLEASE COME WITH US, ENSIGN LORENZ.
WE'VE ARRANGED FOR YOUR GEAR TOO.

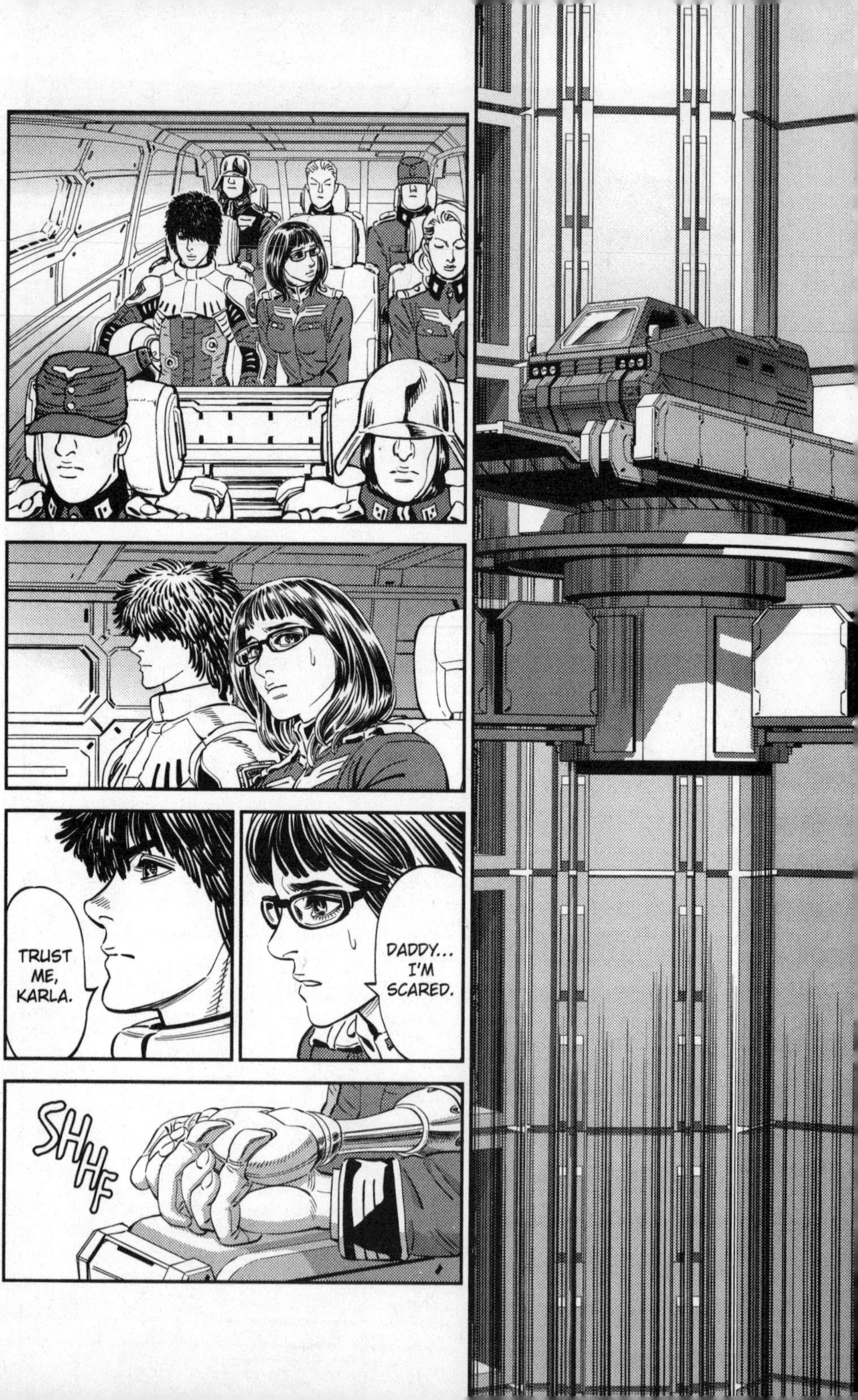
DADDY... I'M SCARED.
TRUST ME, KARLA.
SHHF

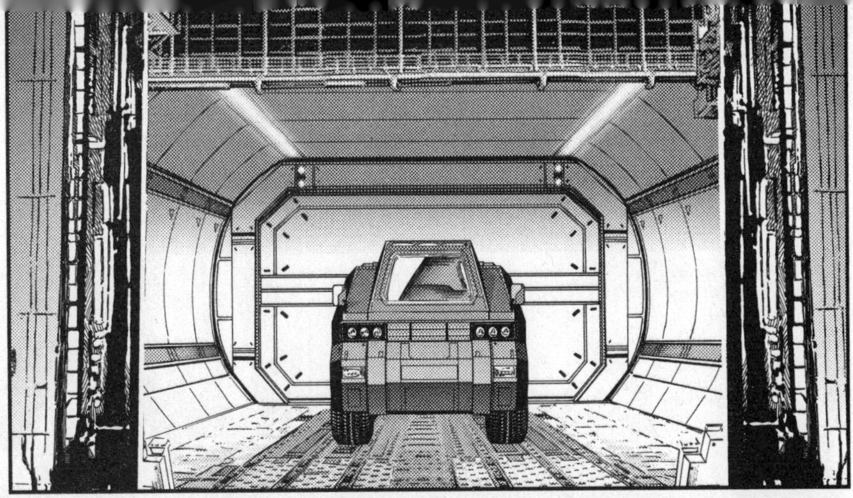
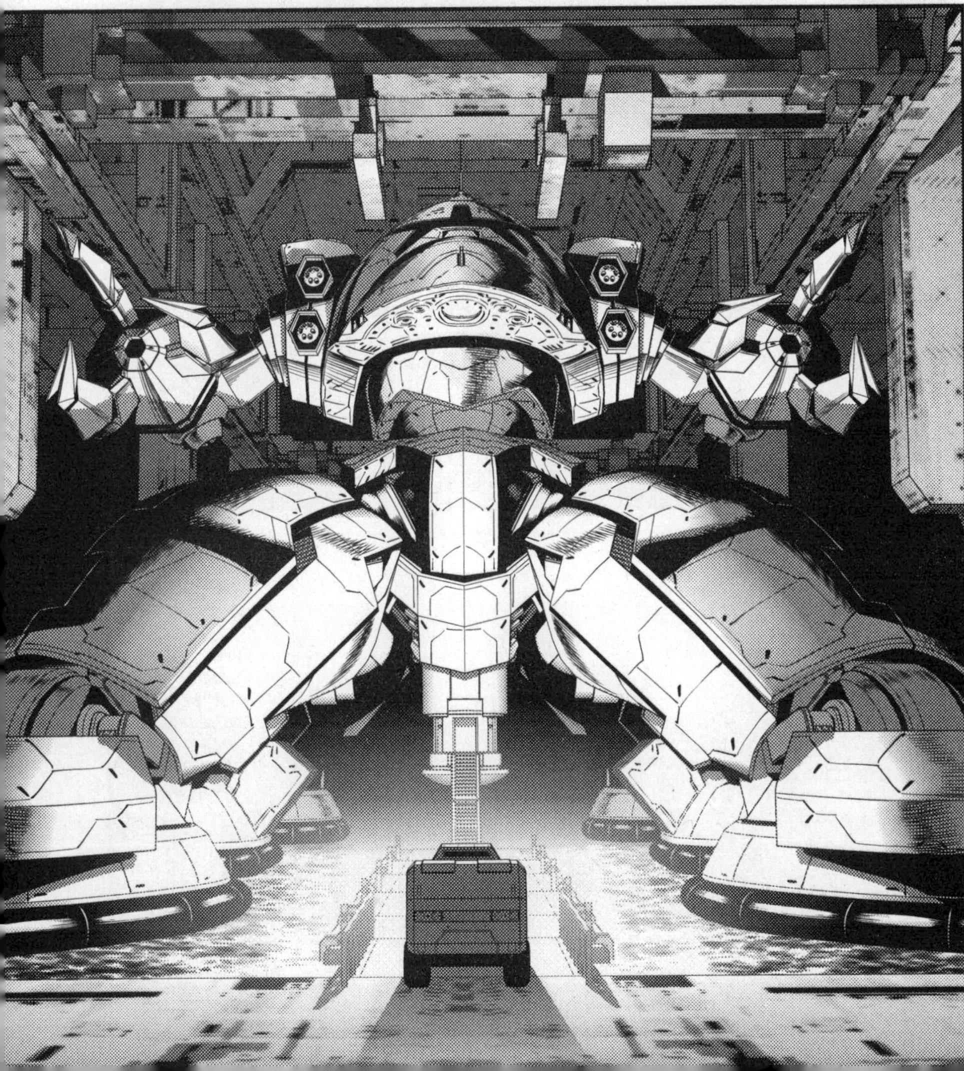

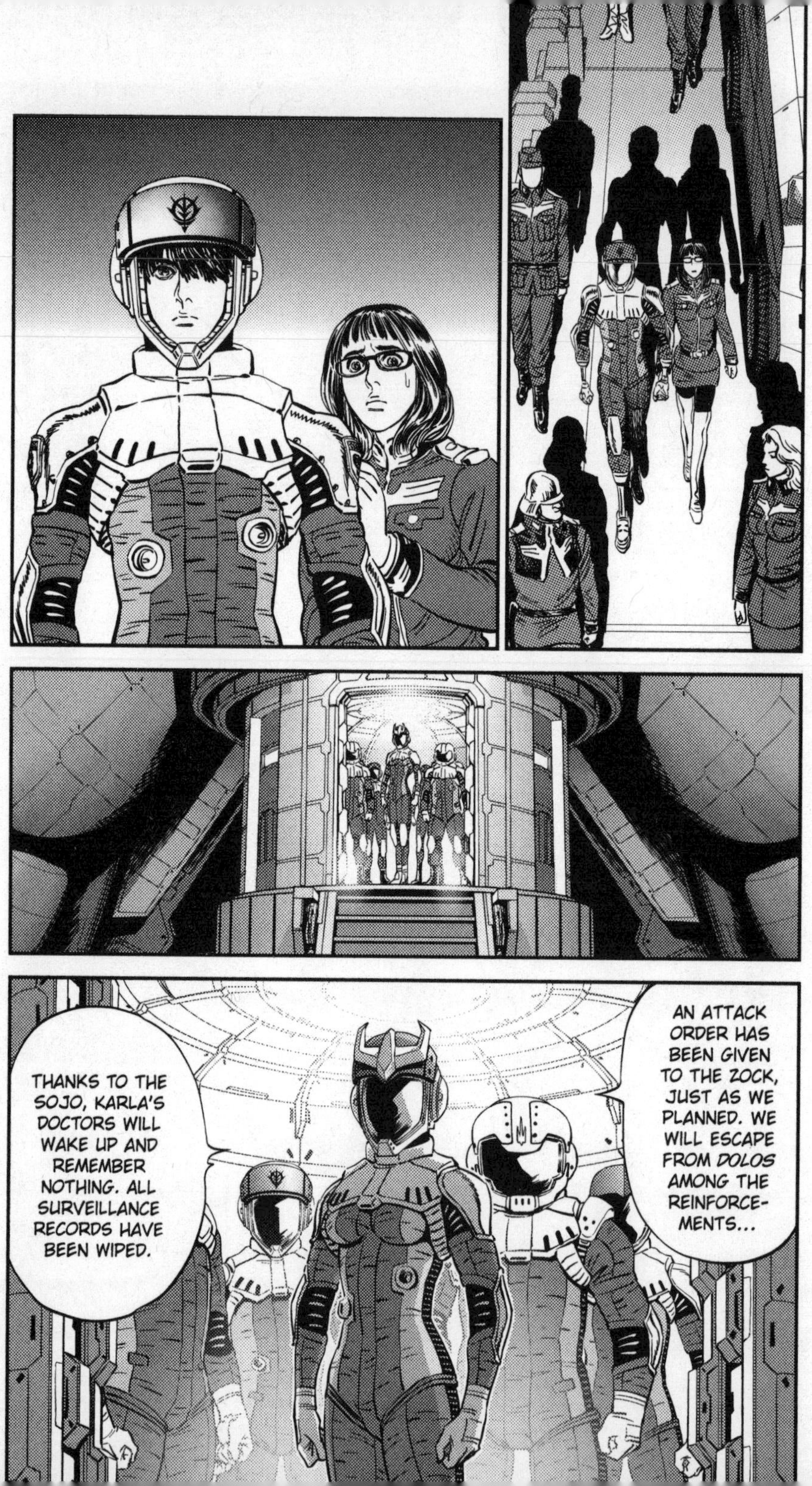
AN ATTACK ORDER HAS BEEN GIVEN TO THE ZOCK, JUST AS WE PLANNED. WE WILL ESCAPE FROM *DOLOS* AMONG THE REINFORCE-MENTS...
THANKS TO THE SOJO, KARLA'S DOCTORS WILL WAKE UP AND REMEMBER NOTHING. ALL SURVEILLANCE RECORDS HAVE BEEN WIPED.

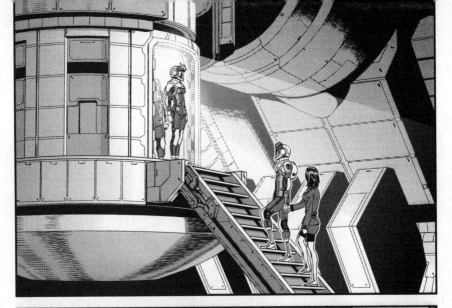

SOJO LEVAN FU'S NEWTYPE ABILITY WILL SOOTHE KARLA'S SOUL AND BRING BACK WHO SHE WAS.
DARYL, IF YOU CHOOSE TO BECOME OUR TRUE GUARDIAN...
...THE PSYCHO ZAKU WILL BE *YOURS.*

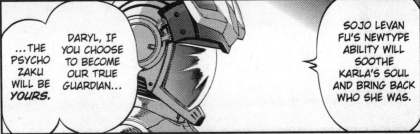

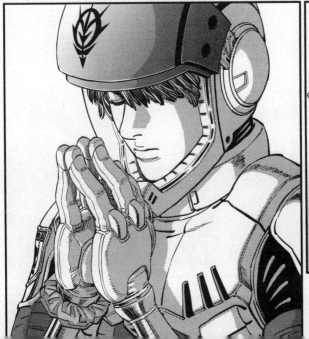

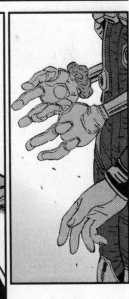

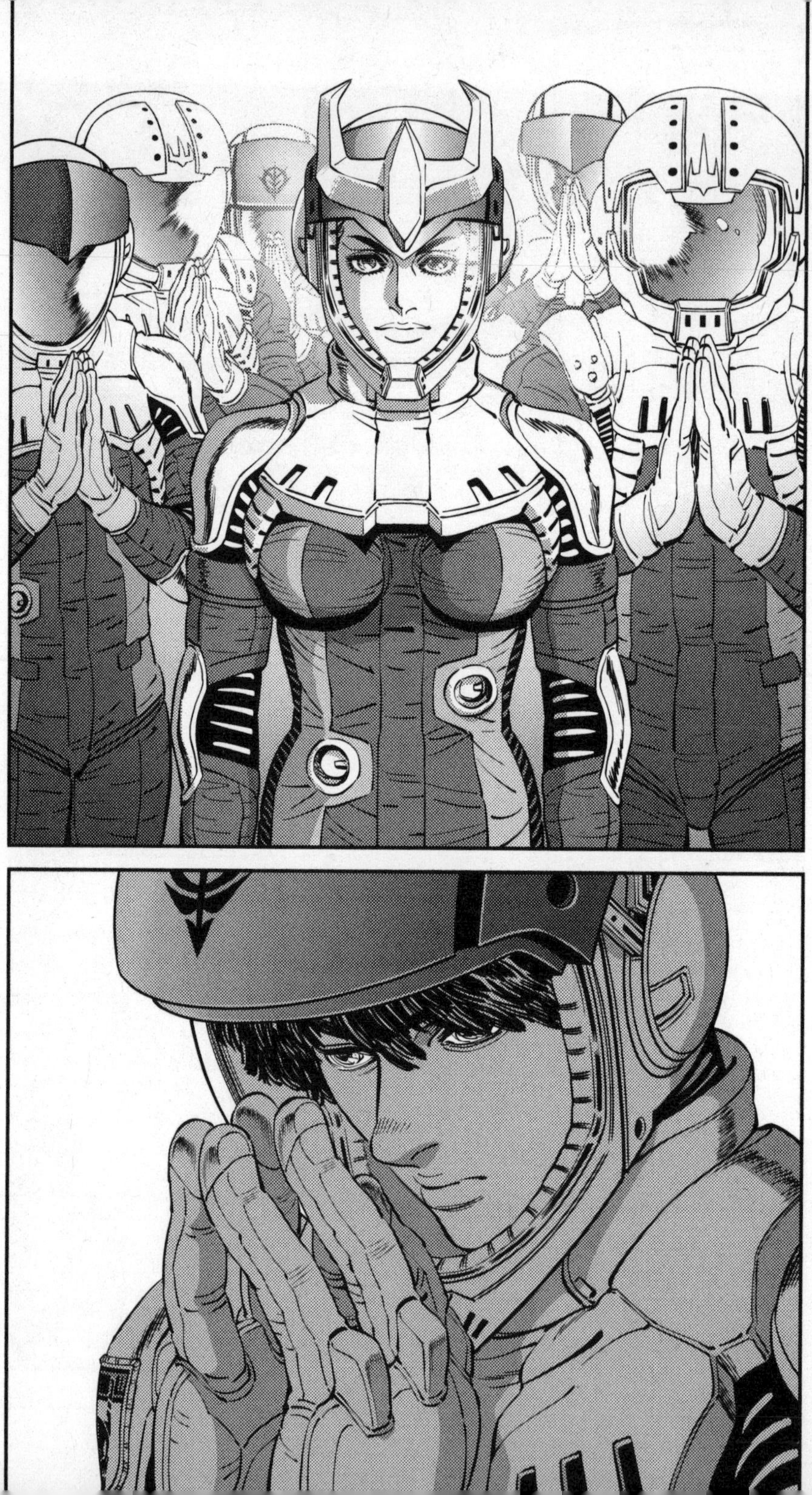

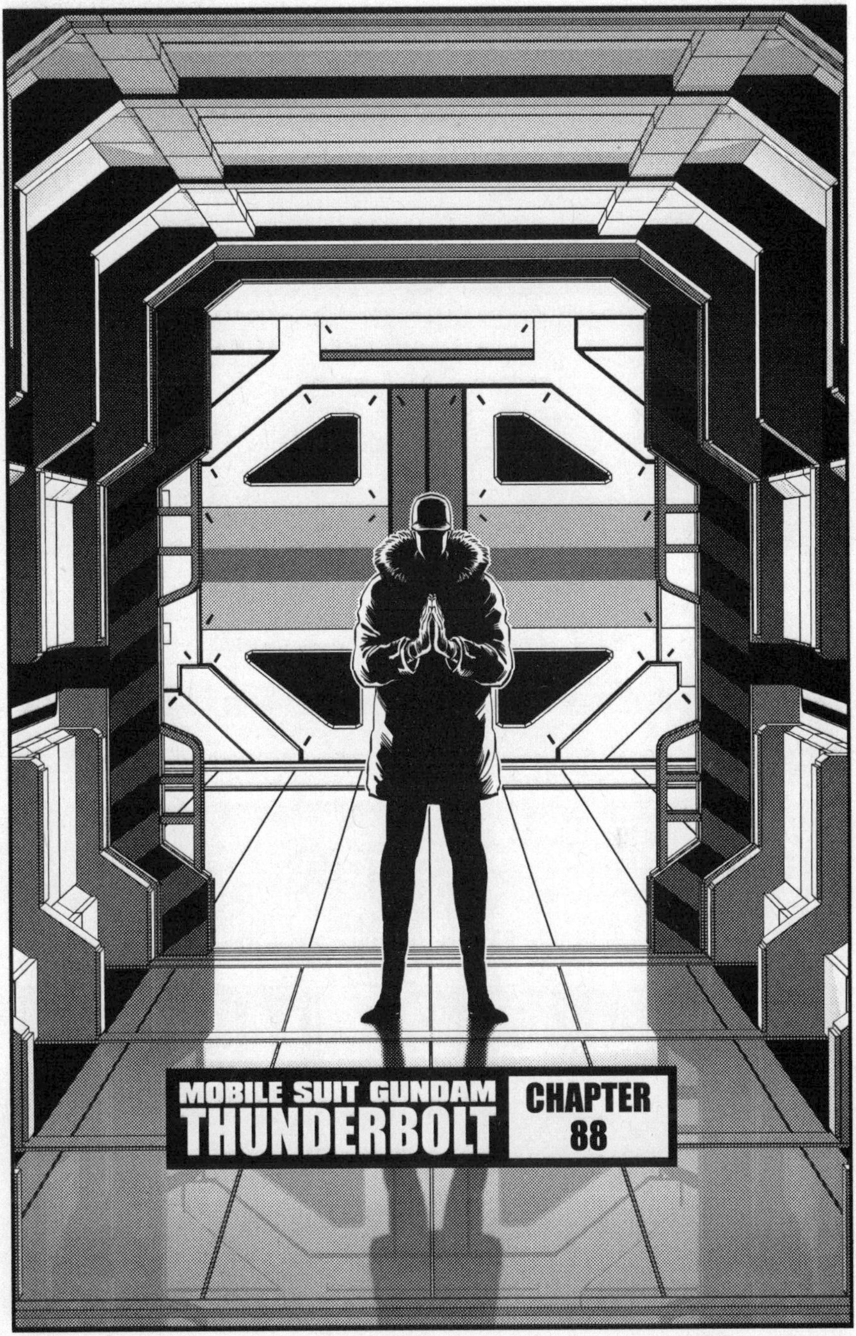
MOBILE SUIT GUNDAM
THUNDERBOLT
CHAPTER
88

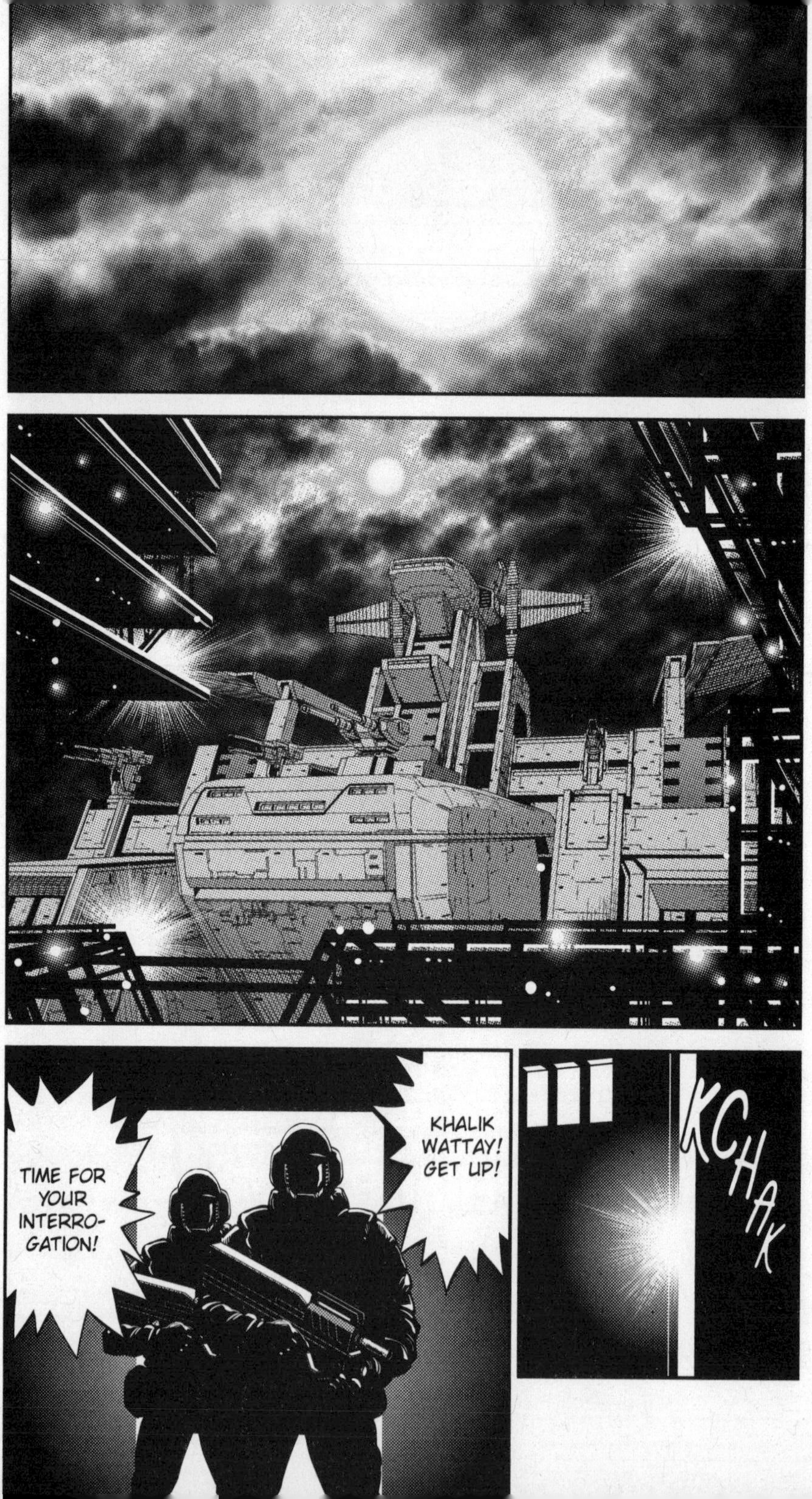
KCHAK
KHALIK WATTAY! GET UP!
TIME FOR YOUR INTERRO-GATION!

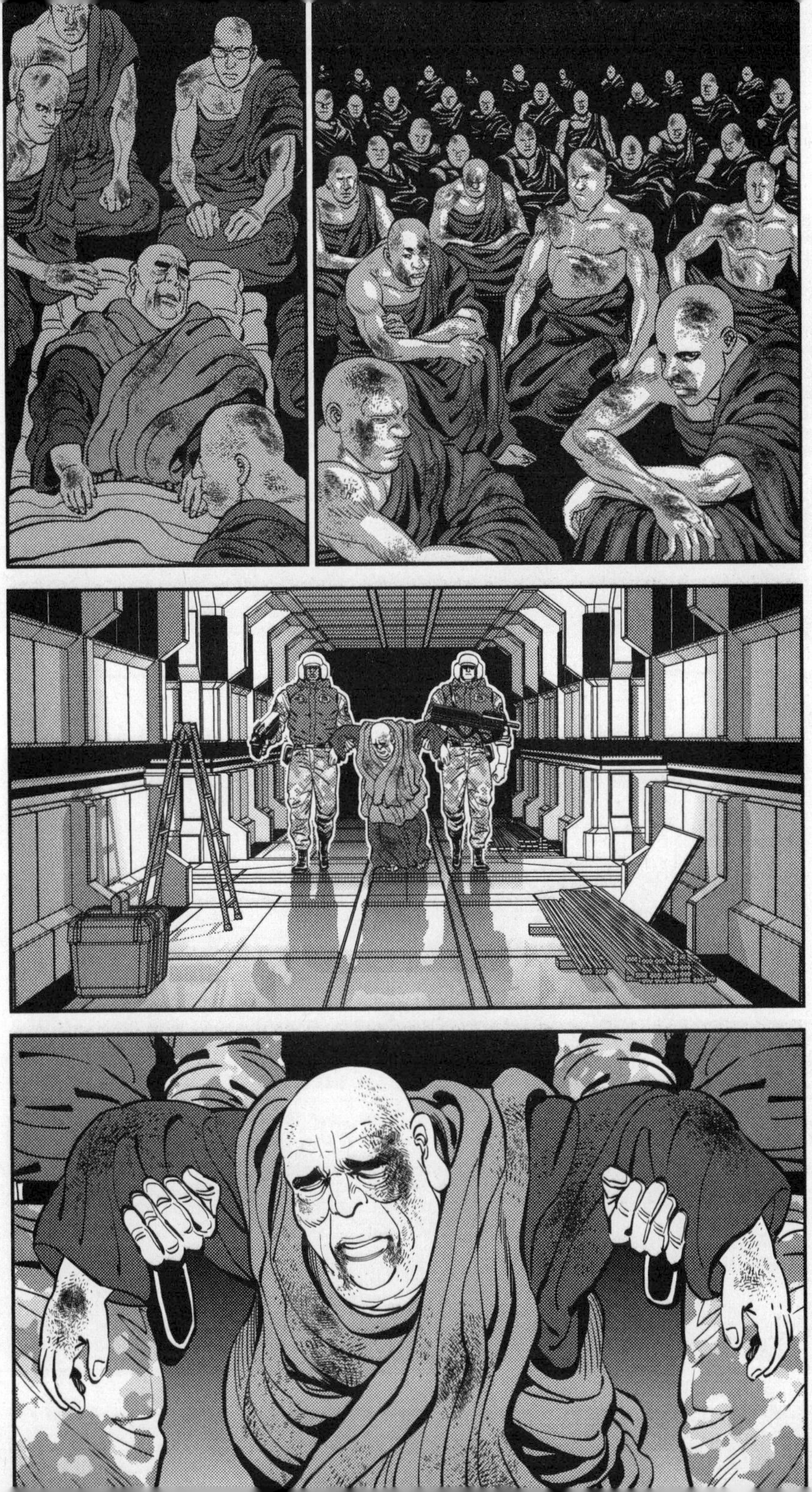

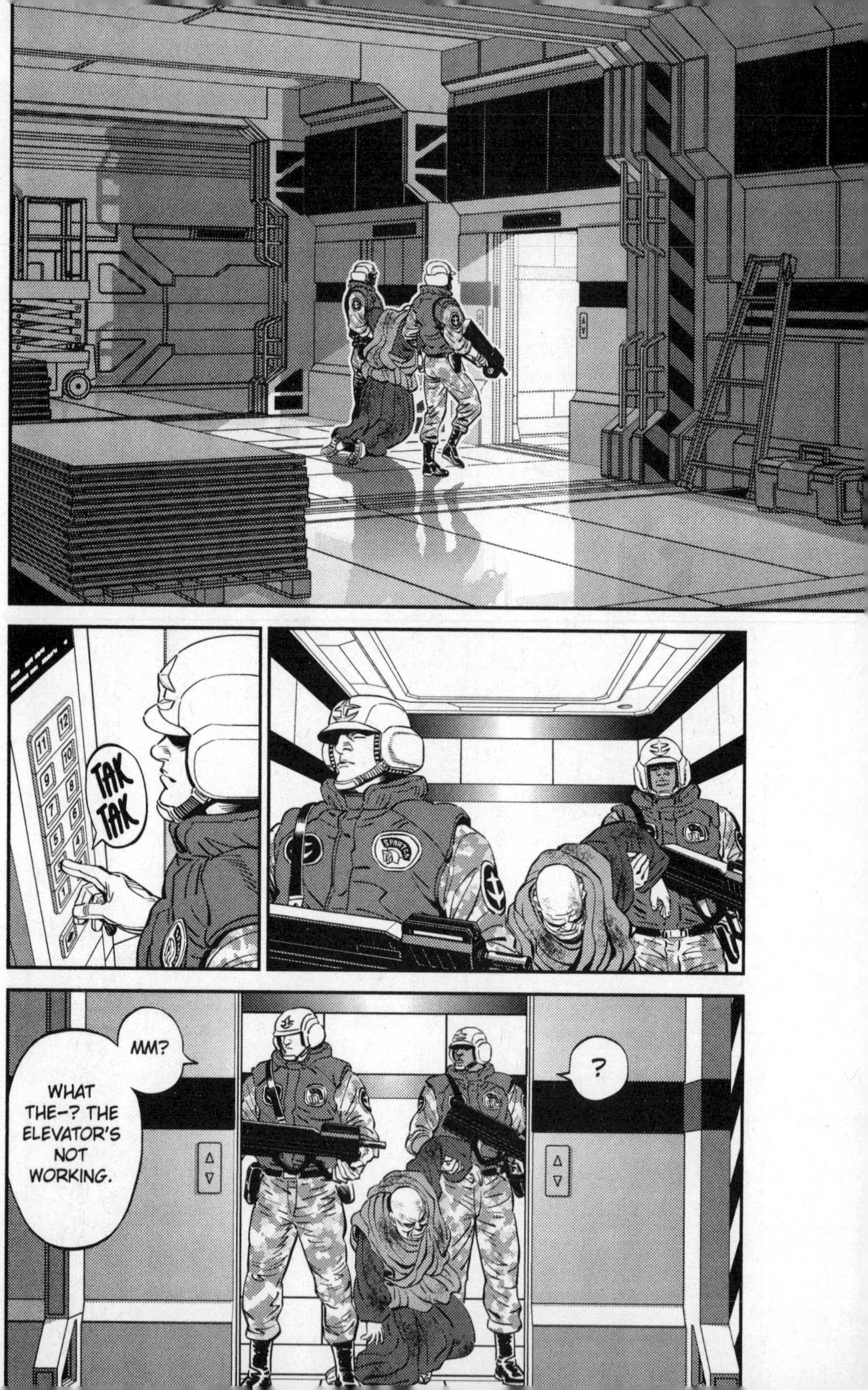
TAK TAK
?
MM?
WHAT THE-? THE ELEVATOR'S NOT WORKING.

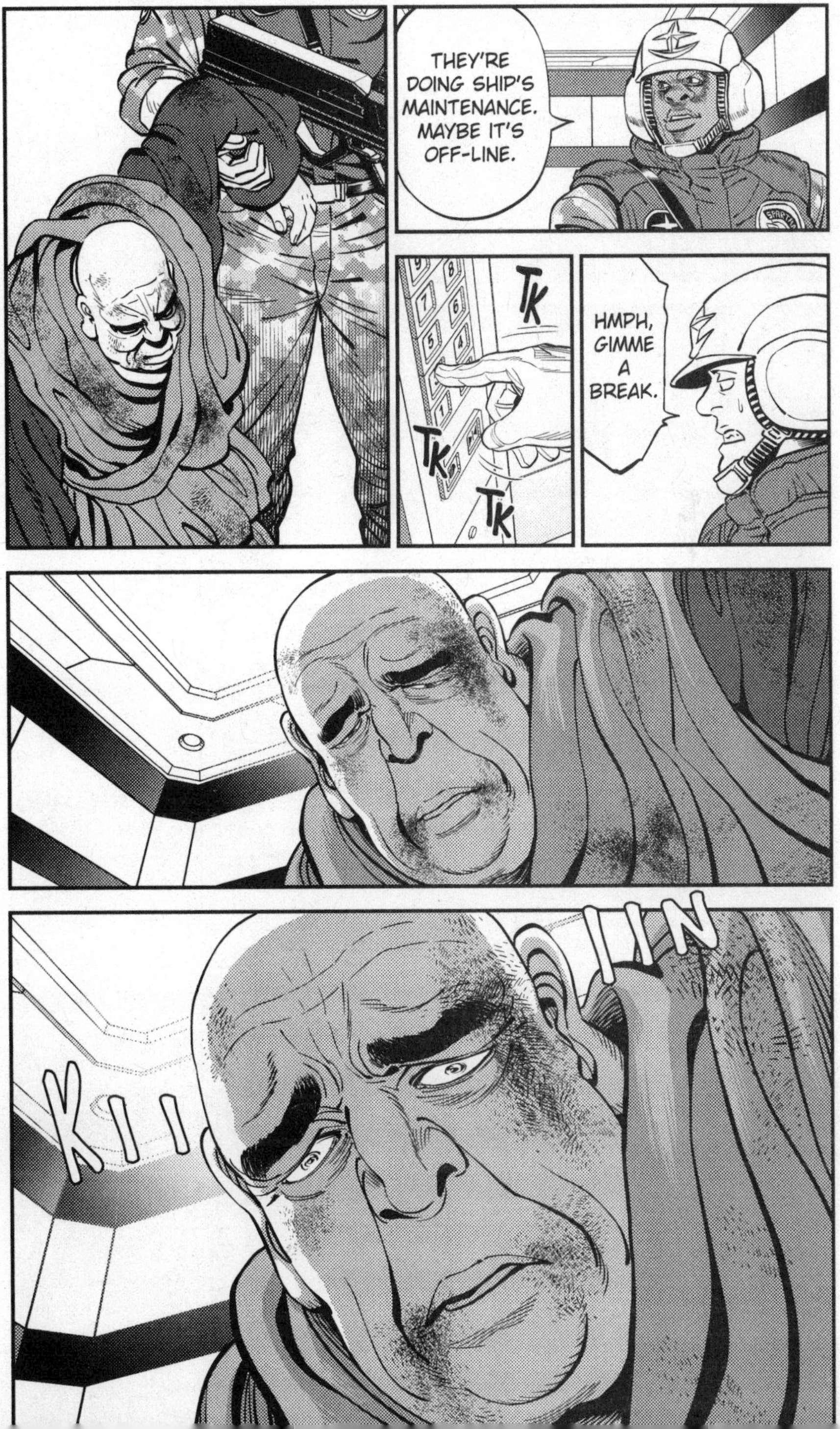
THEY'RE DOING SHIP'S MAINTENANCE. MAYBE IT'S OFF-LINE.
HMPH, GIMME A BREAK.
TK
TK
TK
KIIIIN

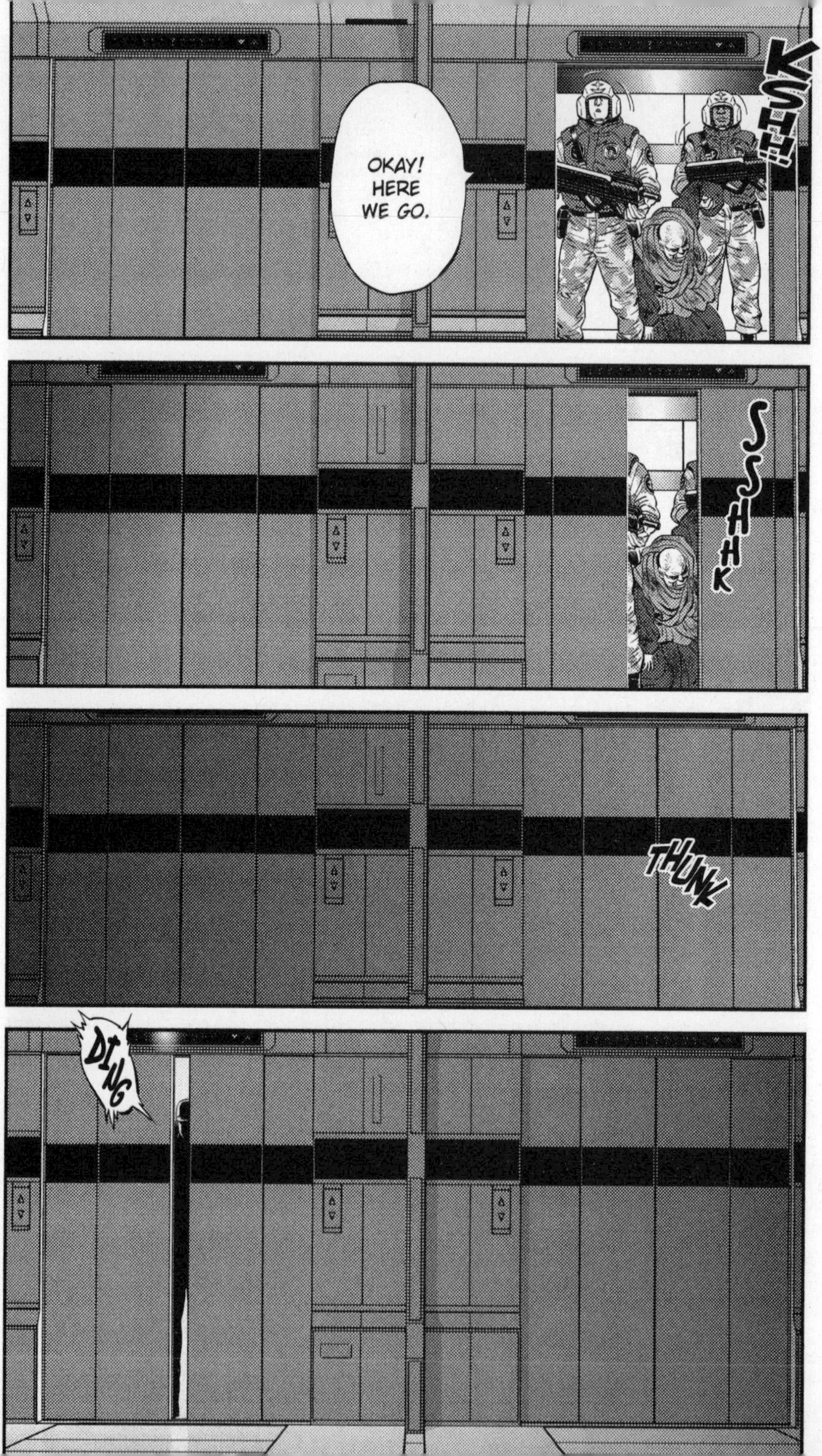
KSHH!!
OKAY! HERE WE GO.
SSHHK
THUNK
DING

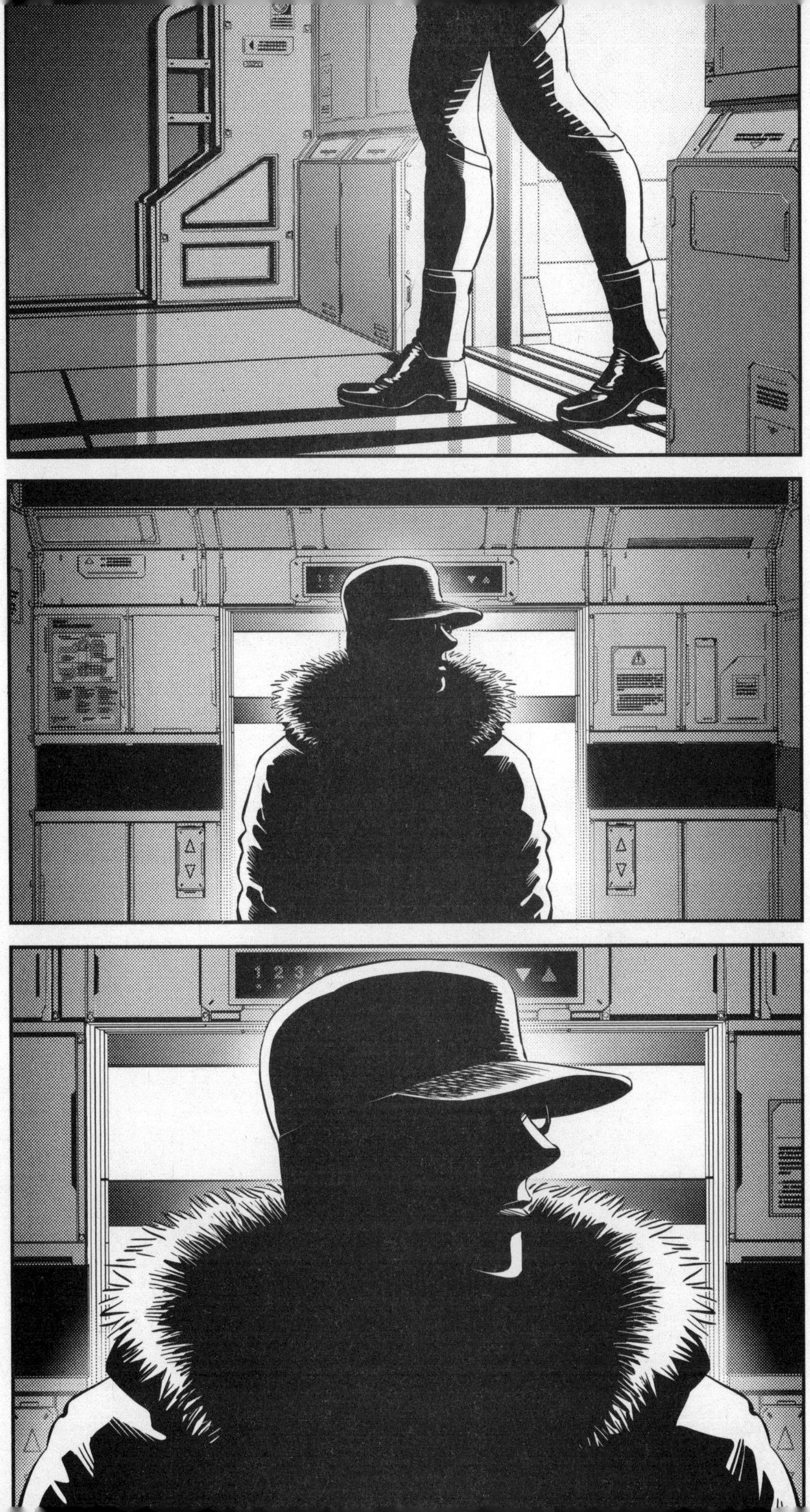

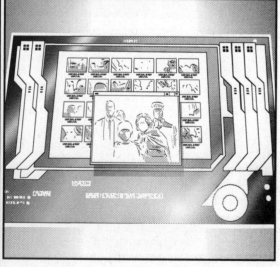

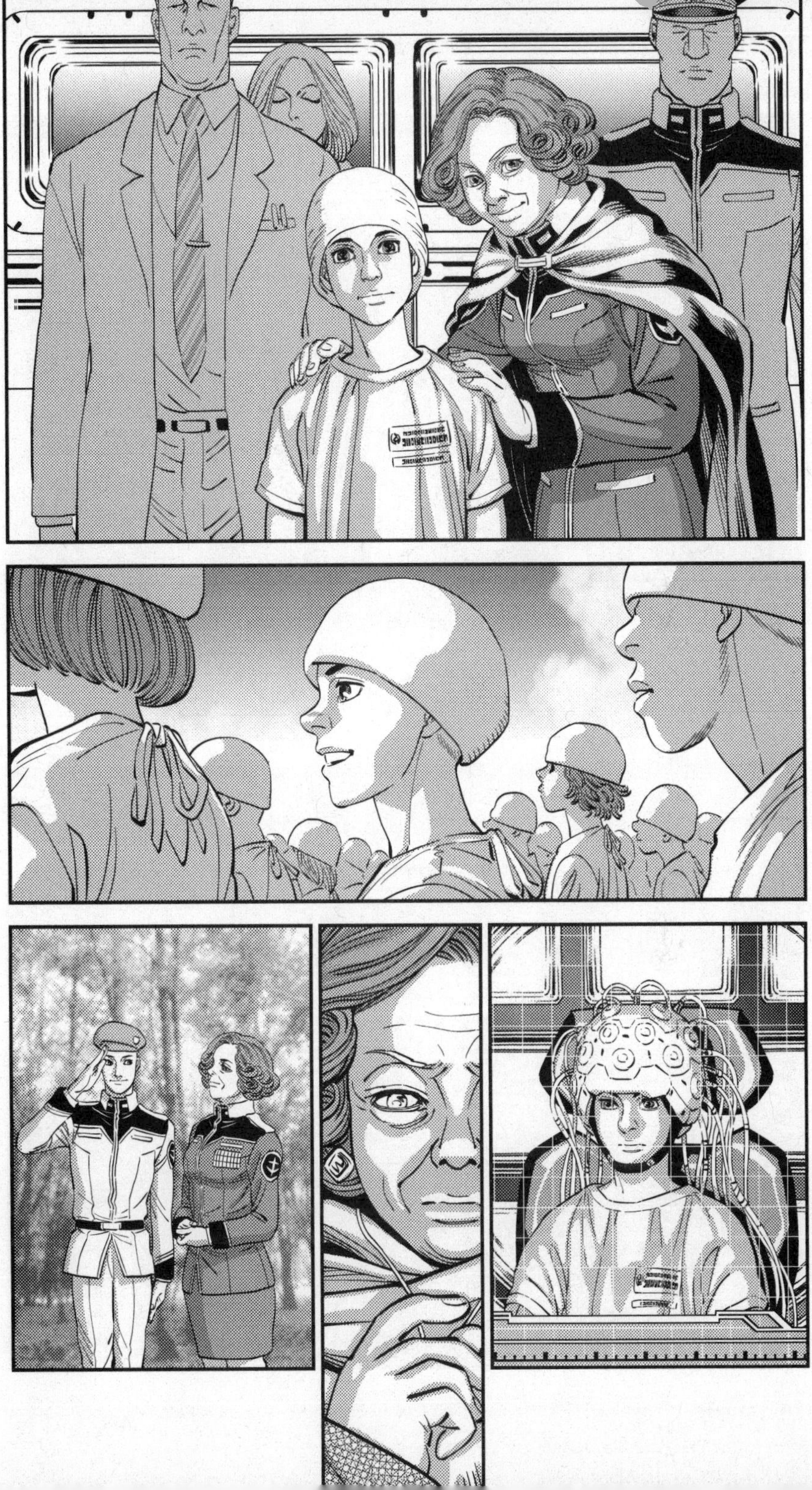

Concentration
Relaxation
DESTRUCTION
00:04:39
144336
385
23%
Connection Level

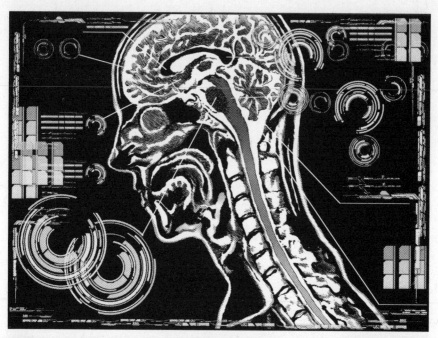

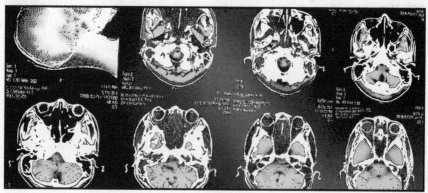

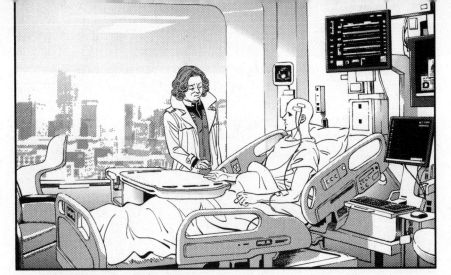

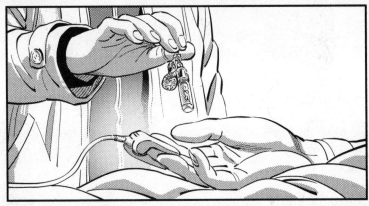

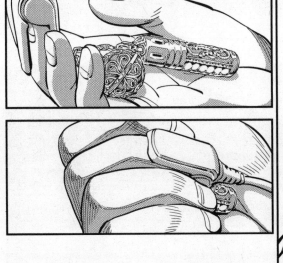

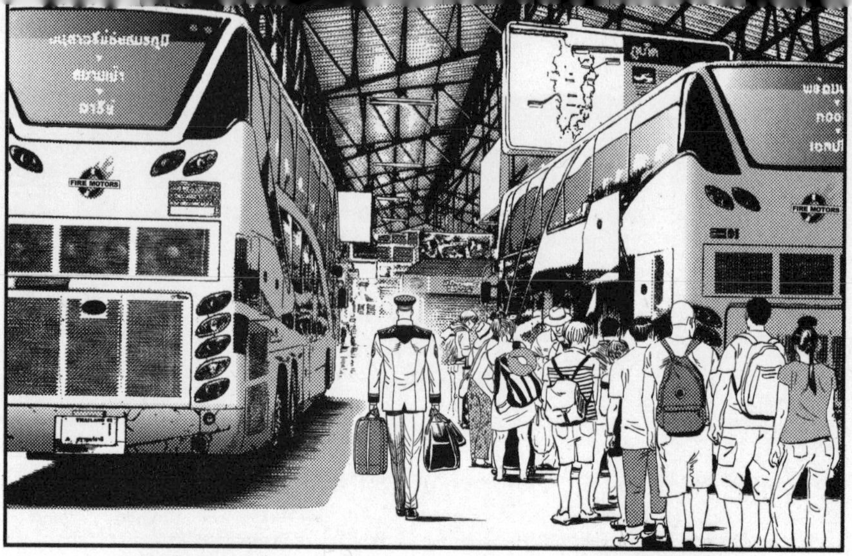
FIRE MOTORS
FIRE MOTORS

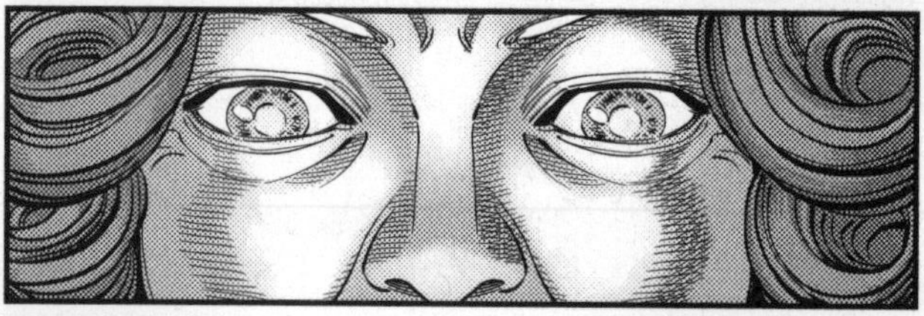

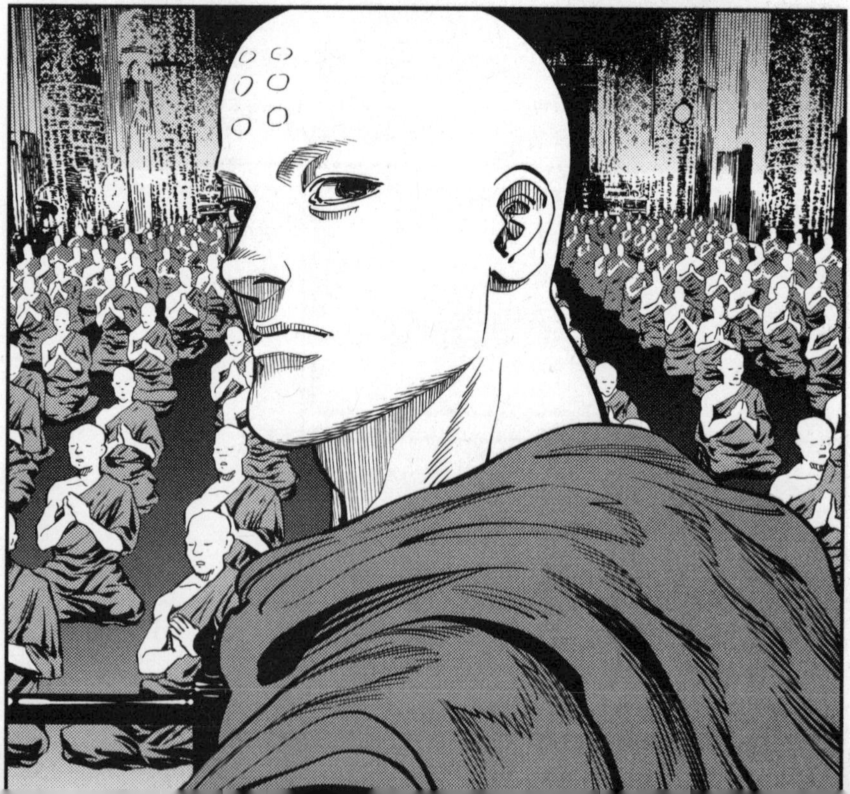

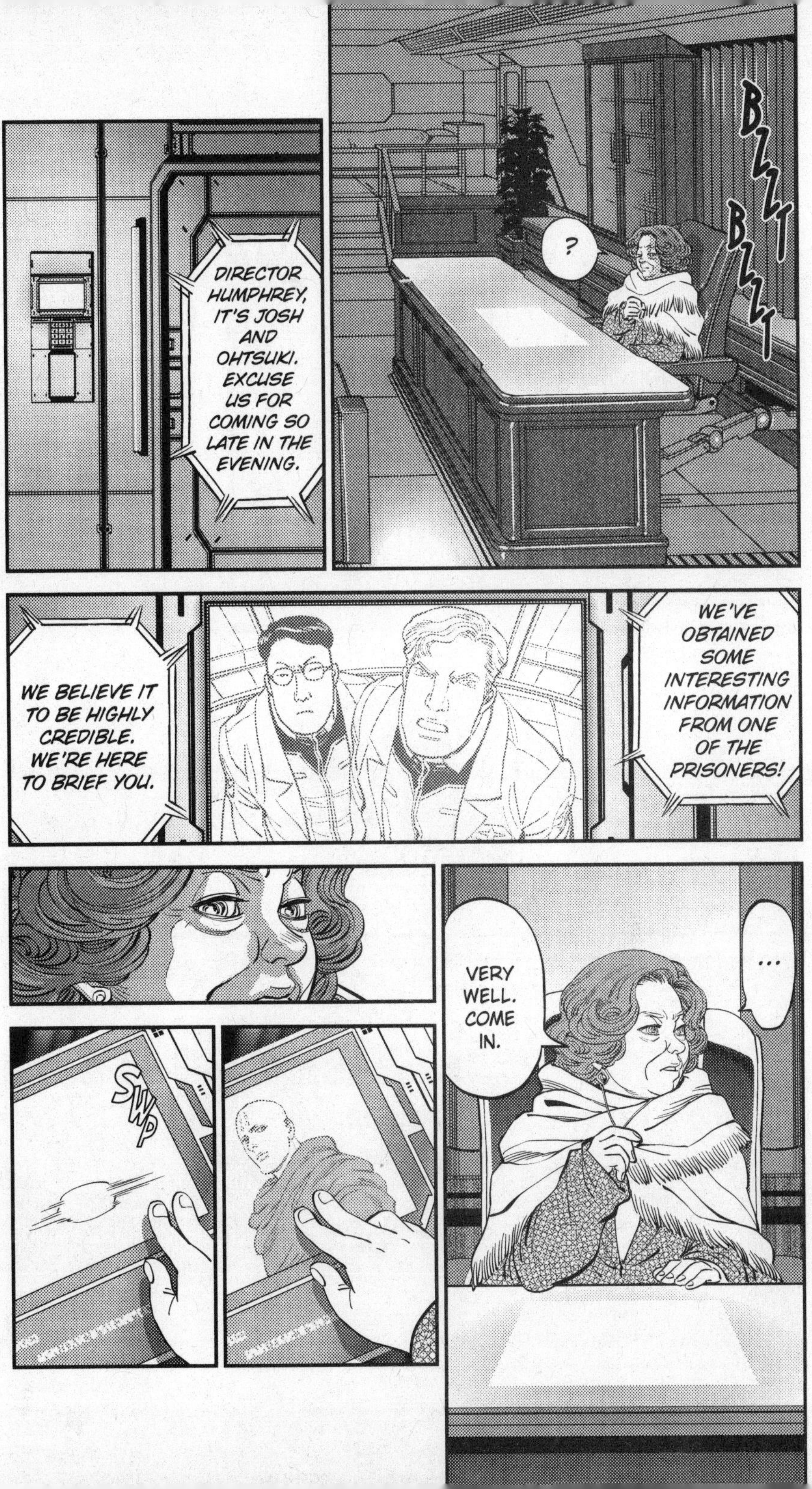
BZZT
BZZT
?
DIRECTOR HUMPHREY, IT'S JOSH AND OHTSUKI. EXCUSE US FOR COMING SO LATE IN THE EVENING.
WE'VE OBTAINED SOME INTERESTING INFORMATION FROM ONE OF THE PRISONERS!
WE BELIEVE IT TO BE HIGHLY CREDIBLE. WE'RE HERE TO BRIEF YOU.
...
VERY WELL. COME IN.
SWP

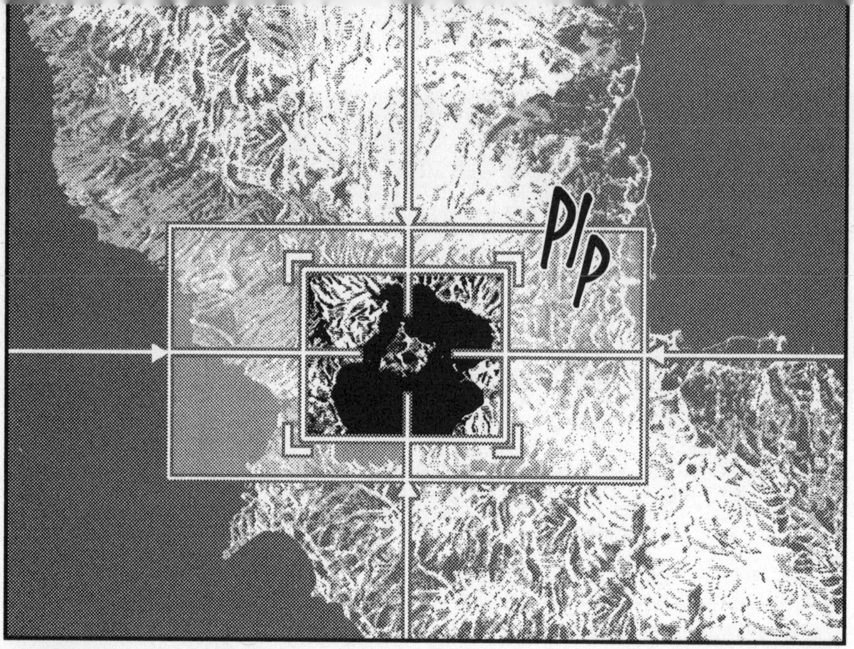
PIP
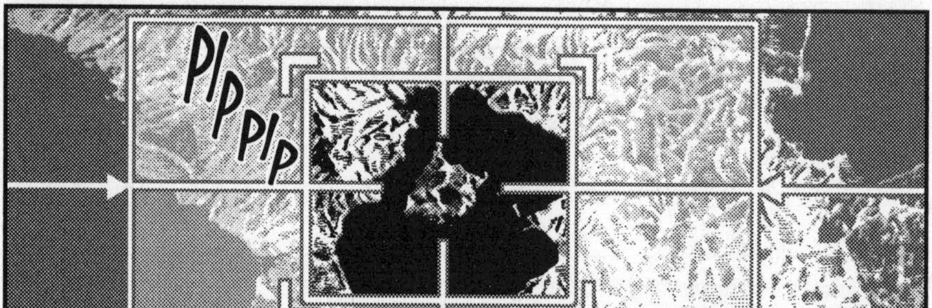
PIP PIP
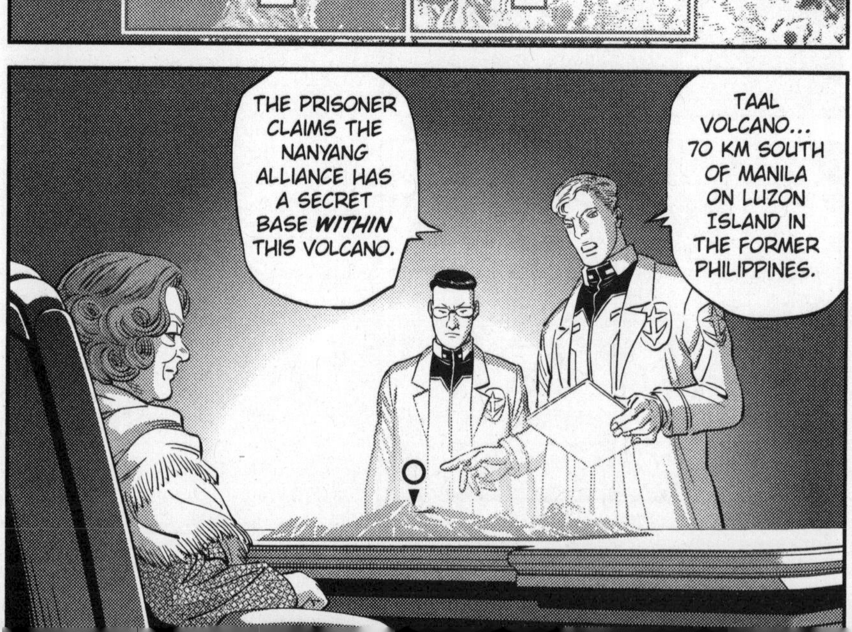
TAAL VOLCANO... 70 KM SOUTH OF MANILA ON LUZON ISLAND IN THE FORMER PHILIPPINES.
THE PRISONER CLAIMS THE NANYANG ALLIANCE HAS A SECRET BASE *WITHIN* THIS VOLCANO.

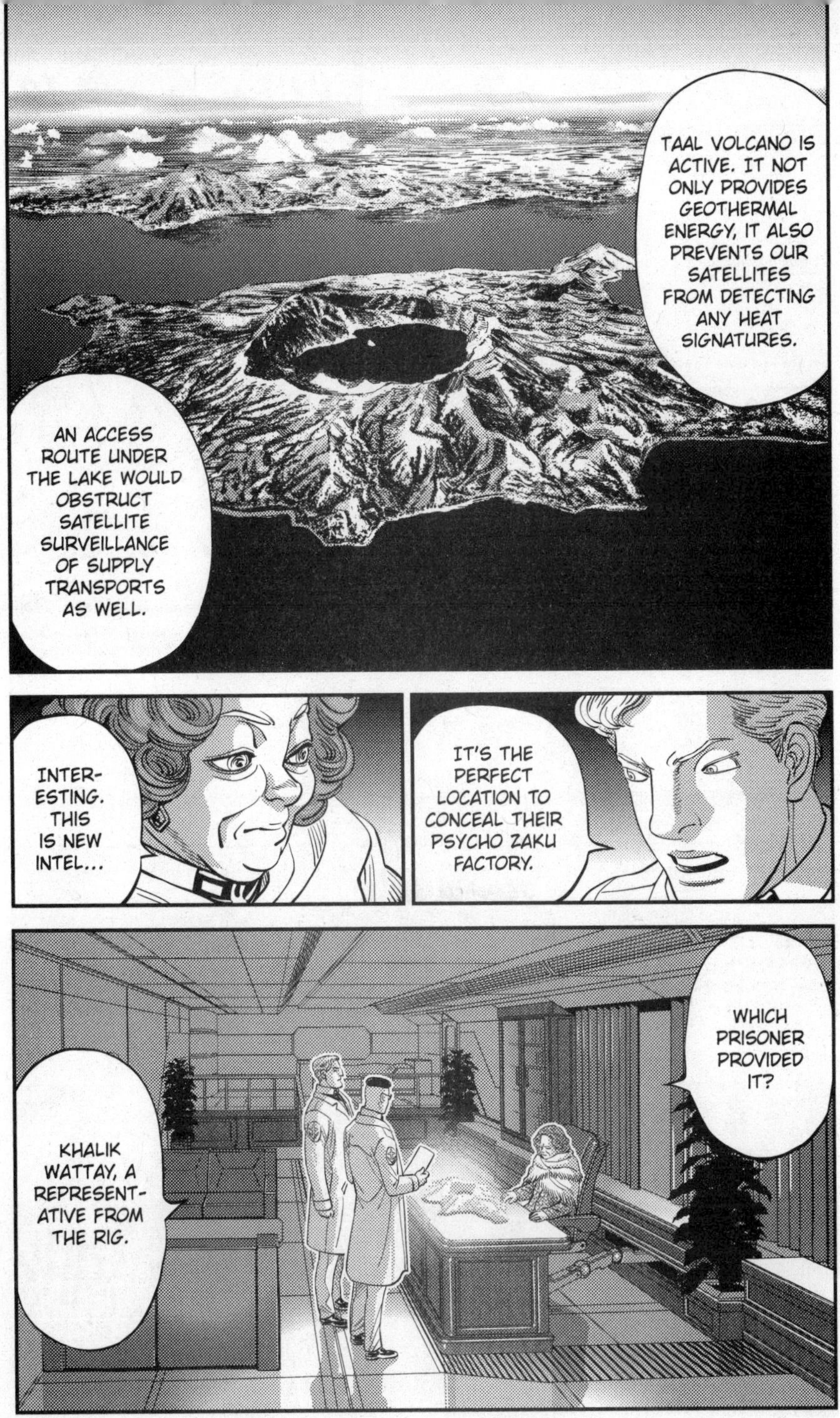
TAAL VOLCANO IS ACTIVE. IT NOT ONLY PROVIDES GEOTHERMAL ENERGY, IT ALSO PREVENTS OUR SATELLITES FROM DETECTING ANY HEAT SIGNATURES.
AN ACCESS ROUTE UNDER THE LAKE WOULD OBSTRUCT SATELLITE SURVEILLANCE OF SUPPLY TRANSPORTS AS WELL.
IT'S THE PERFECT LOCATION TO CONCEAL THEIR PSYCHO ZAKU FACTORY.
INTER-ESTING. THIS IS NEW INTEL...
WHICH PRISONER PROVIDED IT?
KHALIK WATTAY, A REPRESENT-ATIVE FROM THE RIG.

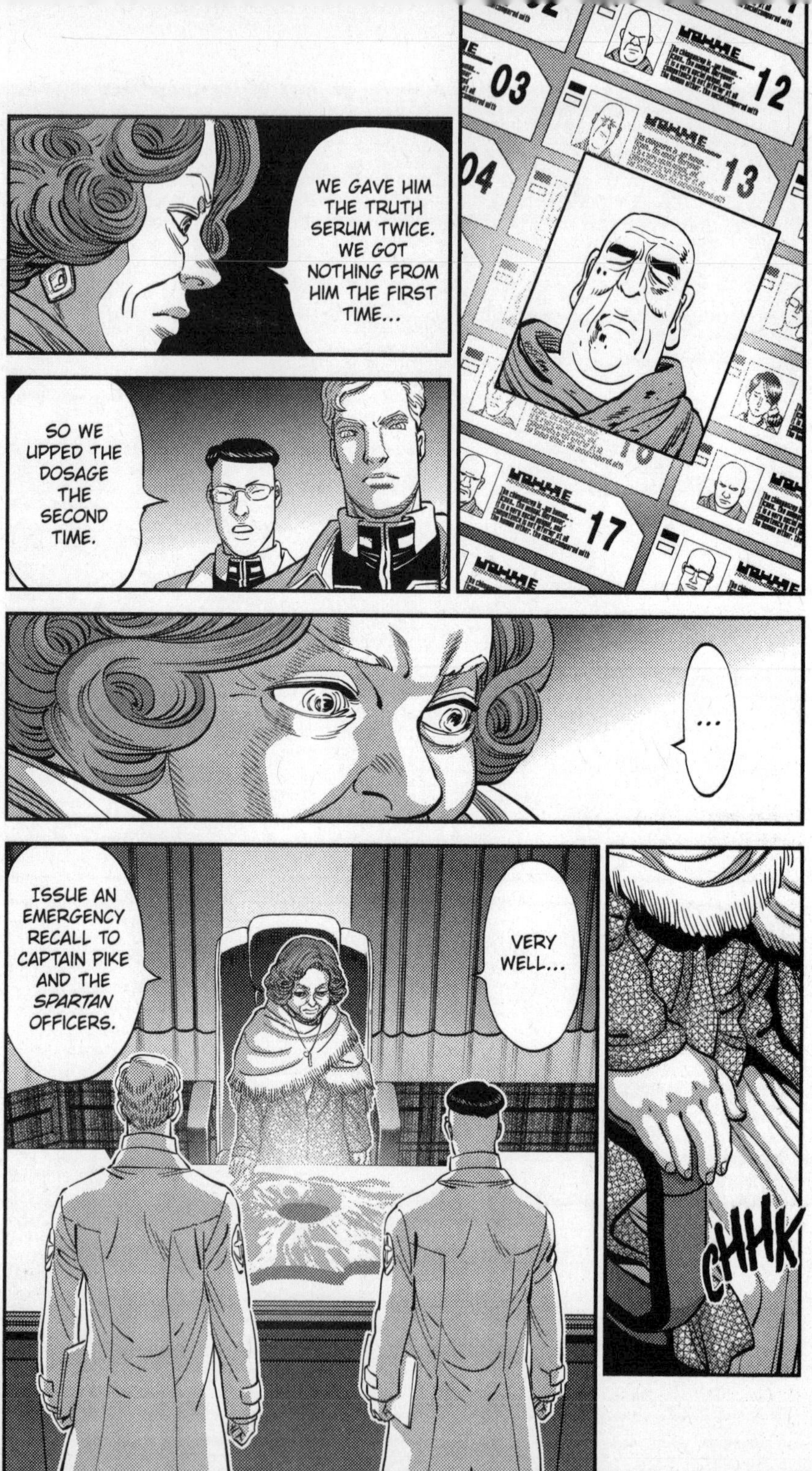
WE GAVE HIM THE TRUTH SERUM TWICE. WE GOT NOTHING FROM HIM THE FIRST TIME...
SO WE UPPED THE DOSAGE THE SECOND TIME.
...
CHHK
VERY WELL...
ISSUE AN EMERGENCY RECALL TO CAPTAIN PIKE AND THE *SPARTAN* OFFICERS.

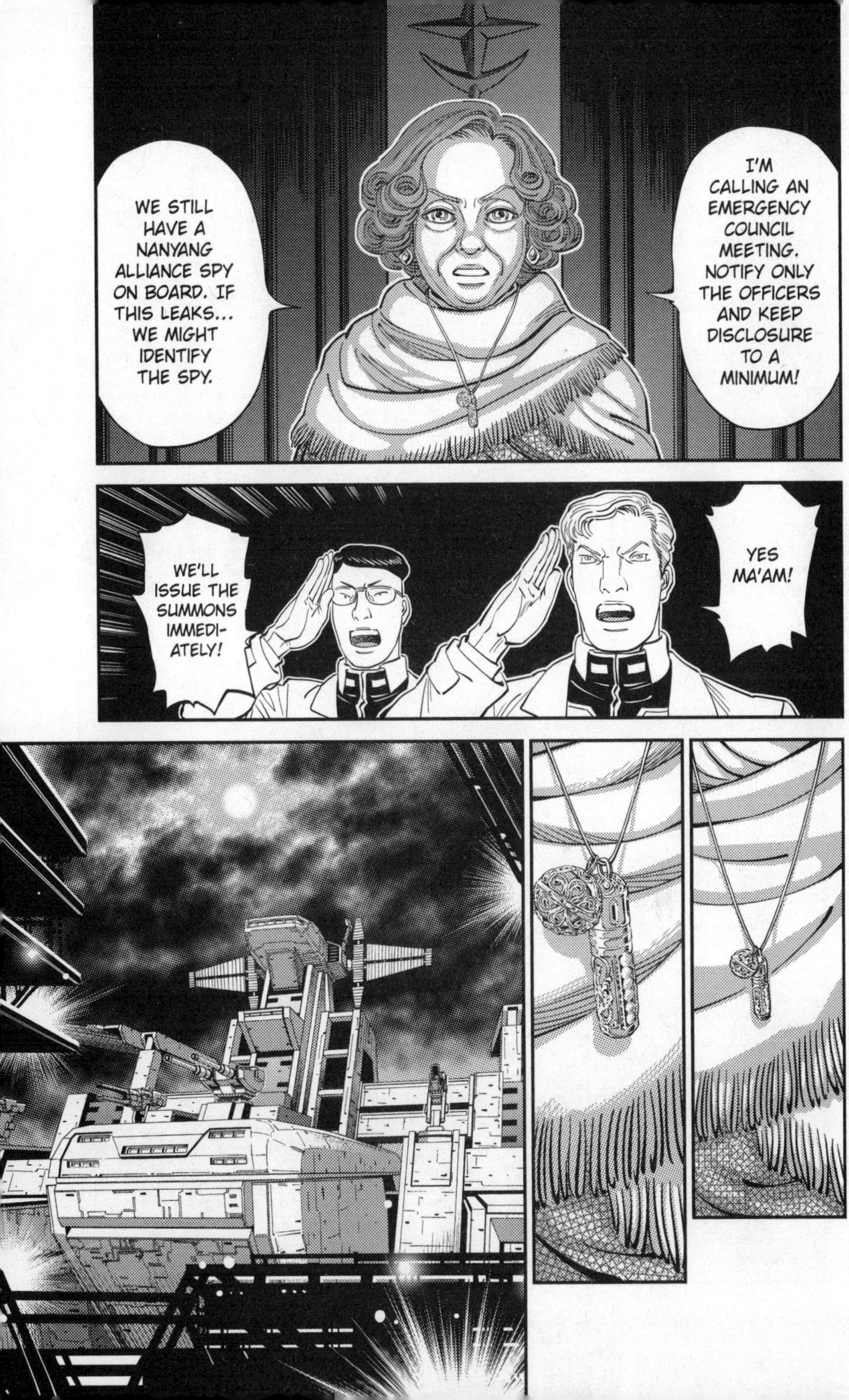
I'M CALLING AN EMERGENCY COUNCIL MEETING. NOTIFY ONLY THE OFFICERS AND KEEP DISCLOSURE TO A MINIMUM!
WE STILL HAVE A NANYANG ALLIANCE SPY ON BOARD. IF THIS LEAKS... WE MIGHT IDENTIFY THE SPY.
YES MA'AM!
WE'LL ISSUE THE SUMMONS IMMEDI-ATELY!

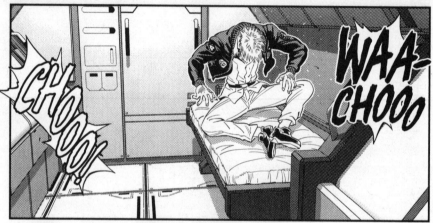

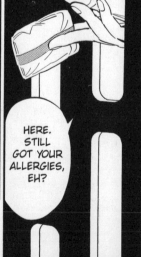

HERE. STILL GOT YOUR ALLERGIES, EH?

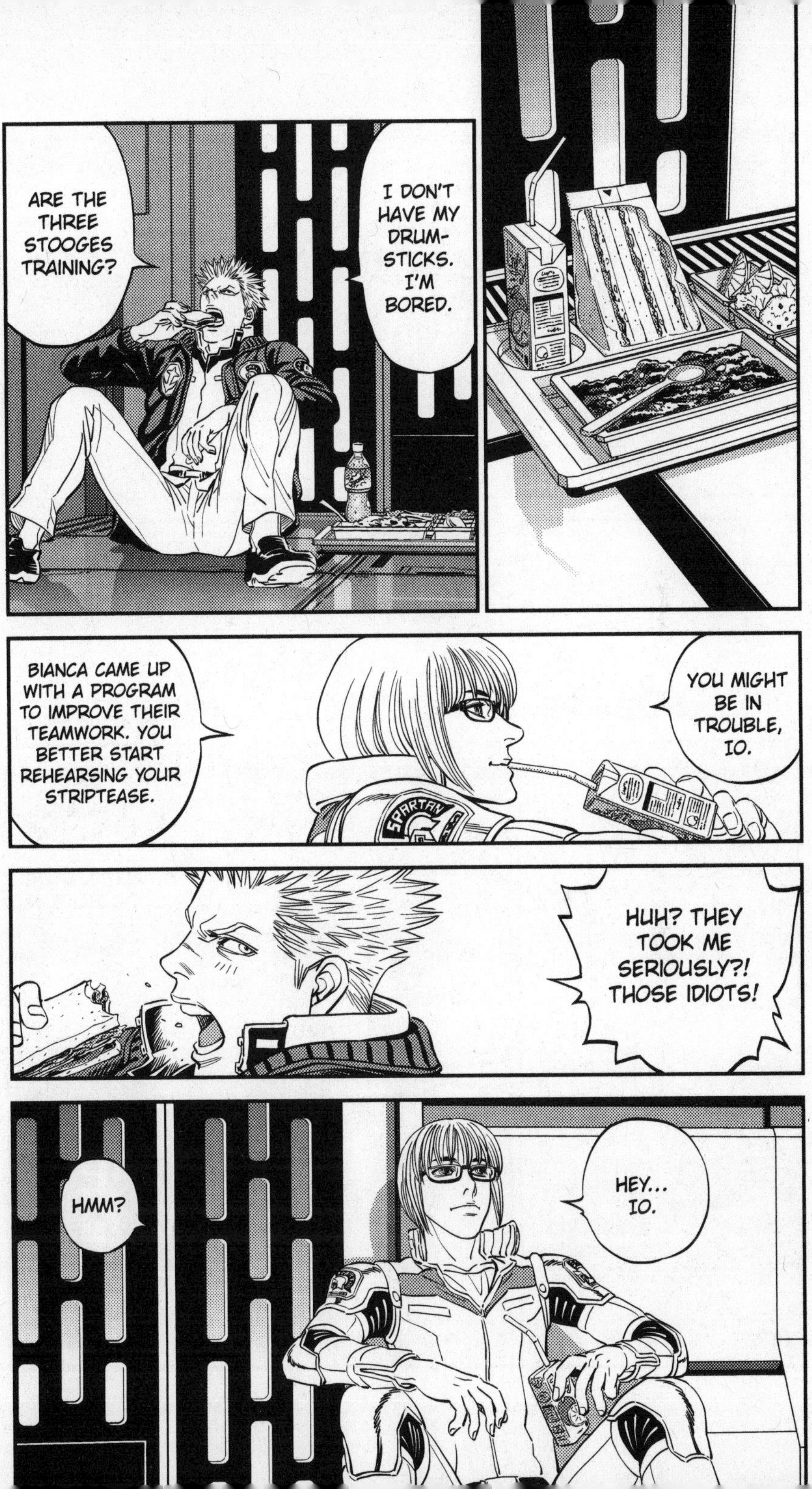
I DON'T HAVE MY DRUM-STICKS. I'M BORED.
ARE THE THREE STOOGES TRAINING?
YOU MIGHT BE IN TROUBLE, IO.
BIANCA CAME UP WITH A PROGRAM TO IMPROVE THEIR TEAMWORK. YOU BETTER START REHEARSING YOUR STRIPTEASE.
HUH? THEY TOOK ME SERIOUSLY?! THOSE IDIOTS!
HEY... IO.
HMM?

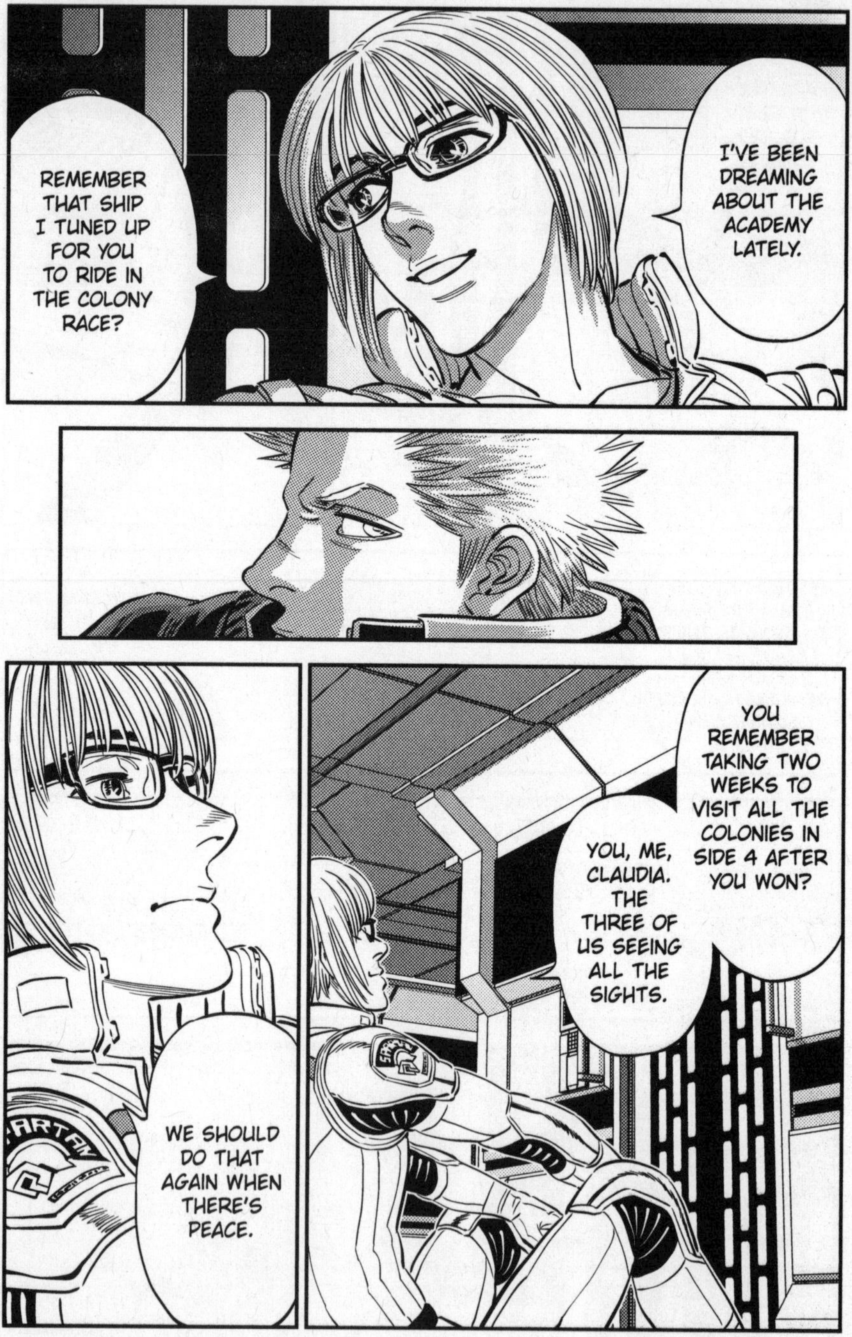
I'VE BEEN DREAMING ABOUT THE ACADEMY LATELY.
REMEMBER THAT SHIP I TUNED UP FOR YOU TO RIDE IN THE COLONY RACE?
YOU REMEMBER TAKING TWO WEEKS TO VISIT ALL THE COLONIES IN SIDE 4 AFTER YOU WON?
YOU, ME, CLAUDIA. THE THREE OF US SEEING ALL THE SIGHTS.
WE SHOULD DO THAT AGAIN WHEN THERE'S PEACE.

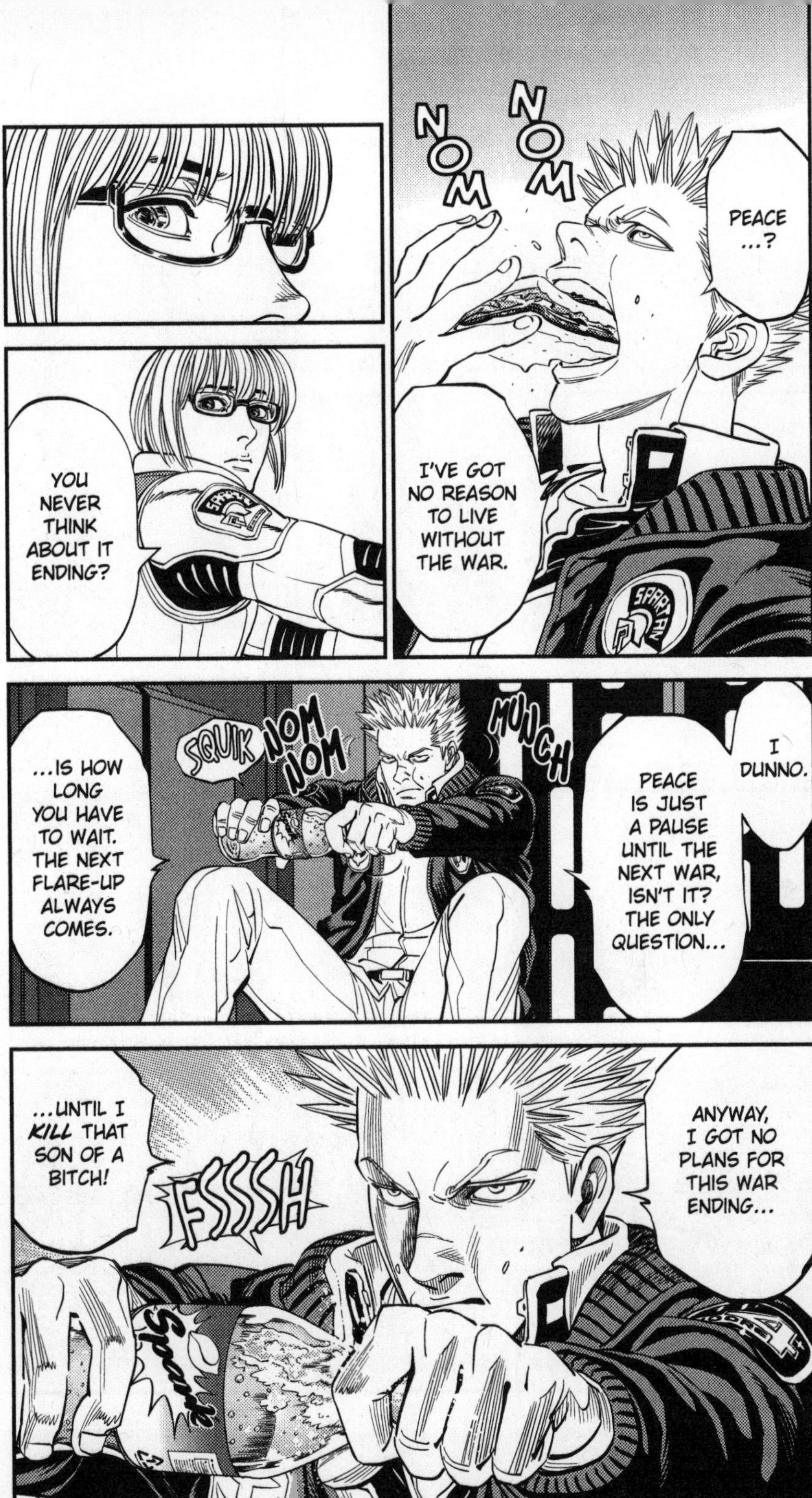
NOM NOM
PEACE ...?
I'VE GOT NO REASON TO LIVE WITHOUT THE WAR.
YOU NEVER THINK ABOUT IT ENDING?
I DUNNO.
PEACE IS JUST A PAUSE UNTIL THE NEXT WAR, ISN'T IT? THE ONLY QUESTION...
MUNCH
NOM NOM
SQUIK
...IS HOW LONG YOU HAVE TO WAIT. THE NEXT FLARE-UP ALWAYS COMES.
ANYWAY, I GOT NO PLANS FOR THIS WAR ENDING...
FSSSH
...UNTIL I *KILL* THAT SON OF A BITCH!

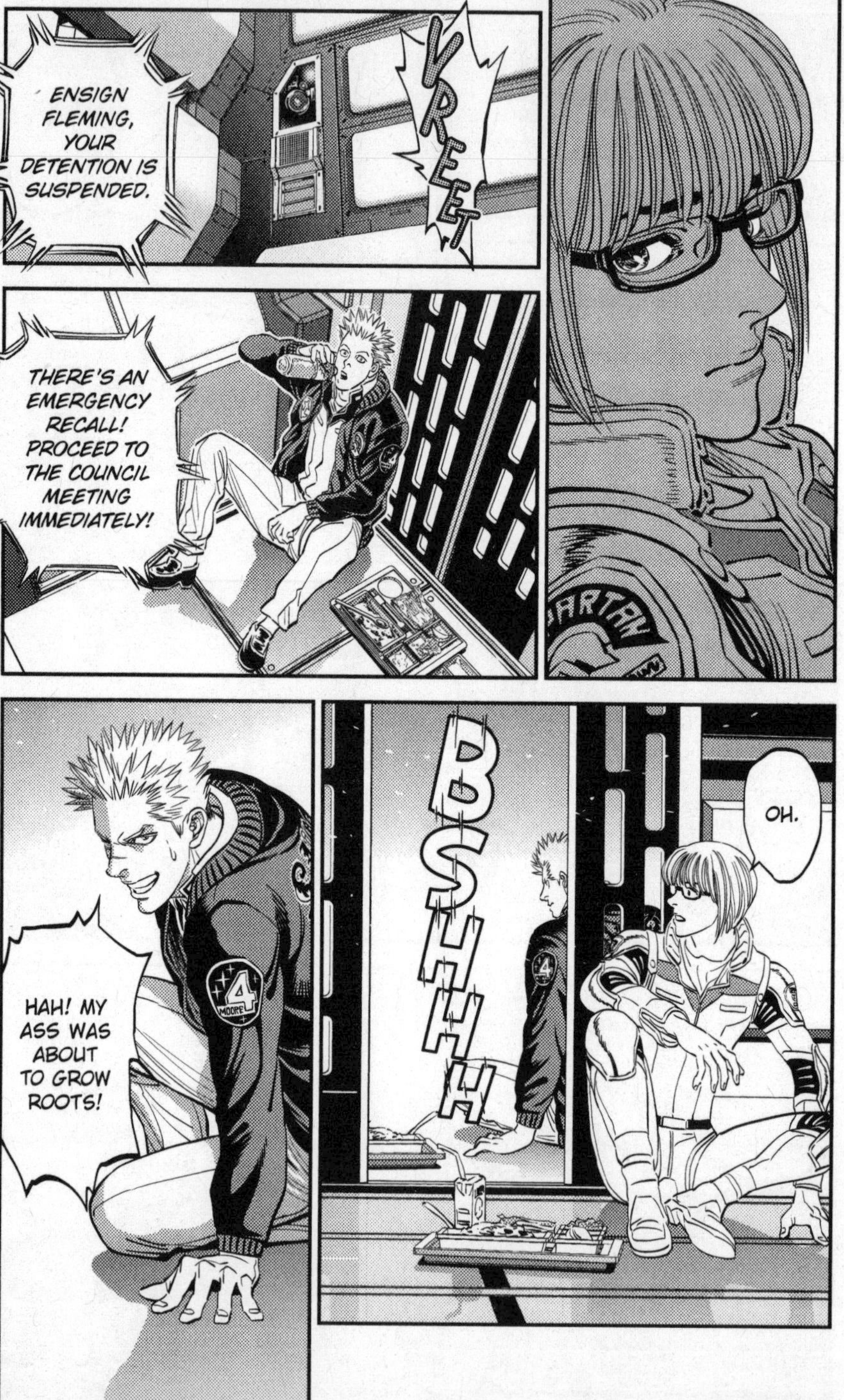
VREET
ENSIGN FLEMING, YOUR DETENTION IS SUSPENDED.
THERE'S AN EMERGENCY RECALL! PROCEED TO THE COUNCIL MEETING IMMEDIATELY!
BSHHHH
OH.
HAH! MY ASS WAS ABOUT TO GROW ROOTS!

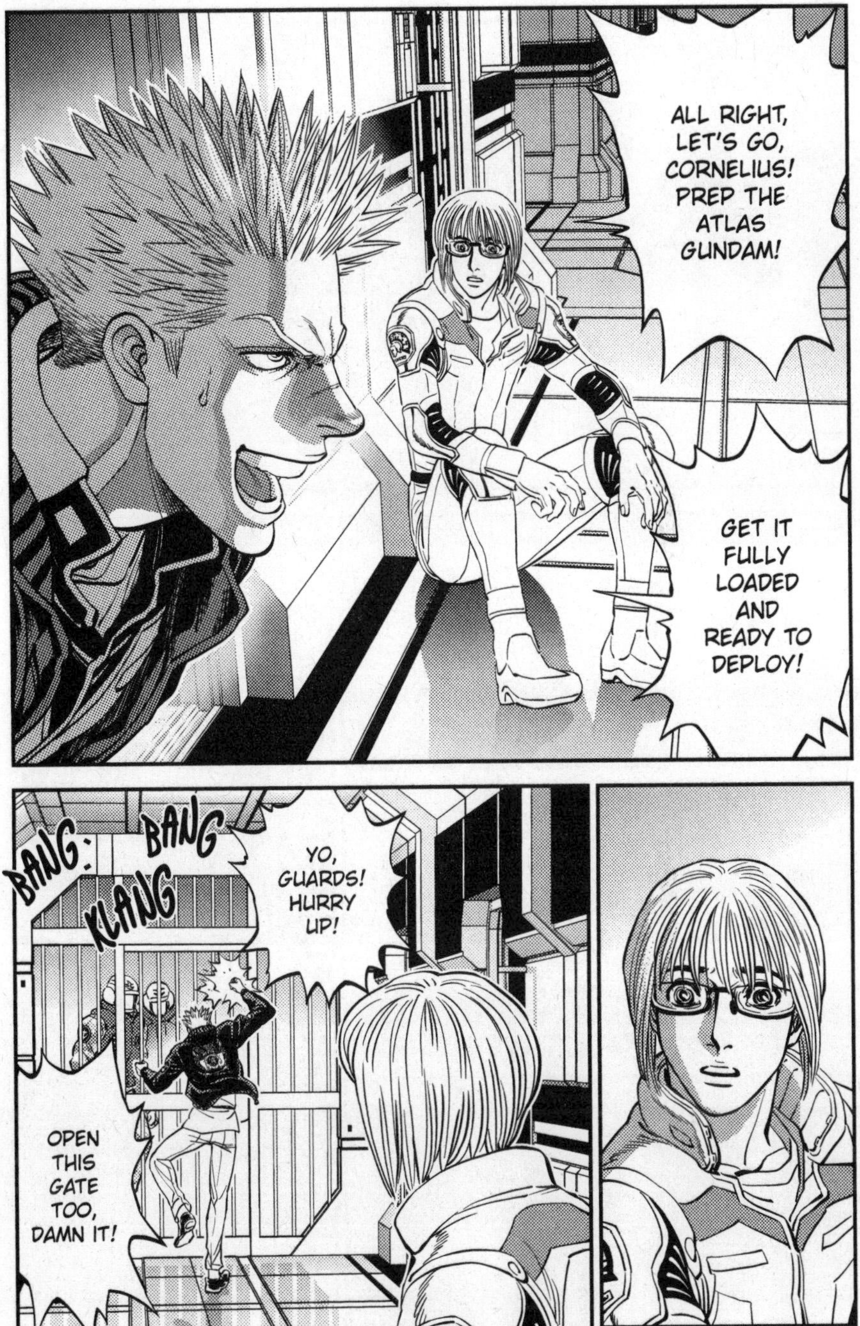
ALL RIGHT, LET'S GO, CORNELIUS! PREP THE ATLAS GUNDAM!
GET IT FULLY LOADED AND READY TO DEPLOY!
YO, GUARDS! HURRY UP!
BANG
BANG
KLANG
OPEN THIS GATE TOO, DAMN IT!

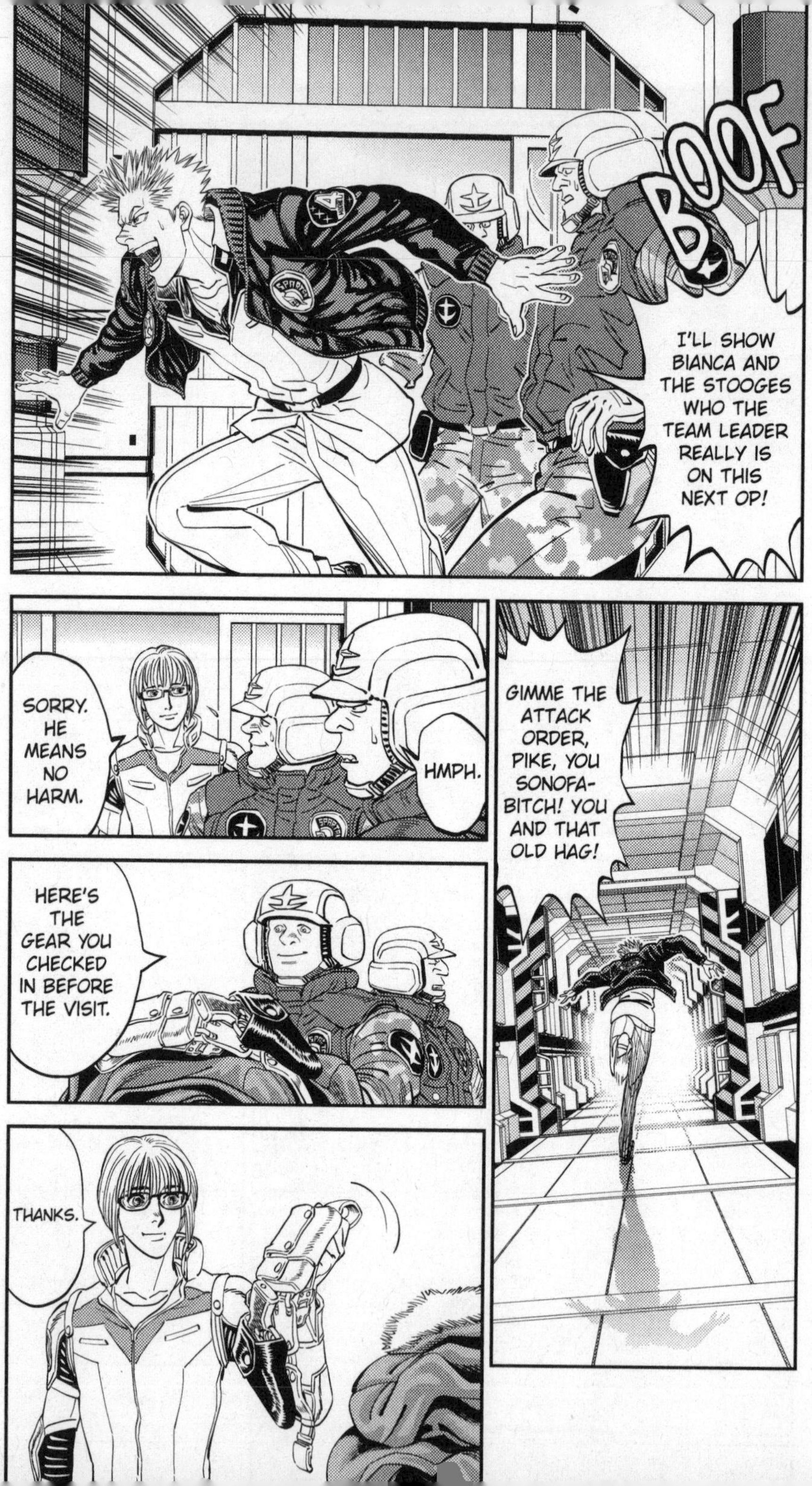
BOOF
I'LL SHOW BIANCA AND THE STOOGES WHO THE TEAM LEADER REALLY IS ON THIS NEXT OP!
GIMME THE ATTACK ORDER, PIKE, YOU SONOFA-BITCH! YOU AND THAT OLD HAG!
HMPH.
SORRY. HE MEANS NO HARM.
HERE'S THE GEAR YOU CHECKED IN BEFORE THE VISIT.
THANKS.

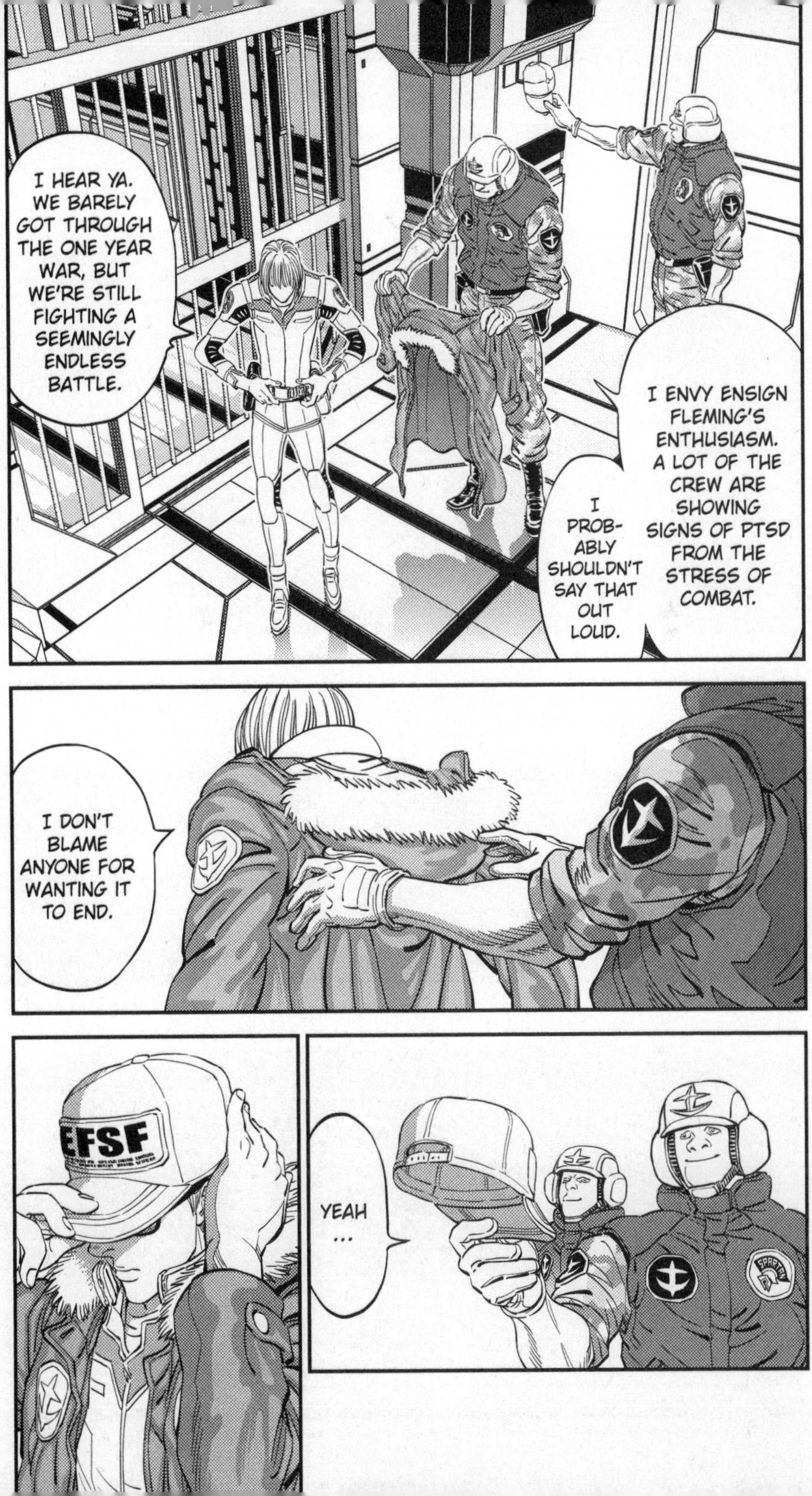
I HEAR YA. WE BARELY GOT THROUGH THE ONE YEAR WAR, BUT WE'RE STILL FIGHTING A SEEMINGLY ENDLESS BATTLE.
I ENVY ENSIGN FLEMING'S ENTHUSIASM. A LOT OF THE CREW ARE SHOWING SIGNS OF PTSD FROM THE STRESS OF COMBAT.
I PROBABLY SHOULDN'T SAY THAT OUT LOUD.
I DON'T BLAME ANYONE FOR WANTING IT TO END.
EFSF
YEAH ...

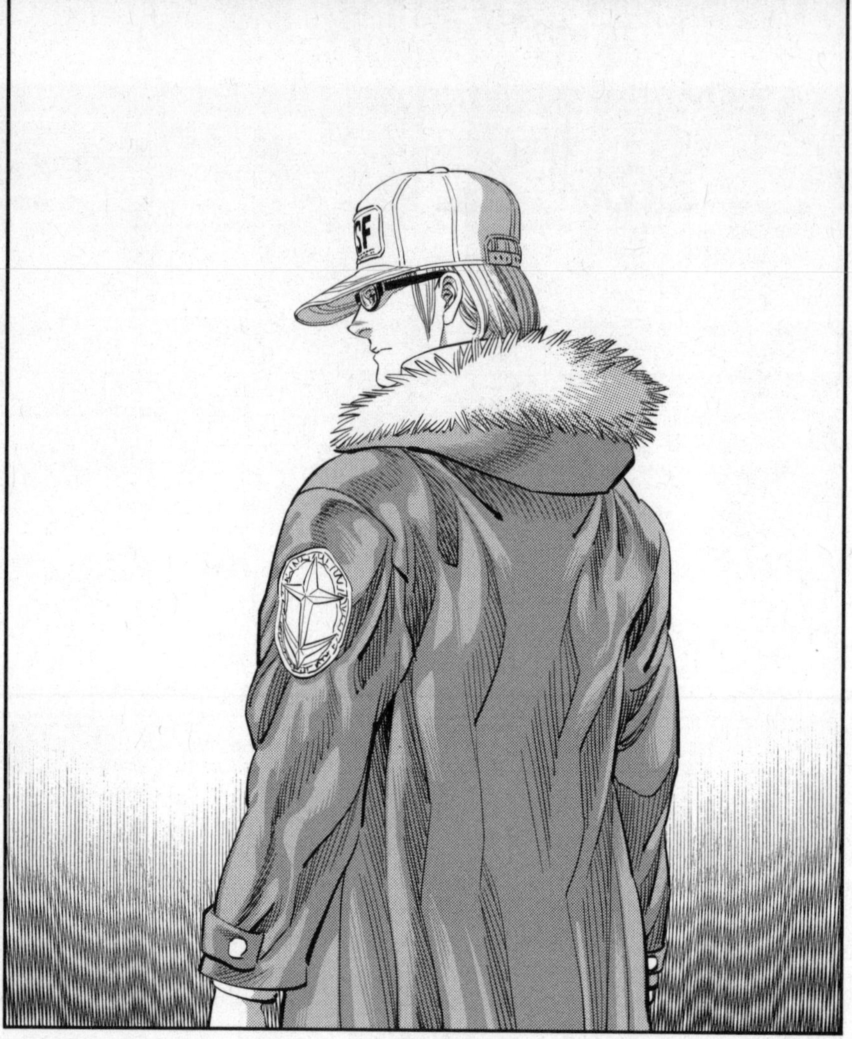

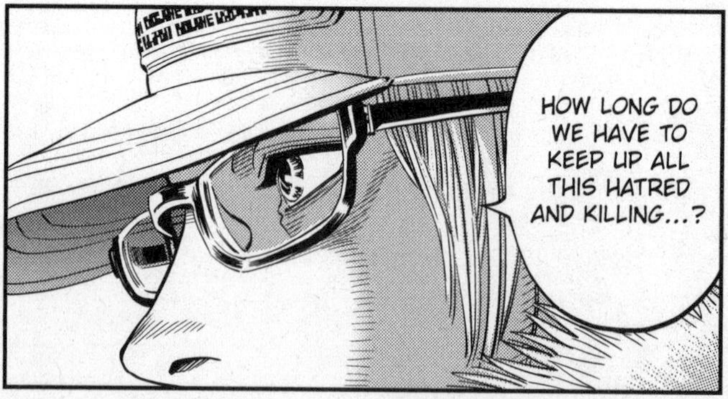
HOW LONG DO WE HAVE TO KEEP UP ALL THIS HATRED AND KILLING...?

MOBILE SUIT GUNDAM - THUNDERBOLT - VOL. 10 - END

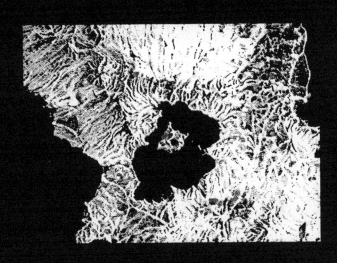

TO BE CONTINUED

STUDIO TOA S.P.A.

Executive Director	**Yasuo Ohtagaki**
Chief	**Sayaka Ohtagaki**
Drawing Staff Lead	**Ju Ishiguchi**
Background Art	**Hikaru Kanefusa**
Drawing Staff	**Ryosuke Sugiyama** **Izumi Yamada** **Shota Sugawa** **Rikuka Kawahara** **Tomomi Sawada**
Production Manager	**Hideki Yamamoto**
Guest Designer	**Takuya Io**
Special Thanks	**Digital Noise Ltd.**

MOBILE SUIT GUNDAM THUNDERBOLT 10

VIZ Signature Edition

STORY AND ART **YASUO OHTAGAKI**
Original Concept by **HAJIME YATATE** and **YOSHIYUKI TOMINO**

Translation **JOE YAMAZAKI**
English Adaptation **STAN!**
Touch-up Art & Lettering **EVAN WALDINGER**
Cover & Design **SHAWN CARRICO**
Editor **MIKE MONTESA**

MOBILE SUIT GUNDAM THUNDERBOLT Vol. 10 by Yasuo OHTAGAKI
Original Concept by Hajime YATATE, Yoshiyuki TOMINO

Original Japanese edition published by SHOGAKUKAN.
English translation rights in the United States of America, Canada, the United Kingdom, Ireland, Australia and New Zealand arranged with SHOGAKUKAN.

ORIGINAL COVER DESIGN / Yoshiyuki SEKI for VOLARE inc.

EDITORIAL COOPERATION / Shinsuke HIRAIWA (Digitalpaint.jp)

Printed in the U.S.A.

Published by VIZ Media, LLC
P.O. Box 77010
San Francisco, CA 94107

10 9 8 7 6 5 4 3 2 1
First printing, February 2019

VIZ MEDIA
viz.com

VIZ SIGNATURE
vizsignature.com

ratings.viz.com RATED T+ OLDER TEEN

PARENTAL ADVISORY
MOBILE SUIT GUNDAM THUNDERBOLT is rated T+ for Older Teen and is recommended for ages 16 and up. This volume contains realistic violence, strong language, mild nudity and some adult themes.

Hey! You're Reading in the Wrong Direction!

This is the *end* of this graphic novel!

To properly enjoy this VIZ graphic novel, please turn it around and begin reading from *right to left.* Unlike English, Japanese is read right to left, so Japanese comics are read in reverse order from the way English comics are typically read.

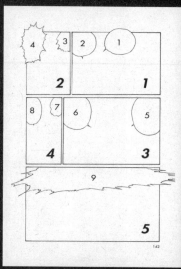

Follow the action this way

This book has been printed in the original Japanese format in order to preserve the orientation of the original artwork. Have fun with it!